Close to the Bone

Close to the Bone
LISA RAY

DOUBLEDAY CANADA

Doubleday Canada and colophon are registered trademarks of
Penguin Random House Canada Limited

Library and Archives Canada Cataloguing in Publication

Title: Close to the bone / Lisa Ray.
Names: Ray, Lisa, 1972- author.
Description: Previously published: 2019.
Identifiers: Canadiana (print) 20200241907 | Canadiana (ebook) 20200241931 |
ISBN 9780385695725 (softcover) | ISBN 9780385695732 (EPUB)
Subjects: LCSH: Ray, Lisa, 1972- | LCSH: Motion picture actors and actresses—
Biography. | LCSH: Cancer. | LCGFT: Autobiographies.
Classification: LCC PN2888.R39 A3 2020 | DDC 791.4302/8092—dc23

Cover design: Kelly Hill
Cover photograph: © Farrokh Chothia

Printed and bound in the USA

Published in Canada by Doubleday Canada,
a division of Penguin Random House Canada Limited

www.penguinrandomhouse.ca

10 9 8 7 6 5 4 3 2 1

Penguin
Random House
DOUBLEDAY CANADA

'It is no measure of health to be well-adjusted
to a profoundly sick society.'
J. Krishnamurti

Prologue

"Illness is the night-side of life, a more onerous citizenship. Everyone who is born holds a dual citizenship, in the kingdom of the well and in the kingdom of the sick. Although we all prefer to use only the good passport, sooner or later each of us is obliged, at least for a spell, to identify ourselves as citizens of that other place."

—Susan Sontag, *Illness as a Metaphor*

THE NIGHT I begin to step into myself, my shoes don't fit.

Everything keeps slipping from my fingers that morning. The shampoo bottle, a teaspoon, my phone: suspended for one surging moment before landing with a clatter on the floor. I stare. Patti Smith is on my playlist today. Her scarred voice cuts through the quiet as sunlight slopes in from a window. I sit on my bed and work through a line of high heels pulled from my closet, trying them on, one by one. They are all pretty and pointy and very bad for pelvic alignment, I've been told. And none of them fit. None.

I always dreaded the red carpet. I had walked it at movie premieres in Toronto and LA, events in Bombay, and I always felt self-conscious: you have to think about how to tilt your head and how to suck in your non-existent gut while photographers click away. You are expected to look flawless. Ambition and judgment wrap around your skin, hug your form. But in the fall of 2009, I do have a gut, and it is swinging beneath a sari-inspired dress in royal purple, specially made for my new body.

My costume designer friend Rashmi Varma dropped off the dress a couple of hours before the debut of my film *Cooking with Stella* at the Toronto International Film Festival. Then, one by one, I tried on pairs of heels from my closet. My feet are bloated. That's what steroids do, and I have been knocking them back by the handful—four days on, four days off. They've also turned my face into a large, round moon. I call this feeling of an extra, elastic skin on top of my skin "my wet suit." These days, I sit on the couch and watch as my belly inflates before my eyes. I study my fingers. They look like kabanosy, the sausages of my child-hood. I marvel at my bloated thighs, saying to my dad, "Look at this. I'm expanding—like a cartoon character!"

And now my feet are swollen, too. For some reason, as I look down at my extra thick ankles, the gravity of the situation hits me: two months ago, I had sat in a tiny supply closet of a room across from a jittery, rab-bit-faced doctor. He spoke very slowly, pausing a long time between each word, as if to gauge my reaction: "You. Have. Multiple. Myeloma."

The doctor reminded me of the rabbit in *Alice in Wonderland*. As he kicked me down the hole, he never said the word cancer. In fact, the signs in the clinic were vague: Hematology Centre. But the pregnant pauses told me I was being inducted into a new club: "Fatal." Pause. "Incurable."

"Oh," I said. "Do you want me to get you some water?"

I know my response might seem strange, but he did look parched. Also, it never occurred to me that I wouldn't get better. Almost as soon as he said cancer (or didn't), I was framing it as just another adventure in a life that had circled the globe for three decades, plucking one experience after the other like cherries from trees. Now cells in my bones were rampaging, multiplying, squeezing out the red blood cells. I had become a junior member of the MM cancer club, diagnosed at thirty-seven, while the average age is sixty-five. *Fatal. Incurable.* But I wasn't scared—not yet, anyway.

Or perhaps deep in my philosophic core I believe nothing is wasted. Not even this.

Steroids, chemo and hospital hallways hadn't burdened that light touch too much. But on the eve of the film premiere, 40 pounds heavier and about to debut my moon face in front of my peers and the international media, I feel just a little bit of self-pity—not because I am ill, but because I can't get into my shoes. I have done everything to avoid being looked at in a certain way and yet here we are: dredging up vanity to encapsulate my life. The irony in this immediately slays the sadness and becomes a strange awakening. Slowly, I emerge from this reverie that I have been in for a long time, living in a disconnect between private pain and public persona. My cancer—which I jokingly call "The Cancer" (you have to laugh, or, as they say, you'll die)—is a rare little orphan cancer of the plasma cells in bone marrow. The marrow is the deepest part of yourself, and I can feel those depths shifting, unmuffling and upending all that is hidden. After years of floating in the wind like a leaf, coming and going, I am ready to feel rooted. After years of trafficking in fantasy, I am ready to toy with truth. I am ready to listen to my bones, this silent support structure deep inside all of us.

Tonight, I will glide on to the red carpet in big shoes with a clunky heel. While one part of me will step forward, another will be at a distance from the lights and the din, wheeling across the sky, watching through a slowly floating lens. I have lived in a way that has transported me through a myriad of worlds, but still, I had never imagined this.

I am composed of all the things seen and known and experienced, the emotions of a life lived close to the bone. I can feel it all expanding in my chest, filling my veins. And now, when I debut a new body on the shimmering opacity of the red carpet, I will reveal how fortunate a thing it is, when life alters you without warning.

1

I WAS BORN to be a nomad. Even as a kid my eyes were focused on the horizon, and my mind floated into a dreamscape which captured my attention more than immediate events around me. I'm sure this is because of my parents. They had rebelled and defied their cultural norms in two countries, and in a third, Canada, built an entirely new life on their own terms. Being a mixed-race couple in a new country forty-five years ago was enough to make them iconoclasts of their time. From them, I inherited the irrational optimism it takes to forge your own unique place in the world. It was passed on in my kaleidoscopic genes and settled in my marrow.

My father was born in a decaying, palatial home in Calcutta, and my mother came from Poland, the land of solid bones. She had the thick wrists of an Eastern European, while I inherited my father's fine, aristocratic frame. "Chicken bones," my mother would intone in her light Polish accent, looking at the two of us, reading side by side on the flowery sofa. "You're both too . . . delicate!" And then she'd add: "Dreamers. I'm stuck with two dreamers!" We would both blink as she marched through our home with a rake or screwdriver in hand, momentarily discomfited before returning to our books; brows knitted, the page tilted just so.

"Dreamer" was an expression of affection, but also one of exasperation. She was taken with the practicalities of life, a woman in constant motion who viewed tidiness and efficiency as a path to personal liberation. Strikingly blonde and spirited, she conjured up a small island of love for our family of three. Her presence was the glue. While fluent in the daily pleasures of life, like cooking and gardening, she had absolutely no interest in intellectual concepts and books. Her frugal, preservationist routine—*Put the used plastic bags under the sink! And glass bottles! Use that old t-shirt as a cleaning rag! Save the newspapers to stuff shoes! Stop, don't throw the teabag away!*—was shaped growing up under communism and the shadow of war but she was fun and frivolous when she chose, and her personality filled our home with visitors, while my father and I would retreat into our corners.

I was more closely aligned to my gentle and introverted father, guardian of culture, more poet than engineer, while my mother kept our family moving smoothly. She did, while we dreamed. Weekends were reserved for meandering conversations on philosophy or "state of the world" discussions, while my mother picked up a wrench and fixed a leaky faucet or squirted oil on the bolts of our lawn mower and cleaned the blades. It was she who turned our backyard into a canning factory every summer, commandeering my father and me to boil and skin bushels of tomatoes, churning them into sauce she stored in Mason jars, sealed and labelled, in our root cellar. Mama regulated our lives by seasons, a tradition passed down through the blood. Long before urban farmers' markets, she would drive me to a farm outside Toronto in Holland Marsh. We would stock up on freshly slaughtered chicken and harvest vegetables from mucky rich black earth, digging with our own hands. Potatoes, carrots, onions, rutabaga were tossed into bushels, the stubbornness of soil caking their forms. Mama would hand me a pair of gumboots and I would stomp into the field with a pitchfork, though I'd have preferred to while away my time reading or lying on the grass. I considered the title "dreamer" a compliment. What else is there to do but dream?

Of course, my mother dreamed, too, and the dreams she shared with my father, articulated or not, were the beginning of my life. My parents were madly in love with each other. But that didn't mean that they always got along, or even that their personalities blended at all. My dad adored my mom. Her fiery nature would perplex and dismay him—especially when she threw the cutlery at him. But they were wrapped in an unthreatened web of loyalty. He felt that she completed him and she felt the same about my dad. There was a dream deep in the core of their relationships, or they never would have ended up in Canada, two young idealists, so far from home.

My father, Salil Ray, dreamed his way out of India. He was the first of his family to leave Calcutta. There were eight children, four boys and four girls. Out of the eight, four have shockingly light eyes set in dark-brown Bengali skin. Over the years, many have commented on my light green eyes, assuming they come from my Polish mother, but in fact, they're from my father. They serve as a reminder of a long-buried quirk of miscegenation.

By all accounts my dad was the quintessential good Indian son: mild-mannered, respectful, strong in studies, his striking features radiating erudition with a hint of rebellion around his questioning, full mouth. In Bengali families, everyone is known by their *daak naam* or pet names, and my father is called Anju, which is short for the girl's name Anjali or Anjana. Why he got a girl's name is a mystery, but it means "divine offering."

My grandfather was a judge, an old-school anglicized Indian working for the British while at the same time still deeply Bengali. He had a thin angular face, with a long patrician nose and appeared as tall and imposing as a banyan tree. He settled his family into an ancestral property inherited from his father in north Calcutta and that home shaped some of my happiest memories. From my visits as a child, I remember him walking with a teak cane, the tap-tap-tap of it as he appeared. Dadu was a strict disciplinarian, and stuck to his routine, waking up early in the morning at five-thirty to go for his walk along the streets and gullies of Shyambazar. When he returned, holding up one end of his dhoti, tapping, I would strategically place myself in his path to get an affectionate pat on my head. There was a magnificent cane planter's chair on the second-floor landing and he would arrange himself there, on his throne, reading *Jugantor*, the Bengali daily newspaper for hours, both feared and revered by his brood.

As a judge, he was frequently transferred from place to place. The lore is that he was professionally so principled and incorruptible that inevitably, no matter where they lived, his life would be threatened in the course of ruling a case. These threats became the signal to move again, and the logistics of moving eight children (referred to as "Top four": Didi, Dada, Anju, Nanu, and "Bottom Four": Shilu, Nilu, Khokon and Khuku) and a home fell to my grandmother. She was a tiny woman with a calm yet formidable personality from a lineage of exceptionally strong, iconoclastic women. Boroma, her grandmother, had ruled over the family like a reigning monarch, earning the title "Queen Victoria." Widowed before she was forty, she defied the norms of the times and single-handedly managed the considerable property left to her by her husband, fighting her in-laws when they attempted to take it away from her. She was known to express her views generously and my father remembers her telling everyone not to waste money on lie-propagating newspapers; predating "alternative news" by nine decades. My grandmother, her granddaughter, was never formally educated, her marriage arranged to my grandfather when she was fourteen. But in her own way, she was just as strong. When the threats became too many, it was she who organized the servants and bearers to move all the family possessions onto the bullock carts and rounded the children onto trains. Before he went to college, my father had grown up in fourteen different villages spread over what is now Bangladesh.

Around the time just before the "Great Divide" or the Partition of India in 1947, the family was stationed in a small town in what would become East Pakistan, and later Bangladesh. As a Hindu, my grandfather had to move his family to India before the final date of Independence. Day after day he waited for his official transfer order, rumours whipping his peers into a fervour, panic filling pockets of space around him. It finally arrived. The family rushed to the railway station to catch the train to Calcutta, leaving an hour before midnight on 15 August 1947. Later, my father heard stories of horror and bloodshed; of neighbours dragged from the very next train.

At Sealdah station in Calcutta, a single taxi couldn't accommodate all the children and the family's belongings. So, my grandparents took the younger children with them to Boroma's house in Kalighat, leaving my father and his elder brother with a pile of baggage and a promise to pick them up after delivering the rest of the clan safely.

I imagine the disorientation of these two boys, how they tried to appear brave while around them a perfect mess of humanity swirled and thronged. Coolies, refugees, men and women setting new courses for their lives. Scents of hope and desperation mingling with their growing hunger and fear.

A Sikh taxi driver approached the lost looking brothers and managed to coax them into his car. He delivered them to Boroma's home in Kalighat—without accepting payment. This human kindness, borne out from a moment of terrible upheaval, stayed with my father. He continues to believe in the good in people.

Eventually the Ray clan settled in an old colonial home in Shyambazar which was originally bought by my great-grandfather to house his sons during their education in Calcutta. Soon a routine of tutors and school, breakfasts of luchis and vegetables restored order and normalcy, while my grandfather resumed work in Independent India. There was load-shedding, water shortage and suffering on the streets of post-Partition Calcutta, but inside the home, indulgent looks over second cups of tea and biscuits from a wired food safe. The family was a soft container that soothed the tremors.

Many of my most enduring, vivid recollections revolve around Horlicks and glucose biscuits and running my hand over the gramophone player in the sitting room. I learned to be watchful in a different way in that home, my eyes following with the shifting moods in the joint family collective, from inquisitive to condemning. For me, Calcutta was brought to life at the level of the senses. Then, standing on the flat roof, at a time when it was no longer day and not yet night, I listened to squalling street cats, understanding the city as a faithful presence when my cousins were called to their baths and schoolbooks and left me alone.

As a child, I took note of the white sacred thread—a ceremonial symbol reserved for Brahmins—worn by my uncles, across the torso from the left shoulder to the waist, when they ate bare-chested in the sweltering summer months. I wondered why the women of the home— my *boudis*—didn't have one. While my father never subscribed to casteism—and in fact remains a spitfire socialist—I was introduced, by virtue of my curiosity, to the concept of Brahmins occupying the top of the caste hierarchy. My family had status, but not necessarily wealth. Rather, my family believed we were the learned class, in contrast to the *Bania*, or business caste, who were traditionally looked upon as more ostentatious, less refined. In my family's eyes, buying an extra pair of

Bata chappals was considered excessive (*Ore baba! Ki atyadhikta!* Oh my gosh, what a show-off!). My father must have imbibed this aspect of his upbringing. He was never concerned with the trappings of success or wealth. If anything, we probably lived a bit below our means, in the modest, comfortable home in the suburbs of Toronto where I grew up.

By all accounts my father had a warmly communal upbringing. He was quiet, but a quick study. Starting from about three years old, he used to sit with his older Didi and Dada when they were studying with a private tutor at home. They let him play with their books so he wouldn't be a nuisance. Apparently, one day when the tutor posed a math question, my father squeaked out the answer and then proceeded to recite the Bengali alphabet. Naturally everyone was startled. "It was not a bad way of learning," my father confessed to me. That tutor later took an interest in my father, cultivating his interest in the written word, even though his only schooling options were doctor–lawyer–engineer. "All of life hinges on moving commas; it is this tiny punctuation mark that alters all meaning," the tutor told my father. "Sounds more like a philosopher, Dad." "Yes," my father agreed. "But he still rapped me on the knuckles a lot."

My father's habits and tastes were ill-suited to India at the time. He valued punctuality and European cinema. His desire to see the world was stronger than the threat of becoming rootless. He decided to leave his homeland at a time when few people did. In 1960, he won several scholarships and chose to "bugger off" to Birmingham University for his PhD on the "Removal of 3, 4 Benzpyrene," a highly carcinogenic chemical from diesel exhaust. The idea in everyone's head, including his own, was that he would get an education and one day return to Calcutta, but this was not his path. He never lived there again.

In England, my dad enjoyed his freedom, and the opportunity to define himself on his own terms, neither completely Eastern nor Western, no longer bending himself to fit a mould. While he worked on his thesis during the day, at night he became head of the university's cineastes' club and would take weekend trips to London theatres. There, he became a devoted follower of the avant-garde cinema blooming in the late 1960s. He adored Kurosawa and the Italian masters. He fell for *The Bicycle Thief* and Goddard's *Breathless*, and of course, the great Indian master, Satyajit Ray. At that time, Ray's films were virtually impossible to see in India, so my father discovered his country's greatest film-maker in England. (Years later, when I read the script for my film *Water*, I was drawn to its warm humanist vision because it reminded me of Ray's films.) I always believed that the secret desire of this gentle chemical engineer was to be a film director.

Having had a taste of it, my dad wanted to see more of the world. He became a member of the Bengali Students' Cultural Society at his university, where groups of young intellectuals would sit in pubs and throw radicalism at one another: opium of the masses, ponderers of utopia. At that time, most Bengali intellectuals were armchair Marxists. They were fascinated by communism, arguing for the humanity of a shared system. They were all especially romantic about the Eastern bloc countries and travelled every summer to one or other on a cultural exchange. I imagine this group of caramel-skinned boys in suits, singing the songs of the revered Bengali poet Rabindranath Tagore for their European comrades and roaming grainy streets afterwards, searching for salvation and the camaraderie of an open bar. In the summer of 1961, my father travelled to Warsaw in Poland.

By this time, my dad was in his early thirties, striking in appearance, but very shy, and a bit of a confirmed bachelor. He wasn't conditioned to look for love outside the confines of a strict Indian family code of conduct. In the back of his mind, he believed that his parents would arrange his marriage at the auspicious moment.

But at a university dance in Warsaw, on his last night of the student cultural tour, he met my mother. Barbara Gallus was a blue-eyed stunner with golden, feathered hair. To my father, she looked like an angel. Standing at the bar, my dad thought, "Let me buy her a whisky; Poles love to drink." He bought her something called "spiritus," which is essentially rubbing alcohol, 90 per cent proof, and sat down next to her. He didn't know that she hated drinking, and always would (this was one of many ways in which my mother, like my father, was an outsider to her own culture). Still, they danced and an attraction was lit, even though neither could speak the other's language.

My dad had to leave the next day. But they kept in touch, sending letters back and forth for a year. When, over the years, I asked how, not knowing each other's language, they kept up the correspondence, my father turned coy. "For Bengalis," he said, "love and beauty is our mother tongue. Love is my first language. But your mother's beauty saved me." I believed him. But I knew there was more to the story. Finally, he told me about an Irish lady who lived in my mother's tiny hamlet. It was she who translated the lovers' letters and began teaching my mother English. I can see this Irish woman—whose name will always remain a mystery—bent over my father's precise writing, my mother beside her, eyes shining, learning the sounds of courtship in another language and laughing through Irish inflected words. The next summer, my father went back to Poland and met my mother's family. They were relatively prosperous, and she lived on the edge of a forest in a pleasant wooden house in Otrębusy, a village to the west of Warsaw. She was the much-adored only child of her parents, the letters of her name, BASIA, fixed to one side of the home in white wood. Finally, on the following summer's visit, I think she just turned to Salil one day and said in her broken English: "All right, now we get married." And my dad went along with it, setting a new course for himself and turning his back on a proposal for a marriage that was waiting for him in India.

But of course, Poland at the time was firmly tucked behind the Iron Curtain, a closed country, and my mother could not easily leave. It was up to her father, my grandfather, who worked for the government, to intervene. He was of French origin, a descendant of Napoleon's army who had marched on Poland and stayed, presumably seduced by local charms. Hence my mother's last name, Gallus, which comes from "Gallic," the generic word for the French. I have only vague memories of him, but enough to know that he loved the finer things in life: rich sauces, generously buttered toast and watercolour paintings. Somehow, through mysterious machinations, he helped my mother get her papers, and she left Poland. She, too, would never live in the country of her birth again.

My parents were married in 1967 at a church in Oxford. It was the opposite of a big Indian wedding: a civil ceremony with three or four friends. In this quiet fashion, they began their life together. My father was working with one of the largest oil companies in the world, Shell, and they lived an idyllic newly-wed existence in a small English cottage in a village called Abbotsford, beyond Oxford. That experience of setting up a life in a foreign place in the 1960s required not just gumption but imagination. I see my parents as artists—as all immigrants must be— in the combination of creativity and risk-taking it took to dream into existence their life. A life created day by day, untethered from the expectations of their families and their cultures.

My mother, ever industrious, not only mastered English but started teaching the subject in a private school. My parents would look back on that time as a free-spirited existence, a time to reinvent themselves. England was experiencing a surge in immigration, and they found themselves surrounded by academics and intellectual exiles from around the world. But there was a professional glass ceiling, too, and my father sensed that his prospects were limited. Then, in 1968, Conservative MP Enoch Powell made his famously xenophobic "Rivers of Blood" speech, warning against the dangers of immigration. The atmosphere in the country was changing just as my dad began to receive job offers from Canadian petroleum companies. My intrepid parents were feeling stifled, and as in any migrant story, that's when you go West.

My parents were both nature lovers too, and though neither had set foot in Canada, they imagined the country as a vast, empty place, with miles of land and wilderness. So, they sold everything, and took a boat to Montreal and, from there, a train to Toronto. They arrived with three suitcases, knowing not a soul but each other. My father had a job lined up as a Consulting Chemical Engineer with Gulf Oil Canada, but they had no place to live. In the immigration office, they filled out their papers and were approved. An official overheard their story, a woman named Silvia Kleinman, and as they were leaving, she asked: "Do you need a place to stay?" Well, yes. "Then come stay in my basement until you get settled."

I look upon this invitation as an expression of how Toronto was at that point in time; a generous, open place, and a match to the ideal in my parents' imaginations. But also, this good fortune seems like a piece of a romantic truth about my parents: they walked in a light together. Their love was so incandescent that it prompted a stranger in an immigration office to offer them a place in her home.

Three years later, on 4 April 1972, I was born in a hospital in the north of Toronto. From all accounts mine was a doubly precarious birth:

I was breach and the cord was wrapped around my neck. Apparently, as I travelled down the birth canal, the umbilical cord tightened, cutting off oxygen and bringing me, ironically, closer to death. I came into the world via an emergency C-section. My mother's incision became badly infected, so she ended up staying in the hospital for a month while I warmed in an incubator. I can only imagine she would remember that time as a vague, confusing haze, except for a rush of anxiety when she thought of her baby girl. Perhaps my birth was her first brush with how life could skid spectacularly out of control. And yet, her baby displayed a tenacity of will that even nurses remarked upon. I imagine her making a silent promise to protect her daughter from the vagaries of fate and circumstance.

My parents named me Lisa Rani Ray. "Lisa" on its own was a bit bland but "Lisa Rani" evokes an inheritance. "Words matter . . . you have the storytelling spirit," my father would later tell me when I sat dangling on his knee. Perhaps that's why he chose "Rani" as my middle name. My dad remembers that as he drove to the hospital—every day after work for a month—to visit us, the radio would always play the song "A Horse with No Name," which if you think about it, is a bit of an odd anthem for a newborn.

On the first part of the journey
I was looking at all the life
There were plants and birds and rocks and things
There was sand and hills and rings
The first thing I met was a fly with a buzz
And the sky with no clouds
The heat was hot and the ground was dry
But the air was full of sound
I've been through the desert on a horse with no name
It felt good to be out of the rain
In the desert you can remember your name
'Cause there ain't no one for to give you no pain

This genesis, along with the forces that shaped my parents' lives, has informed who I am in ways I'm still trying to unravel. I accept that my story began before I was born; that archived within me are all sorts of unknowable things. Like, for instance, my innate distrust of convention which appears to have been passed down to me by my mother and father, whose unusual union, it seemed from the outside, had somehow slipped past the rigid suspicions of two cultures for years. Though my grandfather—my father's father—was initially shocked and angered by his son's marriage to a *phirang*, a foreigner, eventually my mother travelled to India, endeared herself to the family and fell in love with the country. And, it appeared to me during our regular visits to India during my childhood, my father's thronging family had fallen in love with her. She found a kind of connection to India that she had never felt to her own culture. She relished marching through the bazaars of Calcutta and bargaining, dressed in a cotton dress from the local tailor, while my dad hung back, always a little shy to undertake the aggressive negotiations that are part of Indian life. I remember how I wove around my mother on those outings, gaping at how she demanded the best produce from bemused vendors, "*Yeh nahi*... that one. Give me those papayas, behind, behind you. *Tomar pichone*! Don't cheat. Don't cheat me, *dada*!" She bloomed on Indian soil.

But none of us knew then that their marriage had set off an epic eruption behind closed doors. This only came to light a few years ago. My grandfather passed away when my parents had been married for twenty years. But my tiny grandmother soldiered on, in full control of her faculties, free of illness, until she suddenly slipped away in 2010 at the age of ninety-six.

Three of my father's brothers had been living in the Nebubagen Lane home with their wives, and the rest of the siblings gathered there for the reading of the will. My father was in Calcutta (now officially renamed Kolkata in an effort to shed India of its colonial, English legacy) on his winter vacation. As the lawyer read the pages, it slowly became clear that my dad had been written out of the will entirely, very deliberately, because he had married my mother. It was like a hand reaching out from across the ages, casting a shadow on our choices and our lives; a judgment from the past.

This revelation was hard for him because my liberal and tolerant father was suddenly confronted by prejudices he had never known existed.

Mostly, he was sadly surprised by his father, who by all accounts had adored him in every other way, this son who had fulfilled all his duties but one: he didn't marry the woman that his family had chosen for him.

Disappointing as it was, I didn't take this revelation to heart. I was a grown woman when this secret came to light, carrying my own contradictions. By then I knew better than to judge my ancestors who belonged to shifting sands: a different era. Besides, they are still with me, in everything I do, for better or worse. My grandfather had imbibed stories of queens who went to war, of progressive ideals but also of filial duty and sacrifice above all else. My father ended the episode with a sigh. "What can you do, Lisa Rani?" Rani—Queen—varnishing the edge of our pain.

I have learned to balance myself somewhere between two points: in me there is a converging of not just two different cultures and bloodlines, but two varying approaches to life, the pragmatic and the poetic. While this multilayered identity has become my strength, it was to prove vexing and problematic when I was growing up.

2

I AM SEATED in the back seat of our tan Oldsmobile Cutlass, a supreme boat of a car. My mother is driving. Plump legs are stretched out in front of me, clad in green plaid shorts. I am three years old. It's a breezy day but the back of my thighs are stuck to the seat. My mother pulls into the driveway of our old house in the west end of Toronto and shifts the gear-stick into park. Her beige corduroy pants slide smoothly against the vinyl as she gets out of the car and opens the garage door.

I can barely see over the dashboard, but because the driveway is on an incline, I get a clear view of my mother struggling with the handle, her flaxen hair rippling and catching the sun like the wings of a startled bird. Then—and this is the part I have no clear memory of—I've manoeuvred myself into the driver's seat and somehow shifted into reverse. I don't know how I could even reach the pedal, but the car started moving, slowly at first, then more quickly. What I do still recall vividly all these years later is this image; my mother's blue eyes flying open, her body leaping through the air. I remember her wrenching the door open, reaching across me in a tangle of panic and somehow stopping the car.

Apparently I laughed with delight, gripping the steering wheel and enjoying the game. It was a brief moment, but throughout our lives, my mother narrated this story over and over again. She told it with some admiration—her bright and resourceful daughter!—but I could sense that deep down inside, she was a little horrified. The foreshadowing was too stark not to notice: her daughter, age three, trying to get away.

Still, I never questioned her love, and mine was a contented, if solitary, childhood. We lived in an upper-middle-class neighbourhood of detached 1970s houses with big trees and squirrels, chain-link fences dividing our properties. I would ride up and down the driveway on my bike, having been forbidden from crossing the road. There was a park at the end of the block with a tiny creek that ran through it, lined with cattails, and I would surreptitiously walk my bike across the street before scampering into the grass, trampling buttercups in my path. Incredible to think about today, but I spent hours and hours blissfully unchaperoned.

Many of my childhood memories are cast in a hazy and serene light. I played a lot on my own, reading and writing short stories, capturing all the things that caught my attention in a journal. I spun an imaginary world with my dolls and invisible friend Cindy. My father claimed he could hear me conversing for hours on end with "Cindy," lying on a thick purple shag in my room. On that rug, I also dreamed of going to other places from a very young age, flipping through an old-fashioned folio-style atlas, memorizing the names of countries and capitals.

I always joke that I'm resolutely unsocialized. That I never had the problem of growing up "normal." I didn't have a lot of playmates my age, except for my next-door neighbour, Dorothy DeSousa. We grew up together. Dorothy's family was from the Algarve islands, off the coast of Portugal. Most mornings my father would carry me through the gap in the hedges separating our homes and tap on the DeSousas' screen door. I would be deposited into the arms of Dorothy's grandmother, who I called "madrina," or godmother. She prepared breakfast for us both before school and fed me roasted octopus and grilled peppers when we returned in the afternoon, always in the same quilted housecoat. Dorothy was also an only child, but unlike me, she was uncomplicated and a realist at seven. I would convince her to lie beside me in the garden under the plum tree, sprawled on the damp earth, twigs and gnatty fruit raining down on us while we watched the sky.

"Where do you want to go, Dorothy?"

"I can't go anywhere. I have school. You do too."

"No, I mean later."

"We always go to Portugal for summer vacation. You know that."

"No, I mean later in life. Grown up life."

I could feel her shifting uncomfortably beside me.

"Where do *you* want to go?"

"Name the city." I said. "I will go there."

The capital of Kenya is Nairobi.
Jakarta is the capital of Indonesia.

To care nothing for the breathtaking panorama of the world was puzzling. And to know nothing of countries and capitals was cause for instant dismissal. Of course, the opposite was also true; there was nothing more appealing to me, than to have conquered the maps whose lines and creases I had traced in my atlas and on my globe—if not in life, then in imagination. And so, I turned to books.

I was reading passages from my father's collection of paperbacks, like Thomas Mann's *Magic Mountain* or Camus' *The Outsider*, from a precocious age. By the time I was six or seven, I preferred piecing together enormous puzzles on my own and listening to the Beatles, to seeking out company. My dad had a prize collection of LPs, one of the few things he'd brought over from England. The Beatles were his favourite. I remember lying next to my father's enormous, faux wood-clad 1970s stereo system in the living room and singing along. I knew the lyrics to every Beatles song by the age of five. By nine, I wanted to marry John Lennon. If he wouldn't have me, then George Harrison was my back-up plan.

It was my father, more often than not, who tucked me into bed, murmuring my own special, made up Bangla lullaby:

"Lisarani, Lisarani
Monmolali Bulbulnali
Amar Moni Sonar Rani (My golden jewel princess)
Good night. Sleep tight. Tomorrow we will play together."

My neighbourhood was predominantly Italian, with many Portuguese and Eastern European families. There were no other Indian families nearby at the time, but this didn't leave me alienated. Instead, even as a little kid, I enjoyed being marked as different from everyone else. Often people would ask, "What ARE you?" and before I could answer they would offer: Italian? Calabrian? Greek? Persian? Mexican? I'd get defiant and proudly announce my Indian heritage. In my childish way I was challenging this Western perception of Indians as some homogenous monolith—all appearing the same, speaking the same, eating the same food—when the opposite was true. But it was a rather tiresome endeavour for a kid. So if I was in a mood, I'd use an expression I had overheard: "Me? I'm a flower child. An Indian flower child." I rarely laid claim to my Polish ancestry, which is the opposite compulsion of what I've heard most Indian-Canadians describe. Back then, Indian kids would downplay their South Asian "desi" ethnicity, but for me, my unusual background was an interesting feature—I relished playing up my difference.

Summer and spring were my favourite seasons (I've always loved heat; not a useful quality in a Canadian kid). I remember the light reflecting off the blades of grass as I lay on the dirt, watching ants and ladybugs and an entire universe erupt from the earth. I spent solitary hours on a broken yellow swing set in the park, kicking at clouds. Our family made pilgrimages to country fairs and my favourite: African Lion Safari, where the giraffes left a film of slime on the car windows with their thick, purple tongues. Every weekend, my parents would take me out beyond the confines of the city. But our family ritual was walking. Deep in the heart of the Halton area conservation park the spruce grew so thick that I could hear the wind in the canopy while below it was always dark and mossy and still. There my mother taught me which wild mushrooms were edible and which were poisonous. Other families went to church or temple on Sunday; the forest was our cathedral and my playground. We would drive into Caledon, along a two-lane country road, ballads on the radio, the breeze fingering our hair.

"Papa, have you heard of Liechtenstein?"

"Tell me, Lisa Rani."

"It's one of the smallest countries in the world."

"Mmm hmmm."

"The capital is Vadusz . . . the currency is the Swiss franc and the population is 30,000 . . . Papa?"

"Yes, my Lisa Rani?"

"Have you been there?"

"No, Rani."

"Oh. I want to see it. It's not so high on my list, it's not in the top fifteen, but still, I want to see it. Did you know it's doubly landlocked?"

Sometimes we went fishing with very basic poles, lacquered pieces of wood really. My mom would wait until dark to dig in the dirt in our backyard garden for worms. By the bank of a stream, she'd fish out a worm from the bucket, squelch it on to a hook, and tell me where to sit. I would watch the water for the ripple and pull. But when anyone actually caught a fish, I'd recoil at the sight of the hook coming out of the mouth. I always felt that in nature, things were alive and pulsating, beautiful and grotesque at once.

The capital of Greenland is Nuuk.
The capital of Laos is Vientiane.
The capital of Poland is Warsaw.

Yet for all my parents' commitment to the New World, I was really raised in my earliest years by my Polish grandmother, Halina. My dad was busy travelling for his career, and my mother was working, so my grandmother came over from Warsaw, where she and my grandfather were living at the time. She was very stylish, always wearing hats and carrying a different little purse. Every night, she ritually rolled her hair in curlers and applied different creams (Noxzema was her favourite) on her face and neck. The smell was distinctly sickly sweet, but I was riveted by these feminine rites. Granny was all about "elegancki" or "elegance" and beauty. Not surprisingly, my mother (make-up free with her hands in the dirt) and Granny were impatient with each other's world views. My parents were shorn of ritual and pomp; part of coming to Canada meant consciously dropping a lot of those traditions that they'd found stifling in their home countries. But my grandmother loved a little pomp.

Toronto, city of neighbourhoods, has a west end community called Roncesvalles, a long, bustling street of Polish churches and delicatessens selling cabbage rolls out of bins. Now the area is gentrified with yuppie boutiques and millennial bars, but in the 1970s, it was truly Polish. My grandmother, who sniffed at Toronto—"*Nie elegancki!*" she proclaimed—made an exception for Roncesvalles.

She would pull me from the couch, interrupting my cartoons, and dress me up in my most princess-y outfit, then put on her blocky little heels (her idea of fashion was still a little steeped in Communist Poland). In our finery, we would walk to the end of the street on Fenley Drive to catch a bus and then a subway, finally ending up in Roncesvalles. Granny was in her element there. We paraded down the avenue, making sure to be seen, and stopped at her preferred Polish cafe. Granny loved to philosophize with her friends over coffee and *pączek*, a traditional doughnut with the jam peeping out from a little hole, prune or strawberry. The afternoons spent in pursuit of Granny's earthly pleasures were long. Sometimes I would get weary, pounding the pavement after her as she swanned from store to store. I remember getting so tired that I dropped in the street, my princess skirt fanning out around my thighs as I squatted. This particular position irritated her; she would tug me up, with a Polish reprimand. I'm certain that she interpreted my squatting as a display of the heathen part of me, something *Indians* did. She had great disdain for anyone—or anything for that matter—that wasn't Polish.

In the cafe, she cut the *pączek* in half, holding court with the other ladies in their hats and purses. She used to buy the Polish paper, and scan it immediately for any news of tragedy out of India: "See?" she'd point out to me. "There's always people dying in that country!" She accepted my father, but just barely. The digs about the inferiority of India were small, and always in Polish, which my father didn't speak. Her English never improved beyond the basics, so their relationship remained peaceful. My father was always kind to her, despite the fact that in a comically unsophisticated way, Granny was forever trying to condition me away from my Indian side. She used to say to my mother, very dramatically, as if with great concern: "Oh my goodness, do you think some of Salil's relatives have perished in this terrible train accident that took 250 people's lives?" My mom would roll her eyes.

My mother had wandered far from her Polish Catholic roots. She went to church on Christmas, but always reluctantly. Really, she announced as Granny cringed, she was an atheist. My father was a Hindu, but he was more interested in metaphysical philosophy than ritual. He spoke to me from a very young age about the Vedas, how that revealed wisdom coincided with modern scientific theories, the dance of subatomic particles mirroring Shiva's *tandav*. He was also deeply influenced by Tagore's humanist version of life, seeing divinity in all things, particularly in nature. Still, in this fluid, religiously relaxed home, I had been baptized, probably in deference to my grandmother. I can just imagine Nani campaigning for my baptism, slipping in a few references to the new baby's soul burning in hell until my mother said, "All right, all right! We'll baptize her!" Ever practical, she probably thought: "Well, it won't hurt."

Since my mother never went to church if she could help it, usually it was just my grandmother and me. The service was in Latin and suffocatingly solemn. I sat bored in the pew, counting ladies' hats. I dreaded Easter more than anything, when the language became even more dirge-like and the images of a bloody Christ on the cross were violent and haunting. But the other side of my heritage harboured corresponding terrors. In the summers, my parents and I would take the long flight to Calcutta and remain there for several weeks. It would be the height of monsoon when we arrived, the narrow lanes of Calcutta flooded with dull, brown water. To escape the heat and power outages, the snarl of streets clotted with people and the smells of the city, we fled most weekends to stay with extended family in a bungalow in Serampore, an Indo-Danish heritage settlement outside Calcutta, on the banks of the Hooghly river. The matriarch of the house smelled like almonds and carried herself with a natural grace. I never saw her without her head covered by the pallu of her white and red sari. She spent much of the day in a prayer room filled with images of Kali, the favoured goddess of Bengalis. Kali Ma wears a necklace of skulls dripping blood and has six arms; in one of them is a scythe. Her tongue is lolling, and her hair is wild, Medusa-like. My aunt would softly stroke the idol, bathe and dress her lovingly. It fascinated me to watch her turn the terrifying goddess into a reservoir for her affection. In the bungalow, there was dappled light and I could see the muddied current of the river if I stood on my toes on the flat roof, and even hear snatches of songs of the boatmen, paddling across in the rains. When the rain stopped and the sky became mild and pale, I'd run out the door to a large, open field across the street where boys came to play cricket in the evening. There I finger traced words into the grass, smelling the next storm in the air.

"Where were you, Lisa Rani?" one of my relatives would ask when I returned. I hated being interrogated. "*Tumi ki kichhoo bolbey?*" (Do you want to say something?) The grip on my arm increased as I squirmed to get away. "*Bolo*, Lisa Rani?"

"Don't . . . don't . . . don't pinch my wings!" I shrieked as I freed myself, running for the stairs.

Usually, we stayed in the North Calcutta residence, a structure of fading grandeur with my grandparents and many aunts and uncles. The tall house stood in a neighbourhood called Shyambazar, in the northern part of the city that used to be posh but had aged obstinately like a society matron. Inside there were barred windows on the ground floor, and many dark corridors to explore. The streets outside grimy and stained with paan and neglect; the narrow laneway was choked with vendors. I loved the humid, decaying smells of Calcutta. Even as a child, I sensed something behind the spill of many lives staking their claim along crowded pavements and the expanse of the city. Their stories— the ghosts of migrations and lineage—lived in the clang of bells and the sound of the conches from the temple on the corner, the silver toe ring peeping beneath the hem of a saree. On the corner, the ghugni-wallah would come out around four in the afternoon and fry his shingaras (Bengali samosas) in a wok filled with sizzling oil. All around rang the voices of children from the neighbourhood. "Dada! Dada!" they called to him, using the Bengali word for older brother and extending their hands full of pocket change. I wasn't encouraged to mix with these children, so I stood on the roof terrace and watched little boys walking back from school with their arms flung around each other's shoulders. They seemed to be dancing with life.

Men acted as beasts of burden, pulling carts of goods or rickshaws stuffed with people. In those days in India, if you had money, you demonstrated it by your girth. I watched large women wrapped in Tangail cotton sarees, huge vermilion bindis flashing like red signals on their foreheads, being pulled along by a sinewy rickshaw driver, every vein on his arms and legs raised, his bare feet clawing at the ground.

Mama, did you know that Calcutta was the capital of British India from 1772? New Delhi became the capital of India in 1911.

India made sense to me in ways that my sheltered suburban existence in Canada did not. I saw that life was not always equitable and balanced and "nice"—but that it has its own mysterious logic. It planted an attraction to the imperfect. There grew in me, from a very young age, a sort of mythical junkyard; curious, colliding impressions, from the odious to the luminescent. India lived in me as a contrast to Toronto, where I felt everything was clean and orderly but restrained; emotion concealed behind civility and politeness. I could not as a child explain how the winter winds of Canada hollowed me out, the sound reminding me of a desolate existence from a past life. Nor how I resented people in Toronto aggressively minding their own business behind closed doors, when I most craved touch and human connection. Nor how unnatural I felt it was to temper your feelings, your behaviour, your life. In India, I swallowed affection and confounding impressions which fed my inner world. I just loved to see the drama of life played out around me.

In the family home in Nebubagen Lane (anachronistically named after a lemon tree orchard—"lebu"—which in North Calcutta was pronounced with an "n"), I was surrounded by my cousins; their huge, reflective eyes, fingers deftly scooping rice and dal while I awkwardly clanged my spoon against the thali, the plate, during meals. I longed to be able to eat like them, to use my fingers as elegantly to make balls out of my rice and pick the savoury white meat from fish bones with my fingers, but every time I tried, I made a mess and was teased. My father's family also possessed a kind of faith I had never really seen before, different from my granny's orderly churchgoing. With a plethora of schools of thought within Hinduism that people can adhere to, many people in India follow a "guru," or spiritual leader. My grandfather, the rationalist, had banned gurus from the house in his life. But when he died, his offspring ran out, scattering forth as if the lid of a jar had been unscrewed, and found themselves pandits and spiritual guides and astrologers. I was fascinated by their prayers and shrines; I copied their gestures, hands pressed together, and head bowed. But I had to peek from beneath lowered lids for the next cue. It laid in me the tracks to becoming an expert in composite cultures and gestures.

Of course, things get comically sour between kids, too. At every visit, I was upheld as a point of reference for my younger cousins. One of my aunts would announce: "See Lisa Rani? She is so fair! And such a gooooood student!" Light skin was, and unfortunately still is, the height of beauty in India. Not only was I considered "white"—while coveting the brown skin of my cousins—but apparently rich too. My parents always arrived laden with gifts—Swiss chocolates not to be found in the local bazaar and Sony Walkmans, both luxuries in 1980s India—and so we were regarded as very prosperous. From time to time, all of this competitive bragging became just too much. One of my older male cousins, Papul, used to corner me behind the water tank marked with pigeon droppings out of view of any adults, and sneak in a very hard pinch. That would set me off wailing, though I complained to none of the others.

I recall one family outing to a beachside hotel in Puri. I must have been seven or eight. The famous Bengali actress Moon Moon Sen was staying in one of the cottages in the same resort and her name was spoken of with equal amounts of awe and condemnation. This was the tone reserved for all actresses with the exception of her mother, Suchitra Sen. When we collided with her on our way to the beach, I remember being completely mesmerized by her shorts; I'd never seen any of my aunties in anything but sarees or kaftans. She took my father by the arm a few minutes into meeting and led us all down to a wide beach. After the initial shock at her natural ease, it was impossible not to cheer her boldness and ripe abandon as she ran towards the tide, her glossy hair bouncing and streaming behind her, like the mane of a horse galloping to the desert's edge. "She's very colourful," my father offered later over dinner, avoiding my mother's eyes.

Colourful. I would like to be colourful, I thought.

In Calcutta, the world I saw was filtered through my family, and the heart and belly of the family resided in the women of the household. Though traditional Bengali society was patriarchal, the women in my family moved with imperial grace within their domain: the family home. And the kitchen was the one place that tied together all the sprawling lives of the clan. Sometimes it seemed to me all the women of the household, including my mother, came together as one multi-armed goddess in the smoky kitchen; yelling orders, frying fish and dragging children out of the way by the ear. All of us cousins longed to be back in the kitchen when we were chased out. We leaned against the wall, listening to snatches of husky laughter and conversation. My aunts spoke the language of food and nourishment even while aching for more in life. I was also fascinated by their feminine rites: oiling their long black hair, applying *alta* (a traditional red dye) to the edges of their hands and feet and lining the parting of their hair with sindoor. "What does alta smell like?" I asked one of my aunties, burying my face in her palms. They would grab me affectionately with their strong, expressive hands. Hands that, it seemed, never rested, between cutting and cooking, braiding and tapping their foreheads with a gasp of *"Ore baba!"* They were propagators of this magic touch. After every visit, I carried echoes of an allegiance to a country I didn't completely understand. But I loved India. The place completed me.

In the pre-globalized world of the late 1970s and 1980s, there were few people of mixed ethnicities I could identify with. Wherever I went I was always the outsider; the spectator looking in. Yet India was the one place in the world where I felt content, even as an observer. In my head, I was a brown-skinned, doe-eyed, Parle G biscuit—eating *meye*. There were no borders in my mind, though there would be a cost to our choices—both my parents and my own.

The capital of Norway is Oslo.
Canada is the second-largest country by mass after Russia.

Your adolescent years are arguably the most fascinatingly miserable ones of your life. But behind all the reckless, hormone-fuelled angst is secret knowledge. If you survive your teenage self it will become clear, sometime in the future, that those years have laid the foundation for some of the most crucial revelations of adulthood. Life is hard, alienation trains you to value connection, pain is a great teacher. And sadness is the precondition to a tender heart. If someone told me that at fourteen, I would have kicked them in the shins.

I entered adolescence with the plunging force of a waterfall. I ripped my mom's shirts and tied them at my waist, then stalked around looking for confirmation that I didn't belong. I didn't understand at the time that I had made it a mission. I also wanted to shake the world up, fight for truth and justice, and run through anyone who was apathetic about life, or just stood in my way. Sometimes I felt there was a band tightening around my skull (a neon Flashdance headband) making me crazy with the pressure of my thoughts and at other times it was squeezing my chest, making my heart ache with the thought of not living up to all the expectations I had of myself. I was confused. *"I want to change the world."* While at the same time: *"Don't show them who you really are."*

To survive the treacherous currents of high school I became comfortable by splintering into many personae. It was easier to play a role than risk an unguarded moment with other kids who universally terrified me. I was clever and I learned pretty quickly how to subvert the tribal demarcations of high school. I fit in with the nerds and the brainiacs as well as the cool kids. I also played the role of being an "A" student and good immigrant daughter. I was a universal pleaser. High grades and academic awards were an unwavering expectation in my home, but also a point of negotiation: If I was bringing back good grades my parents couldn't really stop me from doing whatever I wanted to do. I used to take my parents' car and go into the city at night and mostly they let me go, intuiting that I was caught in the ritual of forgetting and rediscovering who I was, again and again. It was the first time I began to think: "Perhaps I'm not enough."

I switched out of my local preppy high school, Richview Collegiate, where kids were wearing polo shirts and khaki pants. I couldn't change my skin colour, and I knew just wearing collared shirts wouldn't be enough to fit in. These privileged kids seemed so concerned about doing the right thing, saying the right thing, wearing the right clothes, it was criminal not to try to provoke them. I set aside my need to be understood and set about understanding them. Behind the country club swagger was a group of kids as terrified as I was about life, but secure in the belief that getting ahead in the world was easy; you just had to follow the rules. I once asked a cute boy at a basement party, "What about travel? Seeing the world?" He had his arm around me on the sofa. Friday night entertainment involved drinking beer in one of the kids" basements while the parents were away on a business trip. "Sweet Child of Mine" was playing on the boombox. I really wanted to make out with him, but I needed to know if there was a soul connection.

"I've been to Mexico . . . once."

He leaned in for a kiss.

"I think I have a lot of testosterone."

He pulled, back, confused.

"But . . . you're a girl."

"Yeah. But you know, I can't stand anyone telling me what to do. I don't know what I want to do yet with my life, but it's going to be something important. Right now, I'm just focused on discovering truth. I just know I don't want to get married and have kids. And I really don't like hanging out with other girls."

"What will you do with your life?" the boy asked, completely bewildered.

"What will you do?"

"I'll be a lawyer, like my dad."

"Ah. Well I guess I'll start a support group for mixed-blood kids. I should know. Half Indian, half Polish, totally weird."

"I thought you were Mexican."

Before my first year was over, I convinced myself that this particular high school was boring and it was time to reinvent myself. I changed schools. I thought I was scripting my freedom, but truthfully, the motivation was to leave before strong emotional ties were established. If the world got to know who I really was . . . Game over.

Etobicoke Collegiate Institute was more mixed: Korean, Jamaican, a few Indians. But most of the immigrant kids seemed very eager to become part of the establishment, not challenge it. The world out there was all peaks to be climbed and here I was treading water with future bankers and accountants. But my boyfriend was Greek, and his family owned a pool hall, which seemed tawdry and thrilling.

What is the capital of Greece?
Athens, where Goddess Athena once lived.

India began to feel more and more distant as I grew older and our trips became more infrequent. My connection to our family was limited to shouting my pranams over a crackling phone line and reading a few lines on the onionskin airmail letters my father faithfully kept up. I think that I had been seeking the kind of emotional nourishment I had found in Calcutta in my daily life in Canada. As I passed from childhood into adolescence, I transferred my emotional needs to food. Weekend jaunts with my mother to Kensington market to load up on frozen beef patties or cheese fished out of milky water in plastic buckets and exotic vegetables took on a conflicted air. Food began to be associated with comfort, and then, when I ate too much, I experimented with deprivation. A troubled relationship with food would haunt me for two decades.

I had been chubby as a kid and in my early teens I began to buy fashion magazines. I had inherited thick eyebrows and cat-like eyes from my father. "She looks like Brooke Shields," people told my parents. Those were also the early days of the supermodels: the Cindy Crawfords and Naomi Campbells. My goal wasn't to model. I was too short, too self-conscious, too brainy. Besides, I'd never seen an Indian model before. But I was enraptured by those sinuous curves, the flat tummy and long lean legs of the magazine models. Still, I would tell people I'd be a writer or an academic, the preferred professions for those with social anxiety disorders. Yet, at thirteen or fourteen I set about single-mindedly emulating the images I saw in magazines. And I wanted instant results, which is part of my impatient nature. Years later an Ayurvedic doctor very accurately diagnosed my *dosha* (or mind-body type) as *vata*—the air element. I am definitely "vata": I move fast, ending up here rather than there, often not really knowing how I got there.

For many years I was becoming light as air—anorexic or borderline anorexic, and later it blossomed into bulimia. At fifteen I joined a gym where I worked the step machine obsessively, glancing into the mirrors behind me, almost willing my body to shrink even as I was exercising. It's amazing how quickly my body image became distorted. I slimmed down but slim wasn't enough. I wanted my ribs to show. I had a naturally small waist, but I wanted to sculpt, I wanted to alter. Smaller. Smaller. Dabbing the oil off pizza slices with paper towels. Hiding my mother's pierogis in a napkin. Exercising until I saw lights. Whatever I was, it was never good enough.

I had been brought up with healthy habits and a love of eating. The more my mom saw me shrink, the more she tried to force me to eat. At school, hunger was the uncredited co-star of my day. My mother placed flasks of homemade soup and chilli in my backpack; I would pour out the contents into a neighbour's bush on the way to the bus stop. I was subsisting on a bit of crackers and French fries at lunch and a cigarette every break between classes. I would return home light-headed. I was getting fanatical: no butter, no full-fat milk, very Jane Fonda choices. (Of course, the skinny women we all upheld back in the 1980s, like Jamie Lee Curtis and Jane Fonda, eventually came out, sharing their own secret self-hate that had achieved those bodies.) I simply wouldn't touch the food on my plate, so my mother became surreptitious, secretly putting butter in my food and switching the skim milk to whole. I would catch her and call her out on it, and we argued like political rivals while my father hung back or tried quietly to make peace.

My mother had truly lived with lack. She was a child during the Second World War, and she talked about how often her family didn't have eggs or butter, none of the luxuries of our suburban Canadian life. For her it was absolutely bewildering, watching her own daughter put herself through scarcity by choice. Sometimes she just shook her head. "The oxygen was cut off when she was born—cord around the neck. That's why she's strange. It's not her fault." And, of course, though she never quite articulated it, she was triggered by old anxiety from my difficult birth. The more she flipped out, the more I chafed against her attempts to control. We were locked in an agonizing dance.

We had huge confrontations as she tried to force-feed me, piling the plate higher with pieces of fried chicken and buttered potatoes, demanding that I eat. I remember sitting at the table, chewing and chewing, gathering the food in my cheek, and when she turned her back for a moment, spitting the food into a serviette and hiding it in the folds of the couch. I changed tack and my dissent took a different form. It became silent. I was left to my impulses to scheme and lie, plotting my thinness like a spy.

I must admit that being skinny elevated my self-confidence. I was getting a lot of attention from boys at school, and from men in the clubs

I began to visit late at night. I was socialized to play the mating game, outlining my lips in red and scraping back my hair like the clone-appearing women in those Robert Plant videos. The 1980s endorsed seduction as a legitimate path to power for women. Not fitting in became even more of a priority, because standing out felt even better. While my looks got me noticed, the conversations I had with older men at clubs and bars were surprisingly stimulating. I was finally able to discuss art and culture, Paris and New York. I was in pursuit of interesting people who could expand my perspective beyond this safe, quiet little corner of the world.

Despite the attention, I still carried around images in my head of a chubby face. My face was my struggle; I obsessed over its shape and the fact that I had inherited my father's classic large jaw. I was so focused on my face that I wasn't conscious of my body withering away, even when I got down to 80 pounds. I didn't think there was anything wrong and I couldn't understand the fuss. I was eating lots of lettuce and apples, even chicken once in a while. I wasn't even making myself throw up regularly, only after eating cake or a lot of sweets. At one point, desperate to get to me, they called a close friend of mine, Tina Mann. She told them the more they pushed, the further I'd retreat. I was as stubborn as my mother. I preferred making my own mistakes to being told what to do.

Other nights, I remember hanging out in the upscale neighbour-hood of Yorkville where the bankers and Bay Street boys met after work. The crowded bars and restaurants seemed the ultimate in glam-our at that time. I would dress like a lawyer (or a lawyer's executive assistant), and plant myself at the Bellair Café just to see how much attention I could get. Of course, when you're young and bursting with sexual ripeness there's an allure that makes you the centre of attention no matter how you dress. But as soon as the men sidled up to buy me a drink, I could see that they, too, were poseurs—actors, really—just play-ing a part. Things never got beyond the first drink. The animal ritual was the fascination and the exaggerated story in my head and once it played out, I would leave. At fifteen, I found it strange to have a casual moment with friends my own age. So, I walked into the administration office in order to change high schools again. I think I was constantly trying to goad myself: as soon as I became comfortable, I had to leave, to undermine my ascent, to feed my self-imposed alienation.

High school didn't challenge me. I excelled without trying too hard. My talent for writing exposed what I believed were hypocrisies in the education system. When I wrote something fresh and original, I rarely got top marks. When I customized the words to appeal to the teacher, it was a guaranteed A. I became so good at gaming the system that I eventually got hired to covertly write essays for international students at University of Toronto, many of whom could barely string together a sentence in English. The small company I worked for had an office close to the Toronto reference library and advertised themselves as a "research service." Of course, I loved the subversion of a high schooler getting paid by a university student to get their degree. Every university essay paper I handed in drove home the point that education was not about learning as much as conforming.

My teenage years were not only about searching for revelation but also about concealing parts of myself. I would never admit to my vulnerability. I masked my sensitive nature with cigarettes and sullenness and rage. After reading Herman Hesse's *Siddhartha*, I felt drawn towards Buddhism and spiritual exploration—something my pragmatic mother scoffed at—so I lined my eyes with black, backcombed my hair and hit the clubs in downtown Toronto, a thwarted Buddhist dancing to Duran Duran. But all through an unnamed feeling called for my attention. Today I might define it as the soul's struggle to know itself, the inkling of being part of something bigger than myself.

Given that I would dive into stairwells or bathroom stalls to avoid talking to people—while believing at the same time I was more important than anyone else—I spent my teens largely avoiding sports and group activities as much as I could and instead wrote melancholic poems in my spare time, heavily influenced, no doubt, by all the morose Russian literature I read.

I run against the common grain
Of society's staid notion
That our foremost duty is, I find,
To regulate emotion.

Hence my tongue lies mute to comply
With regulations from above
Who frown upon, I find,
Blasphemies of love.

Of course, I now know that the only reason I could go out there and chase what was wild was because my parents had created a safe haven for me to return to. But it would be years before I'd appreciate just how much my mother anchored the family, the qualities of character it takes to create a home. But even as I snuck out of the house to drive into the club district and chinned a greeting at a bouncer or flirted with older men, or dumped peroxide on my head when my mom refused to let me cut my hair, our family was still the most important thing in my life. In between my episodes of acting out, there were country walks and candid moments on the couch where the love peeked through. I never considered my parents to be part of the bourgeoisie problem. I wore them to the bone, but I loved them deeply. Around that time, I found a role model in a different place: *Vogue*, the bible of every teenage girl. I remember coming across an interview with the French actress Isabelle Adjani. The author had interviewed colleagues and friends who had known Isabelle, and a male friend described her in a way that always stayed with me: "Isabelle is like a cat," he said. "Wherever she goes, she sets up in a corner and makes it her own. And one day you wake up and she's gone."

Rabat is the capital of Morocco.
The capital of Uruguay is Montevideo.

This one throwaway line in a magazine article burrowed deep inside me. I was fascinated: Is it really possible to live like that? I too wanted to be like a cat with no fixed address, crashing in corners and deciding when it was time to move on. I didn't know as I read and reread that article that exactly this life of movement was waiting for me, and that I, too, would make a life of coming and going as I pleased—for better or worse.

3

IN 1991, MY last year of high school, I readied myself to break free of Toronto. I was already taking trips in my mind, sailing over honey-coloured lands, all while sitting in the front row of class. While the teacher droned on about the Upper Canada Rebellion, I sat on my hands to calm a throbbing in the pit of my stomach. I was, even then, seeking a measure of fear—like a war reporter—to feel alive to the adrenaline of going where everyone tells you not to. In the crumbling walls at the back of the parking lot of the 7-Eleven, I saw the ramparts of an ancient city, a whiff of Morocco or Iran. In this way, imagination sustained me as I waited.

Because I was a strong and impatient student, I finished high school a year early and pushed aside all the scholarship offers. I was as uncertain as any sixteen-year-old, but somehow I had in my head the vague idea that maybe a life in academia was for me, chasing some piece of intellectual tinsel in a book-lined room. Anything that limited contact with other humans was enticing. So, it was down to either academia or writing.

But before starting my formal education, I convinced my parents to send me abroad on an unofficial gap year. Given their own restless spirits, it wasn't too difficult to negotiate a travel year with them. Both my mother and father had quietly observed that I simply didn't fit in; those breathless hours on the phone gossiping with girlfriends were never part of my make-up. I had a lot of normal teenage angst, but my parents also understood that my need to explore went beyond that. And in truth, even they didn't fit into the neighbourhood. Today I realize this: suburban life was an excursion for my mom and dad, not a destination.

The idea was that I would travel by myself in Europe in the spring, then meet up with them for a few months of adventure together in Poland and India before starting university in September. In part, they didn't mind sending me off because I wasn't exactly going to be on my own—I was going to spend time with the family of a man who wanted to marry me. The shadow of my parents' long-abandoned cultural beliefs still lingered, and I was always aware of an unspoken conviction, on both my Polish and Indian sides, that marriage was in my future. I wasn't surprised when, at a very young age, I was being pursued as a future wife.

On one of our family trips to Calcutta, we had stayed a few nights at the Holiday Inn on Juhu Beach in Bombay. Bollywood film stars and rich financiers came to this slightly dated hotel to behave badly, throwing their weight around the palm-fringed pool, gold medallions on their chest flashing like a tiger's eyes in the sun. There, in the elevator—or "lift" as they say in Bombay—wedged between my parents, I was spotted by an aide to the scion of a wealthy British-Indian family originally from Kenya. Somehow, between floors, he decided I might make a good wife for his boss. He invited my parents and me to dinner by the pool with V, who was in his late twenties and pleasant enough, if a little nervous. Unbeknownst to him, he had two great marks against him already: he seemed boring and reliable, which is probably why my parents seemed taken with him. Despite her independent streak, my mother still believed a pretty girl should find a husband to look after her. Or perhaps she intuited the fire in my veins and hoped marriage would keep me safe. I recall a thirst to be accepted by my mother despite all my rebellious acting out. So I coolly went along with the plan, enjoying the adventure, while, over the next year, my parents were wooed by V. He invited my family to one of his opulent homes in LA during March break and a plan was made to spend time with his family at one of their homes in north London.

A year later, full of possibilities and en route to Europe, I was prepared to steer myself in a different direction. Before leaving Toronto, I had met a very cute Croatian-Canadian boy closer to my own age at the gym who had told me in passing that he was going to be in Croatia that summer at his family's ancestral village. He had drawn me a map and said: "If you're in the area, come by and visit." Of course, "Come visit me in Croatia" is the kind of invitation that's offered precisely because no one is expected to accept it. Goran didn't know he was dealing with a girl who had spent her childhood memorizing the atlas. I landed in Switzerland, prickly desires like small fish bones in my throat.

In Zurich, I was driven to the home of an ex-Swiss Air stewardess who had a pretty little chalet tucked up in the mountains and who had agreed to chaperone this curious, mixed-blood girl from Canada. She was the friend of a family friend from India, and she welcomed me without reservation. I was to remain with Karen for a few weeks, before travelling to London to meet with V's family and then join my parents in Poland. Karen was a true bohemian and comfortable in her skin in a way I've only seen in European women. I hoarded my impressions of her. She was genial towards me, but impatient with my crust of Canadian politeness. When I made a generic comment about the weather one morning, she responded, "Bah, in summer it's hot, in winter it's cold, what's interesting about that?" without removing her cigarette or looking up. I was delighted. She was to me the height of worldly, mercurial charm. I was fascinated by her wrinkles and long white hair and how she did little to disguise them; I envied her ease. I remember watching her absorption as she peeled an apple, sitting on a picnic bench in her sleeveless dress with her wrinkled arms flapping freely. I was such a restless kid that I was struck by her stillness, something that would become a goal of mine many years later.

But outside the house I was still in Switzerland, trapped in a twee little village and after several days of being hosted, I was bored. Switzerland is a lot like Canada, orderly and scenic, and that was not what I had signed up for. After a week Karen helped me buy a one-way ticket to Belgrade. She drove me down the mountain to the airport in comfortable silence, no need for an explanation between us. "No return ticket . . . good," Karen said. I knew she understood the call away from the familiar.

This was 1991 and Yugoslavia was on the cusp of bloody civil strife. I, however, had no idea of that when I landed, clutching Goran's little hand-drawn map, and took a taxi to the train station. I stepped into the crowd with my suitcase. Here was a place dirtied and a bit bloodied and chaotic, with people darting into traffic on one side and someone shoving a goat into a train car on the other. I savoured the tableaux all around me: gypsies gathered together on one side of the train station; women with their heads covered in black, herding their families through the crowds, the atmosphere thick with chesty smoke.

Once inside the station I discovered the schedules were written in Cyrillic—I couldn't decipher any of the destinations. But somehow or other, because I spoke Polish and gestured wildly at a man behind the counter, a helpful crowd gathered, and I managed to get a train ticket somewhere in the general direction of Goran's village. I had the map and an abiding faith in departures. I boarded, calculating that Goran lived about 200 kilometres away, so the journey shouldn't take more than two hours. I didn't account for the fact the train moved at about 20 kilometres an hour. I was trapped for hours in a crowded car with a huge matriarch in head-to-toe black, her family gathered around her like disciples, staring at me through orange-tinged light. She started to cross-examine me in broken English: "Who are you? Where you go?" I gave her the name of the village and she said: "Where your parents?" then companionably offered me a lemon to suck on when I went silent. I still remember the clickety-clack of that interminable train ride.

I finally reached my destination in Croatia, a village close to Split, the largest coastal town in the country. It was early morning, the sun just breaking. When you fancy yourself a traveller and not a tourist, you develop a taste for disorienting arrivals: it's always early morning or late at night when you stumble into a new place and you are alone except for some solitary cab driver or another misfit like yourself. This very large feeling hits me on every arrival of this nature: I am an insignificant dot. A minuscule part of creation. I remember having one of those moments looking around that empty Croatian village. It was unkempt, like a wild girl gone to seed, bristly grass poking out from the gravel everywhere. Outside the whistle stop was the one taxi and a dusty road. The driver was dozing. I woke him and showed him my map.

When I presented myself at Goran's door at 6 a.m., suitcase at my feet, the palest sky was behind me, turning me into a silhouette. Now that I was here, I had no idea what reception I would get. Goran was quite naturally surprised, and sleepy, patting his hands over his hair self-consciously, but I was immediately welcomed to stay. Yawning young faces emerged from inner rooms to gawk at me over Goran's shoulder. The house was full. There were cousins and kids with indecipherable ties (she's my mother's aunt's second cousin's daughter) spilling out of everywhere, but not a single adult. I was quickly absorbed into that youthful chaos and under the gaze of so many eyes, Goran and I embarked on a whirlwind romance. "After all, there's no spare room so you have to sleep with me." He was an incredibly sexy guy, brooding, with dark, thick floppy hair—almost every man I've been with since then has possessed a variation on this look. But at the time, I had just recently discovered boys in earnest. Goran's family home was a spartan but comfortable three-storey house constructed of simple whitewashed cement set on the side of a hill. Soon word spread and most of the neighbours came by, curious about this Canadian girl who had just showed up. Goran and I were trailed when we linked fingers and walked to the village centre for coffee and to call my parents. The town seemed relatively prosperous—the small iron tables in the cafes were full—though no one seemed preoccupied with work. It was functioning on a typical Eastern European "remittance economy" where family members who had gone abroad sent money back to relatives who stayed behind. You could see the homes built from that money—slightly newer, slightly fresher with television antennas—but still cinderblock and whitewashed with a red roof.

We would swim in the local swimming hole, a scenic bend in the river where a large tree provided an overhanging branch from which the more adventurous boys would launch themselves into the water. It was a fine way for them to preen and show off. We'd walk for miles through cornfields, sometimes for no reason, sometimes to visit an impressive hog. Goran's female cousins showed me how they made dolls out of corn stalks. At night Goran and I slept on a mattress in the loft, whispering in the light of a battery-powered lantern. I remember lying very still next to Goran, holding in my happiness, while the moon spilled drapes of light from a window set high under the roof.

Occasionally convoys of men waving flags and leaning on car horns would wind their way through the villages. "What's that about?" I remember asking Goran. "They're Serbians," he said. Or: "They're

Bosnians." Nobody paid a lot of attention, not understanding that a bloody future was trampling down the horizon. Goran and much of the village came with me to the train station when I had to leave for London. It was never discussed, but I knew V would pick me up at the airport on the other end, and drive me to the family mansion in Tottenham, north London. I remember passing through many sweet, unkempt villages on the train ride back to Belgrade. A mere few weeks later, a bitter and devastating civil war broke out.

But by then I had crossed into a completely different world. As soon as I settled into V's spacious family house, I realized that I was the target of a family campaign to turn me into a good wife. V's mom would wake me up early with chai and lure me sweetly into the kitchen to try to teach me to make puris and rotis. Her small mouth pursed as she tested my talents (my rotis were lousy). I just didn't see the romance in peeling, kneading, flipping and serving and I felt immediately suffocated. At every meal I was watched by this large, extended Gujarati family; I could taste their concern. Also, it was hard for me to starve myself. There was no way to refuse the rice, dal and farsan and reach for just a bit of fruit and yogurt. Suddenly the furniture seemed over-stuffed and the mansion too quiet, drawing my attention to the ants crawling over the windowpane in the kitchen, desperate to get out. This was London after all! I complained to V that I felt stifled, and he agreed to let me stay in one of his apartments in the Docklands, a cool new development at the time, in southeast London.

Once I moved into that flat, I disappeared into the city, which I suspect left sweet, dutiful V a bit deflated but ultimately relieved—I was clearly too maladjusted to be good wife material. He let me stay alone in his flat while he stayed in the Tottenham house. I marvel today at his decency and I'm glad I saved us both from catastrophe by not marrying him.

I remember the flat was very sterile, with round, nautical windows. But I loved this independence to wake whenever I wanted and was instantly intoxicated by London. I made a daily call to my parents—it was never talked about but they understood the marriage scheme was off—before descending into the tube to lose myself in neighbourhoods like Chelsea and Kensington and Notting Hill, where the buildings were bone coloured, stately and pleasingly symmetrical. London had belonged to my parents as well, so it was another skin to try on. And I liked myself in London. I liked the version of myself that appeared—sophisticated and at home in a sprawling city. If I felt small against the grey sky in Hyde Park, or the sturdy cathedrals and monuments, it was all right. Everyone felt their insignificance in London while at the same time intuiting how we are joined to everything that came before, the entire past. London belonged to me as much as anyone else because, really, it belonged to the world. But London was also a muscular and vinegary city with little patience for sentiment. I had to tone down my enthusiasm.

I remember opening a notebook in a sidewalk cafe on King's Road, bursting with so many pleasurable feelings that I had to write them down. "No one should ever have to eat bad food," a fabulously imposing woman tartly concluded to my right. I wrote that down too. I thought these little snatches of life would disappear if I neglected to write them down.

I recall sashaying down King's Road after I checked in the morning that my ribs were showing and my collarbones protruding sharp as needles. By then I was quite thin, getting through the day on fruit and tea with a little milk. My anorexia was my best mate, helping me project confidence and beauty when I was travelling alone in the world. I would wake up and even before showering, smoke a cigarette to keep my appetite down. Then I would look over my journal where I had written down the previous day's calories while running a hand over my belly and thighs, pinching, gathering information that was translated unreliably in my mind. One day a scout from the prestigious agency Models 1 chased me down on King's Road and handed me his card, asking if I wanted to work as a model. "You have wheels on your feet, cha," he joked. I smiled and tucked the card away. I'd never thought about it before. Maybe I felt a little defiant about being told what I should do by someone else. Anyway, my time in London was coming to a close. I had to leave to meet my parents in Warsaw.

We spent only a week or so in Warsaw. It was my first visit to Poland, and it left an impression. My parents had intended for this to be a family pilgrimage to my mother's homeland, an opportunity for me to experience the other half of my heritage. Today I understand Poland was going through an extraordinary transition in 1991. A tentative optimism hung in the air, but as we walked through the city, I began to see a Soviet-era grimness in certain buildings and hunched postures, as well as the occasional breadline with a queue of resigned expressions. It was the year of Lech Walesa, and the older generation was sceptical about whether this democratic transition that had begun in 1989 would bring about real change. Poland was inching towards a market economy, but there were growing pains. Nani, in her well-worn rabbit fur coat, led the charge around the city, punctuating the air with derogatory comments about gypsies and the current shifting social order. Yes, there were more things to buy, more varieties of hats and gloves in the stores, but they were expensive. Who had that kind of money? And the communal ritual of lining up for essentials had not been replaced with new outlets for the older generation to gather at to gossip or complain. Nani stopped abruptly in the middle of the sidewalk to lay her hand on her heart in the universal gesture of mourning. There were beggars in the streets—Beggars!—like in India. Terrible! The weather was still cool, so we pulled sweaters from our suitcases that were piled high in her narrow flat. Every day Nani perfunctorily prepared pots of borscht and laid out bread and butter and cheese in the mornings, and pickled trotters and herrings with dense rye bread for lunch. My father grimaced. Sitting down to this sort of food was like punishment for him. He had never tasted cheese until leaving India, and it was still an acquired taste for him, never mind the terrifying things jiggling around in the jelly on his plate. My mother gave him a look that said, "Keep the peace. I'll make this up to you later."

We did go to the ballet with my grandmother, who was very pleased to take us (my mother was less enthused). Cultural activities were still free or heavily subsidized by the state and I remember sitting between my grandmother and my mother in a dimly opulent, mahogany setting, a rare peace settling amongst us three, watching the dancers sculpt the air. It was achingly beautiful and nostalgic. But sitting there triggered a weird thought: Did people dance while war had ripped through the city? I enjoyed walking through Nowy Świat—literally, "New World"—a posh area with cobblestone streets and outdoor cafes that was trying to recapture the neighbourhood's pre-Second World War integrity, but I felt like

a tourist. I was trying to find something to define my connection to the
country and my "Polishness." I had grown up around the language,
though I rarely spoke it by my teens, but Poland opened an ocean of
sounds inside me, forgotten words pouring through me. I began walking
more slowly to separate myself from the burbling tribe of blonde relatives
to try and hear what the streets were saying. The historic area intersecting
Nowy Świat had been completely razed during the war by German forces
in 1944. I imagined boots in alleyways, high pitched whirring, fear pouring into bricks. I felt a lump forming in my throat, hot as coal. Nani
refused to talk about the war, except the one time she showed me a faded
black-and-white photo of her brother who had mysteriously perished
during that time. I understood why this survivalist town was trying to
bury the past. Does it ever lose its power, I wondered, the terrible emotional toll of war?

One afternoon, my parents and I went on a tour of the Palace of
Culture and Science, a huge, looming Soviet-era building that cast a
shadow over the city. I still remember being struck by the contrast between
the new shopping district and this massive, looming building that seemed
immovable and permanent. Poland was still caught between worlds.

After that week in Warsaw my parents and I flew to Bombay, intending to stay for six months. When I think about it now, it was a strange
decision. Over the years we had stopped in Bombay on our way to
Calcutta, spending a few days and nights in the heaving metropolis.
Bombay is not cordial, nor is it calm. It's a city for having your guts
pulled out, and for feeling the pulse of thronging lives vibrate in your
bones. My parents had taken leave from their cosy lives, to move to a
wild, tough-talking city, made up of everything you are not supposed to
love. Mangoes and magazines are pressed against your car window;
leather shoes and volumes of books run to rot in the salt air. But there
was *something* in that air. It's undeniable. Everyone feels it. It's the
secret heart of possibility that grabs you by the hair.

But the city's allure is not for everyone and it's not immediately clear,
unless you want every belief you hold turned on its head. Or unless you
have that longing scorching your veins. My mother had it, though I didn't
recognize it when I was young and self-absorbed. Maybe all my angst
about not fitting in was more familiar and relatable to my mother than

my father; she was after all, more comfortable in India than anywhere else. Or maybe the fable of Bombay with its notion of self-invention was more of an attraction to my mother than us. Whatever it was, I'm sure now it was my mother who had proposed this sabbatical to my father, expecting no refusal.

We checked into the Holiday Inn on arriving, but we couldn't afford to stay there for long. It has traditionally been difficult to breeze into India as an outsider and find a place to live. It's not like New York or London where immigrant ambitions smooth a well-worn way to find a place to rent. Bombay real estate was (and is) hyper-inflated, and though things were opening up in India as they were in Poland in 1991, the Indian economy was still closed and tightly regulated. A poolside acquaintance from a previous stay at the Holiday Inn, Surinder, had arranged a flat for us, but even after many verbal assurances, he disappeared and it fell apart at the last minute. We found ourselves homeless.

So, within a few days we moved to the ISKCON guest house attached to the Hare Krishna temple, down the street from the hotel. It was my mother's idea and an appropriately incongruous introduction to the city. Outside, the streets of Bombay shrieked and beeped, but inside the International Society for Krishna Consciousness temple compound, it was all benignly glistening white marble. We were given a clean, spacious room designed for foreigners, just down the street from Juhu Beach. I quite enjoyed the dawn chants and bhajans at all hours, and I'd slip my shoes off in the morning to sit on the cool floor during early morning pooja. The devotees were a fascinating lot, dancing with aban-don during pooja, then striding purposefully back and forth from the temple to the offices in orange kurtas and dhotis, friendly and tolerant. There was also a fair mix of foreigners who danced and prostrated their way through the daily routine, the *shikha* or tuft of hair on their bare scalps bobbing like a spiritual antenna; they appeared fragile to me, keeping one hand on malas in their burnt-orange-coloured prayer bag at all times. While I explored the roiling city, my mom made a lot of friends in the ISKCON society and set about nesting with her usual indus-triousness. She somehow smuggled in the ingredients for chicken soup and cooked it up over a little hotplate she purchased in a market. This was quietly indecent, of course, in a vegetarian ashram. This was another of my mother's special skills; bringing the human to the sublime. I suspect the presiding Swami knew but tolerated my mother's indiscretion.

Every morning my mom and I swept across the marble portico and out through the huge gates. My mom stalked off towards the market to stock up on edible contraband, her blonde hair drawing looks from the passing doodh-wallah while I used to go for morning walks on Juhu Beach, a broad stretch of sand lined with the apartments and bungalows of Bollywood stars, and crowded with bhelpuri-wallahs and balloon sellers in the evenings. I was obsessed with exercise at the time, on the cusp of returning to a fully fledged eating disorder and needed regular jogs. It's a well-known fact that people in India have a tendency to stare, even from a distance. The quality of the stare is very unnerving and violating, particularly from men. I used to throw sand at these strange men who would run alongside me, gawking. One day a man jogged up behind me and said, "You should be in the movies." I looked at him disdainfully, preparing for my sand-in-the-face manoeuvre, when he handed me his card. Something in his manner caused me to hold off on my attack. He turned out to be Shekhar Kapur, who was just starting to direct Bollywood films, and would go on to direct Cate Blanchett in the film *Elizabeth*. In Bollywood, he was known for a film called *Mr. India*, and I was vaguely aware of how respected he was already. I expect I appeared very self-confident, but the reality was that I was so reserved I couldn't imagine acting on this opportunity. How was a shy kid from a quiet home going to appear on a movie screen? I'd never even considered acting, especially not in Hindi films, and just the thought of it paralysed me, though I murmured my thanks before jogging away. After he turned, I flicked the card away.

Although we were staying in the ISKCON guest house, our foreign passports enabled us to hang out around the Holiday Inn's pool in the hot summer afternoons, ordering fresh lime sodas. In those days, the pool-side cafe attracted a flashy cast of characters, most of whom had some link to the entertainment business. I watched them flock to the loungers and tables in the late afternoon; the raven-haired women with severely drawn eyebrows, smoking in bright kaftans; the men, modelling them-selves on Feroz Khan, with lacquered hair and dark glasses, their cologne strong enough to close your throat, and a bald, brawny Australian called

Bob Christo who had played the villain in numerous Hindi films and spoke with the strangest accent I'd ever heard. They seemed caricatures come to life, beckoning the waiters with a *filmi* flourish. In this setting, my mother was as eye-catching as a bright feather caught on metal hinge. Quickly and easily, from behind her sunglasses, in a polka-dot swimsuit, my mother befriended everyone. There was Bugsy, a perma-tanned pilot who lived in a bungalow in the Theosophical Housing Colony. He looked particularly good in linen and wore shockingly small swim trunks. I thought of him as the ringmaster; he had a lot of friends in the film and fashion industries and he was one of the first to invite me to a party. "I'm starting to feel like your bloody secretary, my dear," he declared as invitations began flying at me, first getting filtered through Bugsy and later called out from around the poolside. Bombay is a very sociable town, all about the newest young thing. Of course, I accepted. I was too curious not to go, overriding my natural reticence.

Every night seemed a constant, gunfire round of parties in Bombay. There was no design or shape to it. "Plan? No plan, how boring, yaar! Nothing is something, *hai na?*" The party crowd in the early 1990s was devoted to the cause of making every moment count. They each had their own brand of flamboyant glamour; the lipstick was dark and glossy, the neon eye make-up shimmery and perms still trendy. Even for men. Expensive sunglasses perched on the crown of their heads, day and night, a marvellous feat considering they never fell or moved. There weren't many bars or clubs then, so the party caravan would begin around 10 p.m., then move from building to building, picking up new people along the way. "Shit yaar, tell him to slow down," one of the new entrants whined as she tried to line her lips in the back seat. She closed her compact, then noticed me watching. "Red lips run the world," she winked. We all piled into someone's car and drove through the city at night, the tape deck blaring either Bryan Adams or old Bollywood numbers.

I remember how natural it felt to be cruising down Marine Drive, the vitality of the city undiminished at night. Bombayites, starved for open space, made the curvature of the sea-facing promenade an outdoor living room. I saw the crowds perched on the sea wall late into the night as we zoomed past. Malabar Hill, Colaba, Worli, Breach Candy, Bandra—these neighbourhoods were tent poles rising out of the island city, holding up the sky. The buildings were stained and decrepit from the outside. Hard drugs were rare, though some photographers and models would smoke "charas"—hash or marijuana. I was never much of a drinker and for all my experimentation, I never fell into drugs. My penchant for putting myself in strange circumstances meant I needed to be in control to watch things roll out.

Soon I was jumping into taxis alone: "Bhaiya, yeh, this address, take me, leke ana, le jao," infiltrating buildings of upper-class privilege on Warden Road, Nepean Sea Road and the by lanes of Colaba, following someone's direction to take a right at the paan-wallah's stall, past the security guard's salute and entering the elegant drawing rooms of stately families, the guardians of art and good taste in the city. Those homes were filled with imported bevelled glass and ancestors" busts, and also with a varied collection of guests. Newspaper editors and politicians and industrialists, people with the settled grin of having nothing to worry about, and who have the means to make the world bend to their will. I listened a lot, seizing little scraps of wisdom, which I'd recycle during another evening out. "Fitting in is over rated," I'd sigh. Other times a Wodehouseian sentence rose above other voices, "That portly wastrel decamped to London where he's hale and hearty but more irksome than before. What a scabrous nuisance." I stumbled through the ISKCON gates later and later at night. Soon I was returning during the morning bhajans, the clash of cymbals reverberating as I fell into bed. My parents knew they couldn't control my explorations, but they also trusted I wouldn't go too far off track.

I don't remember the music, the views or how the light fell across someone's face, but I remember all those nights blended into a singular, noisy, glittering, tidal impression. At times, it felt like the city itself was alive to its own dazzling self-importance. There was the tall, lanky, chain-smoking son of an old Hindi film producer with a hooked nose and stained, dark lips. He befriended me, perhaps harbouring a secret idea that we might become a couple, but it was not to be. There were intriguing women—beautiful, young spirits telegraphing sexual appeal through their eyes, or older and majestic doing so from behind oversized glasses and glossy hair, their girth layered in fabric. In their mid-thirties to forties, they were that brand of socialite found in every city in the world, ex-models or air flight attendants who had reinvented themselves as either interior designers, or fashion designers. They watched me—"It's feeding hour," I heard one of them say—with a smug knowing. Bombay was all about self-invention, after all, and I was figuring out who I wanted to be.

In Canada people thought Indians were very conservative. I grew up with the stereotype of the Indian taxi driver, the aunties in hairnets, and the hard-working, joyless immigrant story. But in Bombay all those stereotypes were shattered. Here were worldly, audacious, overwrought, vastly engaging people; artists, photographers, writers, risk-takers, a secret society with their own Morse code and morally ambiguous ways. "Always buy the best and spend all your money—don't save it for children, those selfish bastards" was not just drunken advice from a salt-and-pepper cigar-smoker, but a motto of sorts.

I observed pedigreed women sweeping through the cavernous marble lobby of the Taj Hotel when I was invited to meet a new friend for tea at the Sea Lounge, while outside thin, dark-skinned boys haunted the streets. I watched them, avoiding their eyes. Bombay was the most beguilingly atrocious place, built around monstrous contradictions. Maybe just the fact that the city endured was a testament to the presence of something greater than men. But it was the aroma that brought the city most vividly alive; the reek of public urinals and fish and sweat and noxious fumes and cheap perfume embodying all the stirring hopes and losses. This was what you tasted when you left the cool lobby of the Taj or the Oberoi or the Holiday Inn and either you had the appetite for it, or you did not. But really there was no way to understand the city except by binding your day-to-day life with it. Soon I stopped talking about the meaning of life. I became a Bombayite.

During this time, I hardly knew in whose homes I was landing. One of those evenings a stranger—an older Parsi man who looked a lot like a turtle in a polo shirt—said to me: "You really should meet Maureen Wadia. She likes your type."

"What's my type?"

"Half-breed," he said. "She's an Anglo-Indian herself."

"But I'm not . . ."

"Cheers my dear. Let's drink to being in a pretty good place. Just don't be boring and blather on when you go across to meet her."

Someone made a call to someone who knew someone. Soon after, I got a message at the ISKCON guest house from Maureen Wadia, inviting me to a meeting. She was looking for models for her in-house fashion magazine, *Gladrags*. I was told she was a legendary figure in Bombay, an ex-Air India air hostess (it was a well-worn trope that the most chic, ambitious women of the 1960s and 1970s were handpicked to work in the skies; they travelled internationally when it wasn't the norm and ended up marrying influential Indian men). She had married Nusli Wadia, who was part of a prestigious industrial Parsi family who had allegedly made their money in the opium trade way back. Now they had an empire of businesses, whose flagship company was Bombay Dyeing, a textile brand which had cornered the Indian market on bed sheets and towels.

I took a cab and was dropped off outside her security gate of her home in Prabhadevi. I should have asked to be driven to the front door, but I couldn't explain myself in Hindi, so I got out and started trudging up the long, curved driveway. Ahead, I glimpsed a huge bungalow—an immediate flag of extreme wealth. Bombay is a vertical city, but the Wadias' wide, sprawling house was fearlessly horizontal. I saw Maureen come out on to the large porch of the mansion and stand between pillars under a portico. She looked like a silent-era movie star with beautiful, wide set, sleepy doe eyes. She was perfectly exuding regal glamour in a pair of smartly cut pants and a little scarf tied just so.

As I walked towards her, I noticed a pack of dogs appearing from around the side of the house. German shepherds and Rottweilers. At first they didn't seem threatening, but then they appeared to change their mind and ran towards me, barking loudly. I stopped, amused rather than alarmed as they surrounded me. I extended a conciliatory hand towards one of the German shepherds and at that moment, one of the Rottweilers jumped up behind me and bit me on the butt cheek. I let out a loud yelp, and Maureen came dashing down the steps. It really was an out-of-the-ordinary introduction. I was struggling to compose myself before we exchanged a single word, holding my lightly bleeding ass. She guided me into the house, apologizing repeatedly, and opened the door to one of the huge guest washrooms. As I gawked at the gilded taps, she coaxed me to pull down my pants so she could look at the wound. Maureen directed her staff, hovering nearby, to bring a little medical kit. Even as she cleaned my wound, she was charming, her personality washing over me like a warm, buttery light. I was watching the entire episode unfold, detached from the action, wondering how best to describe this veer into the unexpected, and why I wasn't embarrassed. With the bite bandaged and my pants up, we agreed to adjourn for the day. Maureen sent me home in one of her cars. I replayed the scene in the back seat the entire drive. But when I returned to Juhu I decided not to mention the incident. I thought I would likely never hear from her again.

A couple of days later my parents and I left for the beaches of Goa where we had rented a house in Colvale for a week. In the mornings I watched fishermen haul in their nets and young boys make homemade spear guns. We spent our days eating in the beach shacks ("Does that say "fried children" or "chicken"?" my father pointed to a typo on the menu. "Oh sir, it should say chicken. We don't serve children here.") and went swimming in the dark, churning sea. When we returned, there were frantic messages from Maureen at the guest house reception: "Lisa, I'd like to take some photos of you. Can we do it tomorrow?"

Though I loved fashion magazines, I felt oddly neutral about this invitation, an ambivalence that would stalk my whole career. I told my parents and they didn't seem to mind, thinking it a frivolous diversion. But I also think they were reconciled to the fact that I was not going to be herded through life in a manner that was familiar to them. My mom had more practical concerns: modelling is fine for now, but finish university and eventually, marriage! I was still reliant on their support, so I caught my father's eye and didn't argue.

I decided to look upon the shoot as yet another experience to recount to my friend Tina back in Canada and the next morning took a taxi to a photographer's studio in Mahim. Ashok Salian was one of a small group of pioneers in the fledgling modelling and advertising industry in India at the time. He looked like a prophet, with hair that grew like scrub and granny glasses. He smoked constantly and spoke in a booming voice that would inevitably cascade into laughter. I suspect he was high most of the time as anything would set him off: ask for a glass of water and he'd throw back his head and laugh and laugh. I felt I was that much closer to becoming an Isabelle Adjani cat.

It was my first photo shoot, and I had no clue what I was doing. I tottered out in heels, in a bedazzled Bhairavi Jaikishan cat suit I'd been zipped into, and wearing a stiff smile. Ashok grabbed his camera from his assistant. "Let's start." But nothing happened. I was obsidian. A mortified slab. Raising a hand to my hip upset my balance, and I stumbled off the black paper laid down for me on the floor and into a studio wall. *Jidder, jidder, crash.* Ashok paused. I waited for him to shoot me a contemptuous look, then throw down the camera in protest. There was no air in the studio; just the echo of my thoughts: "Oh. My. God. I. Am. So. Clumsy." Suddenly, Ashok's beard began to quiver. He grinned. *I think he grinned.* At least I saw a flash of white teeth through the thicket of facial hair. "Okaaay. Let's try *this*. Be a cat. You know, meeeeee-ow!" and he laughed. I started laughing too; it was a trigger. I walked back to the spot marked with white masking tape and planted my legs the way I'd seen Lynda Carter do as that Amazon with special powers: Wonder Woman. Slowly I began moving fluidly from pose to pose. Here was a space where I could shed my introverted self and create an entirely new personality. I immediately began enjoying myself. I was dressed up in sparkly hot pants and sarees, the choli dripping with crystals and a long, black, fitted catsuit that would make a splash later. Soon I began whipping my hair around, back and forth, thrashing my arms like a dry land backstroke. I suppose it was my version of a spinning transformation: from mild-mannered geek into my superhero alter ego. I had always been fascinated by projecting something I wasn't—ask the men in Toronto. Here, that projection was required. As I posed, I was taking all the images I'd seen in *Vogue,* amplifying them to a subcontinental frequency and enacting them. I was playing also with what it meant to be a woman: this innate talent to blend in, to adapt, a requisite theatricality, a splintering of self. It was easy for me because it wasn't me at all. I didn't have to confront that scared, conflicted young girl who was so unconfident about her gifts and whether she had any to share. Rather, I could put on the mask and be strong and seductive, all the things I never felt. And the make-up made me look a full decade older. I felt safe in front of the camera with the real me hidden away, invulnerable yet ambivalent beneath the armour.

It never occurred to me to get paid, I just thought this was a one-off experience. When Maureen saw the results (it took a few days to process contact sheets in the pre-digital era) she called me up for another shoot, this time at her seaside mansion.

In the early 1990s, India, known for its "no kissing" policy in film, remained conservative seemingly outside a thin slice of open-minded privilege. In contrast, Bombay women struck me as emancipated. The ones I encountered were sensual, assertive and direct. Maureen was known for putting girls in bathing suits, which was considered scandalous. As we shot, Maureen kept up a lively commentary while she hovered, handing me towels, picking up reflectors and adjusting the furniture. "You are a natural, my dear. The camera loves you," she enthused, squatting behind Chien Wein to squint through the lens. It was clear she had an affinity for me, half-breed and outsider, a girl who didn't belong to one group or the other. Before me, she had chosen Aliya Knightly to model for Bombay Dyeing. Aliya was half Indian, half Australian, the daughter of renowned investigative journalist Philip Knightly. Even the photographer was an interloper: Chien Wein Lee of Chinese origin, born and brought up in India who went on to become a close friend. As we chatted during shoots, both Maureen and Chien made me feel like I was part of a small, exclusive club in India, trying in our own way to break the shackle of the country's more traditional ideas about women.

As I crouched by the side of the pool in my high-slit, Baywatch red one-piece, I was drenched, tired and thinking of dinner. Chien Wein was coaxing me into posing for one last roll of film. It was the "magic hour" and the setting sun was lighting my skin with a flattering glow. I narrowed my eyes and arched into a provocative pose feeling silly and giggly, not sexy, while Maureen stood on the periphery of the frame with towels to wrap around me once we got the shot. That picture became the cover that launched what was to become my career as one of India's first "supermodels."

Before I left for Canada, I did a few more shoots for Maureen, hanging out at her house and eating sandwiches by the pool. We quickly developed a bond, despite the gap in our age and experience. I think Maureen was an outsider in her own way, and this had shaped her personality and talent for self-dramatizing. She entertained me with a stream of stories about the small, daily battles with the "staff" and how hard it was to get anything "done in this country." I listened, quietly reflecting at the same time, on how I had felt getting made up and photographed. Less inadequate, for certain. If you had asked at the time if I felt objectified, I would have answered "no." There was no whiff of patriarchal, sexist aggression on those shoots. I was taken with the implausibility of it all—pretending to be a sex bomb! What a lark!

My year abroad was ending, and the University of Toronto beckoned. We packed up our things from the Hare Krishna temple. My mother gave away the hotplate and bought a box of sweets which we carried to the office of the head Swami to thank him. "You are a Bengali, I know you must have a sweet tooth," she said with a sparkle. His bald head bobbed and he parried my mom's cheekiness by handing me a Bhagavad Gita. Someone barged into his cabin and as I listened to the air conditioning rattling, it occurred to me the Swami knew all about my mother's chicken soup and my energetic social life and yet he had tolerated us. Really, he was a kind man and I felt great affection for the entire exuberant bunch.

We returned to our home in Toronto in June 1991. Initially it was a difficult adjustment. I had to tuck away all the excitement I had experienced in Bombay as I picked my courses and waited for fall. Besides, I had no one I could relate my experiences with, and they sounded more and more surreal even to me. We placed little souvenirs brought back in a showcase; I consigned my memories of *Gladrags*, Maureen, the parties and the poolside afternoons to the back of a closet in my mind. Gradually I became excited about the prospect of beginning university and my life of letters. If my life was to be defined by in-betweenness, Toronto was as good as place to be in as any other.

And then, one summer day, a few weeks before university, I stepped into the car for a family picnic, and everything changed.

4

SO MANY OF my summer weekends growing up in Canada were spent lying in a reverie of tall grass that I can't recall if there was anything particularly different at all about that Sunday jaunt in late August 1991. The memory of Bombay had melted into the air and our normal routine had been resumed in earnest. A carelessly squashed bug, my mother finicky about repacking picnic plates just so, me chewing the stem of a foxtail contemplatively and consequently saved the trouble of helping—these were the commonplace experiences of those afternoons. I was likely being a bit sulky as we packed up to drive home. I was impatient to start university in September, without an inkling that stepping towards adulthood would be defined by a series of small and sometimes monumental events.

There was nothing but warm encouragement in the sky as we drove home from the conservation park in Halton on a narrow country road called Highway 10. When we were getting into the car, at the last possible moment, my mother and I switched places and she climbed into the rear of our Honda Civic. Again, I don't remember the reason, but I do remember the click of my seatbelt and the uncomfortable pressure of it stretched across my chest.

My dad had wound up the window and he was talking. What about? Most likely his favourite subject. How entropy—the measure of chaos in the universe—is out to get us anyhow. The road was grey asphalt, straight and smooth. We passed a large golf club, the immaculate grounds stretched for miles on our left. Up ahead in the distance, I saw a car pull into our lane and head straight for us, trying to overtake another car. Suddenly, it appeared the car was not going to pull back, it was still in our lane, head on, coming closer and closer, making no move to avoid us. In the instant I thought it was going to hit us, I knew the world as I had known it would cease to exist. My dad swerved to avoid the car and hit the gravel shoulder. He lost control, spiralling on to a grassy stretch in front of the golf course. The car began to roll. I remember the feeling of weightlessness as we were lifted into the air. Then a whipping and knocking together of bones, and finally landing upside down on a knoll, wheels in the air. I'm told that paramedics cut me free of my seatbelt and dragged me out of my seat, but I only remember coming to consciousness on the grass. Someone said: "Don't move. Don't MOVE!"

It was a sunny day with an endless expanse of green on either side; a beautiful day for an accident. The sky did not crack. It was clear and blue. I blinked at a single fluffy cloud. A rushing sound rose in my head, filling in the background like the ocean until suddenly everything went quiet. Quiet. Quiet enough to hear air quiver and bone break. The paramedics suspected I had a fracture in my neck, so they laid me on a hard board and put me into an ambulance bound for the closest hospital. I had no clue where I was, or that my dad had no injuries except for a cut on his hand. Nor did I know that back at the grassy knoll the keeper of our family, my mother, was lying on her back. The hatchback had flown open when we rolled and, without her seatbelt, my mother was thrown from the car and had fallen to the earth, breaking her neck. Her spine was severed at the C4 and C5 vertebrae.

Sometimes in an unguarded moment I wondered: Did I miss something? Were there any signs? A premonition I had brushed away, like the wings of a dragonfly? Would it have been different, perhaps, if it had been a bleak and grey day? A rusty sky and slick road? And where was Nani's Jesus? Kali ma? All the gods and goddesses? Why didn't they send a warning, blunt and clear as a highway sign?

I woke up in the hospital, still strapped to a board. A doctor came in, steely eyes tempered with concern, and said, "We're going to X-ray your neck to see what's wrong. We suspect there might be some trauma."

"Where is everyone?" I asked.

"I have to tell you," said the doctor, "your mother may not make it."

His words were the heaviest I have known. I caved under their weight. I can see now that in that instant I shut down completely; it was the beginning of a very long emotional hibernation, as well as the end of a belief that I was entitled to get through life unscathed. My yearning to be free, to push into the hard edges of everything was possible because my life had been secure and sweet and idyllic but now suddenly this security had vanished. This is not the way it was supposed to go. I remember a single tear sliding into my collar and then nothing. I lost the capacity to cry.

Then began a season of hospitals, one of many to come in our family history. My mother was immediately airlifted to Sunnybrook Hospital in Toronto where trauma surgeons went to work on fusing her spine together. I had a hairline fracture in my neck, but I was released quite quickly with a foamy neck brace and the advice to take it easy for a couple of months. I deferred my admission to attend the University of Toronto in the fall and spent the next few weeks adjusting to sleeping on my back with a cervical collar; gaze fixed on the ceiling, arms across my chest, like a vampire. While other kids were buying textbooks and decorating dorm rooms, I was in and out of the Intensive Care Unit at Sunnybrook, bracing myself to see my mother slumped in a hospital bed. A C4 injury means paralysis of the body below the clavicle, so she needed assistance to breathe. Tubes crawled in and out of her body, and between the sounds of whooshing and exhaling my mind whispered: *Push it down. Stay strong. Manage.*

Most of all, I cannot not forget my mother's eyes during that time, groggy from the drugs but also lit with terrible discovery. It scared me, the awareness I saw in her gaze, like she had discovered a truth in why all our lives had led to that place. When I rounded the hospital curtains and caught the glint off a jumble of steel machinery behind her, I had to will her into a stranger to me and that's probably how I missed the decision behind her eyes, to hold on, in defiance of everything. I remember pausing in the hallway, outside. "Did I do this?" All those years of whining about how routine and safety bored me. I was the one who had craved disruption, an operatic life, but oh, my GOD. Please. Not this.

My father and I spent all our days in the hospital, driving home late at night on the 401 to sleep. My mom was still with me when I sank into bed thinking: *It's going to be okay, it's not going to be okay*. Morning by morning, task by task, step by step, we numbly crafted some coherence to our days. I was clueless as to how to fix this but at least in the hospital I had purpose. Without the structure of school, I needed something to focus on. At least, in the confines of my mother's ward, I could be useful. I could run to the snack machine and feel useful. I could call the nurse to change my mother's catheter and feel both useful and useless. The problems began when I stopped moving. That's when I would spiral, flooded with feelings I would have to stuff down, way down, often seated on the edge of the toilet. I didn't know then that even as I learned to compartmentalize my pain, the heart break would embed itself in the core of my being. Holding the sadness inside was not more noble; it was inevitable. My dad and I were coping alone together. He did the best he could, and I found a strangely effective balm in stitching myself up from the inside until nothing affected me; even the seams didn't show.

And then, at two, three, four in the morning, the phone would start ringing. When someone you love is in the ICU, a ringing phone sets off only one thought: "Oh, shit. Bad news." Very reluctantly, very timidly, I'd pick up the phone, foggy and bleary-eyed. The callers usually left messages because it took so long to run downstairs to the kitchen phone. The voices on the machine had thick Indian accents: "Hello, I am looking for Leeza Ray." "Is this the residence of Miss Leeza Ray?" "I am calling from the office of Rahul Rawail and we want Lisa Rayji for his next film. Opposite Sunny Deol."

I stared back at the phone mutely.

Other famous Bollywood directors and producers were calling, a laundry list. A "Ghai Sir," a "Ramesh ji," a "Kumar Sa'ab," a "Mister Mukul." It was a surreal situation bordering on the farcical, like a sketch of exceptionally bad taste. It appeared, at the same time that my world had come undone, I was being chased from across the world by the most prominent Hindi film directors of the day.

We thought someone was playing a cruel joke on us. But the calls kept coming, two or three per night, friendly but insistent voices blasting at us from the other side of the world. India is so noisy you can hear all of its ambient clatter in the background of any call. I could practically smell it through the phone, this sensory assault from far away. "What did you do in Bombay?" my father asked, genuinely disconcerted after fielding a call. He had scribbled down the director's name and office number and we both stared down at it, trapped in a strange trance. Those voices and scribbled names in the middle of the night triggered a memory of my parents, the mauve leather sofa and a pirated Bollywood film. Mithun Chakraborty, the dark horse of the industry, is executing intricate dance choreography in a silver metallic disco jumpsuit on our television screen, featuring unsettling pelvic thrusts. The background dancers are dressed like psychotic toddlers. Mithun tosses a microphone from hand to hand. "I am a Dis-co Dan-cer!" he sings, free of irony and care. His hands look like they don't belong in the same frame. He has sensitive hands.

"He was a Naxalite," my father says knowingly.

"What? A gyrating communist rebel wearing a tinsel headband pasted together by a two-year-old?"

"What a sad state of affairs, this Bollywood film industry," sighs my dad.

I nod disdainfully, and get up from the couch. My mom hasn't heard us. She doesn't care about our condescending opinions. She's glued to the screen and Mithun's stellar dance moves, which are chiselling out her eyes. (Once seen, never forgotten.)

For a while, we ignored the messages, concentrating on our new life unfolding in the hospital. My mother was pronounced incapable of movement from the chest down. Paralysed. She struggled to move her upper body, trying to regain use of her hands and fingers. And while she relearned her body and started on the long road to rehabilitation, I had become an instant celebrity in India, only I didn't know it.

It's hard to fathom now, but without the Internet, how would you know that you were famous? How would you know unless somebody picked up the phone and called you? We didn't even have cell phones then (the ones that did exist were as big as submarine sandwiches). In the early 1990s, no one was texting: "Hey, did you know, you're a huge sensation in India!"

———

A few months before, a strange set of circumstances had conspired to turn me into an Indian poster girl. That image Chien Wein Lee had taken of me in a risque red swimsuit was released on the cover of *Gladrags* in India in August 1991. Indian fans are notorious for their ability to fall in love at first sight. Overnight I became an object of adulation, a cover girl for an India that was opening up to new possibilities. Once the fans seized on my *Gladrags* pictures, I was in demand. Later, I heard stories of billboards that caused traffic accidents on Marine Drive. Directors and producers who managed to reach my father or me were salivating, offering Bollywood films and modelling contracts

Yet this was no consolation to me. Back in Toronto, it was touch and go with my mom. We didn't know if she would make it at all. After a few weeks, her condition finally stabilized and she was transferred out of the ICU, wearing a halo ring, a contraption like a crown drilled into the skull. All the while I stood silently by the curtain divider in her room. Doctors bent their heads to whisper to my father and me. Their words admitted nothing, a professionally veiled language that made me feel even more confused. I felt stranded in those hospital rooms. Helpless. Standing on the edge of everything. Trapped in blankness. *Push it down. Stay strong. Manage!*

A large percentage of people who suffer from spinal cord injuries are very active before their accidents and get hurt in the course of a daring activity, like skiing or diving. In her own way, my mother was one of these people. She was vital and restless, the kind of woman who would never stay in one place for long. She used to roll her eyes at my dad and me when we curled up on the sofa. She would rarely sit through an entire movie. "Sitting? How about doing? There's tomato sauce to be made. Come, help me peel the beets. I'm going to bring the laundry in." To see that energy stilled was a huge devastation. Little by little I found temporary relief in the repetition of waking, hospital, dinner, and I focused instead on helping my dad with paperwork required by the lawyers and insurance agents who spoke in low, pacifying voices. I remember my father's mannered, elegant handwriting filling form after form. It was a tort case because the driver responsible for the accident had fled the scene. I'm not even sure he knows what happened.

Something else happened at the site of the accident which was never spoken about. I had a moment of hyper awareness—the realization that the car was going to hit us, a blunt and obvious "Oh, really? Now?" And I was strangely detached from it. In that moment I splintered. Some part of me was left behind there by the side of the highway, while the other part needed to outrun everything, all the fierce attachments that caused me pain. I hadn't yet figured out that a life in pieces is grace; you can put it back together the way you want. That understanding would come much, much later.

Once the initial crisis was over, my mother began the long painful road of healing. The good news was that she was going to make it, the bad news was that she would not be able to walk. Soon we moved from trying to accept the idea of her life as a paraplegic—the initial diagnosis—to one as a quadriplegic. My father and I were exhausted, and when the calls from India came in at night, I would get panicky, hanging up quickly. Then one night the phone rang and it was Maureen. She had tracked me down, but she still didn't know about the accident. I told her, the words feeling bulky in my mouth. She answered back, clear and certain. About a week later, she flew to Toronto.

We didn't have any family in Toronto to call on in this crisis. The three of us were leaning on each other, but it was a lonely time. My parents, it seemed, had the pilgrim spirit in them. Since leaving their families they had become entirely self-reliant and not used to asking for help.

I too have always found it difficult to ask for any kind of support, so it meant the world to me that Maureen came all that distance, showing up at the hospital. Our lives had come undone and in came Maureen, in control, unflappable and managing every situation. Even the doctors seemed both fascinated and cowed by her. She sat on the edge of my mother's bed with perfect flourish and established an immediate intimacy with both my mother and father. In contrast to the stark, intimidating certainty of the doctors was Maureen, adorned with a different sort of certainty—characterized by her expensive pastel suit and sloe-eyed affluence—that somehow or other, things would work out. Watching this play out in the starchy white setting melted something inside me. I was grateful to her. It was simple; in a moment like that, you are deeply grateful for any kindness. I remember Maureen stretching across worn hospital sheets to hold my mother's hand. She had a proposal. I was standing in the doorway, a part of me holding back, watching what felt like a scene from someone else's life. I heard her say in her modulated English to my father, "Send Lisa back to India. I'll look after her."

Of course Maureen had broached the topic with me. Would I come back to India? It was an opportunity to extract myself from the tableau at my mother's bedside. Now that my mother was to be transferred to a rehabilitation hospital there was even less for me to do. In Bombay I could wring myself out and find my feet again. Oh, and of course, I could stay busy modelling for *Gladrags* and Bombay Dyeing.

All this while, my mom was heavily medicated. Speaking through the drugs, she would murmur: "I don't want to live like this." She was forty-nine years old at the time of the accident. But somehow, in a remarkably short period, she called on her tremendous will power and as the drugs eased, she stopped saying that she wanted to die. Looking back, I'm convinced that she faced her illness with ironclad resilience primarily for my father and me—for the ones left standing.

Eventually, she was ready for the transition from the hospital to a rehabilitation centre called Lyndhurst. The hospital season was passing, but now we knew it would be months of therapy before she retrained her body and learned to live in the world again.

In this atmosphere, Maureen's offer wasn't a business proposition but something entirely more personal. "Give Lisa a break from all this," she told my father. She promised to be my guardian, to keep me occupied with a few months" work, and then send me back to Toronto. I knew that in Maureen's company, I would get all-encompassing hospitality. Maybe on the other side of the world I could out-smother the highway, the sound of the gravel and the desire to see my mother made whole again.

And to be honest, I wanted to get the hell out of Toronto. By October I had healed physically, and the neck brace was gone, but my mind was heavy and sluggish. I could feel winter approaching in the air and the shorter, darker, depressing days. For the first time in my life I didn't really have a plan. I imagined exploring this little chunk of time in India, avoiding the snow and the heartache at home. I could return to university later. I pretended it was a gap year. Some kids go to the tourist area of Haliburton County and work in a kids' camp, others go back-packing and volunteering though South America. I would go to Bombay. (I deferred from university so many times in the subsequent years that I had a thick stack of letters from them. They finally gave up on me.)

There were no heart-to-heart chats with my mother during that time. The truth was she was preoccupied with trying to understand her new life, as far as it would be susceptible to understanding. But my dad, with typical generosity, told me to go. "You need to get away. Don't worry about anything here." I was almost seventeen. I see now that I was running away from something than running towards some-thing. It was an ironic kind of serendipity that drove me, the daughter of immigrants, back to India.

But the birth of my success is forever linked in my mind to the accident. You might say my career in India began on the edge of sword: fame on one side and on the other, grief. My mother would never have the use of her legs again. From that 1991 crash until her death in 2008, she would live her life in a wheelchair. And throughout those years, I would keep flying away.

5

THAT'S HOW, IN the winter of 1991, I found myself in a penthouse in Bombay. Maureen bought my ticket from Toronto to Bombay and put me up in one of the flats normally reserved for Bombay Dyeing company executives that had a lavish view of the Arabian Sea. *Where have we landed, sugar plum?* And so I began my strange sabbatical with sea breezes and the odour of things decomposing in the humid heat which reached up to even the twenty-seventh floor of an apartment building called Twin Towers.

Urban India in the early 1990s was very different from what it is today. Aside from some Victorian gothic relics of India's muddled colonial legacy, aesthetically, Bombay at the time appeared to my eyes quite unlovely. I remember that most of the furniture in the expensive apartment was either blocky and practical, polished in a dark wood varnish or, as in the case of a set of dining chairs, looked like they belonged to an aristocrat of faded glory—ornately carved and perpetually dusty. Down below on the streets were squatters and pockets of filth; dark, stunted men squatting mornings on the beach to evacuate their bowels. But from up high, everything looked heady and exotic, and I could float above it all, willing myself into a state of lightness. "I'm so sorry I had to leave," repeated in my mind on the plane ride over.

In the beginning of my stay I was isolated, but I didn't feel lonely. There was a particular flavour to the aloneness of being in a city, surrounded by millions of people, that I enjoyed. I unpacked my sneakers and Canadian wardrobe of jeans and sweatshirts, most of it completely unsuited for the climate. I would soon learn how copiously I could sweat. And later how the effort of keeping white cotton crisp or linen pressed or suede loafers clean in Bombay was the sign of a lifestyle so free of strain and concern, it was a mark of affluence in itself. Maureen visited me to make sure I was comfortable. She brought contraband like bottles of Coca-Cola (the company had been ejected from India in 1977) and Mövenpick ice cream and once the foreign booty was placed in the fridge we sat together on the sofa. "Oh my God, I tell you, this country . . . so small minded . . ." and went on to enumerate a list of grievances, starting with some of the executives at one of her husband's board meetings. While I tried to follow the flow of her words it hit me—beneath the surface of this beautiful woman's life, was alienation and loneliness. Perhaps bringing me to Bombay was as much for herself as for me.

But the more I listened to Maureen's provocations about "bad" and "uncouth" Bombay, the more I felt drawn to the city. I had, after all, already encountered the entire fascinating mess on the trip with my parents, and now, on my own, I was anxious to descend from Twin Towers into the clamorous way the crowds ran down below. What Maureen should have shared was that she was trying to shelter me not from the crowds, but from Bombay Society, the wealthy and influential who were endlessly speculating about this mysterious woman on the cover of her magazine, "Leeza Ray." Though I was free to come and go, I felt I was hazarding her disapproval when I took the building lift down and ventured into the streets. I took a cab to Mohammed Ali road and saw men stirring pots in splashes of light. In Lower Parel, close to the railway tracks, both men and women laboured in dark rooms in a wake of sparks. I peeked into dingy one-roomed tenements in areas I couldn't name. I was trying to place myself in the city, so I walked. The more I walked, the more I felt I was not in a fixed state, but just a bundle of energy losing the definition of myself.

I kept busy working for Maureen. She put me on a contract, something, like Rs 1,00,000 (about $2000) a month which was a generous amount for the time. She had me do a Bombay Dyeing calendar by Chien Wien Lee, and a shoot with Karan Kapoor, one of the sons of legendary gentleman-actor Shashi Kapoor. Karan's mother was English actress Jennifer Kendal-Kapoor, and his dirty blonde hair and blue eyes identified him as outsider despite his Indian lineage. We used to hang out at Chien's office in Readymoney terrace in Worli, which he shared with Karan's brother, Kunal, a leading ad-maker. Modelling was not yet considered a respectable profession in India. Girls from good families wouldn't do it, but mixed-blood Anglo-Indians were already freed from the bondage of societal conventions. Women like me didn't belong to that highly codified traditional society, nor were we Westerners exactly.

But all of that was beginning to change. By the time I began modelling, India was loosening up, and there were a handful of girls who were becoming stars. These girls became the country's version of the 1980s supermodels—the Cindy Crawfords and Linda Evangelistas of India. In the typical super-sizing of India, you couldn't just be a model; you had to be a supermodel—the world's *best*. Back then, models were becoming like movie stars, and the public waited for every new ad like it was a new release in a theatre.

The red swimsuit image cover heralded an emergence of perilous possibility. When liberalization started in 1991, it was confined to the "metros," towards the thin upper-middle-class section of society, the city dwellers. There wasn't yet a lot of provocative imagery in India, but that red swimsuit had helped awaken a hunger for it. Maureen put me on more *Gladrags* covers as soon as I arrived. I was always very high glam with the red lips and big hair. Tight-fitting outfits and plunging necklines emphasized the curves and the fantasy. For the general Indian audience, still modest, still un-moneyed, the look was both terrifying and impossibly aspirational, almost inaccessible: a true pin-up. This converged with a kind of haughty, unavailable quality in the photos to create a particular image of me in the public's eye.

A large part of me shrank away from the attention. I feared I'd been promoted beyond my worth. Bombay, right off the bat, began to solidify those adolescent feelings of being an imposter. But in a way, disconnection is a perfect state for a model: the job requires distance between the self and the image of the self, and I was already very good at existing in that distance.

Either way, tired and bruised from Canada, I was ready for distraction. Those early days now seem like an unwritten instruction manual:

How to Turn an Outsider into a Pin-up Queen aka How to Avoid Yourself. A car and driver would pull up to my building and drive me the studio. My bags would be carried through the studio to my "green room," which was often that; painted a sickly pale green, smelling vaguely of fried onions. I carried a very good, very toxic air freshener. I started knowing what kind of coffee I wanted, and I expected it, pronto. "Spot!" I'd yell and the spot boy (not always a boy, more often than not a middle-aged man with jaundiced eyes) would bound in with my special mug. Once I had the coffee, the make-up artist and hairdresser would begin working on me. The film industry union at that time had defined some archaic and illogical rules: women cannot be make-up artists and men cannot be hair stylists. I was fond of my early make-up "dadas" drawn from lower-middle-class neighbourhoods like Bhayandar and Thane but their class-conscious, conservative upbringing made them shy or deferential around women. So, morning chit-chat fell to the hairdresser, and she'd begin by breezily stirring the pot in the tradition of every nosy auntie while she combed the knots from my hair. There were time-honoured ways of passing along information in Bombay and she would tell me a certain very famous, very sexy, "*besharam*" movie star was making inquiries, and that other Bollywood heroines were feeling threatened. Inhabiting the glamour world meant entanglement in an amazing game; coolly assessing utility of the other, wanting whatever the other has, and then pursuing single-mindedly, all of which brought together movie stars and starlets, starlets and thugs into a hardscrabble, bubbling stew. "Didi, don't be so quick-quick to go when they call . . . *thora sa naatak hi chahiye*," —put on the drama—my hairdresser advised when I would spring up from my chair. "Eh, *chokra*, madam is not ready, come back later," she'd yell, sending off the assistant who had come to call me to set. I would laugh and say something bland, but on the inside, I felt like I was a happy-go-lucky puppy nosing in a rival pack. I watched the hairdresser through the mirror when her back was to me. I would have to be vigilant.

Make-up and hair could take up to two hours. In those days the make-up dadas blotted out your entire face with heavy Kryolan pancake and drew your features back in Kabuki-style. "Cutting" used to describe the addition of depth to your face which involved drawing lines in a darker shade down the sides of your nose or shading your cheeks by painting triangles under cheekbones. "*Didi, aur cutting cha-hiye? Aur lippis-stick?*" (*Do you want more cutting? More lipstick?*) This seems unforgivably heavy-handed to our eyes today—and it is—but the lighting was much harsher, so subtle make-up washed you out. Fashion and advertising images were wrestled to life by a whole crew of unruly characters, from the beauty squad backstagers to the photographer's multiple lighting assistants. Observing these shoots, even for a short while, would cure you of the conceit that these images are real or representative in any way. When I came along, the concept of someone else doing a model's hair and make-up was relatively new; till a few years back, models carried their own make-up kits to shoots. It's actually quite gruelling to sit still in a make-up chair, under the hot lights of a vanity, for so long. Today, I have little patience with all the waiting required by my profession, but back then I immediately found an equilibrium. I think I wanted to turn modelling into a job that I could be proud of, so I told myself: Be the most patient model in the world. This, of course, is part of the pathology of perfection—the good A-grade student becomes the good model.

Long before models had their own stylists, designers would come in with racks of their own clothes and do the styling themselves. They were larger-than-life characters, and pioneers in their fields. Being gay was still taboo in mainstream India, but the modelling and fashion world formed a spirit of community that was a safe and inclusive zone. Designer James Ferreira, in particular, was a thrilling combination of campy wit and sensitivity. He would swan in to a shoot, smoking, voice gravelly and emphatic: "Lisa darling, I designed something these stupid Indians will not understand! Our country is so stupid! I wish they would just open their eyes to beauty and stop being so conservative because everyone is sucking cock anyway!" I'd listen to this diatribe, spellbound. "They just hide it! Believe me, my child—*I know*!"

I would soon find myself in a jumble of exiles—from Steve McCurry to the scandal-linked Pamela Bordes—at his historic Khotachiwadi Lane cottage, lounging on antique furniture, listening to James' latest antics. He was allegedly having an affair with his head tailor, his "masterji," but he appeared to be always trawling for his next lover. Needless

to say, I had never met anyone like him. In those days I was excited to
see myself on billboards and my name in print, but when the dissonance
of Bombay became too much, I retreated to James' cottage for his
East Indian wedding rice and spicy curries as a way to find sustenance,
comfort and acceptance.

A subtler, new kind of cool was moving into the striving city. A
prohibition-style jazz bar was opened up by an enterprising A.D. Singh
on the rooftop terrace of an unmarked building in Flora Fountain, in
a members-only Parsi club called the Ripon Club. If you knew about
it, you climbed the worn rickety stairs to an old, caged Parisian-style lift
and rose to the rooftop. There, under a starless sky, all of Bombay's
ad and creative professionals mixed with models and photographers
on the roof into the early hours, drinking and listening to live jazz. We
would fete our coolness and sip wine, eyes skidding from face to face.

"People with great taste get very competitive about the company they
keep," a long-limbed art director had encroached on our small knot, looking me over.

"And the toilet paper they use to wipe their asses," dead-panned
Farrokh Chothia.

I met Farrokh Chothia, one of the country's foremost photographers (who trained with legendary American portrait photographer
Mary-Ellen Mark), on that rooftop when he was a young talent rising
through the ranks. We bonded over our mutual taste for the zany and
Fellini and joking about our inner torment, and he soon became one
of my closest friends. He's a Parsi—a small but prominent community
descended from Persian Zoroastrians who emigrated to India centuries
ago to avoid persecution. Parsis are known for a sense of professional
honesty and eccentric conduct and this blatant ethnic profiling fits
FC to a T. And so those Thursday nights at the Ripon provided a delicious refuge and a place for my mind to loiter. I felt I was standing at
the edge of change and was thrilled to be included.

And the city to me really was a jazz score. I came alive under the
lights of the studios, improvising expressions and undulating my body,
building to a crescendo until the hours of posing and poking got under
my skin. Then I was all horns and trumpets and traffic noises, blaring
out my mood swing. A confusion of thoughts breached out from me in

syncopated patterns, joining the noisy and bizarre stream of voices and clatter, nothing melodic about it until I returned to solitude in my Bombay Dyeing flat and woke up the next morning, craving it all again once more.

Maureen was my informal agent, but there were no agencies as such, no concept of managing models. We were our own managers, lawyers and agents. We negotiated our own contracts and schmoozed with the clients. We were friends with the photographers and designers, more family than colleagues. Often, on a day off, a photographer friend and I would go into the studio to collaborate on something beyond the money-making principle that drove the city. We wanted to create art for its own sake, pulling out of the depths of ourselves the dark and grotesque and transforming it through light and shadow. My pain, smoking up the cavern of my chest, found expression through afternoons contorting myself into new shapes for the camera. It was also a way to bring the personal into the professional, and to convince ourselves we were artists.

It was a frontier time for the modelling industry, and an exhilarating one. A few months after arriving I began accepting outside offers to model, in pursuit of a shared single interest: the creation of beauty. Like many models of the early 1990s, I was not mercenary in my approach to business. Often, to get paid, I had to call clients over and over on a landline that would keep getting cut. Sometimes, I wouldn't get paid at all. But the work was constant, and we took a certain pride in our ability to build the industry as we went along. A small group of designers—Hemant Trivedi, Wendell Rodricks, Rohit Bal, J.J. Vallaya, Shahab Durazi, Tarun Tahiliani—photographers and models put together the nuts and bolts of the modern Indian fashion world. The clothes came second (Oh, this infuriated the designers. Ferreira would complain: "People think we're tailors, but we're artists!"), but it was all about the girl in the clothes. The clothes were just there to make the girl look good. We were stars.

There was Mehr Jessia, an elegant Parsi model, very Hepburnish and perhaps the first widely celebrated Indian supermodel. Rachel Reuben, sexy, Jewish, enigmatic and very ambivalent about what she was doing. Anna Bredemeyer, Coleen Khan, Shyamolie Verma, all taking turns to embody the role of muse of the catwalk. Farheen Khan full of blasé sass.

Malaika Arora, tiny and sensual, with a magnificent aura of body confidence. Madhu Sapre, who almost won Miss Universe in 1992, but tripped up on the "What would you do if you were prime minister?" question. I rarely did live fashion shows, being too short and too shy. I didn't have the classic features or poise or the long limbs of many other girls and was simply lucky the beauty ideals of the time favoured me: soft face, curvy body, light skin and eyes. Most of us more or less bumbled into it. There was no plan: somebody saw someone, said, "Hey, you're pretty. Enter this pageant or do this shoot for a friend." Then suddenly, she'd be doing it full-time.

Fashion was a place for outsiders. For a period in the early 1990s, there was a siege of unconventional outcasts. We didn't exactly fit into India and yet we were deeply attached to it, proud of what we thought it could be. Today, the industry has become more codified. The rough edges have been smoothed, and many of the eccentricities squeezed out. Franchises of big American and European modelling agencies have set up shop like so many Burger Kings: Ford India and Elite India alongside home-grown celebrity management agencies. FC tells me that the girls today are different animals. They travel to New York and Paris, working their contacts, wired to the world through their social media posts and phones. I used to make subscriber trunk dialling (STD) calls that dotted the city streets. "They're not like you guys were. You were the last of the flower children," Farrokh told me. "The new generation knows what they want. They're business savvy."

Back then, I was finding my inner cat in the appealingly unregimented pace of Bombay. If I wasn't working, I could just show up at a friend's office where I'd be handed my mug of coffee or tea, and I'd sit around chatting with friends, immediately incorporated into what was going on. I sometimes spent my afternoons at ad agencies, like Ambience, barging into conference rooms during meetings. I'd climb grungy stairwells, to enter studios and observe other girls being shot. I was always absorbing, listening, trying in my way to dissect the whole world. Evenings were often measured out in bowls of fried rice and smoke and animated conversation on someone's terrace, while in the distance dogs barked at a path of crows, the sound marking their sunset flight towards the ocean.

I began to feel like maybe this was my place. Maybe I would stay a little longer. Maybe denial is just a structural defect of the human heart. My nature remained that of the recluse, but it was easier to stay busy and avoid all my pain. Calling home was expensive then, at several US dollars per minute. I preferred to send postcards, perhaps wanting to let my parents know I was okay without engaging in conversation that might reveal the reality of what they were going through.

Maureen had tried to shelter me from an incestuous party scene, but I couldn't resist gate-crashing that Gatsby-ish world and I needed to fill my nights with distraction. "Tout le monde, c'est ici!" I remember a bearded host trilling to everyone who entered, but when I replied in French—having studied it in school in Canada—he guided me to the bar by the elbow. "Don't be naughty and make me look bad in front of everyone." In Bombay's mythology, I would learn, there are no saints or villains; only circumstances shaped by the utility of relationships. I would feel occasional resistance from some sleek socialite or fashionista; just a haughty glance, or the turn of a back. I kept hearing the murmur of strange rumours: *She's much older. She's in her thirties. She has a kid. She does a lot of drugs.* In the time before trolls there was just this— words that cut to the bone. I didn't know this was just a habit of the unhappy rich. They appeared self-possessed, saying things like, "Cutting your hair when you've had plastic surgery distracts everyone from the work you've had done." But smoking on the balcony I would have quiet conversations with strangers who revealed to me more than I wanted to know about sham marriages, brothers succumbing to greed, hearts strained from the effort of keeping debtors at bay, eyes glazed from no longer caring. People liked to confide in me, and I liked to listen, so I learned there was no greater leveller than pain, and especially the sort we hide.

My thoughts turned inwards. I was acutely aware of what I saw and heard around me. I was already walking around with this gnawing feeling of fraudulence, wondering: What the hell am I doing in this situation? They give me money, I'm in a penthouse, all these famous people in India want to meet me, but what have I done? Where's the accomplishment to match the fuss? I had gained access to a world where bonds were established from the womb, though being an "of the moment girl" was enough of a calling card. Beauty was its own resume, it seemed. And there was an undeniably wicked appeal in toying with the attention of the future titans of the city, but all that attention came at a price. I was already fragile, so shouldering innuendo and judgement was harder than it should have been. It chipped away at me day by day. I craved gentleness and empathy, though I hadn't spoken about what I was going through with many people. I was looking for someone who would say, "It's going to be okay." But Bombay is New York. The response is: "Kid, you think you've got problems? I've got problems!"

Maureen was my retreat from the intensity of my life, but she was also complex in her own right. She confided in me her own deeply personal problems, which I found overwhelming. I wanted to continue to idolize her, not become her confidante. But when she played mother figure and clucked her concern, I felt suffocated. I needed both independence and nurturing; I was a bundle of sparking contradictions. Hold me, but not too tight. Look at me, but don't look too closely.

Instead of a hug, I received an offer for a part in a movie with Sanjay Dutt. Sanjay had chased me down personally and his secretary Pankaj Kharbander made it known the actor wanted to "launch me" in a "home production." It was disorienting to have captivated Sanju baba, but he was never anything but extremely decorous with me. He struck me as both a breathless baby bird and a wild spirit, rounded up and caged by civility. He hunched as though exhausted from the effort of being himself and I felt a tenderness for someone who appeared more lost than myself. The offer was a huge honour but I was terrified at the prospect of appearing on film. Sanjay wanted to enrol me in dance and Hindi lessons, but the idea of getting up in front of all these people and doing a Bollywood dance number made me catatonic. Yet my curiosity was strong, and I agreed. The mere rumour that somebody as famous as Dutt was pursuing me for a film created a whole flurry of excitement in the "filmi" press. At a party, I overheard the result of the media maelstrom: sarcastic, cold comments from a group of women I had never met. "Well you know why she signed that movie . . ." "Haan. It's for booze *ka kharcha*!" It had never occurred to me that all of Bombay society would assume I was having an affair with the married Dutt (or that I was an alcoholic). I was horrified to be featured in one of the cattiest columns in *Stardust*, "Neeta's Natter," which wrote things like, "Get wet pets. Rain does that to libidos you know." I was gripped by shame, but I had been so warmly embraced by Sanju's family—his sisters Priya and Anju and his brother-in-law Kumar Gaurav—that I tried hard to quell the noise of uncertainty in my head and go on.

Those days, there was only one major nightclub to let off steam and "go clubbing"—RGs, off Marine Drive, where the rich kids came to slump languidly against the bar; young wolves with sly smiles and expensive watches. A lot of them were studying for their business degrees outside the country, in Boston or London, and when they returned home on their breaks or to join the family business, they were scanning the city for new, inviting faces. I was still the new girl in town. It was a clear path in those days for models and actresses to marry into wealthy families. But I had a clear disadvantage: I simply didn't care who was a textile heir or diamond merchant's son. And I didn't regard marrying into wealth as an aspiration. But neither did I hold it against anyone. "You're lucky. You are so lucky. I think J. is going to invite you to come with us to Ibiza. Your kismet is made. Just watch and learn, babe," a young heiress who resided in a gated palace at Nepean Sea Road breathed in my ear. I had something that electrified the princelings but I also had a mind of my own. "Do you read? Okay but you *must* read something besides Dale Carnegie? I'm talking about writers who set your soul on fire, make you see the world in a different way. What will you do when you come back to India besides joining your father's business. Have you thought about doing something on your *own*?" I think she tried telling me this was not a favourable line of conversation. Be more Linda Evangelista, less Joni Mitchell.

I liked spending time with the ludicrously wealthy; they were both frivolous and smart. But rarely was I open to advice from anyone to tone it down. I preferred standing at the edge of everything, watching. My policy those nights was always: Dance, but don't drink. I knew that I'd have to get up early to shoot for Maureen, or for one of my new gigs and began to say goodnight. One night, a guy I didn't know said: "If you want to go, I'll drop you off at home." He was part of the inner circle, a friend of a friend. There was something brittle and slightly needy about him. I shrugged—why not? I got into his flashy sports car. "Do you mind if we stop at my place?" he asked as we sped along, narrowly missing shrouded figures sleeping on the side of the road. "I just want to get something. You're welcome to come up." I didn't mind, ever curious. We took the elevator to the top of his building which was very plush, with one room spiralling out from the next. "By the way," he said, trying to sound casual. "Do you want to see my shoe collection?" I was thinking: Well, no, not really. Then again, how often does a boy offer to show you his shoe collection? "Okay," I said politely.

He led the way to an inner suite with a huge built-in closet, clearly copied from some rarefied European hotel. Very dramatically, he pushed a door. *Click.* Shelves swung forth to reveal rack upon rack of shoes, shiny and stacked tidily. He looked at me expectantly. There was nothing to do but murmur my approval and lean a little closer to inspect the shoes like they were a row of newborn babies. Suddenly, I felt him against me from behind. "You're so gorgeous. Everybody's talking about you in Bombay," he said breathlessly, pushing his groin into my backside. I grabbed the nearest shoe—one of his shiny loafers—and whacked him across the head with it. He squealed like a kitten and immediately backed off. One thing I learned fast was those coddled guys were rarely tough. I was less scared than annoyed. "I'm going home," I announced. I marched off but couldn't find the elevator. I walked down twenty flights of stairs and hailed a cab, sighing into the night.

The next day, I was laughing about it. I had been naive—again—and I described the incident to my friend Sanjay Narang, who was just back from attending Cornell. He shook his head. The footwear obsessed groper, I found out, happened to be from one of India's most prominent industrial families. Bombay's relationships are tied with webs of gossip, and Sanjay clearly couldn't resist telling the shoe story to a few friends, including, accidentally, the guy's fiancée. She was clearly the forgiving type: decades later, they are still married.

All the sniping and innuendo about my supposed affair with Sanjay Dutt had become too much and I finally decided to drop out of the film. I didn't know how to neutralize the waves of chatter. As much as I tried to laugh it off, to be an irreverent non-conformist, I also wanted to be accepted and liked. After all, I was the Canadian "nice girl." So I turned all my attention to modelling. My gift in this area was a certain adaptability. I was a tabula rasa. I could be any race, any age, good girl or bad girl. Growing up, I had often received compliments from people about my unusual looks, but they only fed my conflicted views about myself. My face was too *gol-gol*. My jawline undefined. My nose looked like a pebble at the end of an anthill. On and on went that voice, muttering inadequacy, drowning out the praise. Nevertheless my face and body were everywhere I turned. I would look at the images, and I knew that they were a mirage. Some people look better in front of the camera, and some look worse. I'm in the former category. I'm simply lucky that I'm very photogenic. But I couldn't relate to those images because someone else had decided which woman, from the vast array within me, I should be.

I now have the vocabulary for how I felt objectified, but I also feel my modelling at that time had value: my looks and my multi-racial identity were not in cultural discussion anywhere in the world back then. Not Indian enough, not Western enough but undiluted in its challenge to common perceptions at the time. This strange conflict—What was the image and what was me?—and the expectations of perfection I had internalized pushed me into a dark period just six months after my arrival. I started eating compulsively and I gained a lot of weight. Sometimes slouching into a dive for a Konkani thali, sometimes ordering dosa from Shiv Sagar, or stopping the car at Haji Ali Juice Centre to load up on chikoo milkshakes. Without make-up, I was able to continue slinking through the city for food. Kebabs at Bade Miya or sizzlers at Kobe, plates of pav bhaji and sev puri at Swati Snacks, all gave me a temporary sense of relief. Perhaps I was looking for the comfort that food had provided me long ago, in a spirit of eating shared meals, prepared together as a family. Or maybe overeating was an act of defiance. The bulimia that had started as a young teen was still raging. But even regular bouts of vomiting couldn't keep up with my massive intake. Gaining weight was a way to declare that I didn't fit into this world of fashion and beauty, figuratively or literally. My new, heavier body was really me saying: I am not what you think I am. I am not your image of me.

My relationship with Maureen was faltering, too. Towards the end of that first year, I had begun to feel that she was too controlling. There was no air around her—to be silly, to breathe. In Bombay, she had rubbed up a number of people the wrong way and had set herself apart from society. That isolation and separation seemed increasingly oppressive to me. Today, however, I understand something crucial about Maureen. Behind everything, the litany of complaints about male executives and others not "getting it," was the universal feminine struggle to be taken seriously. In a sense, Maureen's experiences were part of the collective of us all; shared by every working woman in India demanding to be respected professionally—and having one's value and worth emancipated from the "husband–father" figure. Certainly, Maureen's story played out against a backdrop of luxury and money, but as I was learning, that did nothing to cushion the spirit. In fact, my time with Maureen confirmed something I had suspected for sometime: extreme wealth does not solve the soul's questions. One morning, purely on impulse, I left the Twin Towers apartment for good, speed packing one single, overstuffed suitcase without even sending her word. I moved into a friend's empty apartment in Bandra on Bandstand facing the Arabian sea. I had slipped to a much lower floor, closer to land and the water and people's emotional geographies. I could see fishermen's boats bobbing on the crust of the ocean. I pushed open windows to the not insignificant company of the breeze. I have to keep moving, I told myself. This has been a pattern in my life: invite in a dominating person, and then— finally and messily—break away. I was afraid to confront Maureen, but I felt, again, the call of freedom, knotted with my self-sabotaging reflexes. James later told me she sent the police looking for me. I'm certain it was out of concern. Today I see clearly the generosity of Maureen's spirit, offering during that difficult time to not only be my guardian, but my friend. But I was uninitiated in the art of receiving, and I couldn't recognize grace.

However, unbeknownst to me, I became a pawn in one of Maureen's private battles. I was approached by Parmeshwar Godrej, businesswoman and Maureen's great rival. Parmeshwar's husband, Adi, is one of India's biggest philanthropists, and regularly features in *Forbes'* list of most powerful billionaires. Maureen and Parmeshwar had been competitors for decades, even back in their air hostess days. Perhaps to spite Maureen, Parmeshwar approached me to model for Evita soap.

Even though it was a different "brand category" it still felt like I was leaving Pepsi for Coke. By this time I had already gained a lot of weight and I was on a course to unravel; I needed a break, but in a fog, I agreed to do the Godrej shoot and signed a contract. Then, finding myself in free fall, I turned on my heels and immediately flew back to Canada.

At home in Toronto, I returned to a series of messages insisting that I fly back to do the shoot. The Godrejs of course tracked me down and sent me a first-class ticket through Sam Balsara, the head of Madison ad agency who was in charge of the campaign. Sam coaxed me to fly back to India for a couple of days. Part of me was thrilled by the badass-ery of this extravagance. Somehow, it reaffirmed that I was important enough to be flown back and forth, giving me some twisted sense of value. I barely said hello to my parents and flew back. But when I arrived at the shoot and saw the bathing suits on the rack I gripped the back of a chair with white-knuckled fingers, burning with humiliation. I had put on so much weight that the girl from *Gladrags* had disappeared. They wanted something sleek and sexy and I wasn't that Lisa.

I don't know how I survived that shoot, eels in my belly, but I did. And then I flew back to Canada again. Watching the landing from my seat, I liked the feeling of outrunning the wind. I remember walking through Pearson International Airport, before being stopped by one of the immigration officers who asked: "So what do you do?"

I froze, as I would for many years, at that line: What do you do?

It felt like a challenge, the words undoing me. I didn't know what I did. Things were so strange in my life. I couldn't bring myself to say: "I'm a very famous model in India." I thought he would look at me and see this fat, round-faced girl, and laugh.

What do you do?

I didn't know what to write when I was filling in my travel docu-ment. I couldn't say "model" so I had written "professional scuba diver" believing it the best option. But when the officer questioned me, it sounded too much like "Who are you?" I couldn't answer him. I couldn't speak at all. He watched me struggling silently, and I could see alarm bells going off on his face. He began cross-examining me. I was pulled over and officials searched my luggage. Why was a kid like me flying first class? I looked like a student smuggling hash. I was grateful, really, that they were thinking of me as a student: at least I was something they could identify. An hour later, they let me go. My dad was waiting for me. I didn't tell him what had happened.

People with spinal cord injuries have a classic posture where the chest caves in. I think of it as a blow to the chest from God. My mother, I now saw, had this too: her upper body curved like a spoon. She was just coming out of Lyndhurst and returning home in a wheelchair. She had a little bit of movement in her arms but couldn't use her fingers. The steroids had caused a small hump on her back. I registered intellectually that this was my mother, but I couldn't reconcile the body in front of me with my mother. "You look tired. Are you eating enough? Don't lie to me. Tell me the truth." Her voice announced her spirit was intact, her concern circling me as always. And that got me right in the stomach.

But instead of cheering her bravery I got impatient with her. Her way of coping was to try to control her environment even more than before. Because she couldn't do a lot of things for herself, she would ask me or my father to do them for her. But we never got it quite right. It wasn't enough to simply make the tea for her, she had to explain how to do it exactly, in pedantic sequence: *First take out the teapot, put in the teabag. Only fill three-quarters of the pot with water!* She would make me show her that the teabag was only half submerged. *Don't let it boil too long. Take it off. Wait, wait, wait!*

Even as she drove me nuts, this reminder of the maternal bossiness she'd shown her whole life brought out the exasperated affection that defined our relationship. She was still the centre of action. In a sense, things revolved around her even more now. But I also missed her and felt guilty for missing her when she was right there in front of me. Only later did I realize that my mother continued to be the engine that kept our family running.

My father had taken early retirement and was dedicated to her full-time. That's my model of a relationship: total devotion. I just assumed that's how things are between couples. My parents were so engaged with each other that I felt I couldn't burden them with my hollow preoccupations. They might have had some inkling of what was going on—I had written some letters alluding to my unhappiness—but we were all too busy to confront my troubles. My father was renovating the house to make it more wheelchair accessible. My mother had to be transferred in and out of bed, and equipment needed to be purchased, nurses had to be hired. Dad had to learn about changing her catheter, which was essential to prevent infection. Somehow, I had thought that things would get better with time. Instead, an entirely new set of complications cropped up in place of the initial fear of those post-accident days.

As an only child, you live so much in your own head. An indigenous healer in Canada I would meet decades later calls this "the bad summer theatre of the mind"—the amateur theatrics going on and on, dressing our thoughts with shabby costumes and fake moustaches, dwelling on trauma. During this visit to Canada, I felt trapped. My summer theatre was in full swing. I was pushing away feelings and trying to manage my mind like a manic stage manager. I remember this version of myself, speed walking, poker-faced. Stomach pulled in tightly—never let your tummy relax—the efforts and tension of containing and controlling. Holding and tightening physically was the only way I knew how to control the waves of deep grief and shame. The effort had an effect on my voice—it became high-pitched and breathless. Words often stuck on my teeth, and behind it all the performance droned on and on, without a curtain call.

Bombay suddenly seemed appealing. The calls were still coming. This Lisa continued carving her stardom halfway across the world. Home was sad and stressful. I was now eighteen years old, and I did what I did best. I flew away like a leaf.

6

I WAS EIGHTEEN when I returned to live on my own in Bombay in 1993. "Maybe," that little voice in the back of my mind spoke, "in the maze of this city is an answer." Emerging from the airport, inhaling the humid air full of exhaust and stale sweat signalled new beginnings, the start of a new life. I got the impression Bombay remembered me, that I had made the cut, though it was too early and too dark to see anything. Sanjay Narang, my friend who lived in a spacious home behind a high wall, sent a driver to pick me up. I had landed in the middle of summer. My heart thrummed as we sped past potholes. It's not rational, this love I have for decay and cities peeling at the edges, where you are under constant threat of something coming loose and conking you on the head. These are the places where your senses sharpen and where you come to find what you want or what you think you need. Canada and my secret sorrows were forgotten in a great swell of possibility.

It should be said, I have always lived with a faith that things will work out. I believe I was born with it, this positivity bias. Even when all evidence says "retreat," I forge forward, continuing without overthinking consequences. This might come across as bravery or fearlessness (or lunacy) but I think what it is is old-fashioned moxie: the audacity to go out there and take chances. Life is either for you or against you, and this belief, I think, drives all of human experience.

And with this belief, I set about creating a rough sketch of how I wanted to remake my life in Bombay. I had arrived at the start of an era of strange, political headwinds. The city was reeling from the 1992 communal riots. Bombay had burned, been ripped apart and a simmering rage contributed to a surge in popular support for the far-right Shiv Sena party, which advocated a strong pro-Marathi ideology. Nonetheless, the key was still in the ignition, and business continued as usual, so the work flowed. After phone calls to a trio of creative women—Yvonne, Divya and Anjana ("*Kameeni*, where have you been?! Ok, *chal*, don't say, but you want to work, *na*? was Anjana's response)—who all worked at Ambience, an influential ad agency co-founded by Elsie Nanji, as well as to Wendell Rodricks and Farrokh, I found myself on the cover of *Femina* magazine. This announced my return. I didn't have to hustle. It was a time when a tinge of inaccessibility or faint aura of mystery, not unlike what I imagined contributed to the allure of all those classic Italian actresses of the 1960s I admired, added to your desirability. But friends in the fashion and ad industry saw it differently and began to dub me a sort of errant runaway model. "You have a habit of walking into everything like you are blindfolded," my friend Sujata Assomull sighed. "But still you come out okay." "Pulling a Lisa," as Sujata put it, meant you never knew when someone would leave and when they would show up. Or when they would cancel a shoot, often at the last possible moment. "You're lucky you have something a cameraman will fall over backwards to capture," I was told by a photographer. "Such a beauty you are on camera! Spit, spit, as my amma would say."

"That's just genetics—proportions—*toh kya kare*. I'm just a fraud." I had to get used to having my looks dissected and discussed again.

Away from the lens, I found a "PG" or paying-guest accommodation (a room in a family home with a hotplate) with terrazzo tiles and white curtain-framed windows in Bandra, a leafy suburb. It wasn't an easy sell. I may have been famous, but landlords were not impressed by these credentials. I had to smile demurely to convince my potential landlord I would be a trustworthy tenant. "My" building was just around the corner from Pali Naka, the boisterous market where the residents of Pali Hill—sometimes called the Beverly Hills of Bombay—shopped for their vegetables and Crocin and where the domestic staff exchanged gossip about their infamous households that titillated and implicated each other. I described my new neighbourhood to my parents over the phone from an ISD booth, waving a handful of rupee notes at the attendant when the line began clicking.

Bandra was a former fishing village and a Catholic colony. Old, sagging bungalows with stained-glass windows and curved balconies kept vigil behind rustling leaves on quiet side streets. New apartment blocks were springing up like the patches of lichen and moss that crept up the sides of these Christian cottages, the contrast between these worlds etched against the coconut palms in sharp relief. The names of these modest buildings amused me no end. They hinted at a grand, slightly delusional vision: God's Gift, Lancelot House, Eternity, Valhalla, Royal Manor, and the intriguing Mary's Palace (I never figured out whether there was a Mary who resided there, or if Mary referred to *the* Mary, mother of Jesus). I loved those leaf-dappled streets with their bakeries and crosses and Christian aunties haggling for fresh fish in cotton nightgowns. The luxury of strolling in Bombay was not lost on me, where every step was normally circumscribed, where time was not to be wasted on any irrelevant action. And then there was the question of "fairness." The majority of women avoided the sun and used creams to keep their skin white. I on the other hand, craved a darker skin tone.

After the lapsed intimacy with Maureen Wadia, I took to the street life of Bandra to craft a sense of belonging. There were the kabadi-wallahs on the corner, selling faded *Stardust* magazines and even some *Femina*s and old *Gladrags* with "Leeza Ray" on the cover. I loved the rattle of the doodh-wallah's bicycle in the morning as he delivered plastic packets of Amul milk, which I learned to boil on my hotplate and then add to my morning tea. Quietude. Even the scarred tabby that came to nap amongst the potted plants on my balcony was forcing me to slow down and savour. The small, quiet voice in my head was heard, though it would take me years still to trust and to listen to it. But this part of my life gave me respite from the other.

I was still trying to make sense of my celebrity status in those first few weeks. Whenever I saw my name or photograph on a magazine cover or newspaper, I'd get a little electric thrill, thinking: "That's me." But at the same time the Indian media's spotlight rendered the "Lisa Ray" I read about unrecognizable. At least I didn't recognize her. "Lisa: Lithe and Lethal," "Hot," "Gorgeous Lisa's Curves" shrieked the headlines. In popular culture at the time, you fell into one of two female archetypes: the vampy seductress or the virginal heroine. I saw myself described as a haughty "diva" who seemed to lead an impossibly glamorous (and vapid) life, getting mobbed at events and allegedly having multiple affairs. And then there was the other "me," a protagonist in my own Fellini film, desirous of exploring and figuring it out as I went along. I was watching the drama of my own life unfold, playing my role and observing at the same time. When I was roaming the streets, usually people didn't recognize me; mainly because famous personalities in India didn't walk alone on the road but also, scrubbed free of warpaint, I looked nothing like the girl in the magazines or the vixen whose images were plastered on hostel walls and in the windows of small-town beauty salons. To this day, I must confess, I never really learned how to do my own make-up. I've been worked on by some of the best in the world and managed to pick up zero beauty skills along the way. Then there was my hair which was frizzy in the heat and I didn't bother grooming. Left to my own devices, I was a slob, wearing worn t-shirts and shapeless sweatpants or casual chikankari kurtas. Part of me had just no interest in fashion—I loved beautiful clothes but more to admire than to wear—and I was also, as ever, using my body to express my defiance. A friend of mine, a male model, once said: "It's in your interest to always look great, Lisa. Don't forget you're selling yourself. You're your own product!" My throat constricted. I took pride in what I was doing, but I hadn't come to terms with the idea that I was a commodity. And more than that, the rigid standards women were expected to adhere to enveloped me, like a translucent haze, clouding the looks of others so all they perceived in me was an illusion.

I remember an afternoon with Chien Wien Lee at his office in Worli. There was a group of us and the bantering was fluid and free. I was naturally more comfortable around men, not quite fitting in with many of the women I came across. In truth, I enjoyed intimidating them, women who measured themselves by their circle of friends, and how well you married. I was disdainful of ladies who didn't work, who relied on husbands or fathers, kitty party card players who dropped the kids off to school in heels. The women my ads appealed to. It wasn't simply that I couldn't relate; I was uncomfortable and walled off from my femininity except when called upon on to use it for the camera, like a fake accent cultivated by an actor.

Back to the afternoon. We were all lounging on sofas and cushions strewn on the floor. The group of young creative mavericks of those days wore their hair long and their white cotton shirts untucked, and slurped their tea. I envied the easy pride of these men.

I began by saying, "It's all a big circle game, life, like Joni sang . . . do you believe that? Birth and death and . . . "

"Yes, yes . . ."

"Circles . . . and curves. I don't know about circles but I see curves. Amazing curves. And a scenic view . . . such scenic beauty like no one in India has ever seen!"

They all laughed. It was a flippant, foolish remark but it singed. There was no refuge for me from this casual sexism. And it laid bare our differences. If I protested, I took myself "too seriously," or else, one of the boys would explain to me in a tone reserved for the very young, that given I posed for "bold" photos, these remarks were to be taken in my stride. It was, in fact, a compliment. Didn't women exist to be admired? And they were, after all, my friends. They were not out to demolish me, just patronize me . . . Just joking, yaar. Chill, it was a joke. Feeling little hot stabs of anger, I started playing with my hair, wrapping its length around my index finger and chewing aggressively on the ends when an impulse transformed the moment. My fingers moved rapidly, braiding the entire length of my hair. By the time another photographer began his recital, (Arre yaar, you should have seen this *chutiya* client brief, so derivative man) I was standing in front of Chien, who had been smoking quietly.

"Take this." I handed him a pair of scissors from his desk.

Chien had a dogged way of laughing at everything.

"People think I'm weird because I love change."

I pulled on the end of my braid so it was perpendicular from my head like the swinging bridge in Rishikesh. In that moment I had become Indian—how else would I be able to execute this gesture with the perfect dramatic flourish.

"Cut it off."

I saw something congeal in Chien's face, not exactly concern but an understanding that there were slippery layers of meaning in me and what I was asking. Conversation had paused in the room. Without saying it, everyone understood what cutting my hair would mean. My identity was built on fantasy. The men in this room did not want to confront the messy reality of their objects of desire.

"You will look like a garbage person!" one of the boys mimicked in the voice of a disapproving auntie.

Yes. But I would not be complicit in my dehumanization.

"Cut it," I told Chien.

And he did.

The short hair didn't end my career. Instead, I was introduced to the world of hair patches, wigs, and extensions. I never realized they were in such demand but I soon discovered that most of the girls used them. Due in part to my loner nature (and after learning to tune out the drone of gossip from my hairdressers), I was always late to adopt the essential tricks of showmanship. And yet, while trying to salvage some part of myself, subconsciously, I was also objectifying myself, and cruelly. All through this time, I was exercising obsessively to keep thin, doing aerobics and lifting heavy weights—aggressive and angry exercise. Ten the Health Spa (I gym, do you?) had just opened in Bandra. I started attending step aerobics classes by Leena Talwalkar, held in a bare room with strange smells in a residential building. The class bustled with pretty housewives, bangles jingling as they tied their hair back, and fresh-faced young actresses. Ranks of importance were established through whispers and pointed looks. The "working girls" were the intruders into this world, both admired and judged. When I was recognized the other women would quickly shield their surprise, though from the looks they exchanged I understood that they saw me to be younger, far shorter and overall less impressive than they imagined. My first impulse was to stick out my tongue. I remember seeing a young, lanky Tabu, sweating through a class and leaving quietly with her gaze lowered to avoid stares. I would give back a stink stream or a sweet, friendly smile, depending on my mood.

In the postcards I wrote to my parents I painted a marvellous life, never touching on our shared trauma or the fact that, a few months into my arrival, I was out of control, spiralling out of balance. The contrast between my inner and outer worlds was exclusively mine to avoid. My vata nature was deranged. All the choices I made to fill my inner mania filled me with even more wind. I had become so thin that I was nearly floating away. I'd make sure an hour was carved out daily for a workout, even though I was often working fourteen hours at a time. The holistic practices that have come to be associated with India today were nowhere on the horizon in the Bombay of the '90s. Yoga was boring and uncool, and meditation was reserved for babas or religious freaks. Finding meditative practices in Bombay at the time took more effort than calling for a laserdisc player from your local smuggler.

While I was longing for something I couldn't name, something that might complete me, I made my peace with the classic entertainment-industry lifestyle, where everyone subsists on coffee and cigarettes. I'd started smoking in high school, but it really cemented itself when I was working on sets. Sets are all about hurry-up-and-wait. You sit around for hours at a time, drinking cup after cup of tea, smoking in your green room or in one of the plastic chairs set down by your spot boy on the set. A lot of us smoked. It was actually odd if someone *didn't*. During a creative high point, it was always there, the cigarette, wedged between all the middle and index fingers in the room, the air full of hauteur, stained studio walls melting into the background.

"You don't think people have had enough of you? Silly cow. You are doing *every* campaign this year. I'm *sure* the other girls *love* you."

"I don't give a hoot."

"Hoot? Oh, that's cuuute. Is that a Canada thing? Something farmers say? Never mind, I don't want to know. Okay, what's the look today? Madhuri meets Studio 54? Or drag queen a la Zeenat Aman, from *Hare Ram, Hare Krishna*? Or are we doing straight, sexed-up, smoke show Lisa Ray?"

The conversation was filled with subversion, we were shaking up conventions in India at the time, and loving it. Deeply aware of correct behaviour but never enslaved to it. I would gaze around at languorous limbs, a beautifully painted toe. There were many of these moments when I would feel right about myself and my place in the world. But like everything, they were fleeting and not permanent.

———

The bulimia intensified sometime in this period. India is such a food centric culture, and everywhere you go, people want to feed you. Indians are very disdainful of Western parties or events where food isn't served in volume. Cocktails and nibbles would get a raised eyebrow in India at that time: *Why are you being so* kanjoos?

By the mid-1990s , the country was opening up to global influences. Evenings could begin at a great five-star hotel restaurant, where a huge buffet with everything from channa masala to pasta al pomodoro would be waiting. After all that grand food in a grand setting, I'd dash home, kneel in front of the toilet and stick two fingers down my throat. This became a matter of routine, several times a week. In the beginning, I could throw up with one finger, but after a while I had compromised my gag reflex and one finger wasn't enough. Soon, two fingers didn't do the job either. It wasn't long before I needed to shove my entire fist down my throat to bring up the food.

I had set random rules and regulations about portions and forbidden foods that perpetually ran through my eating disordered brain. I remember being on location for a television spot being shot in Mauritius, with its blue water and beautiful people, a mixture of Indian, African and French. Every morning, we woke to a particularly tempting buffet of fresh fruit, pancakes, and every kind of breakfast food. I allowed myself just a little bit of cheese, a small portion of fruit and some juice. Of course, hunger was a constant companion. Sometimes I'd break and have a piece of waffle or, God forbid, an omelette. Moments later, despite the cameras rolling, I'd stop the action and run to my room and force myself to throw up until I had rid my body of whatever suste-nance I had taken in. By the time I finished, I had red eyes and tears running down my cheeks. Then I'd wipe myself off, call for a make-up touch-up and walk back to the set, to put on the image for the cameras.

Other days, ravenous and defeated by my campaign of starvation, I'd swing to the opposite extreme, stuffing my face. I was caught in the pathology of the perfectionist: if something was off in my day—a shoot didn't go exactly as I wanted, my face looked too round in the polaroid, or someone said something that I interpreted as disparaging—I'd feel

entirely unworthy. Outwardly, I would turn to ice, putting on my cold-
est and haughtiest face, while inwardly, I could feel a typhoon begin to
gather in my belly. I would become restless and impatient to leave. At
home, I would drink big bottles of Coke and order as much rich food
as I could. I'd eat it fast and mindlessly, filling the hole inside me, feeding the self-doubt. I remember that sensation of lying back on my
futon, so stuffed I could barely breathe, my belly filled like a tomb. So
I would throw it all up, violently, enjoying each stab of pain, imagining I could hear my insides tear. My dark, destructive impulses made
me feel special, like I was brave and misunderstood. "Only the brave
will survive in fashion," was the sort of implicit slogan I abided by.
There were no pillars to hold me up, to make me feel safe. The pathway to self-destruction was not just clear but rather appealing.

Bulimics are very secretive, and I thought I hid it well. I'm sure
there were people who perceived what was going on, but nobody spoke
to me about it. I'm sure I was too defensive to engage. The men who
pursued me didn't really pay attention, and for them, the more I was
celebrated, at whatever cost, the better. When you become famous at
the age of sixteen there is a real danger you remain trapped by an over-
cooked version of yourself; in my case it was as a receptacle for men's
desires. One afternoon, I was having coffee in suburban five-star hotel
coffee shop. I was sitting on my own, hiding in full view in a ripped
t-shirt, my hair in disarray. I eavesdropped on a conversation between
two young men at the table next to me. I could sense their curious
glances out of my peripheral vision. There's a specifically Indian way of
getting attention by raising eyebrows and nodding your chin. I saw one
guy do the eyebrow nudge my way and then say to his friend in Hindi,
"Hey, look at her. She's not bad, huh."

The other guy regarded me coolly and asserted, "She's okay." He
turned back to his friend, "But she's no Lisa Ray."

I was amused. I have recounted this experience many times since.
I had become embedded in the pop culture of India, and yet, that person was some separate entity. The real me could never measure up to
the imaginary me.

———

Everyone knows about anthropologists who, in the process of observing their subjects, adopt their habits, values and lifestyle. I think these are my people. From my outsider position, I became immersed in Bombay to the point where I could almost pass as a local. "Where did you go to school? Scottish or Xavier's?" I started being asked.

But on the practical side of matters, I had to learn how to communicate, and not only because the Devanagari script was written above arches on government buildings. Hindi resonates deeply with me and with dozens of vivid and imaginative phrases for lovers that capture the spectrum of desire, it struck me as not just practical but a language of *ishq*, an agent of romance. Bollywood film producers or directors of impressive persistence who tried to convince me to sign their projects would wave away protestations of "But my Hindi is weak." I'd hear a pause, then a rustle of realignment on the other side of the phone. I'd picture them leaning back on cracked leather chairs, a cupboard of silver jubilee trophies behind him, flicking away my unworldliness with thick, ringed fingers. "Arre, don't worry. Look at Sridevi. Even she couldn't speak Hindi. Look at her now."

None of them asked if I wanted to be Sridevi—I most certainly did not—so that was that. But I did want to learn the language just the same and for its own sake. I engaged the same Hindi tutor who had begun training me for the Sanjay Dutt film. Masterji was an exacting, nut-coloured man, who showed up in a freshly laundered white kurta twice a week to correct my Hindi pronunciation. He was used to impressing with his formal elevated language skills. He never showed it, but I'm sure he was dismayed not only by my *jungli* ways but also by the Catholic family I was living with. They looked at him blankly when he greeted them with a "khamagani" type flourish. Their Hindi was worse than mine. Before every class I explained that as I was no longer interested in becoming a Hindi film actress, Masterji should teach me prosaic phrases like "Bring the food and put it on the table," or "Give these clothes to the dhobi." Masterji nodded while finishing his glass of water, wiped his face calmly with a checked handkerchief and proceed to make me repeat:

Main Amrika se aae hoon (I have come from America—and no matter how much I explained that Canada was a different country, in his mind "foreign" meant "Amrika").

Maine modelling ki hai, isliye mujhe camera se koi dar nahin (I have modelled therefore I am not scared of the camera).

Main yeh dono kalayein achchi tarah se seekh loon (I pray to god that I may learn both these arts soon).

Main dil lagakar, din raat mehnat karoongi aur duniya ko dikha doongi ki ek videshi ladki hone ke bawajood main ek behtareen kalakar ban sakti hoon (I will work hard day and night to prove to the world that in spite of being a foreign girl I can be a very fine actress).

Fortunately, in Bombay, you can manage without perfect fluency in Hindi, as the version commonly spoken on the street is a mishmash of dialects and *tapori* slang. My friends spoke mainly in English with some Hindi words sprinkled in, a dubious language dubbed "Hinglish." But more than the language, I wanted the accent. As I started absorbing the cadence, I added expressive hand gestures. "You sound *phoren*, you look like a phirang," were hung around my neck. But I didn't consider them compliments. I wanted to step across boundaries, find another story to hold me. First I became fluent in the technicolour slang used in Bombay: "*Aati kya?*" "First class, boss." Then I trained myself to use simpler English words. Then I learned to change the order of my words in a sentence. I became a Bombayite. "What yaar? Shameless he is, yaar. Where are you? Backside?" I began to soften my spine and flop against floor cushions, then liberate my feet from worn-down Kolhapuri chappals, and prop the soles of my bare feet against the driver's arm rest in the car. My Polish granny had always covered her feet with stockings and slippers even at home. Because, according to her, bare feet were obscene and a sign of savagery, something only the poor and foreign were unable to conceal. Eventually I lost my Canadian accent completely—it made me feel gratified and isolated— forswearing any identifiable speaking cadence. My father couldn't recognize my voice when I called Toronto.

With the accent emerged a new person—at times pliant and coquettish, and at other times harsh and crude, a self-confessed *goondi*, or female thug. I quickly learned there was no single way to be any one of my identities. I remember having it out with a young Nepali security guard in my building. He was new, it was his first night of duty and he made the mistake of asking who I was. A black wave rose from my liver and I slapped him across the face. I pummelled him. I was screaming *gaalis* and threats in a burst that brought all the Catholic neighbours to stare over the potted plants in their windows. I wanted to eviscerate him with my hands and with my words. He had not stuck to the codes of propriety because he thought I was a foreigner; but no, of course it was more than that. When I lost control, the rage that poured through me had little to do with that present moment.

"Saala bhenchot, main ek jharoo tere gaand mein daal kar mor banaungi." (Translation: "Sisterfucker, I'm going to shove a broom up your ass and turn you into a peacock.")

His khaki uniform hung from his thin frame and his eyes registered an exaggerated caricature of shock. He was frightened. And young. And confused by a world where all accepted notions of behaviour had just disappeared.

I felt terrible. I bit back my own tears, walking away into a suffocating night. I was following the script—rise in anger to defend your honour when challenged—but I felt more in the wrong than ever before. I'd traded one cultural story for another by moving to India, but had lost sight of something essential in the process.

Bombay was still reeling from the horrors of the 1992 Hindu–Muslim riots. The riots had revealed poisonous prejudices on both sides that ran deep enough for homes and people to be set ablaze. My friend Ali described agonized screams carried on the wind all the way to the terrace of his posh Pali Hill building, where he and his family had retreated uneasily while the city burned. The aftermath of communal violence was still to be ascertained but one thing was clear, Bombay had changed, though the impact on nightlife in 1993 could not be fully gauged yet. But the attraction to the freedom that the cover of night brought was on the wane. Religious tensions flared, and the city itself seemed flammable but the professional partiers still clung to a version of life that remained a giddy parade. Instead of finding a safe way to scream, a way to release the city's collective angst, we continued to come together in an endless pageant of excess to lose ourselves. It could have been any city, but my experience of this ritual played out in Bombay.

From my corner of the room behind the velvet rope, sometimes I was dropped into a moment where I saw them, Bombay's Beautiful people, from a far. *"Eh, Meena Kumari, band karo yeh drama,"* my friends would chide, referencing the proclaimed "Tragedy Queen" of Indian cinema. Turn up the house music and have a drink and stop being so boring. But I was fascinated by the spectacle.

7

I DON'T REMEMBER why or how I found myself on a potholed road to Shirdi, a five-hour drive into rural Maharashtra from Bombay. But I remember what happened when I got there: all the clawing thoughts, the eight million stories in my head called it a day. I walked through the chaotic streets barefoot, in the direction of the mandir, my mind emptying itself with each step. Going on a darshan, the chance to witness that which is holy, was the one part of my life that should have felt unreachably alien, but oddly enough it was the only time when I felt my essence take flight. There was a world I had missed, believing the whole world was out there. This was a trip that took me inwards. And that was the beginning of an important awakening.

Shirdi is just one of hundreds of such sites in India that attracts pilgrims and seekers. Shirdi Sai Baba was a spiritual master, whose teachings incorporated elements of both Hinduism and Islam. He lived an itinerant life, wandering for long periods, occasionally taking refuge under a neem tree. A shrine sprang up in the hamlet of Shirdi after his death, soon becoming a popular pilgrimage. After that first visit, I started making regular trips, soothed right at the outset by the drive through endless fields sliced with ditches. I would cover my head with a chunni before entering the temple to receive a sprinkling of water from the priests. A bare room next door housed various artefacts Sai Baba had kept during his lifetime: a low stool; dented and aged utensils; a heavy metallic tumbler. I sat on the bare floor losing track of time, but feeling I was peeling back centuries of skin. I didn't have words to describe it, so I never shared my experiences, but I never returned the same. Driving back from Shirdi, a poem I learned as a child ran through my head:

Who has seen the wind
Neither you nor I
But when the trees bow down their heads
The wind is passing by.

Determined to hold on to the calm and sanctity of prayerfulness, I began visiting pilgrimage sites around India. Whenever I travelled on work, I'd slip away to a local site of worship. These spiritual side trips took on more and more significance in my life. I covered my head and visited dargahs, temples, monasteries, gurdwaras and churches, always feeling like I was standing on the periphery of something, before silence would gently blanket all the habits of my mind. In those delicious moments, both my mind and spirit faced each other in silent, dazed celebration. I had stumbled upon peace.

But the truth is growing in consciousness is hard work. It's not about blissing out but the ability to emancipate yourself from others' opinions and uncage your awareness. And in order to do that, you have to confront the rawness of the pain of your many selves. Not everyone is ready for that calibre of pain. I wasn't at that point. But resting peacefully was a good start.

Pretty soon the act of touching my fingers lightly to my forehead, and then between my heart—the gesture of devotion—became automatic. One afternoon a friend observed me making the gesture as we drove to South Bombay, first as we passed Haji Ali, a shimmering white mosque set on an islet, one of Bombay's iconic landmarks, and then each time I saw a Hindu temple and smaller, roadside shrines. There was no favouritism in my developing spiritual galaxy. "You half-breeds really are confused, aren't you?" she said. I replied with a smile. "I'm just scrambled, not hard-boiled."

Even as I blended into Bombay, I remained perturbed about the social inequality that normally hits an outsider at the moment of arrival. You might say it was my lingering Canadian worldview that kept bumping up against India's social complexities and the gaps between my two cultures made me very self-righteous. I'd go to splendid dinner parties and lecture guests on how we needed to lift the poor out of the slums. "How can we seal ourselves in our cars, with the poor tapping and scratching at the windows? How can we tune them out? Doesn't India progress economically only when everyone progresses?" I looked around to see everyone smiling tightly; they did not, their smiles said, think this was worthwhile dinner conversation.

When I finished with poverty, I'd start ranting about the pollutants. Rape culture was not the headline news it is today, but with the ongoing ascent of Bal Thackeray and his right-wing party, the Shiv Sena, the liberal, pluralistic, accepted way of life of Bombay was under threat. Suddenly independent career women were viewed through a chauvin-istic lens. "Our freedom is under threat!" I would pound the table. I was right, but I was also a colossal bore. The guests would contract into a defensive ball away from me. My friends would roll their eyes. "Mother Teresa, don't you need to use the loo?"

After a while, I grew numb to the poverty. Of course, I became as much of a hypocrite as the others, stuffing olives and pate in our mouths, though I didn't believe I was influenced by a "Western bias." I never felt India was a "developing world." It was my world and I loved it, which is why I was fired by ideas of social justice, but I stopped dragging social issues around. Instead I put my faith in small everyday actions of redistributing my overflowing rations, tipping extra, paying for my staff's kids' education, and listening closely to what needs to be done just because I could. Kindness giving birth to compassion, giving way, per-haps one day, to an epidemic of empathy. I was told it's a waste of time to think of these things, "You don't know what you are dealing with, don't encourage them, you phirangs will spoil the marketplace." On days when I had to bribe an MTNL worker to fix my phone connection and he returned to my door several times that same day with an expanding group of fellow employees, hurt that I had neglected to include them in this wonderful game, I thought it true. The ongoing struggle for me in Bombay was with apathy and the *chalta hai* attitude that comes with facing an onslaught of unacceptable social problems day after day.

I have a good analogy for how easy it is to be lulled into privilege. At one point, I was caught in the gossamer first strands of romance with the son of a prominent business potentate and we flew to Goa for a weekend. One moonlit night, he told me to hop into his jeep. Jeeps aren't allowed on the beaches in Goa, but there we were, racing along the shore in the darkness. I could see the shapes of thousands of crabs, drawn by the light of our headlights. They glistened for a moment before I heard the crackle and crunch of the tiny creatures being crushed under our wheels. On the surface, this was a romantic evening, and a perfect indulgence—beautiful man, the beach a luminescent dessert under the milky moon. But in order to serve our pleasure, we treated thousands of creatures as the playthings of circumstance. We were reckless because we could be. I smiled over dinner even as the image of little crushed bodies catching the light like broken ice crept into my heart.

By 1994, I had been living in Bombay for a few years, making the occasional trip to visit my parents. On one of those trips, eager the whole time to return, I realized I had made enough money to buy a flat in Bandra. With a place of my own I could have my parents ride out the winter months with me. This time, my parents returned to Bombay with me to help search for a flat and I could afford to check them into a five-star hotel. It was their first time back after the accident and an enduring testament to their grit and sense of adventure that that trip established an annual ritual of travelling to Bombay once a year—quite a logistical challenge with my mother's wheelchair. With the help of my lawyer friend, Dilip Jhangiani, we found the perfect Bandra flat on the top floor of a small Catholic building called Ave Maria.

During this time, I was contentedly single. Considering my name was synonymous with seductive temptress, my life wasn't exactly high on passion. I had dated both of Maureen's sons—not at the same time—and after that consented to the odd dinner date, always bringing along a girlfriend.

Privately, I joked about sex symbols as the third gender—sidelined and excluded because we were expected to date only the fabulously famous or wealthy, which in my mind equated to fabulously narcissistic. Then one night, through a friend, I ended up at an expensive Italian restaurant, which was in the swanky Leela Kempinski Hotel. There were three men at the table—one acquaintance and two strangers. I remember being preoccupied with what to order and trying to gauge when I could leave the table. Living with an eating disorder required a lot of cryptic information and counterintelligence-level secrecy. I became paranoid when I was out for dinner unless I knew there was a bathroom close by where I could purge. It took me a while to figure out the floor plan before I could relax enough to notice the guy sitting quietly next to me. He was interesting looking: not at all traditionally handsome; a solid, thick-set body; gap-toothed; powerful eyes. Multiple *kala dhaaga*s, the threads given by a priest after prayer, were tied around his wrists; the black strings considered a protection, and a blessing.

He leaned over and said: "Can you tell me what I should order? I normally just eat rice and dal." I thought: Here's a man who's either trying to play me like a violin, or else he genuinely doesn't take himself too seriously. In contrast to the circles I moved in, his simplicity broke through. He wasn't like the rest of them, preening in loafers and flashy patterned shirts. He seemed shy but when his pager went off and he looked down, moving it beneath the tablecloth, I caught a glimpse of something else; mildness giving away to a hooded gaze. The darkness I glimpsed in him at that moment drew me in more than anything else.

He was secretive and street smart and jarringly unsuitable for me in every way. We began to go for lunch together, always in Juhu. Two strangers in a hotel, smiling at each other in awkward silence. I observed him while he chewed, feeling myself pulled into this peculiar mating dance charged with dark energy. Mr X, as I'll call him, had a candour and an odd chivalric reticence. He always insisted his Bihari driver pick me up and drop me back on our lunch dates at the Sun and Sand and the Holiday Inn, but when I turned to say goodbye he'd already be on his phone, something unreadable shading his expression. On our fifth date, he said, "I like you a lot. I'd like to sleep with you." Did he really say that? I had to laugh at his forwardness. I had no intention of sleeping with him, but I was taken with his extremes. Here was a guy who wasn't playing strange games; there would be no groping in the shoe closet. But I also felt myself teetering on the edge of turmoil, courting drama and crisis. Mr X was clearly enmeshed in shadowy dealings. Soon, my good girl intentions vanished, and we became romantically involved.

It was glorious to fully dissolve into another in the way of the sweeping love stories I had read about. It was also a relief to have a confidante,
but only gradually did I learn the scope of Mr X's influence. He was
something of a Fixit baba in Bombay. He told me he worked in "crisis
management." For example, if a movie star bought a plot of land and
wanted clearance so he could build on it, he'd call Mr X who would get it
done with a few phone calls, all the while sipping serenely from a can of
Coke. "I love my country, but you know we live in an ass-kissing society,"
he would say with undisguised glee. "I'm just a simple villager," he'd say,
like a man used to hauling pots of water, which was blatantly untrue, but
he seemed to take pleasure in contrasting his rustic ways with my sophis-
tication. Another famous star would call to smooth things over whenever
his drunk antics got out of hand. Everyone knew Mr X, it seemed, but he
was rarely seen out at parties or events.

Mr X inducted me into how his business was conducted in the city. He
would organize entertainment evenings at one of his bungalows for
high-ranking police officers one night, and politicians the next. Prostitutes
were brought in and imported alcohol served, though X himself didn't
drink. He would narrate his account of these evenings to me in the manner of sharing a day at the office, treating the men's keenness on raunchy
activities as an endearing and forgivable indulgence, like naughty school-
boys. "Was it a veg or a non-veg night?" I'd ask, referring to the quality
of entertainment.

His other passion was shikar, hunting wild boar. I remember
accompanying him on a moonlit hunt, powerful flashlights sweeping
the forest, the darker-than-darkness figure of a boar, a graveness over-
taking my heart as I watched the animal jerking and gasping for its
last breath. I had worn a light pink salwar kameez on that trip. I balled
it up as soon I got home the next day and flung it out of my window in
an attempt to yank the memory from my mind.

These details would only emerge later, but in the beginning all I
knew was that I felt safe with him—for me, he was stable, and present.
Everyone knew the underworld was infiltrating the Hindi film industry,
and many actors and producers were dealing with phone calls from
"Bhai," the notorious gangster Dawood Ibrahim. You could feel the overwhelming rush of a whole new revolver culture in the city. Wise-guys

and Bombay's demi-monde were falling to the concrete in police encounters and gang warfare and quite a few film producers were caught in the
crossfire of extortion and intimidation. It seemed a little dangerous,
though I enjoyed the frisson of the unpredictability of life. At the same
time, and this was a new thought for me, having Mr X around filled me
with a naive notion that he was steering me clear of the rocks. His
mantra was, "I'll take care of everything." He sent officials to escort me
through the airport every time I travelled, causing me mild embarrassment. As material proof, he carried a gun.

A few months into our relationship, I boarded a flight for work. I
remember saying goodbye and how much it hurt, an outsized pain at the
separation. When I reached the hotel, he had already left me a phone
message to tell me he was getting married: to a serious girlfriend I had
not heard of before. It was a sudden crack in a still night, a revelation—
no, an existing reality—that escalated too quickly and too overwhelm-
ingly to digest. I was shattered, as if I'd been punched deep down in my
insecurities. Now the feeling of somehow being unworthy had spilled
over from my professional life into my love life. I immediately broke off
my relationship with him understanding he had had a long-term girlfriend the entire time we were together. I replaced the dead flowers in
my flat and willed myself into working and travelling obsessively. But
all the while I was shrinking into myself like crumpled foil. Somehow,
months later, Mr X. crept back in my life. He whispered in low tones,
convincing me we were in a pool of light together. I had no power of
refusal in me when it came to love. I could not resist a mechanical yes
to all he proposed. He told me, "I'll make it work so we can be together."
Very soon, a new Lisa grew to cover the old, the one who would never
have consented to becoming the "other woman." To be so profoundly
out of solidarity with another woman. To betray both her and myself.
To be the mistress of a married man.

This relationship continued for most of my time in Bombay—it was
like a never-ending hike through the bad lands of my self-esteem, a
psychological desert where laughter was short and scornful. Mr X soon
became possessive and controlling. He interfered in my work life, my
friendships and even dictated the way I looked. I thought that was how
love worked. "My mother always said, 'Never trust a woman with light

eyes—*billi ke jaise,*'" he would laugh affably. We fuelled each other's insecurities, sparked each other's fuses. There were fights (he was never physically abusive though I would throw things) and nuclear abuses dropped from my lips. I lashed out with a vehemence reserved for the one you love. And he loved seeing me come unhinged. I see now that I had invited it in and take responsibility for my role in it all. I was the IT girl full of self-loathing. "Will you remember me as a ray of sunshine, or a dark, moody devil?" I asked Mr X during a peaceful moment on one of our frequent trips to Goa. His voice was soft. A loving voice. "When are you planning on dying, baby?" he asked from behind lowered lids. At the zenith of my popularity and desirability, deep down I felt totally unworthy of all of it, even of a fair, loving relationship.

Thinking of that time still brings up evidence of damage, pumps my blood with panic and guilt. How is it that these memories of abusive love are always there? Circling, circling quietly in our atoms. A reminder of our volcanic layers of human mistakes. And it's okay. It's okay to have been through what we experienced. There's no way to get to where you need to go otherwise. It's the only way I know. And it's okay.

My career had taken off in India. I was enjoying myself in large part because I was constantly on the move. For the first few years, I remember packing chicken jungli sandwiches from Candies or Birdy's for a location shoot in Alibagh or Lonavala or Madh Island and eating them in the car on the drive before the mayo went bad. Shooting on "location" also meant peeing behind shrubbery or in a village home. But by the mid-1990s, clients wanted increasingly glamorous locations that changed every season, along with the budgets. I was flying to the Seychelles, the Maldives, Mauritius, Switzerland, the United Kingdom. It was also the dawn of the age of celebrity endorsements in India. Somewhere around 1999 Aishwarya Rai was signed by Longines and Shah Rukh Khan by Omega. Then Rado called and I signed a contract to be their official ambassador. The endorsement meant making public appearances at stores and launching new watch models as the face of the brand in India. It also meant frequent trips to smaller towns and cities I would not normally visit: Ludhiana, Mangalore, Patna and Kochi.

Venturing outside the pandemonium of Bombay is what brought a tingle in the lining of my skin. How can I describe India except to say it defies definition? I soaked it in on my extensive work travels and felt the experiences as intimately as the lines in my palms. I stored a mosaic of all I saw and felt, fragment by gathered fragment. I nourished myself to excess on India and its majestic, scarred landscape, and recognized myself in all its dichotomies.

Those were the glory days of advertising in India. Fashion was beginning to boom. A corporatized beauty industry was also taking hold of the country, flourishing in the obsession with beauty pageants and Miss India winners. I had great respect for Sathya Saran, the editor of *Femina* magazine which sponsored the contest, but the beauty pageant culture with its toothy smiles and exaggerated femininity was difficult for me to digest. In North America, beauty pageants were something of a joke, and brought to mind Dallas-style bouffants and spray-tanned legs. But the Miss India crown was coveted as much as a monarchic accession. ("A life in a day, a month as a lifetime, and now a year which could transform all her tomorrows," said the *Times of India* ad for the Miss India contest.) Winning was a smooth catwalk to wealth, success and national respect. It truly puzzled me. Bright and intelligent women became all fluttery and bloodless during the contest. It was like a conjurer's trick, the swift disappearance of their personalities.

I was familiar with a lot of the girls who participated and won in those formative years. I also knew several of the Miss India grooming team. It was the beginning of the packaging of beauty queens. At the time, vanity was still considered indulgent; women needed to be attractive enough to get married, but after that automatically dissolve their sense of self to become mothers and wives. So, in a roundabout way, the growing glorification of beauty contests signalled a step towards self-definition, and emancipation for women in India. I could appreciate the winds of change that it symbolized, if not the more commercially driven efforts to corral concepts of beauty into an Indian version of Barbie.

It was also a lucrative business. I enjoyed watching the show unfold. I was in Goa during one of the final rounds of the seminal Miss India contest which pitted the crowd-favourite Aishwarya Rai against dark horse Sushmita Sen. It was like an afternoon at the Derby, the way the audience placed their bets and reduced the girls' chances to their parts and features. I recall crowning Ash when she won the swimsuit round. Every move and moment was breathlessly reported, like a UN summit. It was a new landscape to be curious about. Pradeep Guha presided over the event. He was the CEO of the Times of India group and positioned himself as a benevolent czar and impresario by influencing not only ad revenue but also content. He introduced a popular tabloid culture dubbed "Page 3" through *Bombay Times*. He was also the publisher of *Femina* magazine. This was his show.

After crowning Ash, I found a group of friends on the beach making sarcastic comments, "No one behave normally—we are all under the spell of the Femina Miss India contest," while I watched dazzling faces pass by, faces which seemed burdened with too much make-up. Pradeep walked up to me with a drink in his hand. This was a signal to separate from the group.

"Would you ever want to be Miss India?"

I was taken aback, but I understood veiled language, admitting nothing but implying everything.

"But . . . I'm technically not Indian. I mean, I am . . . I think of myself as Indian . . . but I have a Canadian passport."

"Yes well . . ."

The offer was obfuscated in his shrug, but the implication was clear. But for me, it was too absurd a thought to entertain. Strangely, I thought of my grandfather with a carpet of old newspapers decaying at his feet precipitating a retreat far from the crowds to a spot on the sand. I squinted into the salty air. I was also being altered like these girls. But increasingly, I couldn't relate to this way of owning dreams, to consent to be sized up and cut down. These bright young women I saw were wild and lush, wide-hipped, with eyes like teardrops and full of inherited graces, and here they were being distilled and squeezed into a mould that travelled well—it would impress the world outside India—but also take them so far from themselves.

"You are mad. Why didn't you say yes?" My girlfriend had sat down next to me on the sand. "Come on. Don't you want to be a beauty queen?"

"I'm already a Rani," I said, looking out at the savage and beautiful sea.

Ad films in the 1990s weren't just disposable promotion, but glamorous little snippets, as engaging and well-produced as movie trailers; short movies, with big budgets. People paid attention and talked about them, following the output of the models like they were actors. "Did you see Lisa in the Garden Silk Sarees ad? Then after that, she did the Lakme ad. I liked her in the Sprite ad too. But I'll always remember her wrapped in towels as the Bombay Dyeing girl!" There was a lot of exchange between Hindi films and the world of advertising; the same DOP or director who worked on a feature had no problem doing a quick, hit ad film. There was no loss of status in moving back and forth. One of my favourite DOPs to work with was Ashok Mehta, of the rakish Australian outback hat. He had worked his way from tea boy to super technician status through talent and chutzpah. His lighting was unearthly: the way you imagine the world when you're in love.

I did an ad for the iconic brand Garden Vareli Sarees—popularly known as Garden Sarees—in which I twirled in slow motion as the pallu of my saree fluttered poetically in the breeze (the saree flutter is a popular image in Indian cinema). The jingle was composed by A.R. Rahman which should say something about the calibre of talent in ads those days. It was directed by my friend Ashish Sawhney, sensitive and witty, the grandson of Ismat Chughtai. He was one of my first friends to come out and has gone on to becoming a vocal supporter of LGBTQIA rights in India. The ad made a huge impact. People will still tell me: "I remember you in that Garden Sarees ad!" When I was in treatment for cancer, a friend called me to say the ad was on TV again in India. I called the head of Garden Sarees, a formidable woman, and said, "I hear you're running the ads again. I know I did them a long time ago, but India has changed, and surely by now there's such a thing as 'residuals'?" Immediately, she told me she too had experienced a bout of cancer. And she cut me a cheque, which I donated to an Indian charity.

This is what I love about India: while the way of getting things done is so labyrinthine, there's humanity at the core. Perhaps not the system, but the *people* surprise you. From my early experiences I like to tell people that everything you hear about India is true, as well as its opposite. There is no better place in the world to challenge your everyday assumptions about pretty much everything.

There were still no stylists at the time, though my friends Hemant Trivedi and Wendell Rodricks, Rohit Bal, Shahab Durazi and James worked with photographers on campaigns to design "looks," but a new generation of make-up artists with light fingers and contemporary sensibilities was beginning to remedy the old ways. Mickey Contractor, Cory Walia, Michelle Tung, Kapil Bhalla, Jojo, Vipul Bhagat, Subhash Vagal, usually called "Subu" within the industry, and Anil Chinnappa, better known to insiders as "Bondu" were all starting to blossom and thrive. They sounded the death knell for pancake and shading through "cutting." I remember shooting for the coveted Lakme ad with my friend Farrokh. The images were lovely. When I saw the result, the copy read: "When they call me soft-spoken, are they referring to my lips?" Really? Soft-spoken? Yet the play of tension between real versus ideal and the valorization of modesty in women rubbed me the wrong way. I arrived at FC's studio and climbed into a wicker basket. We were such close friends, with such strenuous loyalty between us, I felt safe enough to regress.

"Take me to John Irving," I whined in a baby voice from under the lid.

To FC I had confessed my heart's desire to be a writer. He had developed a close bond with John Irving while assisting him with his research in India for *A Son of the Circus* so it felt only natural that I should make this peevish demand for an audience with a man for whose company I would exchange an evening with every Bollywood celebrity.

I was more or less on a set working as a model or "personality" every single day. I was now in my mid-twenties and had clocked up eight years in Bombay. I was still charmed when I saw kids stow themselves away in the trees during a location shoot, clinging to branches to get the best view, cupping their hands over their mouths to giggle and whisper to each other. But I was getting tired. Sometimes I would wake in the night, the hotel room distorted and wavy, wondering where I was. Outside of work there were demands on my time to attend events like Umang, the Bombay Police's annual cultural event, or a garba evening organized by a local MP. Refusal was out of the question. In the previous five years, I hadn't had a single day off. And the days were long. There was no concept of "turn-around" time or strictly enforced time limits on how long a human could reasonably be expected to toil. I felt for the lighting men, the junior artistes, all the technicians on a suffocating set without whom none of the fantasy would be possible. But I was too exhausted to advocate for them. When the work is like that, you almost forget it even happened. Your body wades through the days, while your mind sees everything through a pool of water or blacks out. "Wow, that's a skill, talking non-stop." I said to my make-up artist Hameed once during a location shoot. "But Lisa, I haven't said anything for the last half hour." I was hearing things. A low, breath-less whine poured through my ears that I mistook for voices. That morning in fact, I asked Hameed to begin working on my face while I was semi-conscious, lying in bed. I was simply too burned out to get up at 4 a.m. At that time, popular names went from job to job, putting your face behind everything, from soap to sarees to cars to washing powder to music videos to editorials on the cover of *Elle* magazine (which entered the Indian mar-ket in 1996). When the music channel and satellite television revolution came to India, I was offered a job as a veejay for *BPL Oye* on home-grown music channel Channel V, and co-hosted my own film review show called *Star Biz*. Life was gleaming with opportunity and for every "no," another offer would grow in its place. My position seemed assured, as if it would last no matter how much I toyed with it. I was still less interested in the commercial aspects of my career than this idealistic notion that I was part of a creative revolution. When I was working. I became a bride of the camera. A fever would summon a doctor to the set, shots would be given, and strips of antibiotics tucked into my spot boy's bag, alongside my gum and tiny Ganesha and whatever book I was reading. I wanted to be someone else, a better version of myself, not just in appearance, and the industry helped mould me. At times I was haunted by the thought that there were now so many other girls waiting for the chance I'd been given. Even though I had never wanted to be a model, I worked very hard at it, turned it into a passion and enjoyed all its fleeting pleasures.

I did a few music videos, including an iconic one for the legendary Sufi vocalist Nusrat Fateh Ali Khan. I had always enjoyed the showy rhythm of those Hindi film qawwalis, the soaring notes, and stylized, expressive gestures, but without really understanding the mystical tradition until I moved to India. Then, the Sufi, the fakir, the mystic became romantic objects of fascination for me. How is it possible, this utter devotion to the divine, and how is it that you sing to the untold stories of my soul? Those streamers of sound transported me. The air, the earth, the crow, the kabadi-wallah whistling roadside were all mine. Life unwrapped itself, revealed itself to be shining. Of course, I would be a part of his video, no questions asked.

The aesthetic was dreamy but also very straight: no irony allowed. The song was "Afreen, Afreen" (O most beautiful one) and there I was, walking the desert in billowing fabric, being pursued by a hunky male model named Himanshu. Of course, in the Sufi tradition, all praise of the beautiful one is of the beloved, or God. Music videos in India were at the height of their popularity but I'm still not sure why this haunting meditation on divine love ended up being visualized by Ken Ghosh in the deserts of Rajasthan. But I enjoyed Ken's light-hearted approach to work and was happy to film with him, even in 40-plus degree weather where the camera lens was in danger of melting. I also didn't anticipate the video would become such a hit, that I would be known thereafter as the Afreen girl—even now, decades after its release. But one person who took the shoot very seriously was Himanshu. He really wanted to break out of modelling and become an actor. In one shot, he was supposed to walk off into the desert, so the director set up a crane. Off went Himanshu, overacting to the hilt, wiping his brow, falling and stumbling in the sand for dramatic effect. The director got his shot, and they began to disassemble the crane. But Himanshu was still walking off into the desert, becoming this tiny little dot in the distance. "Oh no, we forgot to yell "cut," said the director. "He's going to end up in Pakistan!"

I was still being ardently pursued professionally by some of the biggest names in Bollywood at the time. Boney Kapoor, Mukul Anand, even Salman Khan persistently chased me down. I was still struggling with my shyness, which was exacerbated by my ongoing relationship with Mr X, who was becoming increasingly paranoid and possessive, proving his mettle as an emotional terrorist. The spirit had not moved me to say "yes" to any of the offers for many reasons. I couldn't imagine gyrating with Govinda to any of his hit dance songs like "Ande ka Funda." (I admit it, while I sang along to those songs in my car and delighted in the absurdist cheer which many mainstream Bollywood films of that era spread, it was not for me to dance with Govinda or his counterparts.) I had a strange naivety for an Indian celebrity at the time, believing in the power of cinema to elevate, to move people, to tell a story worth remembering. Even if there was no terrific story to tell, at the very least I needed a story which was meaningful, or perhaps just sensible, to say "yes."

The other thing that made me hesitate was the lack of bound scripts. Most films were narrated by the director during a meeting and if you signed on you were handed your dialogue for the day on the set, scribbled on a sheet by the writer in a corner. This was unthinkable for me with my weak Hindi. I was also nervous about the time commitment. Sometimes these films could take months, running into years, depending on the availability of the male star. Everything revolved around the lead actor, and more than likely, he was involved in multiple projects. So, it was possible an actress could shoot a few days, and then do nothing for six months but wait around. I wasn't interested in shackling my freedom to a Bollywood actor.

It wasn't so much the statecraft that was hard for me, it was the role that a woman was required to slip into during meetings, one that conferred all the power on a male actor. Act demure and coquettish, "eat your tongue," laugh at their jokes, diminish yourself. Do whatever it takes to glorify the man in the room. Have your lines ready when they "humble brag" or feign any sort of humility. "Oh, no ji . . . you are still the biggest star . . . critics don't know anything, they are so . . . critical and the public loves you. *Kya zabardast acting kiye hai aap!* I've always been such a fan . . . my whole family, we are all fans . . . I used to bunk school when your film released." I just couldn't comply. I wouldn't do it. I had not understood the value of the stoical tolerance practiced by successful actresses of that era who put up with a male star's tantrums. There were alternative models of exercising strength as a woman in India. It takes tremendous skill to navigate patriarchal structures, and power for women at that time lay largely behind the throne. But I was too damn hot-headed. "*Pataakha* she is," I heard before the door shut behind me once. I was a difficult girl. I also must admit to being just wicked enough to want to see what came of my provocations. I loved that I was chased as much as I loved to say "no." But my mental forces and fortitude were getting sapped by the unending need to dazzle and perform, or to rebel against it. I was running on depleted, irritation splotched and mirrored across my face.

I eventually caved a bit and engaged a film secretary, Ajit Dewani, who also managed one of my favourite actresses, Manisha Koirala, to take meetings on my behalf. But I could never relate with Ajitji. He was polite yet hard to read and he simply couldn't fathom my habit of saying "no" to lucrative offers. "Lisaji, don't mind, but Bollywood is all about saying "yes." *Yeh different concept ka filmon, aap baad mein kijiye.* We must cash in on the moment, isn't it?" Whenever I felt judged, I responded with sarcasm or chilly indifference. Ajitji was later gunned down outside his office in an alleged underworld hit. By then I was numb to all manner of ghastly fates. All of Bombay was awash with terror.

In the misogynistic studio system, women are more disposable than men. We were "newspaper items," I remember hearing, "hot until next day's news." There were always rumours about what each heroine had done to get where she was, but of course the reputations of the men remained unscathed—or rather were burnished with each affair. A strict code of Omerta was observed in the film industry, creating a culture of silence and silencing around any sort of scandal or sexual harassment. There were cliques and "camps" formed by film dynasties or successful producers and directors that functioned as safe havens or oppressors, depending on whether you were "in" or "out." Women were pitted against other women in that age-old narrative that "females" are catty, gossipy, bitchy and full of judgement. Popular media fuelled imagined rivalries, setting Rani against Karisma, Madhuri against Sridevi, Kajol against Preity, all of which reinforced a system of belief that kept women feeling insecure and unworthy; that kept us "in our place." I think about that now. I think about the conversation about "starlets" like Mamta Kulkarni and how differently I judged her, compared to Kajol. I believed my status and my reputation at the time were a spell protecting me from any sort of predatory sexual advances, and that my primary power came from saying "no," which made me somehow not only more desirable but superior to other actresses. I stopped going to meetings with producers, much less the ones linked to the underworld. And with Mr X in my corner, I was further sheltered from the sleazy side of the business. The truth was this: I had aligned myself with a thuggish, powerful man in order to survive. I had compromised myself, just in a different way. No one, not any of us, man or woman, comes out unscathed.

Then there were the film magazines, with their garish headlines and slightly blurry, off-centre photos, which were already writing about me, before I'd done a single film. I could handle the personal attacks, but when a publication one day wrote about my family, I was an island shore hit with a pure and overwhelming flood. I could no longer contain my rage; I was bent on suing them. My lawyer grimly explained that filing a case against the magazine meant the entire media house would not be able to write about me.

"Wonderful," I enthused, "that's exactly what I want!"

"But your career. Don't you need to be written about?"

That made me pause. Very few things are as debilitating as someone thinking they know how to define you. But I was amused at how even strait-laced professionals not connected with the entertainment business believed that even bad publicity is good publicity. I went to court and got an injunction. The actual case didn't come up for trial for another twenty years, but that's another story.

While I was putting off Bollywood, I kept getting offers to perform in live stage shows. Eventually, I decided I should try one, just for the experience of it. So I joined the carnival for one night. I came on stage at the Andheri Sports Complex in a net and feather outfit that looked like a figure skater had mated with an egret. I stood in front of 50,000 people and did a little choreographed dance to "Afreen." Really, mostly I just walked here and there on the stage, swaying my hips. But somehow, that was enough. I still remember that ear-shattering roar from the crowd. It was a high, egging me on to return for an encore. For stars, touring with a show is highly lucrative. I finished my dance, and someone handed me two plastic shopping bags of cash. That was how business was done in the 1990s.

8

WHEN I WAS young, Bollywood films were an antidote to the insular-
ity of growing up in a largely white neighbourhood in Toronto. There
was a time to be polite and there was a time to unleash your inner
Bollywood. It wasn't so much about the films themselves as the need to
find a window, to frame my family's unique identity through a fantasti-
cal lens. Of course, I had a crush on Sunny Deol after *Betaab,* while my
mother preferred the more swashbuckling heroes. But it was my strikingly blonde mother's fondness for those infuriating dance numbers
and the fact that she was stilled by them when she was fit and well and
not confined to her wheelchair, that endures most vividly in my mind.
Not the rambling plots or expressive costumes, but their effect on her.

Back in Toronto, there was an Indian food store, a "Patel" store,
crammed with atta, old *Stardust* magazines (which were much coveted),
lurid orange jalebis, chyawanprash and papads, not far from our house,
where my parents used to go to buy their spices and their vegetables—
brinjal, karela, bhindi and drumsticks. Very particular flavours, almost
like "eating a dandelion," my mom once said. Over time, she became
passionate about Indian food, and at some point, she abandoned the
pickled pork feet and cabbage rolls for the tastes of the subcontinent,
exchanging recipes with the Patel Store owner, Rupali. The store rented
pirated videotapes of the latest Hindi films, and sometimes we'd bring
one home. My father could usually only last a quarter of a tape or so
before muttering "rubbish" and stalking off, leaving my mother and me

alone. I tried to follow him but it was like trying to tear your eyes away from the pulsing lights of a highway accident. Those were the days of Sridevi's *Mr India* and my mother's favourite, *Nagina*, a film where Sridevi played a shape-shifting venomous snake bent on revenge.

There are good films, there are bad films and then, there are Bollywood films. Bollywood is a self-referencing phenomenon. While contemporary Bollywood had most definitely evolved in story-telling prowess (and I prefer to call it Hindi films now) for most of its history, the typical ingredients in any film have been song-and-dance numbers, nubile young heroine(s) and macho hero(es), and a story charged with lots of melodrama and family values. But what really makes a Bollywood film is attitude. Bollywood films are full of confidence, and their primary objective is to entertain. The expression "paisa vasool" or "get your money's worth" captures it perfectly and that's the whole point. You might be in the mood for a romance, someone else wants drama or action, so just in case—we'll put it all in! Something for everyone. Bollywood films are the original interactive entertainment—you're not expected to be a passive watcher. Even if you hate it, you *must engage.*

Seated with my parents on our maroon sofa, the 1980s hit films starring Mithun, Padmini, Sunny, Amrita and Rishi unspooling on the VCR, it always struck me that Bollywood films appeal to the most child-like aspects of ourselves. Children want glittery shiny things, and they want fun moments to go on forever: "Do it again! Do it again!" That used to be the Bollywood vibe. They'd do six or seven songs, then throw in some more. Bollywood films hold a trance-like grip over all Indians, even the ones who claim not to watch or like them. They are more evocative of an emotional state, or cultural identity, than pure entertainment. But Bollywood in the 1990s was a rather shadowy industry, rife with whispers of IT raids, money-laundering allegations and underworld ties. Even as I was being wooed and flattered with offerings of big signing amounts to play the lead heroine, I was also cautioned by friends connected to the industry to stay away. Everyone warned me and I was not warned. It was an unkind business, but I was deep in the spectacle, feeling wild and awake to its power.

In ranks of importance in Hindi films, the heroine's place is sacrosanct. When you even used the word "heroine," the first person who came to mind was Rekha of the flawless, fluffed eyebrows. She was exquisite and a perfectly cultivated image of Indian femininity and desirability. I just couldn't envision myself as a heroine, the costumes alone looked like a nuisance. Those chiffon sarees worn on snowy mountain tops and tight, dresses in the 90s. How do you pee? But in spite of my sheer determination to do things my way and my best efforts at self-sabotage, I was still, for the longest time, flooded with offers for films. I was, much to my pleasure, starting to get a reputation as erratic and unwilling to compromise or massage egos. Aishwarya was the first of my contemporaries to focus on films. And she was definitely heroine material, deeply admired while at the same time a bit icy and remote.

So rather than dive right into Bollywood, I decided to make my first film in south India. This is a rite of passage for many Bollywood heroines: do a couple of south Indian films in "Tollywood" to test the waters before going northward. At the time, the south Indian film industry was considered more organized and efficient than chaotic Bollywood. Producers paid the stars well, actresses were treated with respect and they looked upon it as a safe training ground. And, in accordance with the country's complicated racial politics, south Indian audiences love north Indian actresses because of their light skin.

It occurred to me that I was not a fixed, predictable, static identity, one that anyone could point to and say, "This is who you are. Now and always." That fluidity was my strength, though it "negatively affects your image," I was told. "You need to be either the vamp or the sweet, virginal lead. You decide." Rather than decide, I accepted an offer to do a Tamil film, triggered by my Alice in Wonderland tendency: This is so crazy I have to do it! The hero was Sarath Kumar, a moustachioed actor who would also go on to start a political party in Tamil Nadu in 2007. I'd be lying if I told you I remember the plot, but the title was *Nethaji*. I figured that I could have a blast, make some cash, and dine on dosas. It wouldn't be like a Hindi film, making headline news around the country, inviting national attention. Of course, I couldn't speak Tamil but neither could a lot of Tollywood heroines. A dialogue coach takes a stab at teaching the actors their lines, but the education is half-hearted because everything is dubbed. I realized quickly that all

I needed to know was the gist of the scene, and the first few syllables. If I couldn't manage those, I'd just repeat: "One-a, two-a, three-a . . ." in my singsong all-purpose Indian accent, feigning either general indignation or lust. I even practiced my expressions in the mirror of my hotel room, throwing my eyebrows into it. The final result would be dubbed by a Tamil voice-over actress in a studio months later.

I arrived in Chennai (at that time known as Madras) and eased myself into the slower rhythm of the steamy port city. Tamilians consider themselves discerning and evolved, intellectually and culturally. It's an understated place in contrast to north India. I've observed fantastically wealthy businessmen wear the cheapest plastic sandals and simple white cotton lungis in the south. But when it comes to their films—all bets are off. They put Bollywood, with its glitzy melodrama and spontaneous mass dance scenes, to shame.

My first day on set, the costume designer presented me with the blindingly lurid yellow saree that would be my outfit for the shot. It was a kind of yellow that doesn't occur in nature, and there were nine yards of it. They also wanted to dress me like I was twelve, with two little pigtails. Finding the whole look ugly and vaguely fetishist, I fought against it at first ("Sir cannot request me to wear saffron. It is the sacred colour of holy men. And I am but a heroine, go ask sir to change the sari"). I remember the dress designer handing me my petticoat. Then he handed me my choli, or blouse, for the saree. It was so padded in the bust that it could have stood by itself. The conical chest was uniquely weaponized; it didn't just look like it could shoot darts at a target, it looked like a dart. I held it up and sighed. The padding was becoming the norm in Bollywood films too, even in the ads I'd done. I don't love that kind of trickery, but maybe it really is more flattering to have a full bosom in a saree. Then he handed me what looked like a pair of spandex biking shorts. "Oh," I said. "Where does this go?" I held up this strange garment and turned it around to see a huge plastic bottom sewn into the back. Down south, the curvaceous silhouette rules: the bigger the better. I was very thin at the time, and extremely conscious of my weight. I found it humiliating. I'd worked so hard to stay thin and now they were telling me my body was still wrong. I fought against the bum shorts, but I really had no choice. They wanted curvy, and they got it.

The choreographer and I were not fast friends. My thinking was: "Hey, I'm just having an experience here. Don't make me work so hard!" But he wanted some seriously acrobatic, extravagant, cirque du Soleil dance numbers. He didn't care that I couldn't really dance. The choreographer would get on the megaphone, and yell for all the background dancers to take their marks and line up. I didn't know what the hell I was doing. In the rehearsal before the cameras rolled, I'd pick up the steps slowly, imitating what the choreographer's female assistant did, and think that I finally had it down. Then out would come the megaphone and suddenly, the dance sequence I had been practicing would be sped up to some supersonic, unrecognizable version of itself. "Go! Go! Go!" the choreographer would shout. *"Heep-a! Amm-a! Strong-a!"* Because it's all in the hips, you know. He would grow increasingly exasperated with me as I tried to throw my hips side to side. I didn't think it was too bad, really, but apparently it just wasn't "sharp-a" enough. "Sharp-a movement!" he'd bellow into the megaphone as I stumbled around the set. In the end, I was mostly just carried around by male dancers, like Marilyn Monroe in "Diamonds Are a Girl's Best Friend."

I did a few more south Indian films, including one that was a western, complete with cowboy boots and spurs brought in from Houston. For that film, called *Takkari Donga*, the director recreated a dusty frontier town in Ramoji Film City, a huge studio outside Hyderabad. It was surreal: an authentic hardscrabble town, lifted from a John Wayne movie, but populated by all these Kannada men dressed in checked shirts and cowboy hats, speaking Telugu and tripping on their spurs. I loved working with the hero of that project, the talented and introverted Mahesh Babu, whose father, Krishna, was the original superstar of Telugu cinema's idli westerns. The film turned out pleasantly watchable and went on to become a hit.

In my late twenties, just when I believed I had chased off all film offers, I was approached by Mahesh and Mukesh Bhatt. Collectively the outspoken director and his producer brother were known as the Bhatt camp. They offered me a film to be directed by Vikram Bhatt (no relation), a young director who seemed to want to break with the Hindi film formula. He had a worldly outlook, an acerbic wit and an interest in films outside of India, which was rare for the time. He was also fascinated by dark, moody thrillers, and Bollywood at that time generally did not do dark or moody. Bhatt had a script for a film called *Kasoor*, a remake of a Glenn Close movie (a lot of Hindi films at the time were "inspired by" or blatantly copied Hollywood film plots). I couldn't believe there was a Hindi film that revolved around a female character, so I agreed to do it. I played a lonely, young lawyer Simran Bhargav, and Aftab Shivdasani was my client. I really enjoyed working on the film, even though I didn't know the first thing about acting. "Mindblowing!" Vikram would intone dramatically after each scene was canned, in cheerful mimicry of a typical Bollywood director. However much he joked, Vikram's understanding of human nature was canny and profound. He carefully extracted a performance from me, scene by scene, day by day. Close to the end of filming, on a vast set built to look like a swamp, something clicked. We were shooting the climax of the film. Simran, my character, is confronted with the harsh truth of how profoundly she has been betrayed by the man she loves. Vikram set the scene and I lowered myself into the tank of murky water. As the slate clapped and was removed, I felt my breath catch in my chest and suddenly I was pulsating with anger and grief, feeling like blood was running out of the ends of my hair. I was gripped by wave after wave of emotion in take after take, shaking and wailing. It was dangerous, I thought from the safety of my dressing room, to access those feelings.

Vikram and I used to sit side by side on the set, brooding in comfortable silence. We watched a technician wheel an industrial sized fan on to the set. His forearms were sinewy, covered with curly black hair. A woman from the art department was decorating the set, fiddling with chair placement, gesturing at others to pull up a carpet and carry it a few inches to the left. When she spotted the wind machine she began smoothing her curls reflexively while simultaneously telegraphing her displeasure with a bang of her palm to her forehead. "*Nahin dada, nahin.* Take it away. *Le jao, dada. Le jao, le jao, LE JAO!*" She must have imagined all her props somersaulting through the air like apparitions. I watched the technician grow sulky and walk away as I used to when I was angry with my mom, rubber chappals slapping the floor. This decision to use a fan capable of significant destruction—or not— was Vikram's call. I looked at him out of the corner of my eyes but he was quiet, behind tented fingers. Contemplating the shot? The little drama that unfolded? Lunch? Suddenly he spoke, "Leesa-ji, you are the sort who will do something because you want to, not because it's the popular thing to do. But I'm not sure if it's because you're protecting yourself from getting hurt, or from an impulse to provoke. Maybe a bit of both, hmm? But you know that's what's so cool about film. Say what you need to say and how you need to say it." My eyes must have dilated like a cat coming out of the shadows. He called for the giant fan to be brought back on set which was a distraction from how uncomfortable it made me to be seen in such transparent terms. But Vikram, like his mentor Mahesh Bhatt, made me start to like myself in spite of my flaws. At times he directed me to "use your own pain" in a scene. I hadn't known this sort of self-knowledge could be used in acting. I started seeing the attraction to the craft.

My only trouble was getting my dialogues in advance. I wheedled the dialogue writer, Girish Dhamija, into sending my lines a day or two before I was expected on set. I had a long, wordy courtroom scene, which, after my anguish turned to threats, I received by fax at midnight. I stayed up the entire night, "mugging" my lines. Irrfan Khan played the opposing lawyer and complimented me after the scene. Vikram, as well as I, favoured naturalistic, truthful performance, which was generally ridiculed as "wooden" or "non-performance" at the time.

But the film was a hit. It made money and the songs by Nadeem–Shravan in particular became quite popular. Due to my "good kismet," I signed a second film with the Bhatts, scheduled to be shot in Ooty. I shot a few scenes in Bombay for the film, but Mr X was becoming increasingly paranoid and he didn't want me to go on location for more than a month. I was so naive that I believed I was putting my relationship first by consenting to his wishes. I put out of my mind the fact that Mr X was married and dropped out of the movie. The part went to Bipasha Basu, who was dating Dino Morea, the male lead, whom I had once played opposite in *Takkari Donga*. I had grudging respect for Bipasha who unapologetically flaunted her ambition and appetites. She appeared to be more of an Isabelle Adjani cat than me. She would not allow a man to call the shots. The film, called *Raaz*, became a huge hit, and catapulted Bipasha to new heights of stardom.

I didn't feel regret: I still didn't know if film was what I wanted. In fact, acting in films still filled me with anxiety and dread. But I wasn't sure *what* I wanted. Perhaps I knew intuitively at that time that I was saving myself—that if I'd gone on to be very successful in Bollywood, I'd have been extinguished. I certainly feel that is a central truth in my journey today. But the industry does lull you into a kind of comfort, it straps you down with garlands of praise and money until it becomes difficult to leave even if you never wanted to be there in the first place.

With my skill for adaptability, the cultural cues of India had seeped into my skin. It had been nine years since I'd left Canada. I had seen 9/11 from an obscure hotel room while filming in Kerala. My mother was suffering bouts of depression, but she had stabilized physically. I had an apartment on the top floor of a compact Catholic building with tree top views. My parents used to come and go, staying with me for the entire winter season. India at the time had no concept of "accessibility," but my mother loved visiting. What Bombay lacked in handicapped awareness, it made up for in cheerful and obliging manpower. In a way, she had more freedom in India because she had staff orbiting around her. If she wanted to go for a drive, she'd tell the driver and he'd take her down in the lift and transfer her into the car. Drivers are used to taking orders and my mom was used to giving them.

She also just loved the communal way of life. First thing in the morning the doorbell would chime, signalling the appearance of the nariyal-wallah who would drop off tender green coconuts sloshing with sweet water outside the door. Then the doodh-wallah would come, bringing the milk, which needed to be boiled. Then the fruit-wallah. The sabzi-wallah. The fishmonger or Koli woman. Then the dhobi. My mother delighted in all of this, the incessant ringing of the doorbell, the men and women squatting in the hallway, their fingers picking and plucking and wiping. "Ji madamji, how-r-u? Me, verry fine. *Dekho, madamji, kitne fresh-fresh sabzi . . . tamatar, piyaaz, baigan . . .*" Our maid wheeled her into the doorway, from where she selected the produce, and carried on with all the people who came in and out all day. I'd pass by her in the morning on my way out as she asked to inspect the weights from the hand scale of a bemused vendor, piles of vegetables peeking through burlap sacks. The aroma of kari patta and wet spinach wafted into the lift. "Which wallah is this one?" I teased as I descended. "It's *Punk*-aaaj," she would call back, her accented voice reverberating through the building. She knew all their names. She was more engaged with the world and always in the throes of "organizing," which took her places she could not normally go. Without her ability to court everyday life in India, my life would have run to ruin, moss would have grown on the walls, the electricity would have been cut and thuggish rats, carriers of disease and Ganesha, would have repossessed our flat. I'm convinced of it.

After the second Bhatt film fell apart, I felt lost. I recognized that mainstream films were not for me, but the experimental art films I wanted to explore were not being offered. These were just a few of dozens of signs telling me: It is time to gather and shape your longings.

"Let's see what the grand conductor in the sky has in store for you next," said FC when he saw me moping. "You know it's like that. He will make you confront yourself and your issues again and again until you clear it all out." This sounded deadly. I wasn't ready.

I was impatient to know what would come next; for life to interfere and take me by the hand as it had done before. In the meantime, I had an eclectic mix of friends: one group of fiercely intelligent, blunt individuals who were as enraged by the status quo as I was even though we were part of it, and another bunch who believed it was a moral code to dress well and that the presence of beauty was the only way to uplift the spirit. I had many things to feel good about. I could discuss poetry and politics in Delhi with Soli Sorabjee (the attorney general at the time) who I'd met on a flight and bonded with over our mutual affection for jazz. In the course of fervently collecting modern Indian art as an antidote to my mother's middle-class pragmatism I became friends with Nisha Jamwal, a talented artist and designer, who was as mercurial as me. Together we curated an art exhibition, which led to our befriending a number of the city's "decrepit old men," as we affectionately referred to that old establishment, and those dinner conversations became a kind of education. I learned about articulating ideas powerfully and provocatively, about sparring, debate, repartee, graceful flirting encased in poetry, *shayari*, and song. I recall one evening at an elderly Parsi gentlemen's home. The soup course had just been served by gloved attendants. As we picked up our spoons, our host leaned over.

"You've been working with that vulgar, vacuous group for so long, I imagine it would affect you, but it hasn't. There's something in you. You will get where you need if you paddle slowly. Remember: paddle slowly."

I nodded gravely, not understanding at all. At the bottom of the soup bowl was an engraving. On closer inspection it appeared to be a man and goat in a late stage of arousal. That night I dreamed I was blushing lotus flowers while the sun squinted a river of light at my feet, the old Parsi's words reverberating like a prayer: "Remember to never be the smartest person in the room. If you are—change rooms."

I was filming in Jaipur when I got the call; there had been a break-in at home in Bombay. "We are okay," my dad said on the phone, but I refused to believe it, a sense of dread lingering like a strong mint in my mouth. I flew home early, burst through the front door, expecting the worst. A close friend, Ashwini Kakkar, was in the living room, my mom flushed from another retelling of the incident. The police had come and gone, and the house appeared normal. From what I gathered, a delivery boy arrived with a bouquet at our building in the early evening. It was for "Leeza Ray" he told the security guard, who waved him into the darkened lift. At the door, he forced himself past my father, pulled out a small but lethal scythe and meticulously roped him up. "Where is safe? Where is US money?" He had been tipped off. He was a kid, brazen but twitchy. Apparently, my mom wheeled up to him and firmly told him to back down from this terrible idea. The kid, thrown by my mom, pressed the blade to her throat and threatened, "Tell me or I kill you." My mother pressed forward into the rusty edge, "Kill me? Yes. Yes, yes, you must PLEASE KILL ME! Look at me; look at what I've become. Kill me, please."

I could imagine the kid begin to back away, confused at this veer into the unexpected. From what he could gather, his mission had been hijacked by this blonde phirang woman who was now recruiting him;

he would be her soldier and end her pain. He stumbled, rubbery-lipped and backed away. Dropping the knife, he made a run for it down the building stairs.

Call me crazy but, in my head, the darkness of the situation in my head became quite funny. My mother, confronting a thief was both unnerving and darkly comic. She was not shaken by the incident; I was in awe of her refusal to be diminished by it. My dad, quite frankly, was numb. I was mad. I was angry as hell. I had not revealed the details of my relationship with Mr X to my parents, but I called him: "Find out who's behind this. Tell your cop friends to make him suffer." There was an idea our driver had passed on information. Mr X had him picked up for "questioning" by the Bandra police and stationed armed body-guards outside our door. "But I don't want them." "Think of them as baby-sitters," he grunted. When my parents tried to broach the topic of my mysterious relationship and connections, I refused to discuss it. And I refused to put iron grills on our windows as a security precaution. "Ruins the view," was my terse response.

I woke up one morning to the realization I had not seen a sunset for the past five years; I had been working, with my back to the sun or travel-ling to the next location.

And because I would not give myself permission to stop, I had no choice but to swing to the other extreme by urgently withdrawing. With me, there was no other way. I'd never felt worthy enough to dedicate extended periods of time to savour, to wallow in a slow and deliberate pace of life, to let Bombay continue its marathon sprint without me. It was unfathomable at the time. But by simply barricading myself in my Bandra apartment, I didn't have to think about the next morning. Or the next. The decision was made. My friend Nisha joined me in this exper-iment in going nowhere. She brought the ingredients for quiche, bits of scribbled paper falling out of her bag. The next day she took her rings off and left her bag at home. We had both experienced bone-crushing tragedies which made us extraordinarily good at laughing. And silliness came easily to us during that time. We both needed a break from the efforts of remaking our lives.

This sequestered period also turned into my earliest brush with Kintsugi or Kintsukuroi, the Japanese philosophy of repairing broken pottery with gold lacquer, although it would be years before I would see an example. I was in Hong Kong at the time, walking on Hollywood Road, sweating and dismayed by all the glass and steel, until I spotted a Raku-fired bowl in the window of an art gallery. It called to me like a rare, endangered species: the body of the bowl the colour of dry, cracked earth, delicately veined with the faint evidence of an artist's craftsmanship. Shearing through its centre, extending from lip to lip was an irregular, gleaming line, like a lightning bolt articulated in gold. "Kintsukuroi" said the banner in the gallery, "the Japanese Art of Golden Repair." It was the most arresting thing I'd seen because it spoke to that part of me that believed your life is your raw material as well as the part that always asked: Why? Why hide our wounds and pain when they're the things that connect us? But that would come later, much later.

In Kintsukuroi, I finally discovered both an image and a way of thinking to represent what life would teach me; it's only when things fall apart can we remake ourselves with a deeper and more enduring beauty. We are, in fact, more beautiful for having been broken. Sure, at times in my life it would appear I took almost unholy pleasure in wounding myself, but this acceptance of change restored a measure of sanity and proportion to the tricky art of living. Shouldn't we all pay homage to the idea that there is a place for "better than new"? I know now that it has become the theme of my life. It wasn't always like that, however, and I had no word at the time in Bombay to describe this strange effort, which seemed, from the outside, just a bit insane.

There was a large, unsightly crack in the wall of my sitting room, where I had had the shelving ripped out. Nisha gravitated towards it immediately: "I'm going to paint it, Binkie," was all she said. Cans of paint were delivered. Nisha started with just one flower. "But where did it come from?" she asked the room when she took a step back. She then began painting a single vine, threading the flower to the fissure across the wall. Then the vine grew to snake through a grove of succulent plants, and behind the leaves was a peacock and then an entire galaxy emerged, with both the moon and a sun. We painted without pause for days. I copied Nisha, using both fingertips and broad gestures. The paint was warm and creamy, seeping into my flesh. We dragged a wooden ladder to the centre of the room, I held it while Nisha, standing on tip-toes, extended a quivering paintbrush up to the ceiling. We were wrapped in a delirium of colour. Eventually we covered all four walls and the ceiling with a vivid world that warmed our tired hearts. Stoned from all the opened cans of paint and in retreat from the world, I didn't have to adapt to any rules of conduct. I danced, showered once a week and let my eyebrows grow in. I listened to leaves gossiping in the morning breeze, and observed the streetlights laminating every window in the building across from mine in the evening. Looking back, this period would be a turning point in my life, though nothing was resolved, least of all my restlessness.

I still think of myself as an introvert, which probably seems strange. Here's my definition: an extrovert enjoys being around people, while an introvert can play at enjoying people, but eventually becomes entirely drained. The extrovert is fuelled by other people; the introvert depleted. While I could be social and bubbly and take up a lot of room, I never realized I needed to recharge in solitude in order to go back out there the next day. My work had required me to swing so far to extroversion that I was short-circuiting. I needed to wrap myself in silence. And books.

During my self-imposed exile I set a goal to lose myself in words. I read every book I owned. Each and every one, making lists of words that I didn't understand. I was surrounded by towering authors: Herman Melville, R.K. Narayan, Tennesse Williams, Manto, Salman Rushdie, Baudelaire, Rohinton Mistry, Kamala Das, Gabriel Garcia Marquez, Tom Robbins, Wordsworth, T.S. Eliot. When I finished with them, I sent my driver to the footpath booksellers at Churchgate. He returned with a Kala Niketan plastic bag of mildewed books: Ralph Waldo Emerson, Henry David Thoreau and Walt Whitman embossed on the spines.

"I went to the woods because I wished to live deliberately, to front only the essential facts of life and see if I could not learn what it had to teach, and not, when I came to die, discover I had not lived."

Thoreau. Words like a lifebuoy. I clung to this trio of writers. To feast on their minds. To make this cloud of words my own. I became a full-time reader.

It was a strange and lovely period for me. But I was still not considering my injuries deeply. I allowed myself again to be wooed by my compulsion to keep busy. Nisha had triggered this by redecorating the apartment. I threw myself into the project by renting a melamine machine and spraying down her mural and then finding other things to melamine. We forged endless inside jokes that wove us closer together. Nisha and I spent our afternoons socializing with our head carpenter Mishraji (who called me "Lazare" and sometimes "Lazarus") and discussing the nuances of wood polish in Hindi.

"How do you say 'burl' in Hindi?"

"Binkie?"

"What, Nish?"

"I'm so glad we took this time. It has lightened the crushing, oppressive darkness of life. I'm deeply satisfied. And we did it without alcohol."

"But a lot of melamine," I said, "which I suspect has a similar effect."

Towards the end of this time, I got a call from Ajay Virmani, a Toronto businessman connected to the film industry who had tracked me down in India. "The director Deepa Mehta wants to meet you about a project." Of course I knew Deepa's work. I had seen *Earth*, one of her Elements trilogy, and it was soul-moving work. And her *Fire* had awakened the possibility of a new sort of cinema. These were stories worth telling, and told well. I jumped at the offer. The exile was over.

In India at the time, an art film had negative connotations—boring, depressing and, worst of all, unprofitable—I was only being offered big, mainstream juicy roles, but I had a strong feeling that if I were to try acting on a smaller, more human scale, and explore the imperfections of the human psyche instead of being pressured into appearing perfect, I might find a renewed passion for my work. After all, world cinema was my enduring love (along with books); Wong Kar-wai had just released *In the Mood for Love*, and the Cohen Brothers, David Lynch, Gus Van Sant had been masterfully plumbing the secretive, maze-like depths of our nature for years.

Deepa's message from out of the blue seemed too serendipitous to be true. But I must admit that our first meeting was inauspicious, to say the least. I considered myself a down-to-earth girl and not a Bombay princess, but I had lost touch with normal. I strutted into the five-star hotel with three cell phones and just short of an entourage. My driver came in and sat nearby; an assistant sat not far from him. Deepa and I were opposite each other in a lounge. I thought, "This is what a film director looks like." Her kohl-lined eyes can pin you like a butterfly, and her cigarette-gravelly voice immediately commands attention.

Deepa doesn't do formal auditions with actors; she generally just wants to spend time with them, and have a conversation. Her speech was direct but with silences during which I stirred my tea and chewed my lip. I was oblivious to the fact that this was, for all intents and purposes, my one shot. I laid out my three phones to one side. One would ring, and I'd glance at it, then put it down, unanswered. The other would ring. Pick it up, put it down. Finally, Deepa fixed me with those eyes and asked: "Do you really need three phones?" I said: "Well I can turn off this one and that one, but not this one." The third was my hotline. It was the number given by Mr X and he would shake down the city if I didn't answer.

We talked about Bombay, and we talked about film. "I'm thinking of doing something funny and light. I need some lightness in my life," Deepa said. "Me too!" I felt like shouting. The film she had written was called *Bollywood/Hollywood*, an affectionately wry tribute that used the oversized elements of any Bollywood film to gently satirize the genre. I would play Sunita, a Toronto call girl who agrees to help out (for a fee) a young Indian man whose parents insist he find an Indian fiancée. A family comedy with a dash of *Pretty Woman* and some song and dance numbers seemed like a wild concoction, and a perfect merging of my two sides. At the end of our meeting, Deepa told me that she had watched *Kasoor* and saw something in me she liked. Then she left, seeming more than a little annoyed.

I went away more certain than ever that independent film was the direction in which I wanted to go. My faith worked again, and despite the rocky meeting, Deepa offered me the part. In preparation, I starved myself. I told myself that I was making a Western film and Western actresses have to be very thin. I was fixated on my face, which I was convinced looked too wide for the screen. Every day I stood in front of a mirror, judging the cut of my cheekbones, groaning with distaste as I angled my body this way and that. Regularly climbing on to the weighing scale, convinced my success was reliant on my performance at the gym. I was satisfyingly wispy at less than a hundred pounds by the time I flew to Toronto. I was put up in a hotel downtown, giving me the strange sensation of being a tourist in my hometown. But it had been so long since I'd lived there that, in a way, I was. In the morning I ran my hands over my hip bones, feeling rather pleased. Before going on set we were planning on lengthy rehearsals, a novel idea for me but exciting: I would follow Deepa to the lair of creativity.

But when I showed up on the first day Deepa's eyes widened in surprise. On the second day of rehearsals, she pulled me aside. "I'm concerned about how you look," she said. "You need to put on some weight." She was the first person, other than my parents, who had ever said that to me. Deepa is a blunt force, in the best way possible. "You're not looking right for the role. I insist you gain weight, or we'll have to recast." David Hamilton, Deepa's partner in life and film, was sent to broach the subject with me. I was devastated. Finally, I had a part in a film I respected, working with a director I'd always admired—it was my homecoming, and I was ruining it. I murmured that I would do my best. As I left the set that day, Ajay Virmani, who was co-producing the film, found me in the parking lot. "We want to launch you here," he said. "But we want to launch the best Lisa Ray possible and you're just not looking healthy. If this isn't the right time, we will think about another project later."

It was an intervention, and it worked. I finally had to confront the fact that something was going on. I knew what I was doing was unhealthy but this compulsive behaviour had become my way of regulating a life where so much else seemed out of control. On many levels, I was comfortable with life rolling out in an organic, unplanned way. But somehow, food had become the place where I expressed my unacknowledged horror as well as my way of asserting some agency in my life. I did begin to eat more healthily, and I gained enough weight to satisfy everyone. But my eating disorder would continue to rear its head many times over the years.

The rehearsals were enthralling. Deepa spoke of film acting, using language in a way I hadn't heard before. She loves actors and she directs with subtlety and an unobtrusive hand. She gifted me Uta

Hagen's *Respect for Acting*. She would try to get me to access the deepest places in myself, asking, "How would you feel in this situation? Let's talk it through." Here's what I want to say about acting—not becoming a "star"—you have to have the fever for it. It's too hard and thankless. The countless hours of preparation, self-doubt, waiting idle, replaying the scene you just filmed, knowing you could do it differently, better. You walk through many muddy pools in your mind. But I had the burning. Not to be a great and flawless actor. The process it takes to embody a different life, that's what gripped me most.

I was all in. But the problem was my accent. It was completely Indian. To find my Canadian accent, I had to follow people around in Toronto and eavesdrop on conversations, repeating their sentences. It wasn't merely the accent, even the rhythm and lilt of my speech were distinctly subcontinental. This was peculiar and nerve-racking for Deepa's assistant who became one of my prime victims. She wore a beanie even though it was summer, was just out of university, very sincere and a bit overwhelmed that I was stalking her. I slipped into my observer mode, fascinated by the other actors going about their processes. Kulbhushan Kharbanda, who played my father, was given a sequence near the end of the film where he was supposed to come out and sing a rousing chorus of "My India is the best!" I watched him walking around the set, muttering to himself, working his way to the place where he would nail this song. When the shot was taken, he sang so openly and without inhibition. I was still so inhibited, so terrified of doing the wrong thing that I was quite stiff as an actor. The best acting comes out of the ability to let go of control and calculation. I was able to do that, to an extent, in my private life, jetting off on a whim. But on set, something was weighing me down besides caution, and the fear of looking bad. Nonetheless it was here that I fell in love with acting, recognizing that I could never act without making the effort to clear whatever was holding me back.

The set was very different from Bollywood sets where unspoken hierarchies keep camaraderie at bay. I was nervous to be working with Deepa; I would come in shaking with stage fright, but then, I could sit around and have a laugh with the grips, letting off steam. "I'm not difficult or starry . . . I'm just socially awkward," I joked with the girls in the make-up department, who had been forewarned a "Bollywood actress" would be in their chairs. I found myself relaxing. *Bollywood/ Hollywood* was a "crossover film," an emerging form of cinema at the time that bridged cultural borders. I'm sure I came off as a crossover creature, a Canadian girl on paper who was famous in India. I wasn't sure where to align myself, with the Indians or the Canadians. Moushumi Chatterjee, an Indian star who played the mother of my love interest, Rahul Khanna (Rahul"ji," as I call him, has become a close friend since then, his ironic take on the world, and matter-of-fact "tongue or no tongue" discussion before our kissing scene endearing him to me many times over), happens to be related to my father's all-time favourite singer and music composer, Hemanta Mukhopadhyay. As a kid, whenever I heard Hemanta-da's velvety voice swell from the record player I knew Dad was sliding into a nostalgic mood. And now on the set every time I looked at her, Hemanta-da voice started singing in my head in Bengali, very plaintive and sad. But there was nothing remotely melancholy about Moushumi. She had a unique talent of appearing commanding and far-cical at the same time, both on and off the set. She was used to being pampered and trailed by a spot boy, make-up artist and umbrella-carrying assistant. That sort of entourage doesn't happen on a government-funded Canadian film. She'd sit in the trailer complaining to the hairdresser, and then call me over and whisper to me in Hindi: "These people are so strange! They're making my hair so *plain!*" But I understood her, as much as the make-up artist, who was trying to help create an authentic charac-ter for the film. One day on the set it struck me: this is the sort of job where if you do your part right, it should look effortless, like anyone can do it, but if you do it wrong, everyone will know.

Deepa soon became a mentor. Deep inside I yearned for that mother figure, a female mentor, and with her long dark hair, and no-nonsense maternal love, she was it. I remember asking her: "What do you think I should do next?" I was really looking for an answer to that old ques-tion that used to bedevil me: What's it all about? And: Am I any good? Am I any good at acting? Am I any good at life? Am I any good?

She looked at me and said: "I don't know how you survive in that town, Bombay. It doesn't feel like it's for you." Deepa's roots were in Amritsar and though home for her was Toronto, she spent a lot of time in Delhi, where her mother is based. Bombay is a taste many north Indians never acquire; the walls wheat-pasted with film posters, the stink of human sewage and crowds, the sight of men clinging to the sides of local trains, the frenzied compression, are all experiences as unfamiliar to a citizen of Delhi as to someone from outside India. But most of all, Deepa was not impressed by the flashy posturing of the film industry.

Working with Deepa had also opened up another possibility in me: that of using protest as a path. The protest that had balled up in my throat began as a desire to defend against the world's slights and inability to peer beneath the surface of appearance. Perhaps I was even choked with my own shortcomings, but I quickly became attracted to the possibility of protest taking form through film and art.

After the film wrapped, I went back to Bombay. Deepa came to town to meet with the film's composer. We caught up over coffee in a hotel and afterwards she said, "I need to get a cab to this meeting." I was a bit horrified on her behalf because no one I knew in Bombay got around in cabs. I offered my car and driver, and she gave me a "you're-crazy" glance. As I watched her climb into that cab, I heard a tiny voice in my head say, "You have a shallow understanding of yourself if you think you're not a Bombay Diva because you sure as hell have become one." I looked around and realized I had all the trappings of indulged celebrity. I had two Persian cats, Pinky and Porky; magazine editors would come in and photograph me in my apartment. It was fun until it wasn't. I was in my late twenties, and I had hollowed out. It felt futile to continue and futile to stop. The goddess of wealth, Lakshmi, was embossed in the city's psyche, hovering in small shrines set in walls on worn landings. She seemed to say: "Put your faith in me." Many Bombayites were enviably secure in their faith because it was stupid to be concerned about anything other than making a success of yourself. Perhaps they were right. Perhaps there was no secret knowledge, buried in the arteries of Bombay, to be had. Perhaps a cabbage was a cabbage, the world ran on influence and money was material enlightenment. But no; if I'd learned anything it was that there was another reality running beneath that which I knew, and Bombay was not the final resting place for my soul.

After completing *Bollywood/Hollywood*, I got an offer to do a little screwball comedy called *Ball and Chain* that was shooting in Austin,

Texas, over the summer of 2001. The film was another culture-clash comedy about two Americans from Indian families who get engaged just to keep their parents from locking them into arranged marriages. It was a bit of a romp and I grabbed it. The relationship with Mr X was suffocating and I wanted to get away. In Austin I was introduced to one of the producers of the film. He was a young British Indian I'll call A, who spoke in pastel tones, the opposite of the alpha masculinity I'd become accustomed to in Bollywood. He was also a loner. We bonded over our outsider status.

Austin was a huge culture shock: very granola and vegan, the home of Whole Foods. I had never been exposed to an American southwestern university town. At times, I found the casual interactions and directness of the American crew totally unfamiliar, if not shocking. It made me realize how I had internalized the hierarchies and subtle prejudices of India. Kal Penn, who went on to accrue fame in the Harold & Kumar movies, and much later worked in the White House under Obama, was one of the actors. I remember him announcing at the end of one shooting day, "Let's go swimming tomorrow! Let's waterski!" and the next day off they went, actors and crew, like a family picnic. I never did things like that in my world. It sounded like great fun, but I couldn't let my guard down enough to join in.

Instead, A would invite me out for dinner on my days off. He always chose a restaurant far from the hotel where the cast stayed. Everyone could tell my life was complicated and I didn't want to raise any more eyebrows than necessary. He began to win my trust , which fed a growing attraction. When he invited me to visit him in London after the film wrapped, I pictured Mr X, his expression agog with disbelief. I imagined myself flattened by his Pajero, his driver hightailing it through Bombay traffic, while Mr X craned his head out the window with a hangdog expression on his face: "I told you not to talk to strange men."

I didn't think he'd actually run me over, but I also knew then that I would leave Bombay. It had become an increasingly hostile environment, doused in fear and coercion, with dons pulling strings and ordering hits from Dubai and Malaysia. My personal life mirrored the state of the city. Mr X used to call constantly to check up on me. It was a form of mental abuse I had become entirely conditioned to. Never mind that he would threaten people around me and follow up the threats with visits by menacing young men, including sending goons to the home of a talent coordinator once, a move that both shamed and thrilled me. Towards the end of the film shoot I finally snapped out of it. I was in all possibility influenced by the clean, free-spirited vibe of Austin, so that one day I woke up with a shudder of embarrassment at my stupidity in getting involved with a hoodlum. A hoodlum! The years of my fetishizing wise-guy behaviour and living in my own Scorsese film were done. Over. Hard as flint, I called him from Austin.

"I'm not coming back."

I hung up before any more could be said. I had finally severed my ties to him. I called A over the hotel phone, "Let's get drunk. Let's celebrate . . . the end of the film."

From Austin I flew to Toronto for the Film Festival—my first Canadian red carpet. *Bollywood/Hollywood* was getting a premiere at the Elgin theatre. Before the premiere, I went to a restaurant in Yorkville with Tina Mann, my childhood friend. Our meal finished, I told her to drop me off at the screening, so I hopped into her Hyundai and off we drove. I heard the ring of my phone from the bottom of my bag. When I answered, a publicist for the film screamed: "Where are you? The stretch limo with the entire cast is circling the building waiting for you!" Oops! I really hadn't known it was such a big deal. I just wanted to get in there and see the film. Tina threw the car into reverse on Yonge St. I hopped out of the Hyundai and tripped over my hem into the stretch limo. Maybe my entrance wasn't all that flash, but it didn't matter because I was ready to move on. It was a strange homecoming; I already had my eye on leaving. Before the screening ended, I had decided I would accept A's invitation to visit him in London. But really, I was activating the harrowing journey back to myself.

9

IF YOU HAVE ever encountered the Himalayan mask of Mahakala you won't soon forget its screaming open mouth and silver fangs.

I know this mask well; I wore it for years.

It was how I had survived Bombay, where outrageous behaviour was a kind of protection. I employed this different persona often on sets—speaking in a different manner (okay, yelling) and gesturing in a certain way that's all exaggeration, but is required to get what you need. On a set, the mask can be powerful and theatrical but on a day-to-day basis, the habits of the mask seep into you on a darker and more subterranean level. It also becomes very, very exhausting. You begin to lose sight of who you are beneath it. In part, that was why I did not return to India in September 2001. I left in order to remember my own face and body. I left because I was thirty years old, and I had no idea who I was.

When I decided to take up A's invitation to visit London that September it was a way to begin lightly stepping away from the mask. In Bombay I had lived on a diet of bedlam and inflated drama, and having tasted it, wanted something different. India was an experiment that had changed me, although perhaps not enough: I still had this thing about losing myself in a relationship. Even though I needed to be alone, there had to be someone in my life who was a safe place to return to. A and I merged into an immediate intimacy. Of course, I was merely trading in my weakness for bad boys for manners and civilized dates, which is another sort of mask.

A lived in Kensington, around the corner from Holland Park, and when I first arrived, I chose a small, mouldy hotel with oppressive floral wallpaper in the area. When he left the city for a few days' work, I spent my time exploring the borough. London hugged closer to the top of my head than India, and instilled in me a sense of containment, making me feel like the little Kyoto Garden in the park, reassuringly and invitingly peaceful behind a low fence. Evenings alone in my tiny hotel room, I would watch old *Tom and Jerry* cartoons and exhale the mood of the day. I fell asleep thinking about how the door of a coffee shop had been held open for me by a stranger and how being here seemed eminently right.

The following day, I returned to the same coffee shop on High Street and settled next to a window to watch people pass on the pavement outside. Here, they walked with terse but purposeful strides, clothes muted to suit the available light. Englishwomen, to my eyes, were tall and reedy and seemed to prefer un-showy, low heels. These were the days before Russian émigrés moved into Kensington, when it was mainly populated by Anglo-Saxon Londoners with a sprinkling of South East Asians who also dressed in severe cuts and grey layers. I'd never seen so many variations of grey, and I tried to name them as they passed: dove grey, cloud grey, African parrot grey, Delhi pollution grey . . . Needing a coat, I walked into one of the High Street boutiques, next to Oxfam. The salesgirl was as long as a leek with a short bob. She tried to sell me a dark blue hooded pea coat.

"This one says, "I'm a lot of fun but I've got secrets.""

"No thank you. I just want something in grey."

London had a sense of rightness and propriety in direct contrast to Bombay. In those first few weeks, I was under the spell of fresh love, which has a terrible habit of imbuing a vitality into the most ordinary things. I pushed my hands deep into my pockets while stalking around the city. I thought about how it felt to be perceived through A's eyes; like a delicate morsel or a baby bird slipped out of the nest. Sure, he liked to pontificate, saying things like, "The first decade of the new millennium will be characterized by a state of denial." Nor did I like how he framed the events of my life—the details of which I shared like thrilling episodes of a crime series with winks and short laughs—like a tragic opera. But I really did like the version of myself that was summoned forth when he looked at me.

He also possessed the one quality I found completely irresistible: he lived in a different city. London had always exerted a pull. But to answer it I would have to walk away from my house, career and the grip of not only Bombay but India, a place I loved where everyone knew my name. There was a part of myself that was used to being famous—I had after all been pursued and made to feel like a golden girl for more than a decade. You can't help but believe your desirability will last forever. I could have spun my fame on and on, into new opportunities and creative endeavours, secure in having built a "brand." But maybe that was the reason I had been dropped into this intriguing but speculative relationship; it would have been impossible to leave otherwise.

Also, I have to face it—romantic love was a hedge against self-doubt. I had no current film commitments in India. I was still ambassador for Rado watches, but they made few demands on my time. I was ready to uproot myself. I preferred to not consider too deeply the pros and cons before making big moves. It was more interesting for me to fling myself off a cliff and figure it out on the way down.

I called my parents.

"Pappy, I'm moving to London."

"Oh, good." He was characteristically calm and unsurprised. "But did you lock the door of the Bombay flat?" he asked, familiar with my cavalier ways.

"I'm not sure," I said, thinking not only of the flat that I would not return to, but the life I was leaving behind.

My new flat was on a beautiful, tree-lined street close to Holland Park, seemingly to me, the best, most magical place in the world. I strolled through it daily. The landlord gave me a huge skeleton key which I kept misplacing that first year. I was just not used to looking after the small details of life. The only thing I had brought with me was a Jackson tissue box. It was something common and small that I was in the habit of carrying for shoots. I placed it by the bed. On the side were listed suggestions for use:

— handkerchief

— make-up remover

— car steering wiper

— spects cleaner

— and for what not

Long after the tissues were used, I kept the box. It reminded me of India.

I missed India but knew London was my place now. I could breathe easier even with new distractions and different kinds of commotions. And the task of building another life came easily to me. I'm not detached but I have never felt tightly bound to any one place in the way I've heard others describe it. Every day I walked the city, in larger and larger circles radiating outwards from my bachelorette, getting to know its fading memories, its scheming ambitions, its flower and newspaper vendors. When I returned in the evening, the soles of my feet ached pleasantly.

Very quickly, I discovered the consequences of being pampered for so long. It was like I'd been hatched from an egg at thirty. There were things I had simply never learned, surrounded by staff in India all that time. I remember standing in front of the washer and dryer in my building, utterly flummoxed. Where does the soap go? I hadn't done my own laundry . . . ever. And I no longer had a driver idling outside my door, special privileges or armed bodyguards (as Mr X had provided at the height of his paranoia). At first, I took the tube, as everyone does, descending underground. Then one morning I decided I had had enough of travelling beneath the surface of the city. I was still greedy for the sights and sounds of the city and didn't want to disappear into its bowels like a scurrying animal. I wanted to remain at ground level where I could take in everything. I became obsessed with the need to feel the presence of great thinkers who had walked before me in London, as a sort of substitute, perhaps, for the pilgrimages and deities I had left behind in India.

I started studying bus routes and asking directions until I only travelled on double-deckers, even if it meant leaving for my destination two hours ahead of time. I always took the same spot: upper level at the rear, right side. Under the cover of the crowd, I could observe the range of skin tones on display without being accused of staring. I wondered how the Poles would react if I broke into their bitch-fest about their English foreman in a flawless Polski accent. I listened in on two Nigerians, their accents like their skin, smooth as the satin chrome finish on a Leica lens. "They eat money. Currency Eaters." When I looked around there was no singular way of belonging. I loved the cultural hodgepodge of London buses. Hanging on to the rails or tucked in amongst the warm bodies, my hybrid identity found a common home.

"What? WHY?" A's voice was incredulous. "Don't be ridiculous darling, take the car." He was in his favoured long, grey wool overcoat and I wore a sweater that swallowed our linked fingers. It was a relief to be able to walk hand in hand with a lover down the street after years of hiding. But that tinge of smugness in his voice was beginning to irritate me. We were beginning to struggle to find common ground. He also didn't seem to understand what I saw in the common and the everyday. He belonged to the tribe of clean-haired people with professional goals and immaculate fingernails.

Suddenly I felt him jerk my arm.

"Darling, pay attention! You were about to walk straight into a puddle."

"I want to get my feet wet."

There's a large portion of the Indian immigrant community in London that's very plugged into Bollywood. I knew at the time that it would be easy for me to tap into that world, making money on appearances, waving from a stage or cutting the ribbon at a shop opening. I found the "desi" scene interesting but odd: not Indian, not English but a homeboy amalgamation of cultures and remixed music with brown people connected to India, but many of whom had never been there. What they knew of it was glazed over with decades-old memories from their parents or over-the-top Bollywood films that fed a complicated nostalgia.

I also avoided the places where people I knew from India came to do their shopping—places like Oxford St., Leicester Square, Harrods. The Dorchester and Nobu were also out of bounds. The odd time I ran into an old friend from the social circuit, I was awkward. The accents made me homesick, but in them I also heard echoes of my old life. "She didn't "hello" me," a Bombay-based businessman pronounced with consternation after I skittered out of a restaurant. I felt bad but I needed my space.

For a brief time, I supplemented my savings with a bit of radio work for BBC Asia as a sort of celebrity commentator, but I quickly stopped. I was searching for something deeply personal that didn't play into my established identity. I had come to remove the mask. I wasn't ready to put it back on.

I liked to downplay my practical side, but living off my savings in complete anonymity was feasible because I had made good money and invested well on the advice of some of my more financially savvy friends. It enabled my freedom, so I could take myself to places important to me. I lost entire days in the Victoria and Albert Museum and lingered until closing time at the Tate, dizzy from nearness with all that art. I took Kathak lessons in a class with pre-teens at Bharatiya Vidya Bhavan, pretending to be a foreigner with a passion for the form. I saw a dance performance by Akram Khan, a man with feet and hands of gold. I started writing, filling notebooks in my narrow, cosy flat, using the wide window ledge as a desk. The sashed windows were too tall to clean so dust sprinkled on my arm like pollen when I heaved the glass open for air. I wrote to my parents on postcards, with elaborate details of everything I saw and felt.

I spent my first Christmas "in the West" back in Toronto. I had by then proceeded to more regular, but short visits. I sought to strengthen intimacy with my parents through other means: writing and longer, more frequent phone calls. There was a quiet comfort to be had in our regular talks. On the phone, my mom now had the luxury to tell me to eat more leafy vegetables. "No cheating," she breathed. In her overbearing tone I heard warmth and tenderness and how important it was for her to feed me. I threw my frozen Waitrose meals away.

One day I took a winding bus route to Birkbeck University and signed up for a bunch of night courses on subjects I found intriguing, including: How to Write Poetry—Form and Feeling. I loved these classes where I sat in a room full of men and women topped with unkempt hair and stained cardigans in the way of the leisured class—or the very poor in London. I could never quite tell. Hours passed discussing the metres and rhyming patterns of poets. I didn't want to miss out, as I had in Austin when everyone went waterskiing without me. So, I joined the group in the pub after class. "I think I'm aroused by Wordsworth," I announced after a few drinks. I joined in the laughter and conversation, but I was always nervous about the inevitable questions: Who are you? Where are you from? What's your story? Often, I would simply make myself up, trying to deflect attention, not wanting to explain the convoluted story behind the strange stardom I had left behind. Once when my Bengali blood was stirred by Tagore's poetry during class I almost gave myself away so I invented a character for myself: "My father's Italian and my mom's English but they sent me off to Canada and I've come back to be an artist." It was a lame attempt at a postmodern reinvention that someone had to have seen through.

I remember the feeling of returning home to my flat satiated by those classes. Night came too soon in the winter. I found myself walking home on echoing streets eerily lit, a scarf wound around my neck, sometimes spooked, sometimes moon drunk, my mind full of ideas and things I'd heard during class.

"Did you know horses cannot see the colour orange?"

I wrote that down in my notebook on the ledge.

But back in India, the press was speculating on my disappearance. The Internet had made it easier for friends to send me links to tabloid articles: "Where has Lisa Ray gone?" Rumours and whispers rippled with sordid excitement: "She ran away because she's a drug addict." "She had an abusive boyfriend." One friend told me that the rumour was that I was living like a bag lady in London. "How did she fall so far?" But I was no longer absorbed in my own importance. It left me unperturbed in my new life. Bombay no longer had its teeth in me.

Meanwhile, Deepa and David would send me messages and updates on the success of *Bollywood/Hollywood*, describing billboards all over the city, and solid reviews. The film led to a number of offers from Canadian film-makers, which I politely refused. I'm not congenitally built to make decisions that "cash in." I've always been far more attracted to the mischievous possibilities of doing what is not expected; refusing to stick to what should be done. This time I felt a strong pull to remain in London and train and I listened to it. *Bollywood/Hollywood* had shown me that I had much to learn about the craft, and to do that,

I needed to be cut off from that "Lisa Ray" that existed in two places now, Canada and India, both disconnected from me. London was my neutral territory.

After starring in movies and walking the red carpet at the Toronto International Film Festival, I decided to become a student. It was a decision that arose from solitude—which I cherished, and was realizing was my truth north guide. I started taking night classes in acting all over London, spreading myself out at different locations every night of the week (Tuesday nights were at Central, CSSD, Wednesday night in Hoxton). In London, acting is considered a trade or a vocation. A kid can grow up to be a plumber or a performer, without judgment. Acting is neither placed on a pedestal nor disreputable. I made friends at the classes and followed them into darkened spaces—everywhere from the National Theatre on the Southbank to basements in East London—to watch the stage and be transformed by it. London was freedom. For the first time I felt like borrowing a Hindi film trope: rising from a sunroof and whipping my hair around in the wind.

My first summer in the city, I took a course in Shakespeare at Oxford with BADA, the British American Dramatic Academy. Once a year, the Academy brings over American acting students. I wasn't one of those, but I wrote persuasive letters until BADA agreed to let me attend. Oxford, where my parents had begun their life together, was a fantasy for me. It was an idyllic summer, the sky blue as a cornflower when I stepped off the Oxford tube. Before the course began, I signed up for tours of most of the colleges, including Christchurch, and found myself rooted to the spot, gaping at buildings that looked like visitors from another time. I was in a state of rapture, which would have been embarrassing to my former self, but now I threw myself with abandon into learning about palimpsests and the shadows of the buildings that had existed before, layer upon layer, outlines revealed under the faces of the gargoyles. I was geeking out on everything. I even called my father and got directions to the church where my parents had been married. It was a sweet, charming little building, modestly decorated. This seemed exactly perfect, an ode to their coming together, shorn of adornment and very pure.

Alan Rickman and Ben Kingsley came to speak. I was older than most of the students, and more experienced so I aligned myself with the teachers, especially one named Bill, a brilliant actor. We met often over lunch on the grounds, discussing "passion" and "intention." He tutored from a room in a turret in Balliol College from where he conducted one-on-one sessions for students as part of the curriculum. One day, I arrived early for an appointment and saw another student, a dark-haired girl exit his room. Tears were streaming down her cheeks. She wasn't distressed but transported. When I opened the door, Bill was waiting. He said: "Did you see her?" I nodded. "She's a soprano. Everything she does is infused with delirious passion. She guzzles it and then sings it out. I want *you* to feel what it is like to be unleashed. Rip aside your civility and show me passion. I'm not seeing that in your performances right now at all." Shakespearean text is all about illuminating universal cruelties and mysteries, how life is imperfect and unfair but beautiful all the same. Bill pushed for that quality to shine through in performance too. Something in me resisted. It felt uncomfortable. We began working on my monologue, breaking down layers of meaning behind the words. Bill was pushing me, breaking me down as well in the process. "Again," he intoned after I stumbled. I threw my pages into the air. "I'm trying to SPARKLE, dammit, fuck, fuck, fuck, FUCK!" "YES, Lisa. I want you to feel. Take that emotion and put it in the text. Kill all your demons and let your angels die too. You've surely heard that before? Acting is all about what's happening within you—nothing to do with the mirror."

What was I missing? What was I doing wrong? I repeated the lines again and again, doggedly, like I was scraping paint off a brick wall. The atmosphere in the turret had turned oppressive.

"Remember," Bill intoned, "do your work and then, let go."

He let that soak in.

"What do you feel?"

"I feel . . . I feel like no artist should tolerate reality." It was a bullshit line that sounded appropriately "luvvie" for the moment, something I'd heard in another acting class.

"Good."

"And . . . I feel like I need to pee."

It appeared that this was a different sort of sport, this acting. But I wasn't ready for radical acceptance of my flaws—not yet. My self-imposed distance from my inner life, feelings and, most significantly, the wounded bits, made it painfully difficult to locate that passion. I was travelling slipstream behind so many disguises, it was getting hard to see what was real. Author Parker J. Palmer has said: "Violence is what happens when we don't know what to do with our suffering." In my case the violence had been turned on myself largely, using sarcasm mixed with perfectionism and a work ethic that drove me to work like a slave cutting temples out of rock. I had made a contract to avoid myself. And I was very good and imaginative at it. But the process of acting is one of self-revelation: you must agree to turn your skin inside out, to have your heart wrung out and your eyes pried a little wider open. For me, criticism was very painful; I didn't know how to use it. In India, criticism was only ever toxic: a photographer complaining that I'd gained too much weight would send word around town, and I'd panic, redoubling my efforts at physical perfection. Scrutiny meant an opportunity to push the star off the pedestal, cut her down to size. Because of this, I had built up a secret self-loathing that had hardened inside me. This had made me very defensive about criticism, which makes for a lousy student. It had taken ten years to calcify, so it wasn't going to dissolve in one night or even one semester. I was ready to lose it though; it was painful, carrying around this crushing, leaden feeling of never being good enough.

While I took my acting classes and lived my days like a student, evenings were reserved for luxuries and elevated experiences. I lived well in London. A and I would go out for dinners regularly to faultless little bistros and starred restaurants with dim lighting where he asked for sparkling water and I learned about wine pairings. His friends were all like him, eaten up with their accomplishments, but slyly well-mannered about it. They were solicitous, always asking about my parents whenever we met though I'd never spoken of them. They valued handmade artefacts and jute runners representative of the "dignity of labour," supported "philanthropic organizations" (never "charities"), writing cheques only once they had established its fiscal responsibility. "I'm on the board of Oxfam. You both must come to the next gala," was the cue to be lavish in both your gratitude and admiration. I would just gape at them, or bite down on my lower lip to hide a smile. It was all very amusing to me, this pantomime. And at times, irritating. It appeared those nights of formal dining were lessons in becoming the perfect society hostess and more than that, a way to map the boundaries of engagement between us.

"Please don't pound the table," A would intone evenly. I hadn't even realized I'd brought my hand down in the middle of an impassioned discussion on women's rights in India. His sense of righting a wrong would become a cue for the others to turn studiously to the menu even though we had all ordered already; glances were exchanged. What they were witnessing was the slow mutation of love into something else. "I'm sorry that was a tatty move. I'm not quite as singularly focused on propriety as you. I'm passionate and I get carried away," I heard myself say in my newly minted London voice. "Maybe life isn't always that subtle." I was beginning to recognize both in and out of acting class that words—when wielded with an unbearable politeness—can be worse than any insult.

I began to contemplate taking a degree in acting. Though I had a deeply embedded suspicion of authority and structured learning, drama school seemed to be an entry into new creative ways of seeing the world. I squashed my inner resistance. But I couldn't picture myself signing up for a full-fledged three-year programme. I was already in my early thirties, and I was looking for a condensed one-year course. I shortlisted a few accredited schools, including the London Academy of Music and Dramatic Art (LAMDA), Webber Douglas Academy of Dramatic Art and the Academy of Live and Recorded Arts (ALRA). The last had piqued my interest because at the end of the day I did love the camera. The programme also seemed less stuffy than the more traditional schools. In preparation, I read a lot of theory about acting, and every school contradicted the next. One said: Learn your lines and rehearse, rehearse, rehearse! Another advocated: Don't learn your lines! They should spring from deep within you.

I definitely had an instinct for acting but it hadn't been tested on the stage. I was trying to apply the principles I had learned as a screen actor over the years to standing in front of a panel for an audition. But I had never auditioned for anything in my life. In I went with my prepared pieces: a classical monologue from *Macbeth*, and a contemporary scene from *Top Girls*. The English accent did not immediately come to me, and I struggled with my voice. England is known for voice work, and English actors are renowned for modulation. But I was still using my strange Hindi-Canadian-Bollywood-comes-to-Kensington accent. I didn't know what the hell I was doing at those auditions, and I must have been appallingly bad, but shockingly, I got some callbacks. Webber Douglas thought I needed to do a two-year programme to work on my voice, and LAMDA also offered me a two-year slot. (The acronyms still amuse me for some reason.) But when ALRA offered to take me for a one-year programme, I didn't have to think twice. It was the first accredited drama school in the United Kingdom to offer training in all media.

So, I returned to school full-time, eleven years after high school. In the beginning what I was most excited about was the building: a former asylum in south London with a vast Gothic edifice and romantic looking towers. I had a free pass to wander the little narrow grotto-like hallways, all twisting and winding. The taps ran cold all year long and everything on hinges creaked. It really was the perfect setting for a drama school if you think about it: grand and macabre enough to feed our imagination. And it shook out of me a memory, of my mother using the downstairs toilet—reserved for the "servants"—in the old Shyambazar house, much to the horror of everyone. Emerging triumphantly, my mom declared to no one in particular, "I liked it, so romantic, with a view of the sky," alerting my grandfather to the task of repairing a broken roof.

In my first week, I took a class that required us to climb three sets of stairs to a sloped-roofed turret. The next time we had the class, the location had changed. "Sorry," said the professor, quite casually. "I just felt a presence in that other room." Turns out the building was originally built for girls orphaned by the Crimean War and who had lived in terrible conditions. One of the girls, Charlotte Jane Bennett had perished in a fire when she was deliberately locked in a bathroom. Apparently she haunts the building still. I imagine her startling the bejesus out of Lieutenant-Colonel Oreste Pinto, the "spy catcher" between one of his infamous interrogations during the Second World War, when the Royal Victoria

Patriotic building became an MI5 detention house. It was a place of tall stories. I loved it.

Our post-graduate group was mixed: some were in their twenties, a few much older, experienced students in their forties and me, in between. I tried to quash my feelings of fraudulence as I watched the other students warming up before class, most of whom could sing or dance or play the piano. I didn't have any of those skills but I was really open and enthusiastic. I was ready. Many years had led up to this moment. I still consider my experience of drama school to be a life lesson: toss away your preconceptions, and just be present every day.

I would wake up extra early each morning, leap on the bus, and show up at school before anyone else. I didn't register the dark days, the lack of sun during that time. Slowly this taste for the process of acting triggered my overachieving mentality. I became obsessed with investigating characters, peeling back patterns and personality to expose the vulnerable skeleton of our needs and desires; understanding what forces drive people. I discovered that the process doesn't necessarily have anything to do with the end result, that the process itself could be the reward. (Do your work and then let go. How simple and how terrifying!) What I was beginning to love was finding a portal in yourself, an emotional keyhole in order to melt into another life. Perhaps my obsession with embodying someone else was another form of escape. But still, these investigations helped me, ever so slowly, to understand myself, and why I had made the choices I had.

I remember lying on my back, pushing my breath lower into my body, lower than my diaphragm, lower and lower into myself. My stomach expanded more and more, like a balloon, with each breath. "Elongate your breath. Good. Now we are going to access those places we don't want to. Let the breath travel. Deep into your lungs. Good. Now send your beneath below your diaphragm, go deep into your pelvis. Go. Deeper. Let your body breathe itself." Our voice teacher warned us this technique could release long buried emotion, but his voice was mild and soothing as he said it. I inhaled deeply and there they were: pitiless, powerful feelings from another world. To face these feelings was to risk being borne away on a wild beast. A memory of the accident flashed. I remember leaping up from the floor, running blindly through the courtyard until I couldn't hold it back any more. I threw back my head and howled. I heaved myself on to my knees, willing myself to be empty of this feeling. Make it stop. Let it go.

Eventually I gathered myself and walked back to class, dazed, pausing at the window. Our voice teacher was speaking as if I'd never left the room: "What's that thing? Wedged between imagination and imperfect recall? That's your character." Over the months, the work became more and more internal and more and more difficult to translate to the outside world. We were asked to sieve through memory to find emotional triggers or sense memories to evoke a truthful reaction in a scene. Every day my emotional muscles were getting a workout. I spent a fair amount of time crumpled on the floor, weeping, in the dark wings of the theatre. Studying the performing arts appeared to be a draining and dangerous occupation, but actually, these exercises were setting the foundation for reclaiming and repairing my spirit. At one point, we had to learn stage fighting. Obviously, one of my last incarnations was in the medieval ages, and I was a knight. That's the only way I can explain my lifelong fascination with fencing. It was hard, and tedious to learn the intricate footwork. Every second is coordinated and choreographed. For me, this was tough because I still wasn't completely in my body. I struggled not to get slashed or take out the eyes of my fellow actors as we moved around the gym area of this magnificent, three-hundred-year-old hall, lined with beautiful stained-glass windows and an elaborate hammer-beamed ceiling. What strange figures we must have made, leaping around in sword fights; perhaps we were the ones menacing and disturbing the ghost of poor Charlotte.

I had by then let my guard down with the other students and shared my personal history. I wanted to be part of a community. We'd gather in the canteen for a communal meal at lunch, like restaurant staff before service. I have to admit I hated the bland, dry sandwiches they served. One of the older students, Sean, noticed the faces I made. He had a way of bantering with me that did not raise the spectre of judgement or self-criticism within me anymore. It was a way to unleash my inner rude boy. It was pure fun.

"Ah here's the maharani who gave up everything to come down to earth with us common blokes. Don't like the food? You shouldn't have left the palace."

"Ah, if you fall, fall splendidly, I say. I am looking for a manservant though, but I notice your teeth are not crooked enough!"

"It was a pleasure chatting with you, miss. Now fuck off!"

"Address me on bended knee!" I would bellow back . . . and on and on.

The fencing was part of my campaign to reclaim my physical self. Those years in London were the first time I really began to examine the disconnection between my self and my body, and the damage this relationship had incurred over the years. In India, I'd become an expert at absorbing cultural conventions. As much as I seemed to be free-spirited and liberated, the female body in India is still meant to be covered, to titillate within the narrowest understanding of femininity. Topping those circumstances with my own insecurities, I'd been living with a topsy-turvy sense of my body for fifteen years.

But I really only awoke to this in London. My posture was designed to thrust out my boobs and pull in my waist. When I look at photos of that time, I resemble a Barbie doll, my arms hanging limply from my sides. "Shit," I remember thinking, "I look extraterrestrial. Robotic. Damned. Is that what I've looked like all this time?" It was a brutal reckoning. Drama school was training me to study postures, to recognize where emotion was held in the body; shoulders held back suggested bravado, shoulders collapsing in was an attempt to protect a wounded heart. All this would help define a character. It made me consciously attempt to get back into my body (if I had ever been there at all). The physicality of the training was unknotting old patterns. I had read somewhere that Jessica Lange had trained as a mime in Paris, so I took a course at the Desmond Jones School of Mime and Physical Theatre to improve my craft. In a large open hall, on bare, hard floorboards we would crawl from one end of the room to the other like animals: "Go as a scorpion! Come back as a frog!" It sounded absurd but this was the way I connected with my body, to bind together movement and breath, pick my way back to the raw, natural intelligence of my body. To begin befriending myself.

Am I any good? Am I any good? I wanted to ask our director.

I think the mime is what prepared me, without my knowing, for the introduction to yoga, which has become so fundamental to my life. In London, I had kept up my routine of trudging daily to a gym; this one

was down the street, close to Shepherd's Bush Station. I was still continuing my intense workouts several times a week as I had for years: cardio,
cardio, some strength training and then more cardio. Sweat, I thought,
was the key. I saw signs for yoga class but thought it wouldn't be for me:
I needed to feel the burn. Yoga sounded excruciatingly boring for an
alpha girl like me.

I was quite thin at this time, weighing possibly around ninety
pounds. I was extremely stiff, and one of my acting teachers had told
me: "You have to stretch." He meant it literally, not metaphorically. I
said: "Oh no, I'm inflexible. I can't touch my toes." I gave every excuse
possible when the truth was that I had taken pride in holding myself
taut and undefeated in the face of adversity all those years. My teacher
was not swayed. He said: "Try yoga."

Of course, it's ironic that I started yoga in London after living in India
for a decade. But traditional yoga in India was quite different, rooted in
the guru-shishya tradition, where the student becomes the disciple of
one teacher. It's more worshipful than in the West, and true practitioners
do pilgrimages to sit and absorb in sacred cities like Rishikesh. But I had
never really come across that kind of yoga, or any kind, in my Bombay
bubble. Instead, when I lived in India, I had damaged my knees with
aerobics and lifted at the gym, concepts that were still new to most of the
country. Now, of course, even in India, yoga is being repackaged and
introduced into Indian urban centres the way that gyms were two decades ago.

So I went to my first yoga class—and I hated it. It was excruciating,
and so very boring. And it hurt. Not only was it physically difficult, but
also, I was forced to sit and be still for extended periods of time. That's
when I noticed the thunderclouds passing through my mind. The chatter! Like some supremacist rally had moved into my head. I had no idea
that this constant stream of thoughts and its grip over me could be
transformed. In the beginning I could not shut it down or make sense
of it. Simply being in silence with my body for an hour was torture.
After that first class, it was not my body that alarmed me (though I was
very stiff), but my mind. "We spend so much time aspiring to be strong,
not realizing the glorification of strength covers up something valuable.
To be soft, to be vulnerable, to falter and fumble is true wisdom. This is

how you learn," the teacher said (or something like this) during class while I did an internal eye-roll.

It was quite a reckoning. I'd been working out for more than a decade, and I thought I was in great shape because everyone around me thought I was in great shape. But it turned out I didn't know how to use my body. I had to learn the fundamentals: how to bend, how to allow, how to soften and breathe to create space in my body. I left the first class, thinking: That was awful . . . when do I go back? I knew there was a lot of work to be done. In my family, we didn't have this idea of "working on yourself." After my mom's accident, I remember my father describing the attempts half a dozen psychologists and counsellors made to work with her. "She was impenetrable, a brick wall," he told me. "They had never seen anything like it." She had no concept of therapy and was very set against it. This was her strong-mindedness at work, buoyed by some Eastern European idea of self-reliance. If things get bad, pick yourself up and go on. My mom only believed in the tangible, in things that she could see and touch and feel. The soul was a fable.

But I had always been open to the spiritual side of life. Partially because I felt alien and apart from my surroundings. Partially because I saw everything, even the hair on my pillow, as a question mark. Yoga solidified my tendency towards questioning that had begun with my solitary pilgrimages in India. I hated that first yoga class but I think it was curiosity—What does this mean? Where could this lead?—that brought me back, again and again. Something was shifting inside me. After a few classes, the practice became less aggravating and more soothing. Of course, my alpha self was alive and well, so I also got into the competitive aspect of it: Look at me! I can stretch further than last week! One day I'll do a headstand! It took me a long time to realize that yoga isn't a competitive sport. Years of working hard to get what I want, had thrown me out of balance.

In 2002, as I got into it, and the inner dialogue started dying down a little bit, I began seeking out other kinds of yoga: Hatha, Iyengar—I wanted to sample every type there was. I travelled to every far-flung corner of London's boroughs, slipping into different traditions, until I found Bikram. Sometimes called "hot" yoga, Bikram is an intense practice of twenty-six postures in a room heated to 105 degrees Fahrenheit.

The atmosphere is athletic, even competitive (though it's not supposed to be). There's no gentle, long-haired teacher murmuring: "Listen to your body." Instead it's: "Push, deeper! Hey, you in the bikini! Deeper!" The teacher communicates these directives via microphone, while walking around the room. Early on in the practice, a lot of people feel dizzy or nauseous from the heat. The first time I did it, my head felt light, but I forced myself to push through. I've always loved the heat, and the practice seemed to combine the intensity of working out with the calm of yoga. I had found the perfect yoga for me.

The cultish aspect of the Bikram movement mirrored where I was at. Its founder is Bikram Choudhury, a charismatic, off-the-wall yoga rock star known for his collection of Rolls Royces, earned by bringing yoga to millions, for millions. (Now, a scandal-ridden figure, as seen in the Netflix documentary *Bikram: Yogi, Guru, Predator*, and having been accused of rape and sexual assault.) He is prone to uncompromising pronouncements: "Do the eagle pose, it's good for sex!" "The more you backbend, the younger you become!" "Do this and you'll be young and sexy your whole life!" Bikram Yoga has been franchised around the world, but Choudhury's controversial wild-man energy (no matter that he was born in 1946) is the brand standard.

I became pretty fanatical about the practice. I had to get up at an ungodly hour and take two different bus routes north to a rougher part of town. Here the Sainsburys and Waitroses gave way to halal butchers and Jamaican patty shops. Nurses and security guards and cleaning ladies coming off the graveyard shift were pausing to chat on street corners. They must have been bone-tired, but they were bristling with life, waving their arms, exchanging small talk. I'd watch them from Bread and Roses, a little bakery cafe where I'd sit and drink tea, and bask in the after-effects of the Bikram practice. In the eyes of the west London crowd, these people would be considered poorly off, but it didn't seem to be a condition of their spirit. I lingered as long as I could before leaving for my next gig: drama school. I had been in London two and a half years. Gossip about me had died down in India. There was a new cycle of fury and farce; people had moved on. I was no longer a hot commodity. In Canada, I think they'd written me off. For my part I was firm in my dedication to the theatre, hoping to join a repertory, with perhaps some miming and yoga on the side?

I remember clearly a day in October when I had just passed through the Earl's Court Gate into Holland Park. I registered him first out of the corner of my eye, a lean, long-limbed rangy figure in a worn blue shirt. I noticed him because he wasn't wearing a coat, and it was getting cold. He rose elegantly from where he was squatting on the grass and without a word, fell into step with me. I didn't alter my pace. In fact, I slowed down. I didn't have a habit of chatting with strangers but something about this man drew me to listen to him. It might have been his irregular beauty, his long, finely boned face; his world-weary but gentle air. Or his dark skin that swallowed the light and reflected it back like a still lake. He began telling me his story: He was from an African nation I can't recall now, born into an aristocratic family; sectarian troubles and violence had scattered him and his kinsmen like birds. His poverty in London had not dimmed his inborn sense of noblesse oblige, a notion of gentleman's generosity.

I didn't speak until we reached the opposite end of the park. "This is where I turn to get home." I was touched by his story and felt a strong fellowship. "It was a pleasure chatting with you, miss. You have been so kind to give me your attention. I want to leave you with something in return. I have nothing to offer but a riddle."

He paused.

"What's the furthest a human can travel?"

I scrunched up my face, making quick calculations. Darkness was falling and an evening crowd in long boots and leather shoes were throwing glances as they stepped around us with a coiled impatience.

"Here to Australia. No, wait, London to South Africa?"

He raised a long finger to his temple. "From here—" I watched his finger as it descended, to tap the middle of his bony chest—"to here. That's the longest, most difficult distance a human can travel. And you, young miss, you are on your way." He turned and walked off into the glumness of dusk, as though our allotted time had ended. I never saw him again. But I never forgot him nor the map he drew on his body.

10

SERENDIPITY, FINDING SOMETHING valuable or delightful when you are not looking for it, has been one of the primary shaping forces of my life. The word is believed to have been coined by Horace Walpole, from a letter he wrote to a friend about a Persian story he had read: *The Three Princes of Serendib*. The trio was always making discoveries, by accident, of things they were not in quest of. Serendib was the old Persian name for Sri Lanka before the Brits named it Ceylon. Some people rely on their family or friends for advice or consult oracles and business coaches. I rely on serendipity. I imagine an impish grin on her face every time she places her hands on my shoulder and draws me close, breathing gently in my ear: *Have I got an assignment for you! Here's where you are going next.*

Just before Christmas of 2003, I was tightly cocooned in my drama school world. I had lost all track of days and time. I left my flat in the dark and returned home in the dark. I was consumed with finishing my coursework, perfecting monologues and rehearsing a song for an ensemble performance which filled me with dread. I barely saw A. Postcards to my parents had stopped. But my mom made my father call me once a week, on Friday nights, before I dropped into bed from exhaustion. I was going to spend Christmas with them: I could only think of how much I would sleep. In the middle of this drama school trance, I received an email from Deepa, written in her typically blunt style: "Here's a script. Read it and tell me if you want to be a part of this." The script was called *River Moon*, and as soon as I began to read, I recognized it. This was the film that had made headline news years ago, when I was living in India. This was *Water*, the film she had originally tried to direct in Varanasi in February 2000.

I knew the background of the film from interviews and media articles. In the early 1990s, Deepa had been shooting an episode of the Indiana Jones TV series, set in Varanasi, or Benares, one of the oldest, most sacred places in the world. It contains the entire circle of life: people come to be reborn through yoga and to study the scriptures, and people come to die. An assembly line of bodies is cremated in funeral pyres and the ashes scattered in the waters of the Ganges where pilgrims wash themselves amidst the remains. It's a mystical, effulgent, provocative, sometimes gruesome place.

While shooting, Deepa saw a widow on the river's edge, dressed in widow's white, bent like a prawn. She spoke to the woman, and followed her back to the ashram, a lonely island where widows were exiled. Deepa had never been exposed to this dark tradition. This widow lived on one handful of rice a day, under a small shelter, crowded by other widows, singing to Lord Krishna. This had been her life since her husband died and would be her life forever. Appalled and fascinated, Deepa began to imagine her film. By 2000, Deepa had finished her research and had her script completed: *Water* would be set in British-ruled India of 1938, and tell the story of eight-year-old Chuyia. A child-bride wrenched from her family and sent off to marry a grown man, Chuyia then finds herself suddenly widowed. Her head shaved, she's exiled to the widow's ashram for the rest of her life, shunned by society and sentenced to a life of renunciation. Several great actors had been attached to the prestigious project, including Nandita Das and Shabana Azmi. But on day two of shooting in Varanasi, Hindu nationalists began to protest. Demonstrators took to the streets, tearing down the sets that had been built, and burning an effigy of Deepa. The state government did nothing to help, and officials finally shut down the production.

During this time, the right-wing Bharatiya Janata Party (BJP) was in power. They may have laid the groundwork for the economic liberalization of India, but they had a social agenda that promoted a troubling mindset which could be interpreted as either intolerant or as a siege for political control. Deepa had already made the first two films of her Elements trilogy, *Earth* and *Fire*, the latter a controversial story of forbidden love between two married Hindu women. I'm sure she had made the wrong people nervous or pissed someone off long before she began to make this film about a dark corner of Indian society. In the eyes of her critics, Deepa was presenting a negative view of India to the world. Her film, they feared, would perpetuate an idea of the country as backward or unjust at the exact moment that India was positioning itself on the global stage. It was not the time to acknowledge this shameful custom.

In India, it's actually possible to "rent a crowd"; politicians and powerful people will do so frequently to make a point. I always suspected this was how the sudden riots broke out on that second day. On the first day, Deepa had watched a man rowing back and forth on the Ganges, with a huge rock roped to his waist, calling through a megaphone that he was going to drown himself if they didn't shut down the set. The Indian crew working with Deepa all rolled their eyes and told her to ignore him: he was well known for being paid to protest. Deepa also received messages that if she made the film anywhere in the world, she would be killed for her transgression. And so, she put it away, and made the light comedy *Bollywood/Hollywood*. But devotion to a vision has a way of slipping through society's judgement and years later she had opened the box again and sent the script to me.

I opened the email. Because of all the controversies and death threats, she could not call the script *Water*. She had to disguise it with a different title: "River Moon." But it didn't matter what it was called: it was, and continues to be, one of the best scripts I've ever read. I wept at the end. The elegiac imagery, the pathos and the passion I'd been looking for—everything was there in the script. But crucially, in the character of Kalyani, I saw myself: the quiet rebel, trapped in a role dictated by her appearance yet longing for an unnamed, impossible liberation. I could feel the spirit of the maestro: Indian film-maker Satyajit Ray, my father's favourite director. My own favourite cinema is all about gaps—not the dialogue, but the spaces between words. I love what's not said. As an audience member and as an actor, I find it more challenging to be silent than to be talking all the time. The script was filled with simple silences. I knew I wanted to try to bring those silences to life.

Of course, I was in the middle of a dense one-year course, and drama schools in London have a strict policy of not allowing students to take on any professional work while studying. But if I was interested in acting because I wanted to understand the human condition, then this was the opportunity of a lifetime. Coincidentally, Rado, my one, unwavering professional connection to India, had renewed my contract once again and requested me to fly to India for a series of appearances in Kochi, Amritsar and Jaipur. In more ways than one, my bond with the brand transcended business as usual. Serendipity, along with the watch brand, brought me to Delhi during my break from school. There, I met Deepa—all eyes and a tangle of Fabindia dupatta—in the lobby of the hotel Rado was putting me up in for a few nights before I flew off for my engagements around India, and said, along with my small, inner voice: "Yes. Yes. Yes."

I did an informal screen test that Deepa needed to send to Telefilm, the government agency that helps fund the film industry in Canada. I knew that she would have to sell me as her choice for Kalyani, the young widow who befriends Chuyia and falls in love with a handsome follower of Gandhi. On the surface, I was an unusual casting choice to play a simple village girl who hasn't been exposed to the world. Deepa draped me in a white saree and filmed me from the foot of the luxurious bed in this five-star hotel. I sat there, legs tucked under me, trying to be a simple Hindu widow, on the thick pile carpet with the room service coming in behind the camera. Shortly after, back in Canada, when I was doing the Christmas dishes, I found out that the role of Kalyani was mine.

I returned to London in January 2004 after spending Christmas with my parents. I had told no one about the film as I was scared about my upcoming conversation with the head of the school. I was close to graduating, and I'd spent a lot of money on my courses. It was hard to imagine not getting the diploma. But what if I were forced to choose between school and the film? I went to my principal during lunch to plead my case. I walked into her office with a book Deepa had given me for my preparation—*Perpetual Mourning: Widowhood in Rural India* by Martha Alter Chen. Luckily, the principal knew who Deepa was, and she probably heard the rumblings from my heart. I was trying to throw off my anxiety and flagrantly set a path for myself. Standing in that office, I was asking permission not of the principal but myself to cut through all excuses in order to follow my "highest excitement." "It's the basic organizing principle of the world," I had told my oldest friend Tina when we were teenagers in Toronto. "Without fail follow your highest excitement and everything will fall into place. That and constant change are your friends." I had crossed continents since then and it was time to put my own puffed up words to the test. In the time I stood there, waiting for an answer, I must have appeared both bewildered and as desperate as an addict. I remember staring at her with a fixed look, scratching my arms. Whatever it was it worked. She told me to take the term off, but to return for the final production. I left a different person, my skin rippling with excitement, a huge and invisible possibility growing within. I was in *someone's* good graces that day.

I was heedful about not allowing the next stumbling block—my relationship—get in my way. I had let the will of a man override my desires before; I would not let it happen again. "This is fantastic news, but it feels like you just walk through life blindfolded. There's no planning or goals." Yes. I thought. Finally, you get it. By then, it was clear that A and I had drifted apart. We still put up with each other's moods, but I was beginning to see him as a friend who had overstayed at dinner. I hoped he thought of me the same way so we could part amicably when I returned from filming.

And then, the final stumbling block: language. My Hindi was rooted in Bombay and very rusty. I wanted to make sure I was well-armed with strong language skills not only to serve the authenticity of the film, but because I knew I'd be scrutinized by the Indian population in particular. *Water* was the kind of film I would have loved to do in India but would never have been offered. The practice of profiling in India was still too strong and being labelled a "model" meant Bollywood, not art house. Modelling was about fame and beauty, not the ability to give committed performances. Also, I was not quite Indian enough. All actors hear the "not enough" speech sometime or other: You're not quite tall enough for this part. Your hair isn't the right colour. For me, there was an added "not enough": You're not quite brown enough. You're not quite white enough.

To cut off the criticism at the pass, I immediately signed up for a part-time night course at SOAS, School of Oriental and Asian Sciences, in the heart of Bloomsbury. Though I was fluent in Bombay slang, I had never really learned to read and write Hindi, and I wanted the fundamentals. I enrolled in a beginner's Hindi class. The teacher's name, Lalita, brought to mind a middle-aged Indian woman with glasses and a long plait down her back. I walked into to the classroom and this tall blonde woman announced: "Hi, I'm Lalita!" She was Dutch, and she'd lived in Varanasi and studied not just Hindi but Sanskrit as well, which is like learning Latin. It was her teacher in Varanasi who anointed her with such a quintessentially Indian name. Lalita was in London to get her PhD in the nuances of Hindustani classical music. She didn't feign warmth but was extremely patient, working with me day by day as I endeavoured to unlearn my bad habits. Unlike Masterji she indulged my eccentric requests: "Lalita ji, teach me to say, "The first coffee of the day is a stalwart companion in the face of an unreasonable world."

I called my parents. It looked like I'd have to miss a family visit we had planned around Easter because I'd be filming. I wasn't asking their permission but beneath the excitement was something close to a need.

"You know why I moved here. And I love my courses, I love acting, I love London . . ."

I paused because it felt like something was stuck to the roof of my mouth. I willed myself to continue.

"You know those books that I have always felt most connected to have that feeling . . . of personal necessity. A sense that the writer has no choice but to tell this story." I paused. "This film is that."

There it was. My father immediately understood.

"Yes. And we love you. You are our gypsy. Fly, fly. Keep flying."

I finally learned how to read and write Hindi. I recorded my lines in Hindi, and would listen to them on the Wandsworth Common bus on the way to school, hoping I'd absorb them through osmosis. At home, I'd put on my simple white saree to get used to the garment that Kalyani lived in every day. It had become clear: I couldn't act the part of Kalyani; I had to *become* her. The start of the shoot was drawing close—only two-and-a-half months away. Deepa understood my growing anxiety and dedication; I wanted to push myself into new corners of empathy for this role. She arranged for extra training. I was to leave for India first, where I would work with a theatre director and then visit a holy city in north India, where I could observe Indian widows living in destitution.

In India, I headed straight to Chandigarh, a relatively erudite and well-designed city—some say the only planned city in the country, designed and built by French-Swiss architect and urban planner Le Corbusier. There, in preparation for the role of Kalyani, I was handed over to Neelam Mansingh Chowdhry. Neelam was a childhood friend of Deepa's and a renowned theatre director. She had defied her respectable middle-class Punjabi upbringing to train at the National School of Drama (NSD) and redefined the aesthetics of Indian theatre by translating Lorca and Chekhov for the Indian milieu. Neelam had travelled all over the world with her productions but was rooted in the Punjab. She had the markings of a personal hero for me.

Neelam was entrusted with the task of transforming me into a simple Indian village girl. I arrived in Chandigarh at her home, which had a little sunken open-air theatre in the backyard and I immediately felt I belonged. Her house was located in one of the posh city sectors, behind low walls on a generous swathe of land, but it looked like it should have been elsewhere. There was no imported wallpaper or PVC wall panels or crystal. The structure was low and sprawling and blended into the earth, shaped from terracotta-coloured bricks. I was given a room with a four-poster bed the colour of ebony and piled high with *chadder*s. I wrapped myself in shawls borrowed from Neelam to fight off the north Indian winter chill. I was swaddled from morning to night in a place of magical thinking.

Neelam was everything I envisioned her to be and more. Her face and demeanour are delicate and birdlike, with large green eyes often focused on some distant point as she searches for the right turn of phrase or patiently absorbs a question. She is steeped in culture and curiosity. We formed a very natural bond right from the start; I've always been lucky with female mentors. But she wasn't interested in a lot of theoretical chit-chat about the "craft," and immediately set me off on a series of tasks that would immerse me in the bodily rhythms of Indian women. Her troupe of actors, called "The Company," was partially drawn from men belonging to a village on the outskirts of Chandigarh. They were the ones who taught me the body language of a village girl; how to walk, how to squat, when to lower my head, how to use my eyes. They tied on sarees and demonstrated their version of Indian femininity to me all day long, while I followed them around, miming their movements. These men were *naqqals*, traditional Indian performers expert at quickly transforming from meaty men into female impersonators.

Every day at lunch, I would try to set the table while remaining in character, and the men joined in. I can only image how bizarre we looked, playing village women dance-walking around the table, setting down thalis and spoons. If one of the men adjusted his pallu, I'd do the same. Another would raise the hem of his saree and I'd attempt the same delicate reach. Then one of the men would spontaneously pick up a spoon or a plate to beat out a tune and the lesson would dissolve into nautanki, that folky mash-up between dance party and opera.

While it might have appeared from the outside like monkey-see-monkey-do this time was a scholarship in the art of *Sringara*, one of the nine rasas or flavours that form the basis of most classical Indian arts. Sringara is a sort of emotional pitch created through an amalgamation of love, beauty and grace, weaving together the sacred and the feminine. Every gesture has meaning.

In the script, my character's pivotal relationship was with a child-widow, Chuyia. So Neelam brought in a couple of kids from the village for play dates. I set about trying to recapture my own sense of wonder. If you're not emotionally honest, it's impossible to relate to a child without condescension or exploiting the power of adulthood. And the camera knows when, as an actor, you're not being truthful. I was beginning to truly comprehend the enormity of preparation I'd need for this role; to become Kalyani. I'd sit on the grass in the backyard and play traditional Indian games with the kids like *kiklee*. Clasping hands, Munni, a little girl with crooked bangs, and I twirled around to a song: "*Kiklee klee the, maj mera veer di, dupatta meri mai da . . .*" Let's twirl round and round! The cow belongs to my brother, the chunni belongs to my mother, and to hell with my brother-in-law! Neelam said, "Don't ask me the logic of this song!"

I also spent a lot of time with Neelam's maid, Shobha, who had presided over the household for thirty years. Researching and observing real lives was one my favourite things. It was a sneaky excuse to immerse myself in another's life. And, also, to disappear into another reality. I asked her to teach me everything, and so became her assistant, much to her delight. Traditionally, food in many parts of rural India—particularly in the north—was prepared on a *chulha*, a fire around which the women squat on their haunches. I worked for weeks getting that squat just right; it hurts like hell, and it's really hard to do. I'd be squatting and making chapattis when I'd simply roll backwards like a beach ball. The domestics would all laugh so hard they'd also drop to the ground before pulling me up. I also learned how to sweep using the *jharu*, holding my free arm behind my back while I bent over. It was a serious workout. Shobha would load me up with household chores, giggling the whole time: "An actress who wants to do *mehnat?*" I was the subject of much hilarity to everyone who worked in the house.

At my request, about three quarters of the way through my training, Neelam took me to a local village to spend the day with one of the families. The main home had a thatched roof, smooth walls which were covered with cow dung—gobar—a large courtyard and a small kitchen housed just off the main structure. I joined in the day's endless labour, beginning with gathering bales of hay. The interior of the home was dark; there was no electricity. I spent a lot of time in the kitchen, bent over the chulha, trying not to burn my fingers and perfecting my technique of rolling out rotis and parathas. Children shyly gathered in the doorway, watching as I attempted to grasp large bundles of wheat and insert them into a noisy machine to separate the chaff. I could barely turn the handle on the machine, which evoked gales of laughter from everyone but me.

That visit culminated with the making of cow dung cakes. *Patthiyan* are considered to have antiseptic qualities and a lot of different uses: the dung can be smeared on the ground outside a home to create a clean entranceway; some patties are placed on the side of the huts as insulation; some are burned as fuel. Note to all eco-warriors: cow shit is the ultimate in recycling. You could say; it's the shit. Of course, it's up to the women of the house to get their hands into the big pile of gobar and mix it with hay or straw, shape the cakes and press them into the side of the house. Elbow deep in cow crap, stinking to high heaven, I did have a moment of reckoning: "Okay, I am officially married to this role."

The final step of my preparation, a few weeks before proceeding to the set in Sri Lanka, was a visit to Vrindavan, a sacred city a couple of hours north of Delhi associated with Krishna. Vrindavan is a place where you can still find a large concentration of widow ashrams like the one we would be portraying in *Water*. After the movie was eventually released, some sections of Indian society cried: "But this doesn't exist any more in our country!" Some even said it never existed to begin with. I will always and forever fight them on this point. I bore witness and I have memories of my own. One of my aunts in Calcutta was relegated to wearing white sarees and shunned from elaborate family dinners when I was a girl. I didn't understand at the time, but now I do: she was a widow.

I travelled to Vrindavan with a young assistant director, Vasant Nath. We spent several days sitting in the rear of a cavernous ashram with about two hundred widows, listening to them sing devotional songs. With their own husbands dead, Krishna had become their spiritual husband, and they droned on, crooning to him for eight hours a day. I was so determined to understand these women that I called myself a "widow hunter" to lighten the mood. It was appalling to see how an ancient text—the Manusmriti—persists as a distorted version of itself as a tool to oppress widows and turn them into social pariahs. I saw women of varying ages toiling away in service and prayer in threadbare white sarees. The fabric hung liked dirty bandages from their thin frames. Of course, this is only one of multiple ways in which women are subjugated. But the point of making the film was to explore and reflect underlying patriarchal attitudes, for the institutionalized oppression of women transcends borders and cultures.

My own beliefs draw from a version of Hindu philosophy that recognizes and honours the divinity in everything; that we are all parts of the

same entity, or Brahma. Vrindavan made me question my own tacit acceptance of so many wrongs in the world. But I had to be real: I was dancing
on sharp edges. I was an actress preparing for a film. What sort of impact
could I actually have? But this is why we make films like *Water*, to hopefully nurture a discussion and an awakening of conscience over blind faith.

Mornings and evenings, before and after prayers, Vasant and I
would follow the widows through the streets as they made their way
back to the cramped, cluttered rooms they slept in. I remember how
they walked along the outer edges of the road, furtively, with short
quick steps or a slow, ghostly gait. To me it illustrated, more than anything, the way their spirit had been crushed. They moved through the
world like they were invisible. Many of the widows were quite elderly,
and the bulk of their lives had been spent in this place. Vrindavan is
supposed to be a holy city but you could feel its dark underbelly; something sinister lurked around every corner. I asked them again and again
about their lives, and one after the other gave us the same story: My
husband passed away, and my family can't afford to support me. It's my
fate. One frail shadow of a woman, probably seventy years old, looked
me in the eye and said: "I have to clean my karma." And so to purify
herself, she dedicated her every breath to Krishna. The hardest thing to
see was not her sense of fatalism. It was her blinding belief: *I am wrong.
I caused this. I deserve to suffer.* I wanted to reach for her, touch her, but
I was afraid she would dissolve into nothingness.

The exchange with this woman reminded me of a scene in the
script. Eight-year-old Chuyia has just been widowed. Her family depos-
its her at a widow's ashram ruled by the imperious Madhumati who
tells the child: "In grief we are all sisters here and this house is our
refuge. Our holy books say a wife is part of her husband while he is
alive, right? And when husbands die, wives also half die. How can someone who is half dead feel pain?"

"Because she is half alive," retorts Chuyia.

As soon as I arrived in Sri Lanka. I had an intuition that *Water* was
going to be a transformative experience. In an interview with Emanuel
Levy in 2006, Deepa would note:

Water can flow or water can be stagnant. I set the film in the 1930s but the people in the film live their lives as it was prescribed by a religious text more than 2000 years old. Even today people follow these texts, which is one reason why there continue to be millions of widows. To me, that is a kind of stagnant water. I think traditions shouldn't be that rigid. They should flow like the replenishing kind of water.

I was one of the first of the main cast to land in Colombo. Deepa thought it was a good idea for me to spend time with my co-actors, getting used to the climate and sets. The production design team had already been working for a month to pull together the world of the film. Immediately after arriving in Colombo I drove to the sets to begin immersing myself in the world of the widows of *Water*, just as they were being completed. Sri Lanka is a beautiful land and the locations were almost too lush for the story. My eyes filled with indigo shadows and vibrant green.

Deepa's brother, successful photojournalist Dilip Mehta, had joined us to oversee production design. He had his hands full with the epic undertaking of recreating an Indian village in Sri Lanka, because although the landscape is similar to parts of India, the cultural differences meant everything to do with the widow's world had to be flown in. On a riverbank just outside Colombo, an entire set of bathing ghats had been constructed from scratch by local production designer Errol Kelly. Standing there, I remember conjuring a vision of India of the 1930s. I was both outside the story and deep within it, preparing to embody the experiences of the widows.

At another key location—the widows' home and ashram—workers were hammering and scraping, building the widows' world by ageing the building and bringing in Hindu motifs, piece by piece. The widows had no life outside of the small ashram where they were exiled, and Deepa wanted us to spend a lot of time simply being on the set and feeling its containment. I sat on the under-construction set, keeping my gaze distant and pensive, trying to decipher the feeling of being utterly abandoned, the ache for love separated from hope. As it often happens in the seat-of-the-pants, precarious world of indie films, there was already a major crisis. The girl Deepa had chosen to play the lead had fallen through. In essence, a set was being built and a cast had been assembled for a film about a girl who didn't yet exist.

They put out a casting call in Sri Lanka and saw hundreds of girls. And then they found Sarala, a cherubic eight-year-old from a small coastal village. I'll never forget my first sighting of her arriving at the hotel in off-kilter ponytails and a blue dress. Just a few weeks later, her mother would silently cry behind her hands while watching her daughter's hair being shaved off during the filming of a scene. I was not there but I heard it described by Giles, our DOP. "Don't worry, Ma," Sarala said between shots in Singhalese, half her head tonsured like an indecisive monk, "it's just hair. It will grow back."

She could speak neither English nor Hindi, only her native Singhalese. She learned the entire script phonetically. She would sit with Deepa and go over the lines, word by word, both of them growing frustrated with the translator in between them. Sarala had never before left her village, let alone been exposed to film-making, or the perks of the lifestyle that come with it. Film sets normally have a craft table covered in snacks and once we began filming she'd pop up there while waiting for her next scene, sometimes eating without breathing between bites. She began to gain significant amounts of weight because she had never been around so much food. She got rounder and softer, though her character was supposed to be living on a cup of rice a day. Deepa raised an eyebrow but let her be. She learned really fast that if she asked for things, they'd be brought to her immediately by an assistant director, so she began asking for Coca Cola between shots. I'll always remember Chuyia wrapped in widow whites, perched on the edge of a plastic chair, swinging her legs, and swigging soft drinks between shots. Watching her, I saw traces of myself: a girl from a modest background thrown into a foreign culture of luxury and excess, suddenly the centre of attention. Both of us turned to food for comfort.

Since the *Bollywood/Hollywood* intervention, I had been trying to eat more healthily, and I thought I had a handle on things but I still slipped easily into the patterns of treating meals as some sort of battlefield. I was very sly about protecting my behaviour, and some of my old tricks popped up on set. I began to limit my food intake and exercise in the hotel gym for hours. I justified it to Deepa. "I'm playing a poor Hindu window who survives on only one handful of rice a day. I'm supposed to be skinny!"

She cut me off. "There's such a thing as creative license. I want you to be healthy."

Poor Deepa: one actor packing on the weight, another shedding it. I remember running into Seema Biswas, my co-star, in the hotel gym during the shoot. Seema is an actress I've admired for years, ever since I saw her in *Bandit Queen*. I was sweaty from the treadmill and she was trying to lose weight herself. She said to me: "Oh, I really admire your dedication to the role. I'm so inspired by you! We should work on losing weight together so I can look more like a widow too!"

My profession is perpetually out of balance in this way; it's a great place to hide. My illness was translating into expertise or craft and I was receiving plaudits for it. I look at my eating disorder as a disease, but also as an expression of imbalance, not just in my body, but in my mind. At the same time, my own unbalanced attitudes constantly met up with an imbalance in my environment.

Looking back, it was a dream shoot. A ceasefire of the long gestating civil war in Sri Lanka had coincided with our filming. Even the country was optimistic, and tourists were tentatively testing the waters after years of conflict. All my collaborative drama school training converged together on a set where we worked without ego, more like a theatre company. It was not even about the result, I realized, but cultivating hard work and trust and then letting go. On set, many worlds intersected, with Canadians, Indians, a British DOP and, of course, Sri Lankans in the crew. We worked demanding hours, falling into our beds bleary-eyed after a night shift. I tried to stick to my vow to walk around barefoot most of the time because that was what my character did; cushioned, pedicured feet would never suit Kalyani. So, on my off days, I loped along Galle Face barefoot in my saree and got some looks from local street vendors: "Nutty actress." But I had *become* Kalyani.

All the other actors playing widows had their hair shaved off before we began filming, but in the script, my character's hair gets cut on camera. Deepa had told me that if I couldn't handle it, she'd figure out a way around the cut. But I knew the cutting scene was critical to the film. I also thought it would be a good exercise for me to get my hair lopped off; it was a symbolic way of shedding my recent past. Deepa treaded lightly around the issue because she knew the Indian obsession with hair. Not only are long, thick locks the Hindi film standard, but they're a corner of the feminine ideal. On set, the stylist put extensions in my hair then dyed it to make it more Indian. My Polish genes were playing against me. Deepa was always clucking, "Go lie by the pool and get a tan!" But the dye was gothic dark and I came out resembling Lara Croft. That was not the look anyone was going for, so they had to chemically strip my hair, and put in another shade. By the time we got to the head-shaving scene, my hair was fried and the idea of cutting it off was actually a relief.

The day of the scene there was a little tension on the set. We all knew this was a one-shot deal; it had to be done right the first time. Deepa gave explicit directions to veteran actress Manorama who was playing the widow Madhumati, ruler of the ashram. "Okay, let's get this right. You have to grab her and hack away at her hair. Make sure it's uneven." Then she turned to me, "You okay? You ready for this?"

I nodded, deeply focused on the scene, already in character. Serious. Deepa stood back. "Action!"

In the first take, at the top of the scene, Manorama was supposed to walk in with the scissors, then we'd stop the action, reset and film the cutting action separately. Manorama waddled in. I inhaled, really feeling the scene. But something was off with the lights, and Deepa yelled: "Cut!" She meant "cut the scene" but Manorama thought she'd received the cue to start cutting. She grabbed my head roughly and began shearing my hair like a sheep's.

"Cut! CUT!" cried Deepa, and Manorama began to hack at my head more vigorously. Finally, an assistant had the wherewithal to run between us, shrieking: "Don't cut! Don't cut!"

That moment of high comedy took the edge off. Fortunately, we had got what we needed for the take. The rest of the scene went smoothly. I rubbed my hand over my buzz cut and felt liberated. I didn't know it then, but this baldness was preparation for what was to come years later. But I did learn that day how little stock I had in my hair, that my hair wasn't me either. By extension, I was beginning to understand that my looks weren't me. I got a sense of how free I could feel.

While the subject matter was heavy and we were all very focused, in between scenes, it was a light-hearted set. Sometimes that happens with a film: the cast and crew are eager to counterbalance what's going on screen. John Abraham, who played the young student who falls in love with me, is a real prankster. He also happens to be gorgeous. I've seen the effect he has on women and I was not immune. There was chemistry between us, but neither of us was single. Perhaps his most attractive quality was his goodness; unlike most Hindi film actors, he was respectful towards everyone on set. So we channelled our flirtation into a routine of teasing each other.

His costume consisted of a simple white kurta, spectacles and a dhoti. That last is frankly a bit of an engineering feat if you're not used to it. John had never worn one before. Production got him a dhoti-wallah, an assistant, who would pleat and tie this unwieldy starched garment around his body as he stood still. My most effective form of revenge was to walk by and give it a hard tug. I loved watching John's face crumple as it unravelled and he'd realize he needed to go and stand for another twenty minutes to get rewrapped. (No, he was never naked!)

We all lived and ate together. We took over that town, hanging at the Barefoot Café, shopping at Paradise Road. We would hit the Crescat Plaza, a shopping mall attached to the hotel, and order fresh juices while perusing pirated movies. Of course, there was a major contradiction between our lives in the luxurious hotel and the story we were telling.

What made the shoot so unusual was the complete subjugation of our egos. *Water* wasn't about my role, and it wasn't about my character. We were like a theatre troupe, all in service of the film and in service of Deepa's vision. It's the atmosphere you hope for every time you arrive on a set, but it comes along once in a lifetime. It was almost like a spiritual teaching: you do your dharma, but you're not attached to the results. On set, I saw some version of that tenet in practice in a very pure way. The truth is, making an independent film in those days was a triumph of human will over circumstances. One of life's minor miracles, if you will, because every day something will go wrong, and you won't have the budget to fix it. The beefy Steadicam operator will trip and fall on his first day, dropping the camera. Another camera's lens will get stuck. An actor will get food poisoning and precious days of the schedule will be lost. I've stopped trying to find theories for why the movie worked. We could all feel that something special was being created but we didn't really know. No one ever knows how a film will end up or how it will be received. I came out of it thinking, "Well, even if no one sees this, it will be okay." It was the most satisfying professional experience of my life. And like any memorable experience, I wanted a souvenir: something that would remind me of the things I had learned. It came to me close to the end of the shoot in the middle of a scene. John's character Narayan asks Kalyani how she bears the terrible injustices heaped on her life as a widow. There is a pause while Kalyani looks out the window of their carriage and then she recites a short shloka from the Bhagavad Gita:

Padma patra evam bhasa
Live your life like the lotus flower

I had found a personal mantra. Rising out of a pond, the lotus shrugs off the water that falls on it. It's both part of the murky world and above it. But there's another way to look at it. No mud, no lotus. Through struggle comes freedom.

11

IN THE SUMMER of 2004, I returned to rehearsals for the final graduation production at drama school. I had been away for three and a half months. It was not easy to leave Kalyani and the entire *Water* experience behind. Right after graduation I found representation. I signed with Aude Powell, who became a combination den mother and agent to me. Aude spoke in the most delicious plummy accent. "I want to be you when I grow up Aude," I would tease. Aude had married well so she didn't have to work but she had come from a family of thesps, and "trod the boards" herself so she was devoted to her clients. I remember how much she relished our weekly updates when she would casually slip in reports of Orlando Bloom's weekend antics with her boys at the family castle in Scotland.

After completing drama school and *Water*, I experienced a renewal of faith in myself. I could feel myself becoming more and more immune to outside criticism, more fearless. The drama school training had fired my sense of wonder. I wanted to continue living life being open to each experience to discover what they taught. I just had to be free to follow the way my instinct was leading. And if it led to the edge of more pain, I would try to face it.

My relationship with A had become stifling, so, to buy time, I accepted an offer for a little independent film shoot in Vancouver, a film so small it never got released. I finished that film and decided that I was going to leave London for good. I had no clue where I would go next but abiding faith that something would come along. I returned to London after the shoot to close shop. In my mind, A was already an ex, though he didn't know it. In the last year of our relationship, he had shed his civility, revealing an inflated sense of self. He was never volatile, but I'd gotten a sense of an odd blankness behind his eyes, like an intruder glimpsed through dim light.

Not that I was an easy person to be with. I had my own story: the misjudged artist, un-comprehended by others. We were both inhabiting our own exasperating, constructed realities. So a few days after returning from Vancouver, and just before leaving for a trip to Milan for Rado, I met him for dinner, intending to break it off officially, secretly hoping we could laugh about it and promise to stay in touch without trying to locate a reason for the parting. It would all be tickety-boo, sugar plum. It was so simple; A just had to behave according to my convenience and expectations, and everything would fall into place.

But during that dinner A was very insistent on trying to woo me back, initially trying to appeal to my emotions. As he spoke, his eyes went watery at the corners. When that didn't work, while a waiter cleared the untouched appetisers, he tried appealing to my logic: "We were planning on being together. I told you from the beginning, I believe in committed relationships. We made plans. We have a future." I closed in on myself, contempt spreading into the space between us. I reached for the bread basket, barely listening. I let him have his say, refused dessert and tea, and then told him goodbye. I left the restaurant, and he followed me back to my flat, pleading, "Don't go. Let's try and make this work."

"I'm sorry," I said. "I'm moving on." I shut the front door of the building on him and walked to my room. Because there was a lock on the front door of the building, I often didn't lock the door to my flat. I had always felt quite secure.

I spent an hour or so packing before I lay down in my empty room and went to sleep. Sometime in the middle of the night, I felt a weight on my body. I opened my eyes to a figure in my darkened room. A had climbed up on top of me. I thought I was dreaming. I was fuzzy with sleep. It was the swaying of the bed that had woken me, and suddenly I became aware of a pressure building up in my chest and ribs. He had put his hands around my throat and was squeezing. I looked up and focused on his eyes, and even in the absence of light, I saw the most, terrifying hollow expression. I realized: *He's not there.* I tried to speak to him, choking out the words: "What are you doing?" No reaction. Time slowed down as I fluttered in and out of consciousness, beginning to kick in slow motion as he bore down, squeezing harder. He had an absolute iron grip around my throat, and I felt my kicks get weaker and weaker. My brain was on fire, white specks sparking in the corner of my vision, even as I felt I was slipping into deep waters. Thoughts began passing quickly through my mind: Is this how it's going to end? Really? But I have so much left to do. And then, all of a sudden, a voice rang in my ear: "*No. This is not your time.*" I had almost passed out, but the voice spoke again very clearly: "*You are not going to die.*"

I felt a surge of strength as something curdled in me and I punched him in the face, aiming for his eyes, and he fell off my body. Time crumbled in a cloud of dust. And then suddenly, like a body brought violently to the ocean's surface, air poured into my lungs. I opened my mouth and released a single desperate animal howl. A wave of noise that pounded the air and caused an explosion in my ears. I have no recollection of how I opened the door and bolted, still in my pyjamas, barefoot. It must have been 4.30 or 5 a.m. and I ran and ran and wouldn't stop. I watched the streets waver and splinter in my vision when I stumbled. When I glanced behind, I could see him running after me, down an empty Holland Park street. The road was wet and slick but my legs kept propelling me forward. A car appeared, slowed down and I ran in front of it. The man inside hit the brakes and leaned his head out the window: "Are you all right? Do you need help?"

I turned and could see A coming—not a single hair out of place— and all I could think was: He's going to manipulate and mangle the situation. I was shaking, tiny needles biting into my eyes and body. He's going to gaslight me, and he's going to do it so well that this man is going to believe him and leave me behind on this street.

"Please, get him away from me!" I pleaded. I screamed. I was frantic. Was he coming to finish what he'd started, or had he snapped out of it and was now focused on damage control, to smooth the waters? The man in the car opened the door and pulled me in. He looked down briefly at my bare feet, then he locked the door as A approached and banged on the glass. His face spasmed from anger to a crooked smile.

"Get away from the car," called the stranger, and he peeled away. I never found out the name of this clean-shaven guy, out in the darkness on the edge of morning. His presence of mind and compassion has stayed with me, though I can't even remember the colour of his hair.

He drove me to the police station where I filed a report. An officer named Richardson took pictures of the bruises around my neck and filled out the "Victim Personal Statement" report. Later, I would tuck that report in my Day-Timer to remind myself never to become a victim again. I didn't call my family. I didn't want to tell anyone. I was so used to my hard-earned self-sufficiency that all I thought was: "I can handle this on my own." The cops sent someone to A's house and picked him up. Until then, words were not forming meaning, but I took a deep breath, pulling air from all the empty spaces inside and said, "Make sure this asshole doesn't do this to anyone again. Ever."

I think they charged him with assault, and I was glad. I hoped the incident would go down on his record. I still have the case number—I've carried it around for years—but I never followed up. This may be hard to understand but it's not so unusual in incidents of abuse. I didn't want to circle the shame or slide backwards. I was always looking ahead. But of one thing I was certain: when you end up running down the street in your pyjamas, calling for help, you have to admit that your way of moving through the world is not working. Looking back, I now understand that I was angry but perhaps not angry enough. I feel in some cases, anger is a cover for stilled and silent grief. I used to feel something behind my anger, a tidal wave gathering, and this, huge looming feeling made me shut down, dam it up.

The next day, I was supposed to leave for Milan to shoot an ad for Rado; as was typical in my life, a sudden, swift turning of the page. I made my way back to the apartment and that's when I discovered A had stolen my passport and a large amount of cash. This only fed my desire to flee. I think I was probably in shock as I made another trek to the Canadian consulate for a temporary passport. I used to visit the consulate in London a lot. I genuinely believed I was entitled to cross borders and fly around the globe at will, papers be damned. I'm at my most charming in a crisis so every time I lost my passport, I always managed to have a new one fast-tracked. Once again, the Embassy provided me with a temporary passport overnight. I spent the night in a hotel room to avoid returning to my flat. I landed in Milan on schedule in a top that covered the bruises around my neck. I hadn't told a soul what had happened.

I was a gonzo journalist in my mind. I certainly had a talent for taking the acid swell in my blood from life-altering events, and using that to rewrite the story in my head, reshaping facts into a sort of mental trophy. (*"You remember that time th esociopath wrapped his hands around your neck? Wasn't that a rush?"*) Perhaps I was adept at not holding grudges and moving on swiftly, because everyone I met became characters in my story. And there was always, behind my outward shell, a deeply watchful part of myself, quiet, transcendental, that understood this to be an experience I had to pass through. Observe don't absorb.

I was lightheaded on the plane ride over, trying not to think of the stretch of days ahead. I had never been to Italy before. I should have been excited. I remember the man in the seat next to me flirting outrageously with me and I fell in with it. When I landed, I had one thought only: I need to get through this shoot. I threw my bags on the bed in one of the chic hotels that dot the Piazza del Duomo—"an eight-minute walk from the fashionable shopping area of Via Montenapoleone" according to the brochure. And that's how, a day after almost being strangled to death, I found myself on a set. The lines blurred quickly once I set about distracting myself. I'd been involved in countless shoots in India, but this was my first taste of doing it Italian style. Italians are so finely attuned to beauty and proportion. Their DNA is steeped in another type of bias, a beauty bias; it's not practiced, it's who they are.

I arrived at a big open studio, something very Milanese and haute fashion. The stylist was waiting with a rack of couture gowns. I'd never seen gowns so finely constructed that they were sculptural, and finished with detailed, tasteful embroidery. Still, to my mind, India has the best craftsmanship in the world, and I know of many European couturiers whose celebrated garments are finished discreetly in an Indian work-shop. I said so, watching the stylist in the make-up mirror, adding, "I might have an India bias, but it's true." I think the stylist would have throttled me if he could; he took my discourse as an insult to Italian design. Later I realized it was just Italian passion on display—the hands, the emotion flying like feathers, "Drama, what drama?"—and it turned out to be a good diversion as the make-up artist started covering the bruises on my neck.

The photos were to be shot by an Italian fashion photographer named Marco. When he rolled in about forty-five minutes late, I thought, "Wait, I'm supposed to be the star here!" In India, there's a hierarchy; the star can be late, but never the photographer. Later I realized this was something Marco did on purpose to establish his prominence at a shoot. But there was something about him, an inner stillness, and a frequency of calm that made me forgive him. He was very tall. He had a cleft chin and deep brown eyes but it was his beauti-ful complexion that made him appear like a figure from a Caravaggio painting. He was pale and almost completely poreless—a quintessential northern Italian. He had on a hipster t-shirt with jeans and Converse sneakers, but every item very deliberately chosen, a studied tension between effort and effortless. He was very businesslike, not paying much attention to me. "Hello, how are you?" he said in a soft voice, and without ceremony began to set up.

I immersed myself in the shoot, the attempt on my life already locked away in some back room of my mind. Observing Marco work was a good distraction. There was a theatricality to everything he did: he would ask one of his assistants to shift a light and he'd stand back and look at it, then move it again. Back and forth, back and forth, with these dramatic pauses before each instruction. When we broke for lunch, we all sat at a communal table. Marco took the opposite end from me. I wondered if I had offended him, and I was intrigued. Part of this, I learned later, was a technique to get my attention and part was due to his shyness. His Italian-inflected English was not good, and he felt self-conscious about it.

On the second day of the shoot, he revealed that he was fascinated with India. One of the images he wanted to capture had me dressed as an Indian bride. It turned out gorgeous, but not very Indian. I wore a faded rose-coloured lehenga and choli, a traditional outfit a bride would wear but in understated, muted colours. In general, and until recently, Indians like the big, bloated, sumptuously colourful wedding. As I posed in my Italian-Indian garb, Marco proved himself very knowledgeable about Indian spirituality. He asked me if I was familiar with Osho, if I'd been to Hampi in the south or visited Rishikesh and I was taken by this line of conversation.

Rado had sent a chaperone, a lovely, slender girl called Rafaella. In the most stereotypical terms, the anxious Swiss are very suspicious of the free-wheeling Italians, so they wanted to make sure there were no shenanigans on set. God forbid that their brand ambassadress gets seduced by the photographer. Rafaella took me out for piadina after the first day of the shoot in one of the many espresso bars behind the marble Duomo, close to my hotel.

I remember Rafaella hovering around me as Marco and I began to talk more and more intensely on set. By this time, we were eating next to each other, finding an easy rhythm in the conversation. On the last day of shooting, he asked if he could take a few photographs for his personal collection. He wanted to do something that was less corporate, more his style. I was wearing a very chic, beautifully draped dress, and was perched on the edge of a table. He said, "Okay, now you open your legs just a leeetle . . ."

I remember Rafaella intervening, running up to me and saying, "You don't have to do this."

"It's okay," I said, laughing. "I'm here on the table—let the operation begin!"

Marco continued to direct me, and though there was a room of people watching, it felt like there was only us. When he was behind the camera looking at me as his subject everything else faded away. The edges of reality curled and disappeared. It sounds strange but the way he spoke was so uninhibited yet respectful—"Please, open your legs just a little"—I would have happily done the splits. A great photographer knows how to unleash feeling for the camera.

That night, we all went out for a lovely communal meal of risotto and cotoletta and osso bucco at an *osteria* in a little house. Marco was sitting right opposite me, caught in a finger of light from a pendant. I still remember his Che Guevara eyes in his stylish tortoiseshell glasses. After dinner, a group of us left the restaurant. We stood in the middle of the street waiting to take a taxi back to the hotel. It was a little chilly. Marco took off his jacket and settled it deftly around my shoulders. We exchanged numbers. "If you are ever in Paris, you must come and visit me," he said.

"Of course."

We said goodbye, and I gave him back his jacket before stepping into the taxi.

The next morning, I was changing hotels, from the boutique establishment I'd been put up in to a more modest one on the opposite side of the piazza that I'd be paying for myself. Milan is anchored by the Duomo but it seemed wherever I walked, in whichever direction, I landed up back in front of the cathedral, like it was a hovering deity anticipating my every turn. When I did manage to escape it, I found Milan a place of limited charm, the architecture brutish. The people I saw dressed like fashion plates but were also remote, walking briskly by. Where was the warmth and legendary Italian flirtatious charm? But I had made plans to meet my friend Aarti Sethi—Rado's Delhi-based PR manager—and her husband on the island of Elba in a few days. Elba is an Italian island known for its beaches and as Napoleon's place of exile, which sounded a perfect combination to me. I still had a few days to kill and a strong inducement to stay occupied. When I was too still my mind wandered to places I didn't want to go.

On a whim I sent a message to Marco. He was supposed to be back in Paris but his shoot had been cancelled. We met for espresso lungo then walked and talked. He spoke of spirituality and energy work and esoteric things. He spoke of India through a filter of magic and mystery. He recalled such intimate detail, like the pineapple vine border on a young girl's ghagra, and described the night sky as dark blue silk set with bright diamonds, just like a saree. It was exotic but true. He also described the cities as full of "the cockroaches" and black magic. Hmmm. He seemed to know India in a way I didn't. Until I met Marco, I had thought I was invested in the idea of transformation. But he had made it a way of life, even referring to his profession as meditation. He had "worked" on himself, and at first it sounded like one of those fashion things. He had his Tibetan lama and his own guru, and I pursed my lips sceptically. But he was so transparent and childlike that I was fascinated, too. He was teasing out inclinations in me that I had tucked away. I watched him stalk through the city forcefully, his long trench coat fluttering on his frame like linen on a clothes line. But when he found a facade or cathedral or parkette that pleased him, he stopped, legs wide. He closed his eyes and spread his arms to become part of the world. "It's so super, super bea-u-ti-ful." It was very easy to fall into him, and embark on a whirlwind romance, reinstating the euphoria of a new love. We went back to my hotel room. The wrinkled concierge was very disapproving when I started escorting Marco through the hotel lobby up to my room. And Marco would say in his lyrical Italian-inflected English: "What is wrong with the grandpa? Why is he protesting?"

I never did make it to Elba. I spent two weeks in Milan in the dreamy, fabulous throes of courtship. Overnight, it seemed that the complexion of Milan changed from serious to playful. We spent evenings along the Navigli, strolling up and down the canal, brushing against each other's skin and stopping to "take the dinner" as Marco put it. Our afternoons were full of aperitivos and discussing Osho. We'd lie on our backs, staring at the ceiling, sentences spilling out of us without a pause, circling around our desires. It was easy to be around each other. Marco delighted in my middle name—Rani or Princess. "Raaaani. What are you rani uuuf?" Marco would trill. The mood of the romance made me reflect. "Yes, what am I a rani of? Maybe of all the places that scare me the most? The elusive parts of myself?"

And then we parted. I left reluctantly for India to take care of some business I'd neglected the last few years. My flat had been locked up too long and I was planning on selling it: property in Bombay has a way of gathering moss. Marco returned to Paris. We had a vague plan to meet again down the line, but our schedules made it difficult to know when that might be. I wondered if we really would come together again or if this was an affair destined to remain a sweet memory that became thinner with time. Before he left, Marco touched the side of his nose. "I see you, Rani. You're a gypsy with a taste for first-class travel." It was such a cheesy line, but then everything sounds different in an Italian accent.

I was grappling with the blaring, surging current of life in Bombay when I received a text from Marco. I remember being stuck in traffic, gazing up at looming new buildings from the back of my car. Bombay was changing, and fast. I was beginning to feel like a stranger in my city. Ubiquitous billboards and hoardings displayed new brand names; everyone was busy chattering on cell phones. And out of the old tumult there was fresh vision: new artists, new aesthetics, start-ups, new saree drapes, a subversion of cultural identity in a global age. I was overwhelmed, no longer accustomed to ordering my thoughts in the middle of a million new impressions.

Marco's message was like a tonic. He had told me about Buddhist *tangka*s, the Tibetan Buddhist paintings on cloth that rolled up. He said he was sending me one as a gift, but I needed to go to the airport that night and a friend of his would hand over the fragile item. I showed up at the airport terminal at two in the morning, a bit grumpy, watching arriving passengers push their luggage into knots of welcoming family members. Suddenly, Marco emerged into the crowd, holding an elegant duffel bag and a rolled up tangka. I was completely taken aback. A brazen joy took me by surprise and I jumped into his arms, accepting this grand gesture.

"Raniiii," he exclaimed loud enough to startle the waiting crowd gathered behind barriers. "I brought your tangka," he breathed into my ear and spun me around. When he set me down, I was pointed in the direction of my next adventure, facing Marco. Even as we entered the Taj Hotel at the tip of Bombay—a place so familiar to me, but where I had never before actually checked into a room, much less stayed with a lover—I knew what I was asking. I was asking to be carried away. Not only by him. But by life. I relished the purity of having an intention to move countries, but to allow it to unfold organically.

A week after Marco left, a monsoon storm unleashed its limitless potential for destruction and mayhem on Bombay. The kinetic city came to a standstill in late July 2005 after rains lashed the city and the high tide gave the water no place to recede. My car was literally floating in chest-high water before I managed to flee to the nearby safety of my friend Binaifer's twentieth-floor flat in Bandra. I'd never seen anything like it. People were trapped for days in their cars, there were deaths and, for the first time in recent memory, the airport shut down. Days later when the water finally receded, I took a morning walk, picking my way through carcasses of dogs and flotsam on Carter Road, with a singular thought: when the airport opens, I will buy a ticket to Milan and to Marco, the friend of my fate. And as soon as the airport reopened, I flew away to explore the possibility of extravagant love that had been extended to me, never once struck by the profligacy of my choices.

A large chunk of my early life had been about looking like someone else. That's what I was paid to do, and it had become my comfort zone. A photograph is a staged confluence of make-up, hair and lights; it's a group endeavour. Actually being me, singular and unadorned was a great relief. Yet, it was strange when, in my thirties, my appearance started changing. In spirit, I was very nonchalant about growing older, yet every time I'd take a flight, I'd grab some expensive potion from duty free. My lifestyle and erratic eating habits were taking a toll on my skin. I began to feel the churnings that affect so many performers as they leave their twenties and the freshness of youth behind. The make-up and harsh lighting I'd used for so many years was now starting to show. I had developed adult acne and my complexion was looking sallow. But more than anything, the blemishes were a signal that I was unhealthy on the inside.

When I was newly arrived in Milan, I was fascinated by Italian women, with their innate confidence in their own skin. They have a very individualistic approach to their looks, enhancing their features with light make-up, and refusing to fight ageing with panic gestures like surgery and injections. Untouched is beautiful. One afternoon, I observed a group of Italian women going through their circuit at a spa. First, they would dip themselves in a cold mineral pool then run to the hot sauna. Then they would emerge from the sauna and rub ice all over their bodies, which were a parade of shapes and sizes. This strange ritual passed for an anti-ageing programme and all it did was make them look flushed and alive. No chemicals required; no special potions. "Maybe one day I can be like them," I thought as I ran a towel over my skin. It was a vital shock of oxygen, this idea, that it was my individuality that was sacred, not fitting into an arbitrary standard of beauty.

But it wasn't until I moved to Paris with Marco that I laid down my weapons in my war with eating. Marco was born in Milan but worked a lot in Paris. When I had landed in Milan after the floods, Marco was preparing to drive to Paris. It became our ritual, for a few months, the long drive up north out of Milan, stopping at the Autogrill for *un café* in the fabulous ski resort of Courmayeur before passing Mont Blanc into France and then the long flat stretch across to Paris. Eventually I moved into his tasteful Haussmann Parisian flat, though I would keep travelling for work around the world. It was in Paris that Marco paid attention to my habits. I had conditioned myself to always deny my appetite. Food was offered and I declined. Again and again: "No, thank you. I just ate. No, thanks." But Marco, unlike my previous boyfriends, would call me out. "You have a disease of the spirit," he would say. "It's a denial of life. If you deny yourself food and energy, then you deny life. If your body is empty, your soul is empty." This idea struck deep: how could one be hollow and be whole? Most evenings in Paris we went out and it became a kind of food therapy.

For Marco, the persistent irritant and mortal enemy was denial of enjoyment. Wine was never consumed to become drunk, and danger and aggression were to be found in people who didn't understand beauty. We immersed ourselves fully in the sensual possibilities of eating, the pomp and ritual of a full French meal. One of his favourite experiences was to dress up "to take the dinner." We lived a few blocks away from the Gare du Nord, and opposite the main entrance of the station was the legendary Terminus Nord, at number 23, Rue de Dunkerque—a traditional Parisian Belle Epoque-style brasserie. The ceiling had stained-glass details and the servers wore classic bistro waist aprons and crisp, white shirts. Marco would cut an elegant and imposing figure in his grey Comme des Garcons coat, immediately commanding the attention of the maître d', who would usher us into one of the prime leather banquettes in the back of the restaurant. Marco always grew very solemn and quiet, like someone entering a cathedral. I was expected to follow his lead. The first time he took me there I was wearing the Prada heels he had given me, and I teetered behind him, almost nervously. I sank with relief into the booth and he promptly ordered two glasses of champagne, which he conceded was a tad vulgar, but hey, it was my first time there. Marco's French inflection was almost Parisian and though I couldn't precisely follow what he said to the waiter, I felt secure in the fact that I'd gained access to some exclusive, inner court experience. Just sitting there and gazing around (but never making eye contact), I could feel my cheeks suck in and my lips arrange themselves insouciantly to convey how much I belonged in this setting. The ideal was to look like you just didn't care. When the towering tiered *fruits de mer* arrived, I let the act drop and pretty much gawked. The three-tiered platter held a decorative collection of shellfish: shrimp, mussels, oysters, langoustines and lobsters, still in the shell and cold. A mignotte sauce was placed before each of us, along with lemons and a thick, garlicky reduced butter. My dilemma: how to savour and work my way through these delights and still maintain my cool deportment. When I tried to dip my oyster in the wrong sauce Marco made a low warning noise in the back of his throat until I found the appropriate accompaniment. An image came to mind: I was the seal and Marco was tossing bits of tasty treats my way. I put that away (for the moment) and concentrated on chewing. The taste was beautiful, balanced. I felt I had never truly "tasted" seafood before; it was always masked in sauce or batter. I normally rushed through meals with guilt and panic. Now I could taste the ocean on my tongue. Despite his hipness and spiritual leanings, Marco was still a very traditional Italian man who believed that women, by virtue of gender, should be good at cleaning and cooking. But very quickly, Marco learned that this former Bollywood princess knew nothing of either. So, perhaps to shape me into something more domestic, Marco taught me about preparing food as well as eating it. We moved around the kitchen together, cutting vegetables, preparing the stock for risotto.

"I can't have bread," I'd say.

"Oh, shut your mouth and have some bread," he'd insist casually. And finally, we would sit together over the food we'd prepared. I let myself take a piece of soft, warm baguette, rolling the texture on my tongue. I closed my eyes.

"This tastes like . . ."

"… an apology to your body," said Marco. "And don't put the baguette upside down. It's bad luck."

Living with him, I couldn't easily purge. Marco had been around models all his life and he recognized the signs—the breathless overeating, the long trips to the bathroom. He would coax me away from my worst inclinations. At night we went for long walks across the Seine, avoiding crowds by taking the small side streets. Marco shook off my arm hooked through his and instead took my hand into his coat pocket. He had the long stride of a conqueror and I had to keep up. We were always looking for beautiful things to do, led by his mischievous enthusiasm. If a boat came by, we'd hop on. If we got hungry, he'd say, "Come, Spider, we take the crepe." (He called me Spider because: "You have so many legs and you are spidering all over the world"—a reference to my extensive travel schedule, but also my restless energy.)

My cry of "Carbs!" would be silenced by his powerful eyes.

"Don't behave like a cheap actress," he'd joke, disarming me.

In Paris I was moving towards the idea that life was to be enjoyed and consumed, and that the pursuit of beauty is a legitimate aspect of being alive. I had been in a state of self-denial for a long, long time. Marco also introduced me to the Italian antidote to modern life: *Dolce far niente*. The sweetness of doing nothing. There are virtues associated with taking your time, I was discovering.

During the day, Marco would switch on Radio Monte Carlo and blast Euro tunes. He introduced me to Iggy Pop, plaintive Portuguese fados, and the grainy, languid voice of Italian jazz legend Paolo Conte. I got switched on to Noir Désir at some point, and I'd entreat him to fill the apartment with *Le Vent Nous Portera* on loop. Marco worked his phone, going on and on in his musical Italian. The man could *talk*. Once he had a three-hour conversation, an unrelenting barrage of Italian and French, while I lay in bed, listening. I loved waking up to Marco's cloud of chaos. It was torrential and unpredictable but between us, a gulf of tenderness. He was an artist, eccentric in the ways of people who have original vision. But even he was not immune to the all-consuming demands of the fashion world. It stressed him out. Each season you had to prove yourself as a photographer; that you were chic, modern, relevant and original. "Everything you see today is already done." He would sigh. "Everything people on the street like today, I learned five years ago."

But still it was never enough. The fashion industry took a toll on those both in front of and behind the camera. Sometimes in the evening, to relax, he would smoke a pipe. "There is an art in it, Spider," he'd say to me. "You cannot rush! It's proportion! It's meditation!" One day he bought me my own pipe from Milan. He had changed into hospital scrubs. This was a sign he was done for the day. He taught me how to tamp down the tobacco, lighting and gently sucking on the end of the pipe. But it was tougher than it looked and no matter what I did, I couldn't keep it lit. I got impatient and put it down, feeling lightheaded.

"See Rani, you need to pay attention. It is not like to eat the Chupa Chups!"

I secretly hoped I could throw it into the fireplace one day and call it an accident.

Paris was the closest I'd come to a truly Hemingway-esque experience of life. I felt young, and strong and animal-like. I entered a realm where the world was inexhaustible; life had placed a big hand on its chest and said, "I am all yours." I'd wake up to the neighbour practicing piano and marvel at the endlessly diverting possibilities of the day: a walk through the market at Les Halles, an exhibition on Yves Klein at Centre Pompidou in Beaubourg, a falafel in the Marais. Sometimes I would retrace the steps of Second World War spy, Noor Inayat Khan, who I'd become obsessed with, or just lie in with Marco, he in his NY Rangers sweatshirt, me in a beret. "Why you try so hard to be inelegant, Spider?" "I'm not. I'm wearing this hoping I will spontaneously break into French." Finally, I was in it, living life, lapping it up like the Belle Epoque, absinthe-addicted artist I believed I was in my past life. Marco didn't have a lot of friends—"No time for the temporary people, Rani"—but early on he introduced me to two of his closest compatriots, a couple named Nadama and Krishna. They lived in a flat on the outskirts of Milan with a long balcony of potted plants, the windows covered with aluminium *tapparelle*, or Italian blinds, which Nadama rattled open when we arrived. Before I met them, Marco told me that he regarded Nadama as his "spiritual mother," and I got the distinct impression on my first visit that I was being vetted. The walls of their flat were covered with more of Tibetan tangkas—embroidered silk paintings of the various Buddhas, Shakyamuni, Tara, Manjushri, exotic and frightening to the uninitiated. Nadama, all cat-green eyes and Mediterranean poise, sat cross-legged in the centre of the room, presiding over the space like a monk: full of quiet wisdom and mirth. She had been Marco's history professor in college, but now, in her early sixties, her pursuit was the spirit. Around her, I had the sense of being in the presence of something larger than what was visible. She was a healer and proponent of compassion, but not the limp-wristed variety. Krishna was about ten years younger than Nadama and childlike, with coffee-coloured skin and a Snoopy nose.

At that first meeting, I sat and listened to Nadama hold court, feeling scrutinized and nervous, though Krishna kept bursting into his ho-ho-ho laugh. In her broken English, mixed with Hindi, she dropped many Nada-isms, which I promptly wrote down when I returned to Marco's flat:

— "When you don't have the guts, life makes the decision for you."
— "To get understanding, go back to your nature."
— "Be respected, not respectable."
— "Money is an energy. Hold on too tight, it gets blocked. Circulate it, be generous, monitor your thoughts around it and see the abundance return to you."
— "Trust in existence, and life will teach you. Listen to life what it is showing you and teaching you day by day."
— "Don't go by mind."
— "The world is your field of practice."
— "*Allora*, take three breaths before doing anything."

I also wrote down her recipe for tomato sauce, which may be as important as her spiritual guidance, and goes like this:

— Oil, garlic, tomato sauce, milk, salt, rosemary Borlotti
— On low heat cook together for 20 minutes, put in fresh basil at end

— Add water from pasta

(Simple, but perfect.)

They were followers of Osho, known as Bhagwan Shree Rajneesh. Westerners remember Osho as the controversial Indian spiritual leader who started an ashram in central Oregon in the 1980s (and he is now the central figure in the Netflix documentary *Wild Wild Country*). Idyllic landscape, organic farming and red jumpsuits gave way to claims of corruption and Osho was unceremoniously deported. He died in 1990, but his practices live on all over India, especially at his ashram in Pune where Krishna and Nadama met. Krishna had been living there on and off, having run away from his wealthy family in Amritsar, Punjab, to enter Osho's ashram when he was seventeen. When he met Nadama at the ashram decades later, free love was the policy, so it took a few years before they actually came together as a couple.

"We're not here to be worker ants, Lisa," said Nadama. "Don't take on the aspect of a worker. We're here to grow and experience. To dance with existence. To strengthen the soul."

To strengthen the soul.

In both India and Canada, the question of identity was always linked to work: What do you do? But Nadama and Krishna rarely spoke about their paid jobs, though I pieced together that Krishna had worked for IBM ("I slip in, I slip out"). Nadama said she couldn't touch a computer as it interfered with her energy. We never talked about our work and careers, which was incredibly freeing. At that first meeting, we sat at their kitchen table and chatted over coffee. I was nervous and eager to please, and I spoke too much and too quickly. After we left, Marco told me her verdict: Nadama liked me, even though I talked too much. I should come back the next day for coffee and pasta and we could talk about pain.

Religion had always seemed to me something that people functioned inside of for a limited period of time, like my granny at church. Religious people appeared different outside places of worship. Not always, but often enough. I was always sensitive to this game because it seemed to me another sort of mask. Despite that, I had always felt a tickle in my belly and a strong pull towards spiritual practice, even venturing, in Milan, to sit in the back of churches, waving cheerily at priests during services as they exhorted me to examine my relationship to eternity. I wasn't sure whether I was looking for a path or an exit. But I'd never been in a community of people who emphasized *seeking* above all else. It was a revelation. I began visiting with Nadama and Krishna on my own, often spending an entire day in their kitchen. Nadama was profoundly unimpressed by my important engagements, the influential people I knew, but I think she recognized a particular thirst in me. She also saw the ways I was holding on to emotional pain. "Pain is a teacher and how we grow is through pain. But you are not the pain. What do you think you are? Who is watching the pain?" she told me while stirring the pasta sauce over a gas stove.

"You are the witness. Not the doer. Drop in and just keep watching. Watch your jealousy and your anger and your sadness. Watch it all like a movie." She would answer my questions with more questions, revealing the tricks and games of my own mind. She began encouraging me to meditate. In my head, I had appointed myself one of her spiritual kids.

"You are a people pleaser," Nadama would say. I would open my mouth to offer evidence to the contrary.

Ah-ah-ah. She would hold up a hand. It's not a question. And for the first time I was not embarrassed to not have volunteered the right answer.

It was embodied practice. Some theory, lots of action and no bullshit.

In Nadama and Krishna, I found the embodiment of true rebellion. It meant being emancipated utterly from society's rules and rewards. You will not be admired for your cool leather jacket and radical tattoos and free-speaking ways. Rather the opposite. True rebels are not spoken of well, but they have the inner capacity to not care. Not at all. "Normal is a dryer setting," Krishna quoted from Osho when I entered the kitchen, doubtful. If anything, his irreverent laughter cut a hole right through my brooding.

"You know, Nadama, I used to think acting was about hiding, and I was a natural because I was hiding . . . well, everything, but then I began to realize it's about revealing. Illuminating the inner wounds, all the brokenness. That's what made it tough. But maybe it prepared me for this."

Nadama abruptly left the stove. I saw her pick fresh basil on the balcony. When she returned, she kept her back to me.

"Si."

But I was still using travel as avoidance, she said in her blunt, straightforward way afterwards, over plates of pasta and bread and thickly cut tomatoes. True freedom meant taking a walk inside yourself and saying, "Some of this stuff is not mine. These thoughts are from my grandmother. This opinion of who I am is from society. That's the inheritance of generations of oppression." As layers drop, hopefully, behind it all you catch a glimmer of something. "This is the work of our life," said Nadama another day, while chopping onions. "To become a witness takes more courage and hard work than running away." I began listening to Osho's talks and reading about meditation. He confirmed what I suspected: that life was a great personal experiment. Every experience was an opportunity to grow. There was no negative or positive experience; judging made it so. One day at the kitchen table I announced my intention to visit the Tibetans in McLeod Ganj, as if they were old acquaintances. Perhaps those tangkas of Tara and Manjushri and Padmasambhava had infiltrated my psyche. I had to travel to India for several assignments and I wanted to experience a place that seemed to embrace the reality we spoke of in Nadama's kitchen. She agreed it was a good idea. Marco was busy with his own shoots but cautiously supportive. If you ask me, I think he was even slightly envious of my plan, never having been himself. Spiritual rivals? It happens.

And so, after wrapping up all my assignments in India in the summer of 2005, I packed a duffel with socks and light sweaters and headed north to Dharamshala for the first time. I was hoping to find a meditation course and hang out with other gropers of meaning, eating momos (Tibetan dumplings), discussing the source of perfect happiness. Dharamshala is where the Tibetan government has been exiled since 1960, and where the Dalai Lama has been forced to live most of his life in an unassuming, pale-yellow jumble of buildings containing his offices, chambers for audiences and his personal residence. In the shadow of the Himalayas, the wind whips the prayer flags strung between poles. Dharamshala also means spiritual dwelling or sanctuary. The views of the snow-capped Dhauladhar mountain range and plains of the Kangra valley are not quite of this earth.

The bazaar in McLeod Ganj is dirty and bustling. Tibetan refugees with skin like burnished oak sell prayer beads and steaming momos. Tibetan shawls and trinkets and cheap Chinese-made crocs dangle from the stalls. Giant images of the Dalai Lama and the Karmapa are for sale like Justin Bieber posters; crushingly narrow streets are lined with temples and Internet cafes with names like Moon Peak. When a car or cow charges down the lane you have to jump into a sewer or a monk-filled cafe to avoid being run over. In other words, it is like most other sites of pilgrimage in India where the mundane jostles comfortably up against the sacred. I love these sorts of places where the events of an ordinary day shoulder against the holy expedition in my head. The small, quiet voice in my head egged me on.

But it was the guileless generosity of strangers that struck me the most about the Tibetans. I'd woken up many times over the years smelling new smells and seeing new sights, but this was different. In a community of refugees, I found, inexplicably, a confluence of everything good. Whether a shopkeeper or a monk, I experienced kindness and good-natured humour. Of course not everyone was faultless or had pure intentions, and so the manager at the small guest house where I was staying sent his teenage daughter with me my first morning to perform the Kora—the ritual walking meditation—on a well-worn path, clinging to the side of the mountain around the Dalai Lama's temple compound. We fell in step with other pilgrims spinning prayer wheels and brick-robed monks, people who had lost everything and continued walking. How did they do it? Their faces, cleansed of anger or bitterness, seemed to invite a deeper knowing of this very human experience of being broken, exiled, and vulnerable need not be a condition of spirit. I met His Holiness the Dalai Lama many years later. He is a force of compassion, segueing from a childlike giggle into analytical discourse in a flash, but for me, it has been his followers who have embedded themselves most memorably in my heart.

I sat with hundreds of Tibetans on the floor of Tsuglag Khang, the Dalai Lama's temple, watching their prostrations; folded hands to the crown of the head, to the throat, to the heart, kneel and touch the head to earth. Purifying the body, speech and mind. Bowing to the three treasures, crushing self-centredness, cutting attachment to delusions of ego. It drew me in, this vision of humility. "Is that it, then? Happiness comes from accepting impermanence?" In that place of grit and transcendence, where subtle energy channels entered conversation as casually as Nokia phones, and surrounded by visions of Shakyamuni and Tara, there was an unearthing in me of a buried instinct. *Maybe this impulse I have to mine beneath the surface of appearances is not complete madness*, I reasoned, tucking into a pizza in Namgyal Café, inside his Holiness' monastery, *as I've been made to feel at times*. I wiped my lips, feeling it was a fine meal for this manner of reflection.

"The true and intrinsic nature of mind is love and compassion," Geshe Graham fixed me with his blue eyes. He was a startlingly tall Englishman who had arrived in India via the hippie highway through Afghanistan. He landed up in McLeod Ganj around the time I was born in 1972 and stayed. Geshe is an academic degree awarded after twenty-five years of full-time monastic and philosophical training. I had observed Geshe Graham's distinctly steady gait, the sails of his robe fluttering as he passed through the muddy streets, two heads taller than anyone else. I was a small vessel out at sea, drawn to his majesty cutting through the waves. I struck up a conversation when I saw him next at a small cafe. The following day, I took a taxi down the mountain, descending through dust and heat towards the parceled and suntanned land below, into the main Dharamshala bazaar and bought a pair of size-16 sturdy black shoes. I left them with Tashi, the cafe owner. "These are for Geshe Graham." He nodded solemnly as if it were perfectly natural to feel compelled to replace the worn shoes of a supersized monk.

One day I hiked out of town and into the surrounding mountains. I felt myself melt into them; a complete erosion of self into the moist green landscape. As I left McLeod Ganj behind me, a black dog appeared and began to follow me. He looked well-fed, his coat shiny and long, unlike the other village dogs. When I glanced behind, he turned his snout towards me in a smile. "All right, Kalu, let's go." Kalu means "black one" and I was glad for the company. We walked through fields and deodar groves, the smells of the earth radiating like steam, birds plucking tunes from a faint moon above. My mind stood composed and calm against the sky. Kalu was always just a few paces behind me. As we walked back on a small road winding down through Dharamkot, Kalu stopped in front of the Himalaya tea shop, which was flanked by two gates. On either side of the tea shop were gates. To the left were the austere iron gates to the Dhamma Sikhara Vipassana Centre. On the right, a red-painted gateway with a handwritten board: Tushita Meditation Centre. Kalu paused at the red gates, threw me a look, then entered and trotted away, disappearing around a bend. I stood there for a moment, quizzically picking thorns caught in the sleeves of my sweater. It wasn't until a few years later that I would understand what Kalu had been trying to tell me. How life has a way of charting out a direction for me, and then stands back, waiting for me to pay attention.

I'd only been there for a week or so and was checking my email in one of those cramped Internet cafes when I received a message from Hussain Amarshi, the head of Mongrel Media, the Toronto-based independent Canadian film distributor which was distributing *Water*. Not only was the film accepted to appear at the Toronto International Film Festival (TIFF), that year, Hussain wrote, we had been selected for the opening night gala—could he send me a ticket? The enthusiasm in Hussain's note was compelling: maybe the film had turned out as well as we'd hoped. I flew back to Paris, and to life with Marco, having brushed lightly the essence of Tibetan Buddhist practices and Dharamshala, not then realizing what it would come to mean to me.

12

THE OPENING NIGHT gala screening for *Water* was scheduled for 8 September 2005. A feeling was spiralling from my centre, twisting my stomach in knots. I tasted ribboned guts. My throat was starchy and dry. *Breathe. You keep forgetting to breathe. Why is this so hard, even after so many years?* An entire operation was being mounted—PR, red carpet directions, screening instructions, after-party invites—and I was to play one of the crucial roles. I couldn't just hang on the periphery of the action, passing sarcastic comments. Really though, what I wanted was to lie in my darkened hotel room and eat my way through the mini bar. But no, there was so much to prepare, and I was in an agony of impatience to just get it over with. I had requested my old friend from Goa, Wendell Rodricks, to design me a saree-meets-gown in white, as Deepa had requested all her actors to dress in white. But Marco knew the stylist who dressed Juliette Binoche and she sent over a few exclusive Prada and Dior dresses which he brought along from Paris, just in case. Sometimes, an actor doesn't know what she's going to wear until the day of the red carpet, so it's always nice to have a few options to match whatever mood lands. Marco was excited for the designer dresses, one of which was saree inspired and had been worn by Madonna: "It's very important. Wear the right make-up—less is more. It is better you don't dress like the character. Sell yourself. Be yourself. Wake up. Stop to be a poppet!"

"I hear you, Marco. And it's puppet, not poppet. Poppet is what they call sweet and pretty little girls in England."

"Allora, eet eez the same."

Of course, all I could think was: I don't want to sell myself at all! But the Festival is a marketplace at the end of the day. I just could never get used to being the product on sale. I was put up at the Intercontinental on Bloor Street in the Yorkville arts district, the nerve centre for the Festival before the TIFF Bell Lightbox was built as its permanent home. I was jetlagged and anxious from all the attention, let alone the detailed list of press events which had been slipped under my hotel room door. I just wanted some space to expel the anxiety residing in me like a troublesome djinn. To edge away from the notion of losing myself in others' gazes. At the last minute I decided not to wear the Prada gown and went with Wendell's flowing number to honour Deepa's wishes.

The day of the premiere was a blur of pale impressions. I remember asking for a shawl and getting shot down (*"Ees not elegant, spider"*), and avoiding eye contact as I snatched a cinnamon bun from a passing room service trolley. My parents were coming, and with my mother in a wheelchair, I had appealed to make sure she could come down the red carpet. While I was being wrangled from place to place, a kind publicist named Bonne Smith took over the arrangements to make sure my mother had a good seat. As a stylist pinned me into the white dress, I had a small realization: I'm part of this world. I'm part of the entertainment game and I should feel very privileged to have this experience, rather than scrutinize it from every angle and doubt my place. I think I was trying, just a little, to meditate on the experience, and to live it fully, from inside, as Nadama might.

My on-screen love interest, John Abraham, was there (provoking some jealousy from Marco and hysterical screams from the Bollywood fans who had gathered at the theatre), and the actress who played little Chuyia had been flown in from Sri Lanka. She was very sweet and the most un-self-conscious spark in the experience. In my long white backless gown, I was more comfortable on the red carpet this time, beginning to make sense of the flash of the light bulbs. I finally figured out how to separate the shouting paparazzi from one another and find an actual photographer on whom to focus which made it easier, but it was still a fury of microphones springing in my face and disembodied voices behind blinding lights.

Then, when I paused to pose with John, I saw my parents. My mom had been wheeled to the end of the red carpet and my father stood next to her. He was in a suit—a rare sight in those days—and my mom was wearing a vivid, oil painter–blue blouse, her golden loop earrings and lipstick. They were a vision. My mother's eyes had noted the entire circus, but she was focused on me. They were enjoying the moment and had somehow carved out an intensely private space at this most public of events. They looked proud and abiding, even with my mother shifting from side to side in her chair and I wanted to join them. John saw them too and actually pushed me in their direction. I let out a little scream and let the masquerade drop. I inelegantly skipped past the photographers to my mother and bent low to wrap my arms around her and then stood and hugged my father. I squeezed my mother's hand and didn't want to let go. I was smiling harder than I had in a long time.

After this pause, I was swept off again into the crowd. One of the PR assistants trailed me, trying to readjust the train of my gown which had got twisted. My mom had a place specially set aside at the front of the theatre that she could access in her wheelchair. I was seated in the upper circle balcony with the cast. The entire theatre watched the film in a sort of reverential silence. I could picture my parents" rapt faces. But I didn't meet them again until the after-party. This was their trademark: to move humbly yet uncompromisingly through the world. I always remember them there on the edge of the red carpet, fuss-free and watching from the periphery, yet still finding the best vantage point.

Inside the cavernous Roy Thompson Hall, I watched the film for the first time. I think I wept in the dark. I felt a great sense of achievement but also knew that were I not in it, I would still love this film. It's the kind of cinema that I cherished, imbued with a deep compassion for the human condition. It brought to mind what Akira Kurosawa had said about Satyajit Ray's Apu trilogy: "Not to have seen the cinema of Ray means existing in the world without seeing the sun or the moon." I was thrilled that my father was there, with his love of the deeply observed cinema of Ray, which had so inspired Deepa when making *Water*.

At the end, there was a standing ovation and as we stood in front of the crowd, grinning and bowing, I thought: *This is a once in a lifetime experience. There's something about this film that's different.*

It was during the rounds of parties and press runs that I began to feel unusually drained and exhausted, sinking gratefully into the mattress at the end of the day, my arms and legs spreadeagled like I had fallen from a height. *Splat.* When I think back, I wonder if these were early signs of the illness to come. But it was hard to tell what might have been going on in my body when my schedule was as rigorous as that of a politician on a campaign trail. There had been an explosion of interest in the movie, and we were doing thirty or thirty-five interviews a day with journalists from around the world. A press junket works like this: The media outlets set up in rooms in the hotel and the "talent" is hustled back and forth. If you walk down any corridor of the Intercontinental during TIFF, you'll see bemused, famous faces being wrangled by publicists, marched between suites, everyone anxiously glancing at notebooks and electronic devices, picking at stray strands in their teeth when they think no one is looking. I got used to the strange, artificial atmosphere of intimacy that's created in a six-minute interview in a hotel suite, with untouched trays of food and undrunk coffee. Everyone is exhausted, even the journalists; you can see the strain on their faces as they try to get you to say something you haven't said to the ones who came before. I'd been through the machine on a smaller scale with *Bollywood/Hollywood*, but with *Water*, I immediately gauged that there was a different level of interest in the film. The questions were deeper and the response more real. For five days we were ferried around the Festival and then, without ceremony, we were done. It's a strange sensation when, all of a sudden, everyone fly off and return to their normal routines. The day after you wake, feeling like a jellyfish washed up on the sand.

The film had generated a certain buzz around me as well and I decided it would be a good idea to stay in North America for a while. I'd always loved New York. New Yorkers had the guts to wear their moods, turning the streets into rivers of unquiet emotions. I thrived off that pulse. Besides, I was thinking about hunkering down for the winter, opening a notebook and trying to make sense of the last few months' experiences. Life had become a split screen. Since I was already dividing my time between Paris and Milan, why not add New York to the mix? I'd have to remember they drove on the right side of the road and I'd be in constant peril of forgetting and getting mowed down, but I'd take my chances. Marco had agents in New York too and we decided to make the move together, at least temporarily. So, after TIFF ended, I flew down to New York City and found a great little sublet, an eighth floor walk-up at 12th and 2nd in the East Village, very close to Union Square. From my window, I'd look over my piece of the Apple and muse. This was the best place in the world to discharge all your opinions about the world; the air hung heavy with them. It was also an unusually social time. A few years ago, I'd become friends with Joshua Bell, the greatest violin virtuoso of this age as well as a recording artist and conductor. He performs around the world with a three-hundred-year-old Stradivarius violin, and when I heard him perform at one of his concerts, it was as if there was nothing between me and the sky; I shimmered and melted. We had met in Toronto at TIFF when he'd been there for the beautiful little indie film *The Red Violin*. He lived near my sublet and introduced me to many other artists (every other building in my neighbourhood seemed stuffed with writers and bicycles littering the stairwell). Salman Rushdie had been at the *Water* screening where we discovered we had mutual friends from the Bombay circuit, so occasionally I'd land up at a party with him. I'd met Suketu Mehta back in Bombay through the Soul Fry crew: a group of friends who gathered regularly at the Pali Naka seafood restaurant to share our exploits; since then he'd written a brilliant book called *Maximum City: Bombay Lost and Found*. The book charted his gritty return to Bombay after a twenty-one-year absence, and was a love letter to the city we both know so well. Just because it was nominated for the Pulitzer didn't mean Suketu was above grabbing a beer at the White Horse Tavern in the West Village, where Dylan Thomas drank himself to death. I happily pulled on my long boots that gave me that New York stride. I've always enjoyed the company of writers preoccupied with the headier questions of life, obsessed with how best to describe the uncomfortable bits of ourselves.

Marco loved New York too. He'd arrive from Europe, do a shoot, and then immerse himself in American kitsch. We'd order Daisy BBQ and wander the city, debating who served the best 'amburger, searching for vintage t-shirts with images of 1970s porn stars. At one point, he decided he needed to learn the sitar. "Spider, it is the most bea-u-tiful instrument!" As a surprise, while I was on assignment in India for Rado, I bought him one. It was a huge lump of a thing in a matching wheeled case that I checked at the airport in Delhi and then had to lug up eight floors in the brownstone, pausing at every landing while neighbours greeted me on their way down, but avoided offering help. Marco was thrilled. But how would he learn? Somehow, almost immediately, he found a woman two buildings over who was a sitar teacher. This seemed like a very only-in-New-York moment. I had a Canadian agent to add to the mix, Jennifer Goldhar of the Characters Talent Agency, and while I was sent all over the world to promote *Water* during that period, when I was back in New York, the agency sent me scripts and I hung out with thinkers who played hard at midnight. I shot the occasional small film and also watched a lot of theatre but what I remember most about that time in New York was sitting at my desk, writing. I had with a clear view of the neon sign for Veniero's, the oldest Italian pastry shop in the US, while in the other room Marco plucked at the sitar.

In the middle of all these stimulating diversions I got another email, this one from Deepa in late 2006, telling me that the movie was being submitted by Canada to the Academy for the Best Foreign Film Oscar. This was a huge surprise. The Academy had always stuck to an arcane rule that movies nominated needed to be in the native language of their country, so an Italian film produced outside Italy still had to be shot in Italian. But in the era of globalization, this rule was starting to create problems. The year before, an Italian film shot in Turkish had been disqualified so film-makers had been lobbying for updated regulations. Lo and behold, the rule changed. A year earlier and we wouldn't even have qualified. When I got the call about *Water* being shortlisted for the award, I had just finished a little film called *A Stone's Throw* and, as much as I consider myself an indie alternative girl, I was thrilled to be in a film—my first out of drama school—nominated for an Oscar.

And yet . . . it's hard to believe but being part of an Oscar-nominated film doesn't necessarily translate into a great change in your life overall. It's tricky territory, especially for someone at my level of the game. A huge, established star knows how to make it work to her advantage but for a relatively unknown (and socially dyslexic) actor it can actually add up to a huge pain in the ass. First, it's extremely expensive. You have to hire a stylist, which can cost thousands. I'd never used a publicist, but eventually I hired one out of my own pocket just to handle all the requests. Deepa had to lobby extra hard to get us all invited to the awards ceremony because a limited number of seats and tickets are allocated to the nominees in each category. Deepa wanted her entire cast to be there, and while I was offered a ticket, many others weren't. A hierarchy had emerged from what had been such a warm, collective shoot. I wanted to bring my parents down, but it wasn't feasible. There was no way to get them tickets to attend the ceremony, and the logistics seemed insurmountable. They would have to watch from their living room in Toronto. But the Academy Award nomination did have one immediate, dramatic effect: overnight, I was on the Hollywood radar. I was invited to Los Angeles to meet managers and agents. The calls seemed to arrive daily: The X-Men franchise was sniffing around. I was being considered for a part in *The Kite Runner*. "Come on down!" called Los Angeles.

I wasn't sure what to make of it, or whether I should do anything at all. I'd never imagined myself in Los Angeles which seemed like a land of over-exercised blondes. The LA actors I'd encountered were relentlessly upbeat. Did they have no angst, doubts, shadows in their lives? I'd been living in Europe long enough to find effusiveness rather alarming. ("Awesome" still wasn't part of my vocabulary—neither were "green juice" and "organic yeast.") I was also very suspicious about what I thought of as "the Club-Led" lifestyle where the latest trend is slavishly followed (bubble butts, spirulina, Von Dutch t-shirts, turmeric latte, ayahuasca) and everyone moves around in cliques, like high school. I still felt insecure about myself as an actor. I had, for all intents and purposes, been professionally cosseted up until then, but in LA all bets would be off. It was the biggest, thorniest, most savage playground. Yet I also knew this was a unique opportunity to learn the movie business at the source and I'd never passed up a chance to change locations, so off I went.

I found a sublet through my manager, but it reflected my ambivalence: the house wasn't in Los Angeles proper, but Santa Monica, which was really a little far to be practical, but the kind of distance I needed for my sanity. I got to the little apartment to find a surfboard propped up against one of the walls in the kitchen—very clichéd. It was a cool Cali place in a great walking neighbourhood, which is unusual for LA. I immediately hit the street, asking the first person I saw to direct me to the beach. I walked down Montana Avenue, with its cafes and bookstores, towards crashing waves and the shaggy tops of palms. I arrived to find the sun scattering diamonds across the ocean. I turned my face into the breeze and breathed in freedom and salty, lusty appetites. The wind blew and I stood still.

As an actor you imagine that you'll spend all your time in acting classes or working on meaningful projects and hanging around other "creative types." But then there's the business side, which involves meeting people in suits (in LA "suits" can also mean a subset of men and women in dressed-down but expensive tees, jeans and baseball caps) who can corral and sell your talent. Some of the best actors I knew were very shrewd about this aspect of their lives, in ways I'd avoided. I'd been floating all this while, letting the offers land. Yet again serendipity had led me to this place; I was amused by the entire situation more than anything else. "Here I am again—living someone else's dream." Everyone was vying for each other's attention; it was like a big romantic courtship at first. As soon as I got to LA, I was taken out for lunch and dinner, sometimes two of each a day. ("It's like speed dating," another actor told me.)

One day I had scheduled six or seven meetings in a row at the W Hotel with people who wanted to represent me. I chose a corner banquette. I would not move from there for the next few hours, the table gradually filling with lemonade glasses and coffee cups and contracts casually laid down, "just to go over for you and your lawyer's reference." They were coming and going, singing and dancing about all they could do for me (what I could do for them, the dollar signs in the eyes, was less discussed). Now I realize that kind of position doesn't come around that often, but at the time, it was a little bit of an out-of-body experience. I heard Nadama's voice as my own: "The world is your field of practice. TAKE THREE BREATHS BEFORE DOING ANYTHING."

A manager is a long-term relationship: it's the marriage; agents are the affairs that come and go, according to where you are on the popularity metre. Agents bounce around between agencies, so they look to capitalize on a moment, while the manager is looking at your entire career. The wonderful Danielle Thomas with Untitled Entertainment, an agency that handled Naomi Watts, became my manager. (Who wouldn't want to be associated with that kind of talent!). Danielle is from Texas and she's ballsy as hell. She can take on the boys, is openly gay and talks a mile-a-minute. I chose her because she seemed to get the fact that I was in two worlds, with a substantial profile and fan base on the other side of the planet. LA was just beginning to wake to the possibility of exploiting the Indian market. My agent, Brinda Bhatt, was of Indian origin, and she, too, had a sense of my global cache (her agency, UTA, also represented Johnny Depp, which worked for me). I was surrounded by savvy, strong women. But it was an odd feeling sitting in their offices, listening to them talk: "How do we position her?" "Should we send her here? There?" "How do we exploit and optimize her position?" I existed in the third person, herded from place to place. I wanted to take the full measure of it like any experience but without getting trapped. I was still looking at this as an adventure, not a serious career move.

My days were packed with meetings, morning to night. Every evening, Brinda would courier me scripts and audition pieces, and a schedule of the next day's appointments. Pilot season began shortly after I landed, with thousands of actors descendind on LA to audition for all the new TV series. I would see the others when I drove into the city, in waiting rooms and at the agencies. Most were up in Studio City, not Santa Monica. I lived where Reese Witherspoon lived; any actor that far out of the city didn't have to do a half-dozen look-sees per day—except for me. I had skimped on GPS, believing I could manage without, so I'd print maps the night before and zip along the highway in my rental car every morning. Thank God for traffic jams because that was the only time I got to read the maps and figure out where I was going.

I somehow got shortlisted for the first pilot I auditioned for. But I had been working with an acting teacher in NY who taught his students never to memorize the lines, but "lift them from the page." This technique proved disastrous in the final round of the audition. I stood in the centre of a mini coliseum, studio execs staring down from the bleachers at me, poker-faced. I was carrying my sides which was already considered a no-no and then, instead of "lifting the lines," I ended up dropping everything in a flurry of papers and apologies. When my agent called to ask me how it went, I couldn't stop laughing. It was the best worst audition in the history of auditions, and if you had to blow it, blow it big, I said. Shortly afterwards I was asked to come in and audition for *The Kite Runner* with Marc Forster, another director whose work I admire. He had made *Monster's Ball* with Halle Berry, which earned her an Academy Award for best actress in 2002—the first black actress to win.

In person, Marc is a bit skittish. You can tell his brain is going 200 miles an hour—he's there yet not there. The reading went really well, but the message that came back was one I'd heard before: "She's too pretty for the role. And she doesn't look Afghani enough." My agent's job is to push, so they sent him messages that I could look very ordinary—hell, I could appear any way they want. "He thought you were great, and when he has the right part down the road, he'll call," they said. I thought about a younger version of myself and how she might respond. Instead of feeling belittled, Marc and I started an email correspondence and became friends. LA, which I had expected to be superficial, turned out, from my experiences, to be refreshingly real and gregarious. It was during this time that I met Terence Stamp, the legendary British actor. We shared an agency, and he sent a message saying he'd enjoyed *Water* and wanted to meet. Billy Budd wanted to hang! We used to meet at the Chateau Marmont for brunch on Sundays, which would often run until five-thirty in the evening. Stardom was on Terence's terms: "I always insist they keep me at the Chateau," he said. "I don't stay anywhere else in LA. Take it or leave it."

Terence is as magnetic in person as he is on screen. He knows things, and he loves stories and imparting his knowledge and experience, but he has a great economy of words. He'll just drop a hint of his wisdom here and there, but never paint the entire picture—pulling out the meaning is your job.

He had lived everywhere, including the Osho ashram in Pune for a decade, long after becoming a movie star. He had also become an organic farmer on an island off the coast of England in the 1990s. He'd experimented with Sufi dancing. I was completely enthralled by his stories: I remember actually clapping my hands in childish glee, some heavyweights having a meeting in the corner of the Chateau's court-yard throwing me glances. *"Who is this strange girl and why is she not adhering to the rules of the cool department?"* But here I was with some-one who had made a living as an actor and led a full life off-screen as well. Terence had protected his personal spirit and growth while navi-gating this LA world, even subverting it, working it to his advantage. Terence doesn't use technology—no email, no cell—so our encounters were always face-to-face, intense and utterly personal.

"Just make sure I don't start speaking in an LA accent," I once told him in the middle of our fourth cup of tea.

"Sorry to tell you this but I don't think you have it in you darling."

One morning at the Chateau, I spied Forest Whitaker. He was nomi-nated for best actor for his terrifying portrayal of Idi Amin in *The Last King of Scotland*. I'd been taking some acting classes with Catlin Adams, who had coached Nicole Kidman and Naomi Watts. Fresh in my head was a tenet I'd learned from her: "If life teaches us to suppress our impulses, acting teaches us to follow them." Constant suppression means it's impossible to be open and express what's really going on. Taken to an extreme, it's a justification for actors acting out, but this time Catlin's voice was in my head when I decided that I would accost Forest Whitaker. He's a big, broad, tall man and I rushed up to him (I probably reached his chest) and blurted, "I really admire your work, and I want to introduce myself." He looked at me very directly, radiating quiet dignity, and said, "I've heard of your film. I'd love to see it. Let's do lunch sometime." I came out of there beaming, bounding across the lobby of the Chateau Marmont where everyone else was sprawled across lounge chairs. "Did you see that, Terence! I'm going to have lunch with Forest Whitaker!"

"Of course you are, my dear," he said, as if it were the most normal thing in the world.

I was more thrilled to meet Forest Whitaker than I would have been to meet George Clooney. I instinctively felt he was an actor I could learn from, he just *knew* things. Tibetans believe the deepest knowledge is passed through transmission of energy; sometimes nothing even needs to be said between people for an exchange to happen. I felt certain that simply being in Forest's presence would provide me with insight. We did finally have lunch in Toronto months later, but before that, he sent me a beautiful email:

> Lisa —
>
> When we met I had not had the opportunity to see *Water*. Although I had been made aware of the film's story, the director and some of the actors involved inside it. Over the last number of months, I've not had the luxury to see the many films I have wanted to see. But after meeting you and feeling your spirit I took the opportunity after shooting today to see your film. It is so powerful and your work is beautiful.
>
> I was moved to tears more than once and the honesty clarity subtlety and truth of it were transcendent. Your work was all those things and filled with your spirit. Watching you descend into the river's waters to end your life was disturbing, painful and beautiful at the same time. Thank you for taking me on the journey of the heart that the film took me through and the profound light that it sheds on the subject.
>
> Please send my congratulations to the director for the message and gift of her film. And to the other actors who gave their spirits to it. I will carry with me the final image of the widow at the train station looking to camera making me search for the answer. Leaving me deeply affected by the WATER and the emotions I have been submerged in . . .
>
> All god's blessings and light
>
> Forest

My agents really wanted to push me into mainstream projects whereas I was more inclined to go for little indies. But then they had an offer so big it couldn't be ignored: the Wachowski Brothers were casting for an adaptation of the Japanese manga *Speed Racer*, and they wanted to see me.

The Wachowskis are the mad geniuses behind the Matrix trilogy, and I knew I had to meet them. I went to a huge studio (with an even huger parking lot) on one of LA's palm tree–lined streets. They were conducting mock trials to see how the actors would interact with the CGI. I found myself in a hangar of a room, empty except for a green screen. Out came the Wachowskis, shaking my hand. They were a study in contrasts. Andy was big and beefy, a real Chicago bruiser, very smart but very humble. Meanwhile, Larry was transitioning, going through process of gender re-assignment. (Andy would begin his own transition years later.) They were incredibly attractive, dressed in black and oozing sensuality and emotional intelligence. Larry in particular struck me as a bright, open being, deeply philosophical and intensely focused on the work at hand. It was an intoxicating mix.

I was locked in the studio for twelve hours a day, wearing bodysuits and elaborate costumes, hooked up to machines and harnesses. It was highly technical work and extremely physical. It was also top secret and I had to sign a confidentiality form, so I couldn't explain to Deepa why I had to miss a lot of the pre-Oscar parties and events. She thought I was being haughty, but really, I was flying across a green screen in lycra all day long. Finally, on the day of the Oscars, I had to tell the Wachowskis I needed to leave early. Andy looked up from his monitor: "Oh yeah, the Oscars." They really live in their own cerebral, sci-fi world, unimpressed with the preoccupations of the mainstream, even when their movies make billions.

Because I was working such long hours, I had left everything to the publicists, including dress selection. Marco called from Milan. I was distracted and stressed, unable to concentrate on his words. It was the same with my parents. As I sat in my little apartment, getting worked on by the glam squad, sealed in a self-absorbed actor bubble, I felt unsupported and cranky. This was not boding well. At first the drive to the Oscars was a little bit of a disaster. When I got into the limo with Deepa and a few others from *Water*, I was greeted with a decidedly cool reception. Everyone was silent. Deepa had wanted us to come dressed in sarees. She wanted to pay tribute to the widows whose stories we were representing. I respected the sentiment, but it also seemed like a marketing spin, and, as happens when my mind is cluttered with opinions and commands, I took a defiant route. I wanted to wear something of my own choice. In the end my time was so tight that I ended up wearing a dress I didn't even like that much. It was a rusted bronze colour, and long, and not very well fitted because we didn't have time to alter it properly. I felt okay in it but not terrific, and clearly Deepa disapproved. In the limo I tried to explain that if I'd seemed absent it was because I was working on a project that I couldn't yet discuss. I attempted to break the ice. Gradually, as we drove through LA and approached the traffic and noise that signalled the Oscar zone, the excitement of the event overtook any tension. We had an all-access pass to the great, mad carnival, and it was time to take it in.

Padma patra evam bhasa
Live like the lotus flower

Beeeep! Our driver was blaring his horn at the limo in front of us. There was a massive jam all the way down Hollywood Boulevard. Barriers lined the sides of the street. All the crazies were out with their signs proclaiming love for George Clooney and that the end was nigh. The streets around Kodak Theatre (renamed Dolby Theatre in June 2012) were closed off. Crowds craned to get a look at who was in the limos. The anticipation was building, and a wave of noise from the crowd enveloped the parade of stretch limos. Surreal. At last, we pulled up, the doors opened, and we were deposited into a posse of PR people and publicists, each frazzled and overwhelmed.

The actual red carpet in front of the theatre is not as big as you imagine. It's almost rectangular, wider and shorter. I stepped into the flash-lit stream of celebrities. Cameron Diaz swept in and posed and preened, working the photographers packed in amphitheatre-like rows. A scrum circled Tom Cruise as he walked. At one point, my favourite actor, Gael Garcia Bernal, was within arm's length and I wondered if he would catch me if I swooned. They seemed like holograms; I was sure that if I reached out to touch someone, there would be nothing there. And yet they radiated that very American quality: the pursuit of success as a human birthright, while seemingly pinching themselves on the inside now that they had arrived. This ascension of celebrity

epitomized by the Oscars—to come from obscurity and become globally celebrated and famous—was the taste of omnipotence. Was I in
this private club, drinking in the ferocious showmanship in swigs
(nudge, nudge, wink, wink)? Or split from the pack, taking it in from
the sidelines, wide-eyed with disbelief? I had always kept room in my
heart for the unimaginable. But entering the Kodak Theatre, the air
crackling with influence and power, I felt pulled off balance as if by a
tailwind. Steven Spielberg walked by on the double barrel staircase.
De Niro. Dustin Hoffman. Tom Hanks—all these icons are much
more compact in real life then you might imagine and they seemingly skated past me like we were each executing our choreography
on some bizarre ice rink: Oscars on Ice. I tried to remember Nadama's
advice on embodied practice, how to have a telescopic lens on the
present. Take three breaths. Then talk. But really, it was hard to think
clearly, never mind breathe. I consented to being swept away. I've
never done coke or MDMA, or any recreational drugs for that matter,
but I imagine it feels something like a night at the Academy Awards.
But less dazzling.

All the nominees in our category, Best Foreign Film, were ushered in
together, which meant I got to say a few words to Catherine Deneuve,
who had been nominated for *Persepolis*. She was gracious and elegant,
regal with her long neck. Steven Spielberg walked by and said to me:
"Great film." I have no idea what I said to him; it's entirely possible I was
world-class witty, or that I said absolutely nothing. Everything about that
night is cast in a fuzzy glow. My co-star Seema Biswas and I were seated
a little higher up above the mezzanine, where we could gaze down on the
audience and where people could dart out and get drinks from the bar.
The entire ceremony was a blur. It was also very long and at some point,
I had to pee and then I couldn't get back to my seat until the next break,
which was actually a relief as all the insider action seemed to be happening there, by the wood-paneled bar.

Finally, we came to our category. They read out the nominations,
I saw our film flash on the screen, and then—we lost. I was so high from
the experience that it didn't seem like a loss, but when I saw Deepa
afterwards in the swarm of people exiting the building, she looked
crushed. We had all been invited to the legendary *Vanity Fair*

after-party but Deepa decided she didn't want to go. The limo dropped me back in Santa Monica. I would have to drive myself.

The thing about living in Santa Monica: I could never find my car. It's street parking with all kinds of by laws: Tuesday and Thursday, but not between 3 a.m. and 6 a.m. . . . the rules were impenetrable. I used to have a little log in which I wrote down where I'd parked, so I could run out and move my car to the opposite side of the street before it got towed. But then I'd forget to cross out the most recent spot and then I would find myself in vehicle purgatory, running up and down Montana, peering at license plates. So, naturally, after the Oscars ceremony, I couldn't find my car, and was becoming so stressed that I began yelling into the night, "Where the fuck is my car? Someone help me find my car!" while combing the streets in my Oscar dress. I actually have absolutely no memory of how I made it to the party, except there must be an LA taxi driver out there with a story about a crazy woman who flagged him down in a golden dress because she was late for the *Vanity Fair* party. I mean, lady, haven't you heard of a car service?

Outside, I posed in front of the big *Vanity Fair* logo where the stars are ushered (it's like being in the centre of a dartboard) and the paparazzi clicked obligingly. I went in on my own. The ceremony was over and now I could just take it all in, breathe in the privilege and the power. More than the Oscars, the VF party was packed to the rafters with celebrities, mixed together without hierarchy. I stood still for a moment, watching the light dim. All the Kates were there! Winslet had won something, or maybe it was Blanchett. The people were as beautiful as everyone says, and the celebrity aura made it almost impossible to be nervous because it couldn't possibly be real. I found a corner and accessed a bowl of deep space within me from where I could exhale in my crumpled gown.

I enjoy circling and observing, wallflowering under cover of the crowd. I've always loved that position, and I loved it more with a glass of champagne in my hand. The room was loud. People clutched their Oscars as they walked by. Kirsten Dunst was really rocking out, dancing like the floor was on fire, admirably on her own plane. The milling crowd bumped me, swivelled and bared their dazzling teeth, then parted as I forced my way through, like a Steadicam operator intent on getting the shot. Everyone is trying to figure out who you are, how you fit in and there's a certain amount of canine sniffing to figure it out. But the only person I really wanted to speak to was Sean Penn who I spotted instantly, lurking in the shadows with Dennis Hopper. It was just like high school: the bad boys off in the corner. Sean Penn is the only man who makes me weak in the knees. I love his whole persona, and how his talent is mixed with a little bit of vinegar. I love his rebellious nature. I love what he stands for. I took a glass of champagne, walked up to his table and said, "I've always wanted to meet you."

He looked at me for a moment, like he was trying to place me. Then he patted an empty space beside him. I sat down.

"What are you doing here?" he asked.

"I'm part of *Water*. Have you seen it?"

"No, but I hear it's great."

We chit-chatted a little while. He listens more than he talks. I consciously didn't want to appear to be babbling so I left some long significant silences, during which I got to simply look at his face. He's got those hypnotic actor's eyes. He was smoking, very soft movements with his hands. It might have only been a few moments, but it felt like a long time. He did ask me to go to another party, but I had to pry myself away. It was not going to end well if I stayed. As I got up, leaving a kiss on the cheek, I realized that I had been galvanized in a different direction. The closer I moved to the apex of the entertainment world, those invisible heights, the more I was singed. I walked towards the exit purposefully. In my vast imagining, I saw all those famous faces turn towards me silently as I brushed past and line up like the chorus of a Broadway musical: *Whatever you are looking for here, you don't need it. Whatever you are look for, it's not here. What are you looking for?*

Geez, I thought. What moves you? What do you want to say?

I didn't get the part in *Speed Racer*; it went to Christina Ricci instead, and in a sense it was okay. I loved the Wachowskis but I didn't have passion for the film they were making. I could never say that to my talent team though. "This is how it went in LA, nibble after nibble leading to the big bite," they told me.

I had become disenchanted with the Hollywood scene after just a few months. Be cool, be feminine but not too girly, be ethnic but not too ethnic, be sexy, be smart, be the woman every man desires—the masks demanded of me were endless. Then just a few weeks after the Oscars, in the spring of 2007, a small script crossed my desk: *The World Unseen*. It was going to be directed by a young London-based South African-Indian named Shamim Sarif, based on her own novel. It was just the sort of against-all-odds story that held immediate appeal. And it was female centric to boot. I agreed to go to South Africa. My agents were apoplectic. "You're hot *now*! They love you in the room. Stay in LA!" But to me it was a heartfelt project, a way to pluck myself back into being, no matter how small and obscure. And below the surface maybe I was freaked out and confused and needed an escape route. But it was not just that. "This place is not for you," the voice said, "enjoy it but don't disappear into it." I was, by then, done with even the LA air.

The World Unseen, set in 1950s Cape Town during apartheid and follows two South African women of Indian origin who fall in love in a racist, sexist, homophobic society. I threw myself into the role of this modest, shy unglamorous housewife who starts finding her voice and feeling an attraction to another woman that's never fully expressed. I loved the research, working on the accent, learning about apartheid. I visited Robben Island and eventually stood in the cell where Mandela had been held.

When Marco heard the script, he warned me not to immerse myself too fully in the role. "You can hold back a bit. You don't have to cut your hair off." So what did I do? First thing, when I got to Cape Town, I had my hair cut and dyed black. I had allowed myself to be controlled by men before, and I wanted that to end. Completely. I had to own myself for better or worse. I lived in South Africa for three months, and I still hold that experience dear: in fact, I think that film is my best performance. Outside the life of the film I explored Cape Town, walking up and down Long Street. Discussions on mixed-race identity provoked me to reflect again on my own choices and the struggle that mixed-race—"bridge" individuals—people have. Under apartheid, ethnic groups were cruelly codified in the most inhumane ways. While mixed-race identities were clubbed together as coloured, the most disturbing stories I heard were of the pencil test, where a pencil was pushed through a person's Afro-textured hair to determine racial identity. Families and communities were split according to how "easily" the pencil passed through. Over koeksisters and bobotie, I listened to an unravelling of personal histories, feeling like we were passing stones across a riverbed in the stories of mixed-up identities, of wild dispositions reined in by ethnic policing and the fires you have to set inside and outside yourself to break free. *The enemy of suppression is giving voice to our wounds and injustice. Each voice adds weight until the whole world tilts,* I wrote in my journal. And even though carjackings and violence persisted, I kept walking and walking, feeling my unguarded chest a wearable shrine. I poured myself into my character but I also wanted the whole movie to shine. When I came out on the other end I was drained. On the last day of shooting I couldn't get out of bed. It was very difficult for me to be around people—they gave me this buzzing sensation, as if I could feel what they were thinking. I was one long exposed nerve. I spent a few days lying in bed, staring at the ceiling limply, in this beautiful apartment, very close to the V & A Waterfront docks.

Slowly, Shamim and her partner, Hanan Kattan, who is also CEO of the film company they co-founded, Enlightenment Productions, mothered me out of it, and I returned home. But the episode was a signal and when I flew to Paris to recover, Marco was waiting for me. "You always come to me when you are destroyed," he said. "You don't know how to manage your life."

He was right. He was used to seeing me work or push myself to the point of emotional breakdown or illness. Sure enough, I would wash up, broken and in need of healing, whether it was Milan, Paris or the sublet we hung on to in New York. Though I had been trying, I still hadn't come close to the mythical idea of "balance" or even prioritising my days. *Everything* was on priority and my center could not possibly hold. The regular meditation and yoga were loosening something inside, an edgy hostility that was coming to the surface. What's with that? I thought these practices were supposed help me self-soothe, to calm me the fuck down. Instead, I was overwhelmed by my interior landscape and edging towards eruption. What Marco said came out of a sense of tough love. It amounted to: "I can't help you any more until you start to help yourself." It was true, but it also triggered my ugliest reflex: listen like a disinterested bystander. Then run.

I pre-empted what I thought was inevitable. "Then it's over." I regretted it as soon as I said it. Marco's eyes coarsened while his finger-tips brushed the tip of his nose in an achingly familiar gesture. I was sad, so sad, but I didn't say it. The sadness hung like silk between us. "Okay, Spider. But you keep the possibility of to grow. Always. And don't become extinct. Like the bees." Whatever words and ideas of my own emerged in that moment, I buried.

He had been the type of lover who heard me even when I didn't speak. I had thrown myself into Marco's world. Who would I be now? There floated between us all the meals we would not take, the solilo-quies about becoming a "park ranger," all the Marco-isms on fame, on how beauty lies in proportions. I had fucked up.

I left Paris and flew to Milan, to Nadama and Krishna. They took me in, this broken and weeping version of myself. A week in, the tragic feeling persisted, covering me like a heavy shawl as I moved darkly from the shower and to the sofa. I was sick of it. Nadama made me cof-fee and I sat in their living room and cried fat tears.

"Okay, so now you have reached the basement. Do you have the cour-age to look within? Are you ready to really grow?" she asked me. "Are you ready to make conscious choices, or do you want to keep floating?"

13

LEAVING EUROPE AND Marco was not the end of love. The enduring obsession of my heart, my old flame would always be India. It's
just that when it came to people I didn't fare so well. I asked myself at
the time whether I could continue to praise the path that led me to this
moment; to question my notions about romantic love and to find solace
in the tenuous grief of endings. It was in my hands to cheerfully submit
to the universe not only in times of happiness, but also in loss and ambiguity. It was a new and crucial line of questioning that began while I
was still in Milan, moping from espresso bar to espresso bar, shuddering
after each shot of the dark sludge like an alcoholic. *"Voglio andare a li,"*
I faux-slurred to one of the courteous bartenders, pointing out a cafe on
a map I used to visit with Marco, "I want to go there. *Pronto*! I mean,
adesso." On one of my many cafe crawls through streets peddling visions
of chic, happy couples I began to see how it was a trap; this leasing of
your heart. For all my flowering self-awareness there was still a hungering for connection, for communion, for the emotional excess that comes
from it. But this time, I reined in the impulse to move on to another
adventure, another city, another man. Maybe the biggest laugh is that
love has been here all along? Maybe it was time to pay myself a house
call. Maybe leaving this time wasn't to find adventure, love or freedom.
Maybe it was to find me.

In the summer of 2007, I was called back to Canada. My mother was
ill, and my father asked me to return. I flew to Toronto from Milan,

where I'd been staying with Nadama and Krishna, and sent a message to my talent management in LA: I'm still not coming back. The muscles in my mother's chest weren't strong enough to get rid of mucous from any infection so she was prone to pneumonia. Her breathing had become erratic and she needed to be hospitalized. I drove directly from the airport to Sunnybrook to see her. It was distressing to watch her struggle to breathe. A nurse came around every half an hour to suction the phlegm, sending a tube down my mother's throat. Mom was thin and agitated over being stuck in a hospital bed. But when she saw me, she wasn't interested in discussing her own condition. "What is going on with you?" she croaked immediately. I was very pale, my complexion grey and sickly, and very tired. I shrugged it off as normal; after all, I was going through a break-up, and had just completed a gruelling shoot.

"You must go for a blood test, right now," she insisted. My mother was remarkable that way: she could take control of any situation, stirring up a storm even from a hospital bed. On her face was a look. I knew that squinty look. Before I could protest, I was sent to get a blood test in the very same hospital where she was recovering.

It turned out that my red blood cell count was alarmingly low. "It's just work," I told the doctor, but I was sent for an immediate iron infusion at a hospital in North York. There, I was ushered into the chemo day-care room. It was my first experience in a place like that; little did I know how much time I'd be spending in similar rooms where patients come for their chemotherapy dosing. Most are full of big overstuffed chairs with hand rests, the kind of furniture found in a gentleman's private club. Everything was maroon coloured. At each station, a person sat in the chair, hooked up to an IV pole, watching TV or chatting quietly with a friend or loved one. Only when I noticed that several of the patients were bald did it click: "I'm in a cancer ward." Panic balled up in my chest for a moment, but then I talked myself out of it: It's okay. This is just another experience. Breathe. Take three breaths. Mostly, I didn't want to bring any unnecessary anguish back home. My mom was in the hospital—that was enough for one family to contend with. At home I sat on my childhood bed, knees pressed to my chest and considered my options. I was tough. I could ignore this, look past it, stroll in the opposite direction.

A few days later, I had an appointment with a doctor who was curious about why my red blood cell count was so low. He told me he needed to investigate further with more tests. I said yes, certainly, mmm, hmm, yep. But I never followed up. The iron infusion had boosted my energy, and that seemed good enough. Instead, I stayed with my parents, washing dishes elbow to elbow with the Polish housekeeper, Mom's favourite Latin music in the background, lending ceremony to each mundane chore. I began matching my rhythm to theirs until my mom was better—something that had been inconceivable years ago. But so much had happened that used to be inconceivable. On evening walks around my old neighbourhood I was learning how to savour constancy and silence as seedbeds of resilience, a way to forge meaning from calamity. After she finally stabilized and moved back home, the pneumonia gone, I found myself in Bosnia.

Back in the Balkans after all these years. The mini-series was called *Zone of Separation*, a Canadian drama about the struggle of Bosnian peacekeepers. It had fallen into my lap through my Canadian agent, but I knew a few of the actors, and it seemed like a politically interesting project. It took us two-and-a-half days to reach our obscure location in Bosnia. We were staying in a post-Second World War industrial-looking town in the shadow of the Soviet boot. There was tension in the air anytime we left the set. The area was still scarred from the Bosnian war, and communications weren't well-established; most phones simply didn't work. So I was surprised the day someone walked up and handed me a phone, saying I had a call. I had been standing around with several actors, dressed as UN security peacekeepers, waiting to shoot. It was my father, telling me that my mother had taken a turn for the worse.

I stood there, feeling a section of the sky fall through me. My co-star Allan Hawco, who would go on to fame in the series *The Republic of Doyle*, saw me and took me aside. I explained what was going on and focused on his words. "You know what you need to do," he said. "We support you." And I did know but I felt myself confronted immediately with many issues I'd been pushing aside. I had a responsibility to my family but work had become my enabler; it allowed me to flee the stress of my mother's illness. I spent a few hours in that UN peacekeeper suit walking through the set of a fake war, trying to figure out my next move. I was still stinging from Marco saying: "You have to be willing to give and grow with someone. You cannot use the people who love you as your dumping ground." I decided to leave the series. They had to recast and send someone else to the hinterlands of Bosnia.

I returned to Toronto, brimming. Bosnia had stirred up morbid feelings in me. By the time I arrived, my mom was still in hospital, looking frail but all signs pointed towards improvement. *Women like us are built to endure.* After a few days she had nurses swarming in and out of her room, bringing her warm water, combing her hair on command, unburdening their relationship problems on her, while she presided over it all like the village medicine woman in a flowery nightgown. At night, stretched out on a mattress a head too short, I dreamed she was dancing from her stomach, shaking her hips before a fire like a shamaness. During the day I was present for my dad, living with him, sharing tasteless meals in the beige cafeteria. I had lived in Bombay, New York, Paris, Milan, and now I was back in my childhood bedroom, the purple shag unchanged. *There's no place like home ... You can always come home. Was everyone's life like this then? A tremulous, circular route that brought you back to where you started?* I was sleepwalking in my dreams, expecting to wake up eleven years old. Other things had remained unchanged, like the putty-coloured touch phone in the kitchen, making me jump until I remembered the "ringing prop from the seventies" hanging on the wall. It was a disorienting time. But my agents were still hustling for me and one evening I received a strange call. Months before, when I'd been in LA, I had taken a meeting with some executives from Sony. One of them was the daughter of the late great director Anthony Minghella. She had seen *Water* and wanted to meet me. "Have you seen *Casino Royale?*" she asked me. The film was a huge blockbuster at the time. "I never lie and sometimes it works to my advantage," I said. "So, no, I haven't seen it. It's not really my cup of tea." A few of the other Sony executives hovering nearby laughed a little nervously. "Perhaps we should send you a copy. We're rather proud of it," she said.

"Sure, why not?" I agreed.

"We'd like you to audition for the next one." Only then did I put two and two together. There were Bond posters on every wall. This was a prelim interview for a Bond film. "Really?" I wasn't trying to be coy. Never in my life had I thought I'd be considered for a James Bond film. "I think I'd make a great Bond Girl—not that I've ever seen one!"

In retrospect, this art-house cool was a little misplaced; I should have been simply gracious. Honesty has its place, but probably not on the Sony lot.

Still, it seems I hadn't entirely blown it, because my LA agent said: "They want to see you, like yesterday, in LA, for the Bond film. Marc Forster is directing."

It was a crazy convergence: my failed *Kite Runner* audition, and my great admiration for Marc had met with that awkward first interview at Sony, and now I had an audition for the biggest film of the year. Once again, serendipity had moved the pieces in my life. Now that my mom had stabilized, both my parents were jointly concerned about me: coaxing me out of my exile. "I love to have you here, but you must go back to life," my mother said. "It's because of the cord around your neck," she joked, "it's not your fault you can't stay in one place." I didn't discuss the Bond experience with my family. I had always been secretive about the details of my professional life. If I didn't talk about the auditions, the failures didn't sting so much.

Normally an actor would be expected to arrange one's own travel for an audition but I'd made the shortlist and the studio paid my way. I was given my sides as soon as I landed, which meant I had to learn my lines in the morning and audition in the afternoon. "*Tranquillo, tranquillo*," one of the hotel cleaning staff enjoined as she watched me pacing up and down my suite, repeating the lines over and over. This was the Bond franchise and the stakes were high. A flashy town car picked me up from the Beverly Wiltshire where I was staying. In the studio I sat down in a tiny room with a sofa and a table and about eighteen execs, some sitting on the floor. The only one I knew was Marc, who smiled supportively. They had chosen an actor to read with me who was dashing (check), square jawed (check) and debonair (check)—but was *not* Daniel Craig.

The sides were watermarked with my name and tightly guarded. Any leaks would be traced back to me. Auditions have never been my forte, but I felt I didn't have anything to lose. I had not yet come to terms with a morphing identity and this undesired opportunity I was pushed up against, so I used that angst, sat down and channelled this troubled but determined woman—not merely a spy, but a flesh and blood woman, brimming with silent torment. Very much . . . well, like me. I nailed it. After, they asked me to wait outside for a moment, where a couple of dark-haired, enigmatic actresses were sitting around, awaiting their turns. A few minutes later, Marc came out and said: "Great reading. We'll let you know but it's looking good."

I went back to my hotel, a little dazed. I had another audition for a movie I really wanted to be a part of: *The Wrestler*, directed by Darren Aronofsky. It would turn out to be the film that revived the career of Mickey Rourke, but all I knew at the time was that Aronofsky was a genius. My agents had lined up a bunch of meetings between the audition for the Bond film and the one for *The Wrestler*, and I hadn't found a minute to look at the full script. Still, I had learned my lines and in I went, reading the part of a stripper who becomes the love interest of Rourke's washed-up wrestler. During my audition, something was moving through me; I embodied her loneliness, her toughness. I believe that the best acting should look like anyone can do it—natural and fluid. But of course, there's an alchemy between technique and letting go. This time it came together perfectly.

"Fabulous," said the casting director. "I really like what you did with the character. Very unexpected. What did you think of the script?"

Bluntness seemed to be working in my favour lately, and, naively, I tried it again: "I didn't get a chance to read it."

A shadow moved across her face. "Okay. We'll call Brinda then."

I left the audition feeling deflated and elated at once, worried about my bad judgement, but pleased with my performance. I went to meet my agents. They were waiting for me at the blue astro-turf pool deck of the Standard Hotel. I started to explain about *The Wrestler*, telling them how that was the kind of small, edgy film I was dying to be a part of, when Danielle, my manager, interrupted me: "You've been shortlisted for Bond!" Even as celebratory, kitschy cocktails were ordered, my mind somersaulted into Bombay huckster territory, "shamelessly assuming" that I am, indeed, special while at the same time biting into the gold coin thrown at me. But there was one more thing: Barbara Broccoli, doyenne of the franchise, wanted to meet me.

The next day, I drove across LA in my rental car to meet Barbara at the Santa Monica office of Eon Productions, the British film production company that produces the James Bond films. Her half-brother, Michael Wilson, stood next to her. I immediately sensed just how much the Bond franchise is a family affair, closely guarded and tended. Barbara wanted to know personally anyone who might come close, and possibly sully it. She is an incredible woman, open, accessible, warm; very down to earth, despite having grown up with a great deal of privilege. She gives off a little bit of mothering energy and I was reminded of my long-ago mentor, Maureen Wadia. Barbara and I hit it off to the point where I didn't feel like I was being interviewed at all. She told me some great stories about shooting for various Bond films, and then Michael asked me: "How are you with heights?"

"I'm okay, I think. But tell me there'll be a harness and a big crew!"

And that was it. I went away beaming. It was really a leap-worthy meeting and I drove down to the beach next to the Santa Monica pier to leave some craters in the sand. Even if this goes nowhere, I told myself, what a piece of cinematic history to have experienced.

It turned out, my agent in London, Aude, is a good friend of Barbara Broccoli's, and a little lobby group was formed. Three agents and a manager in LA were working on the studio there, sending messages to Barbara, while my English agent was doing her part from London. But we didn't hear from them. That's that, I thought, and I headed back to Canada. I was enjoying time with my parents, falling into a calming daily rhythm after so many years of erratic schedules. Then, a month later, I came indoors from our backyard garden carrying a sieve of cherry tomatoes to a voicemail in a spy-like British accent: "We'd like you to come to London and screen test with Daniel Craig."

The script arrived by courier with my scenes bookmarked, my name watermarked across the top page. I liked the character: She would be the first Bond Girl that the spy doesn't (immediately) bed. She's out for revenge and they become partners. I had to figure out this South American accent. My acting coach hooked me up with a friend of hers from Chile and I recorded her speaking the lines. I'd walk around listening to those lines on headphones, trying to find the cadence. I went to another Toronto-based acting coach who advised me: "You must reach over and grab a lock of Daniel Craig's hair before you do the scene! Disarm him!" Just thinking about this made me sweat. Not a great look for an unflappable Bond Girl.

I was flown first class to London and put up at a great old hotel, The Landmark in Marylebone, a study in WASP swank. There were Aston Martins and Rolls Royces idling outside, abiding wealth and power in every glittering chandelier and embroidered wing chair. The whole operation was thrillingly top secret and eponymous, it bordered on the farcical. I knew there were two other actresses at the hotel (Olga Kurylenko and Gal Gadot), but I never saw them. We were moved in and out of rooms with the perfect timing of a French farce, never laying eyes on one another. This was a marked difference from traditional auditions where you're placed in a waiting room with your competition, everyone staring each other down. The next day I was driven out to Pinewood Studios, where all the Bond films have been shot as well as *Superman*, parts of the Harry Potter movies and, more intriguingly for me, Kubrick's *Full Metal Jacket*. I walked down the hallowed halls of this "rival to Hollywood with a very English air" in the words of a *Guardian* reviewer. I sat for make-up and then went to wardrobe, where I changed into fatigue pants and a tank top, nothing overly revealing—assassin chic which still, somehow, hinted at formidable sexual prowess.

Ready at last, sitting in the small dressing room with a thin, satin bathrobe over my clothes, I thought: *What am I doing here?* Marc popped his head in the door and gave me a warm hello. Barbara Broccoli appeared too. "Good luck, my dear," she said. I've never had such a respectful audition experience and I'm sure I never will again. Then, suddenly, a red-headed actress appeared in the dressing room: Bond Girl hopeful Gemma Arterton, spilling nervous energy from her audition for the role of Strawberry Fields. She said: "Well, I'm glad that's over."

My internal soundtrack was dimmed a bit on the "I'm a fraud" theme, but when I look back on that moment, I know that I shrank back to peer over a finishing line, and I wonder if it had to do with that red-headed actress. I know how it feels to really give it your all, and up until that point, I'd been giving my everything. But there, in Pinewood Studios, I had the strangest thought: I've cheated somebody else out of this chance by being here. I never wanted this. It fell into my lap, and I don't deserve it. I've gotten this far on luck, on serendipity, but this moment is as far as it goes.

Now, some years later, I have grasped the dynamics behind intentions and our messages: what we put out there is what we get back. But I was always setting myself up for great experiences, and then these nagging self-worth issues would interfere. The story in my head was always: *This isn't for you. This is thoroughly thrilling, but it's not yours.*

The studio was enormous. The scene was taking place in this barren rocky landscape, a set built solely for the auditions. As I took my place, the crew was very gracious, helping me find my mark. And then Daniel Craig walked in. It couldn't have been a more dramatic entrance: he was backlit with a halo of light around him, a perfect specimen outlined in silhouette, just in case I needed to be reminded of where I was. He cleaved the air as I stepped into his line of sight. In a career of them, that was definitely one of those *What-the-fuck?* moments. "*Things are kind of like a movie right now, a movie within a movie,*" I remember thinking. "*Let's see what the script holds.*"

Daniel Craig is very tiny, very physically dense, and he had an aura coming off him from the success of his last film. This was clearly his territory, and he was at ease and focused. I think my first mistake was that I tried to make a buddy out of him. I wanted to imprint myself on him, channel seductive siren, tell him to save the last dance for me. Instead, nervousness overtook me and I started cracking jokes. What I *wanted* to say was: I'm mesmerized by your blue eyes. What I said was: "My, how shiny are your shoes!" I made a shoe joke. Really. This makes me cringe even now. He smiled indulgently, but a rush of energy had exited the room.

"Do you want to run lines?" he asked, very earnest.

"No, no," I said. "Let's go into it."

I think I just wanted to get it done. The scene was poignant and intense. We were hiding under a bridge, pressed against polystyrene rocks moulded by the film's sculptor. No gravel beneath us. How I longed for gravel, something real that would anchor me in the moment. He put his arm around me, and I melted, which was very unprofessional, I admit, and which had never happened to me before. I had all sorts of contingencies in my mind, but I had not set aside one for being physically tormented by my co-star. Then Marc called, "Action!" and we were in the scene.

I think I had been concentrating too much on the accent, which can be fatal. I should have just concentrated on the emotion and added the accent later, but the night before, another acting coach had dropped by my room. She was part of the Bond franchise, there to help us prepare, running lines and working the dialect. Three different acting coaches had all offered their input on these two short scenes. It threw a spanner in my performance. Instead of a passionate flight of oratory, I could hear my South American lilt strangling itself mid-sentence. I started sounding like I'd been in a bar brawl in Edinburgh.

"Forget about the accent," said Marc, after the first take.

As if on cue, my mind clogged up. I'd been practicing so hard at sounding Chilean. Lose the accent? Which of my accents would I choose from now?

There was a pause while everyone prepared for the next scene. I kept trying to goof around with Mr Bond, and while he was only ever kind, I could feel something turning. He didn't go cold, but there was a distance between us, a nameless presence. Even as I regained some footing in the second scene, I couldn't bring him back.

"I've heard about your work, and thank you so much," said Daniel Craig at the end of the audition. Marc gave me a compassionate good-bye, revealing nothing.

I went to the dressing room and took off my make-up, feeling a bit chapped and tumble dried. But the opposite of numb. Defiantly giddy off the adrenaline, like I could climb a tree. The driver who took me back to the hotel let me out and with his cockney accent said: "Good luck, darlin'! Hope to see you back 'ere!" It was a rainy autumn evening in London. I walked around Paddington, the streets slick and reflective with rain, and had a good meal. *How difficult it becomes to relax with yourself when everything is dependent on being in flight from your essence.* It was a strange awakening to have. I went to bed that night thinking: Sometimes we take the wrong train to the right destination, sometimes the right train to the wrong place. And the next day, I got on a train at Paddington to catch my flight back to Canada.

I returned from London to the news that Mom was back in the hospital with pneumonia. This revolving door of illness and recovery was getting to be too much for her. When I saw her, she was drawn and paler than usual. In all her years of struggle with quadriplegia she had refused pain medication. She fought doctors and nurses to accommodate her quirks and impulses, shaking them out of neutrality to an acceptance of her not as a patient but as a human. "Doc, you look at me now, but you should have seen me when I was young. I would ask you to kill me, but I don't want you to get into trouble. How is your daughter?" I read their eyes when they were with her; my mother had the gift of awakening empathy in all sorts of specialists with cool gazes. Watching her with them highlighted something fundamental: the path from "everyone hates me" to "everyone is scared and unsure themselves, so when they appear to not care, it's a coping mechanism—don't take it personally, but don't take it lying down either."

"Please," she said. "I'm tired. Let me go. I've stayed around for you your father, but I've had enough. Let me go."

I had never heard her speak this way before. When I sat with her, she told me how she kept seeing herself disappearing into water. It was as if I could see her doing that right before my eyes, just sinking down, away from me. The doctors told me that it would get progressively harder for her to pull out of the pneumonia, and we should be prepared for the worst. I made a promise to her: "Mom, we're going to spend time together."

But it was difficult. Our relationship had always been charged, as it often is with mothers and daughters with beliefs that were outdated—yet hard to silence just the same. She was the controller; I lived at the knife's edge of myself. Even while prone in bed, from the next room she weighed in on everything, calling out commands to clip specific coupons patiently. We had a string of housekeepers and I'd grow frustrated about how she ordered everyone around. She would ignore my frustration and fuss over me, asking if I was eating enough, telling Magda to make me another sandwich (use the Havarti cheese we bought yesterday) or cut me some fruit (the organic apples) or slip some cod liver oil into my juice. She was just being a mother, and after so many years away, on my own, a deep, unacknowledged part of me wanted that mothering; I was hungry for it, in fact. But another part of me recoiled. I hated being treated like a child. "You think too much, rest your brain. Thinking so much is not good," was one of her refrains which infuriated me. It set me off into a line of protest—"Thinking, is that a bad thing?"—when if I'd stopped to consider, she was saying, albeit in her earthy way, what every other spiritual teacher would echo back at me: *There are other ways to perceive the word than through the mind.* But it was so hard to accept that all the wisdom I needed was right in front of me. And, more than that, she had enough emotional resources for a cruise ship of neuroses. Sometimes I wonder what would have been different if I had spent more time with her. Would I still have gotten tangled in these quirks of hers and miss her incredible courage, her truly superhuman courage?

I don't think I ever accepted what had happened to her. Binding myself to her disability, its struggles and inevitable ending was too painful. I lived outside that reality, concealing the loss behind family banter and bad behaviour. If I wanted to reclaim my mother, I would have to accept her monstrous power wheelchair with the joystick control and what it stirred up inside me. I had taken for granted that she would always be there, even though it was clear that she was slowly lowering herself into the water. My father had told me that we might lose her. So I made the promise: "If you get well, we'll have a great holiday together. I'll take time off from work. We'll really spend some time together." I think she heard me, because, miraculously, she got better.

My eating had been under control for a couple of years. In 2007, I turned thirty-six and I felt a new kind of pressure. The *Times of India* had voted me one of the "Top Ten Most Beautiful Women of the Last Millennium" and this dubious acclaim somehow always slipped into every interview I gave, like a calling card. My image in India, which seemed to chug along without me, was improbably still that of the glamour girl, the pin-up.

I was living on the periphery of Toronto, not integrated into the life of the city. I bought an apartment in the Beaches, a laid-back neighbourhood by Toronto's Lake Ontario. I loved taking walks along the boardwalk and ached to get a dog. I started practicing Moksha Yoga at a studio on Danforth Avenue, a home-grown hot yoga discipline started by Ted Grand and Jessica Robertson, both Canadian and both ex-Bikram teachers. I would take the occasional acting job and I was still flying off to India every few months for work. But now that I was in Toronto, I spent a lot more time with my mom, grasping finally the potency of presence and attention. "Today in yoga class the teacher said that when you receive what's happening, things open up in unexpected ways. Tension in body—and mind—happens when we resist reality and tell ourselves how things *ought to be*." I tried with this new language to communicate what had not been said before with my mom. I would clasp one of her hands in mine, stroking the gauzy skin of her inner arm, the flesh loose and soft. "Don't you want to tell me to eat more veggies or to quit thinking, Mama? All the things you take pleasure in?" I would tease when she closed her eyes. She would smile, her lids fluttering but not opening. She seemed bone-weary. I was also spending a lot more time with myself, experimenting with non-doing, finally taking time to digest my life. I would remain rooted to a meditation cushion on my floor, slow my breath and try to observe the movement of my mind to separate out the "stories" from who I am. It was the best sort of torture.

My thirty-sixth birthday passed, and it turned out that I was still an actress. It shocked me somehow; this little diversion had carried on for almost two decades. But I wasn't sure how to get older in this business. The ways of the ageing Italian women, so free of turmoil, were feeling distant now that I was back in North America. I looked fine with make-up but without it, my complexion was very sallow and mottled. I have no medical proof, but I believe the myeloma was smouldering inside me at this time. I think it was probably there in South Africa too, when I had my mini-breakdown at the end of shooting *A World Unseen*. Something was off. But rather than going to a doctor and figuring it out, I started experimenting with Botox. A friend of mine had been "seeing someone" in Toronto and she looked great. She urged me to go see her dermatologist. "Check him out, see how you feel about him." It was like being set up on a blind date. I was curious and I went for a session. I hate needles, but I really liked the doctor.

I asked: "Do you think this would help me?"

He said: "No, you don't really need it." But then he added, like any smart salesman: "Well, maybe a little here and a little there . . ."

He applied a topical cream to freeze the area on my forehead, then there was a small prick. It didn't really hurt. I made sure the injections were light enough that I could still move my face for my work.

Getting the Botox felt kind of like an affirmation, as if I was tending to myself, starting a self-improvement kick. For years, I had worked hard to be grungy—defiantly so—and to appear very ordinary. But I was thinking: Okay, you've been in the profession for years, maybe it's time to acknowledge that it is your work. This is like doing core exercises, learning your lines, going to meetings. But the most unsettling thing about growing older was the implication that, somehow, I was now grown-up. The idea I might resemble an authority figure was more distressing than the vanity at stake. But the net result was that I ended up looking even more unwell. Whatever health and happiness looked like; this was not it. The Botox had made me stiff, and I was getting paler and paler, all the colour leaching from my skin. I was fixing something superficial when the problem was deep inside me. Life was sending me messages that something was wrong, but I got distracted with redecorating my new place and the outward shell of my skin and body.

And of course, I was waiting to find out about Bond, dissecting the audition with a punishing eye. Everything from the tone of my voice, my accent, to the way I had shaped my eyebrows and how I had greeted Daniel Craig. Had I been too friendly, too eager, not friendly enough, standoffish? No matter what the part, it's absolutely torturous waiting for a response after an audition. There's no way around it. You replay every conversation and every scenario that led to this place, walking around, frowning from the effort of carrying the excesses of your mind. I tend to chew the inside of my cheeks like a particularly tough piece of meat.

Then come the rejection rationalizations, one after the other: I never wanted it. Bond Girls are so retro anyhow, aren't they? Isn't there a curse associated with this coveted role? No serious actress ever goes on to great films after being a Bond Girl. And come on, I don't look like a Bond bimbo anyhow.

Very close to Christmas of 2007, I found out I didn't get it. Aude, my British agent, had a talk with a studio insider. All that was clear was they were not going with me. Then slowly conflicting reports began to roll in: they were going back to retest some other girls. Did I still have a shot? By the time I found out for certain who it was—Olga Kurylenko— I had swung into that comfortable zone in my heart and mind where I could believe it was okay to have lost the part. It was not meant to be, and I was never meant to be an actress in the first place, so I should be grateful for the windfall thus far.

The mechanics of conventional success remain puzzling to me. When I was young, every professional high was echoed by a personal low, often at exactly the same time. Experiencing that early on gave me one insight: How can this be success? I was cured of that driving hunger by living through fame's illusory effects. Racing around the world, crowded with so many decisions and little time to consider had distracted me from seeing where I really needed to go.

The fact I didn't get the role can be viewed two ways: as a negative or a positive. On the negative side, I lost something, an invitation to greater reaches of fame and power. On the positive, I experienced a course correction, a nudge away from all the things that had hijacked my attention for so long. Yet the fallout of having lived in five countries and even more cities was that I had become the professional outsider. It meant, more often than not, missing cultural cues, not completely getting the politics or local humour, automatically dropping into the speaking cadences of wherever I found myself, while knowing I would never fully belong. I recognized it as the exile's age-old struggle but that didn't make it easier.

So, when I was offered the role of a Canadian diplomat in a film called *Cooking with Stella*, directed and written by Deepa's brother, Dilip, it seemed another piece of fortune. I could certainly relate to the character, a half-Indian career diplomat. The film would be shot in Delhi starting in March 2008 on location at the Canadian Embassy. I was to play Maya Chopra, diplomat and wife of Don McKellar's character, an uprooted chef seeking a new culinary obsession. Seema, my wonderful co-star from *Water*, had the juicy lead as the duplicitous chef and mistress of the diplomat's house. It was Dilip's first film, and during rehearsals, it became clear that we had a slight conflict over the vision of the character. Rehearsals were strained, and we were all a little tired from the daily sessions of hashing out the film's vision.

To relieve the stress, I'd begun to do a lot of yoga again. I'd get up at four-thirty in the morning, and my yoga master would come to the room of my hotel. He was short and round, suffused with mirth. "You have chosen this birth and life, welcome to Samsara!" he would begin. Masterji was from the Bihar school of yoga and began teaching me mantras. "All knowledge that a language can never express, that cannot be written in a book or shared comes to you through mantra." (He also, allegedly, after a private class, told my friend, "You cannot do the yoga because of the faaaaate," which apparently referred to less metaphysical matters, "fate" actually meaning "fat" in his accent.) Masterji led me to a class where I'd do Sivananda yoga—a much gentler form than the gruelling hot yoga I'd done in London. I'd meditate a little and then begin my filming. But none of it was helping: I was still pale, exhausted. When I watch *Cooking with Stella* now, I look ill, full stop. Unable to corral this fatigue, I invited Nadama and Krishna to come from Italy and stay with me. It seemed like the invitation of a friend but I can see it now that I needed to be saved, and they were surrogate parents, as well as irreverent co-conspirators.

Hotel living was overwhelming. In India, there's constant engagement every time you walk out of your room; I'd have to nod to at least six people before even getting to the lobby. There's a knock on the door every half an hour either to change a towel or check if everything was good with my minibar. Every employee is instructed to deliver a "Good Morning (Afternoon, Evening, Night) Madam" until the words become a stick poking at your sensitive bits. I wore headphones and dark glasses every time I left my room, but still the staff didn't get the hint. Deepa was on set, too, and she heard my complaining about the transient feeling of hotel living. She had production find me an apartment in a residential area in Greater Kailash 2, a posh south Delhi suburb, quiet and hidden. In the flat were geckos and chick blinds to filter the noise from the street, and a mint green sofa. There, without the constant tapping on my door and air conditioning that made my blood run cold, I went on a very inward journey, reading about one woman's path to becoming a Vedic monk and Ayurvedic master in *The Path of Practise* by Brij Maya Tiwari.

When Nadama arrived, with Krishna in April, the start of the very hot season in India—there's hot, very hot and very hot and rainy—she started leading meditations for me in the mornings, and on my days off from filming I listened to taped Osho discourses. We would blare music and do these ecstatic dances around the living room. Nadama was teaching me to "ground" myself, using certain tai chi movements connected with sending roots into the ground, sandbagging me into the earth, taming that vata, controlling the wind in me. I can only imagine what the neighbours must have thought, watching these astonishing gyrations through the window. There was a temple down the street with an inner sanctum housing idols of Radha and Krishna in festive, candy-coloured garments, draped in tinsel. Every evening, the community bathed a marble Nandi, Shiva's bull, in milk. The evening air was always thick with incense and the clanging of bells.

But away from the hubbub, along the periphery of an outer court-yard was a niche in the brick wall that sheltered a ghee-fed flame. There was something arresting in that little alcove, stained and burnished by smoke—I would stand in front of the diya and stare at that small shock of light, until I felt my own presence subdue.

The film shoot had become almost incidental to that time in Delhi, and even a bit of a nuisance. I was following an Ayurvedic diet, peremp-torily asking for khichri and dahi every day, every meal on set, which perplexed the caterer who laid out a rich and varied keema-paratha-and-biryani spread. I'd do my scenes and rush home to meditate with my friends, not quite recognizing the irony of my savage indignation at being kept away from my compassion and grounding practices. Nadama was always blunt with me. In the past, she'd called me out on my self-ishness, and described my eating disorder as anti-life. "You have to feed the body to work on the spirit," she had told me, and I'd taken it to heart. All those years of dieting—The Zone, the Master Cleanse, the Grapefruit-only diet—had wreaked havoc on my body. I would lie down and she would hover her hands over my body, trying to understand the swirling discontent. "You're cut off. Pieces of you are not joined together. Your pelvis area is cut off from your legs. There's no life in them, no energy," she said.

She was right: I had internalized the varied criticisms from the world, and in doing so had splintered into smaller and smaller bits, like I was under siege from a separatist movement. There were so many *mes*—the model; the daughter; the actress; the seeker; the tease; the rebel—I could not give any one of them autonomy, nor glue them all into one. As soon as we wrapped and finished the shoot, I gave away most of my clothes and gathered some mountain essentials like hiking boots, shawls and a monkey cap. I had been offered a few more films out of Bombay—one to be produced by Aamir Khan—but I wanted to return to Dharamshala, back to the abode of the Dalai Lama.

14

I TRAVELLED TO Dharamshala to dismantle my world, without knowing it at the time. Nadama and Krishna came with me, as fellow dusty-footed travellers and self-appointed chaperones. When they lived in the Osho ashram in Pune, they had made an annual trip to McLeod Ganj to escape the deadening heat of the Indian summers. They still had a circle of friends in this mountain town known as "Little Lhasa" for its exiled Tibetan community. I was grateful for their company and we were all relieved to leave Delhi. The three of us rented a car and driver and we headed north, taking two entire days. As Nadama and Krishna napped, I imagined an aerial view of our car scurrying across wide plains and twisting mountain roads, anticipation singing through my veins all the while. In McLeod Ganj, we checked-in to the Pema Thang guest house, a simple white, two-storey wood-and-brick covered building. With a veggie restaurant and a soaring view over the entire valley, it's a high-end backpacker destination for foreigners, evidenced by the collage of postcards, from Colombia to Norway, proudly displayed in the reception area. The rumour is that it's financed by the town's most prominent citizen, His Holiness the Dalai Lama, and is set on a peak overlooking his temple.

Perhaps it was my state of mind but on entering the guest house cafe and sitting by the panoramic view, I felt a sense of homecoming. The cafe is bright and long and narrow and filled with foreigners in kurtas and cardigans seated on cane chairs and conferring quietly amongst themselves or staring out at the prayer flags fluttering over the Kangra

Valley. The cafe's Tibetan manager was wearing a beige safari suit, moving gently from table to table, honouring this contemplative atmosphere. I felt happier than I'd been in months.

"I'll have the pizza and . . . um . . . momos and carrot cake."

"Just because we are multi-cuisine doesn't mean you have to eat it all at once," he laughed.

I got up early the next morning, drawn by the sound of prayer bells ringing in the mountains. Walking down the narrow, muddy road from the guest house through the cold-filtered morning light, I passed a sign on a post: Ten-Day Silent Meditation Introduction to Buddhism Course. I stopped and walked back. Standing before that sign, I felt odd. Suddenly I was transported, lifted out of my body and just as quickly returned back to form. I had been holding myself on the skin of the water and it was time to get wet. No question in my mind or my body: I needed to do this, whatever it was, this meditation retreat. I rushed back and told Nadama and Krishna. They agreed to wait for ten days and meet me on the other side.

"I don't want to be a maven of discontent any more," I joked.

Nadama nodded solemnly. "What is maven?" asked Krishna. His English was not strong. "What is discontent?"

The next day, I hiked twenty minutes out of McLeod Ganj and stopped short in front of the Himalaya Tea shop, a grin spreading across my face. But of course! I had been delivered to the same red gates that Kalu, my prophetic canine companion, had passed through years before on my first visit. Behind those gates lay the Tushita Meditation Centre. The Buddhist centre is a gathering place for students of the Gelugpa tradition of Tibetan Buddhism. Seekers from around the world gather for the offerings: courses at all levels to anyone interested in Mahayana Buddhism. Practitioners walk the grounds in patterned shawls, wrapped in silence. There's a slightly musty but well-stocked library. Small knots of people practise walking meditation around the pretty little white stupa on the edge of a rolling hill or wander off individually to find a tree under which to sit and parse the ambiguities of life.

I threw my bag on to a thin sunken mattress in my room and entered the main *gompa* with a group of thirty others for further instruction. I was nervous to be part of a group of strangers undertaking this ebb from everyday life. I thought of Nadama and Krishna and what they must be doing; sharing a pizza and beer with one of their old Tibetan friends, warm and content. What was I doing? Signing myself up to sit on bare floors and share a loo with thirty strangers. But for the chance to touch something eternal, I was willing to do that.

A German abbess, in nun's robes and with a pleasingly round bald head, laid out the ground rules of the retreat. "Please, we practice ahimsa, non-harming, here at Tushita. But if you see a monkey, pick up a stone. Don't hit the monkey but they are very naughty. They will steal your food. They will steal your clothes. Now you know why we call the disturbance in your head "monkey mind.""

For ten days, I sat in silence, interspersed with talks on Mahayana Buddhist philosophy. When I came out, I went directly to Nadama and Krishna's suite.

"How was it?" asked Nadama.

"It was the most horrible thing I've ever experienced," I said immediately. "And I have to go back."

Despite the exquisite torture of sitting captive to all my thoughts, I had also felt at home. It was natural, a deep familiarity settling into my bones during extended silence. I took Nadama aside and told her.

"Yes, you felt at home meditating because you did it in a previous life—you have monk energy. But remember, if it's easy, you don't need to relive that life again. Life is to grow and experience something else. Something outside your conditioning in this life and maybe the last one. But it's your decision."

I felt as if the decision had been made for me. Therein began a course of going in and out of the retreat for about six months, ten days in, a few days out, then back again. Nadama went back to Italy but Krishna stayed, undertaking his own mysterious retreats. My time in Tushita during those months sandblasted me. I had felt the fear and done it anyway, tumbling into the deepest corners of myself. Living beyond self-interest, I learned through Tibetan Buddhism and meditation, is not only possible but the ultimate liberation.

Prepare. Do your work. Let. Go.

Years later—because it takes time to imbibe these lessons—I wrote a poem influenced by my time in Tushita:

Is there a way
to talk of the sun
without invoking the moon?
Love without loss,
desire without despair,
without hope.
Arrival without departure.
What follows
can't be easily ignored.
If life is an act of remembrance,
don't forget—
every considered step,
and how well you have
fallen down.

It was deeply unsettling in the beginning. I was entering a strange geography, understanding the terrifying adventure to be held in my head. But luckily the pull inside me was much stronger than my resistance. This was strong medicine, something I'd been seeking my whole life. To some, meditation sounds like entering a claustrophobic room decorated with your greatest failures and disappointments. And they wouldn't be completely wrong. To others who think meditation is all about blissing out, entering altered states, or escaping reality, I invite you to sit on a cushion. Really, I do.

"You see that, those clouds?"

I was startled by our teacher's words. We were on our break, outside on the terrace beneath the cedars, chewing contemplatively. He was breaking the code of lunchtime silence. "Those are your thoughts. Right now the clouds are fluffy and pleasant, maybe tomorrow they will be dark and threatening. But they pass. Your thoughts are the clouds. You are the sky. Vast, radiant, eternal and untouched by the formations passing by."

If I had been told this even a few weeks before, it wouldn't have made an impact. But his words were transformed in the clarity of a fine mountain afternoon, after a morning spent investigating consciousness.

It's very difficult to convey my experience of that time. It took me to places where language fails. The entire schematic diagram of my world was changing as I absorbed talks on "bodhicitta," limitless compassion, non-dualism and the ultimate cure and cessation of suffering and mental afflictions, wisdom-realizing emptiness: the insight that nothing, *nothing* exists independently. "Form is emptiness and emptiness is form" noted the Indian Buddhist philosopher, Nagarjuna. I was also healing my relationships, visualizing unbiased compassion towards both friends and "enemies." But if you had asked me at the time what meditation is, I would have replied: It's simple; you sit and bleed. All you do is sit and bleed it all out. The fear and conditioning that narrows our experience of ourselves and the world, the attachment to the body that we have been fastened into, and the delusion that pain and pleasure are different. It is, after all, all in the mind.

The result of this was all of life became a prayer. I walked out of the red gates after retreat number six and the deodar trees were laced with a soft light that possessed me, filled me with praise for a beautiful, mutilated world. The feeling of grace flared and filled everything, including the annoying, overbearing tourists, down to our collective roots. This is the quality of aliveness I had been groping for my whole life: a direct experience that we were all drawing from the same source. But to get there I had to breathe through waves of pain that shot through my spine, as my folded knees creaked with agony. Every time I wanted to get up and run, I had to stay. When it felt like my fabric would not hold . . . that's when it all made sense.

Through this lens I first interpreted the Four Noble Truths, the essence of Buddha's teachings. Discomfort is unavoidable, but suffering is optional. How then do you find lasting happiness? Laying down your armour is the first step. An unguarded heart is an awakened heart. Learning to open without bias or judgment to both pain and joy, remaining both strong and soft, it was like learning to walk again. I would return to my dorm in the night, thinking about the ways in which the world had hardened me; how I had allowed it. The nights in Tushita clamoured with hidden sounds, crickets and rustles and the sigh of the earth turning over to rest.

Something was made visible to me, developing slowly day after day, like the world's slowest Polaroid. Some of my experiences remain mystical, unexplainable. Tibetans have a policy of not disclosing their realizations. That's a good thing when you're touching places outside most people's acceptable definition of reality. But my greatest takeaway from those months of meditation was this: A human life lived fully awake was available for those who want it. Right here. Right now.

I enjoyed those months, falling off the edge of the world and stepping outside time. The deep empty, as it turns out, was full, even of humour.

"Why don't Buddhists vacuum in the corners? Because they have no attachments!"

"Okay, one more, Tashi-la. Have you heard this one? The Dalai Lama orders a hot dog on the street. He says, "One. With Everything.""

Tashi, who ran the guest house I stayed in between retreats, laughed obligingly at my lame Buddhist jokes. I was in my element. Everywhere, even the muddy marketplace, was alight with gold shadows, all movements natural and unforced. Gradually, the mountains began to frost over with snow. After a lifetime where I could not entirely fathom how to interact with the human species, of being told how dangerous it was to be kind and vulnerable, I had found my place. It was cold and I was wearing an icebreaker over a Tibetan skirt, socked feet in the monks' favoured footwear—Crocs—when I wandered into an Internet cafe and sent a message to almost everyone in my contact list: *I am going to become a Buddhist nun!* I was prepared to shave my head (I'd done it before, after all) and give myself over. I had finally found my home after not belonging for so long. Staying forever seemed perfectly logical at the time—wouldn't you stay, if you had found your own castle in the clouds? Of course, my mass email generated panicked responses, with subject lines like: Top 5 Reasons Not to Become a Buddhist Nun! Read now! Urgent!

As my friend Shamim wrote:

I am just unconvinced by any way that involves a physical enclosing or particular rules (or robes!). Surely, in our unlimited minds, we don't need shaven heads, robes or anything else to mark us out as different (even in a good way).

And are you allowed to have sex?!

Darling, not ready to explain my half-thoughts right now. But we miss you a lot and cannot wait to see you. You don't need

the maroon robes to follow whatever path you choose my love.
You are amazing.

S

xxxxx

I don't know if I could have had such a wandering spirit if my father
wasn't so well-practiced in the art of unconditional love. But of course,
I was also exercising another form of escape. I had taken my usually
obsessive tendencies, my full-on approach to anything new, and translated them into spiritual realms. A spiritual master named Chogyam
Trungpa Rinpoche calls this spiritual materialism—when the desires
we hold in our minds are translated into the spiritual realm rather than
the material one. Instead of wanting a bigger car and a house, we want
enlightenment—but we're still wanting. It's all accumulation.

During this time, I met a woman named Ruth who was leading a
meditation retreat. Originally from the Netherlands, she was a pint-
sized woman with the appearance of a little girl , yet she had dedicated
her entire life to spiritual practice. She ran a school in Sikkim for
underprivileged children. When the school was shut for the holidays,
she'd accept invitations to teach at Buddhist centres, everywhere from
Nepal to Germany. I remember ordering a hot lemon-honey-ginger
tea and wiping down the notched surface of the table, before telling her
of my Buddhist nun plans. "Everything that you love you will eventually lose; it's the all pervasiveness of change. It's so clear. I need to give
up everything now, to cut my attachments, before it's too late." She
listened patiently, then said: "Lisa, you have to be gentler on this journey to get where you want to go. Look at me: I knew this is where I
wanted to be but I had to go back to the Netherlands and do it stage by
stage, step by step." Then she said, "This rapid change is a form of violence. Don't do violence to yourself. Remember, this is the middle
path. Buddhism is practical wisdom. We must be awakened realists. She
paused. "Oh, and did you think you practice only for *yourself*?"

Jumping from one thing to the next—one place, one lover, one
job—had been my life. She was advising me to live the antithesis of the
Nike ad: *Don't just* do *it. Do it slowly. In stages. Just absorb it.* So after
six months, I decided to defer enlisting in a monastery (though I swear,

it's a path I still might follow). Besides, after months of local soupy dishes and momos, I had some cravings that couldn't be met in McLeod Ganj: I really, really wanted a burger.

I flew back to Milan to renew my Indian visa, and I had my burger. I stayed with Nadama and Krishna, who encouraged me to continue with "psycho-spiritual" work. Krishna is a big believer in the idea of good and bad—white or black—energy. It's possible in India to put a spell on whoever bothers you, an age-old revenge drama practice called *jadoo*. Lime threaded with a few chillies swing everywhere, from doorways to the fenders of cars; counteracting the evil eye—the bad energy, the *buri nazar*. The twenty-first-century version of this exists online, where websites advertise "Pure life evil eye *nazar battu* to remove negative energies" or you can find chants on YouTube to "Remove Evil Eye, Black Magic in 4 Minutes." This notion of magic and spell incantations did not, in my mind, run contrary to the life of the intellect, and in fact, could coexist in a darkly intoxicating cocktail only to be found in the subcontinent, where blurring the boundaries between different realms is an art. Nadama and Krishna were convinced that I'd picked up—or someone had specially ordered—black energy. I tried to wrap my head around this notion. I began to think there was something to this concept of carrying a hidden non-lethal disease that influenced your fate. Perhaps this black magic was actually the spirit memory of unresolved emotional pain—carrying around the mother who abandoned you, for instance—and India, quite naturally, had the cure-all spiritual technology. "Black" was code for non-duality, right? Because really, all colours were absorbed in black. In the end, I pushed aside all my attempts at rationalizing, seated at Nadama's kitchen table, laden with pastry and coffee and tarot cards. "We must clean out the energy, just wash it out," said Krishna, as if we were discussing hosing down garden furniture. So when he suggested a road trip through India, I jumped. "Just say yes and figure it out later." Whatever the motivation, his suggestion legitimized my longing to return. I would leave first and wait a few days for Krishna to join me.

On the flight back to Delhi from Milan, I thought: Wouldn't it be cool, wouldn't it be perfect if these were signs in real life, like the ones in airplane toilets telling you to lock the door, or fasten your seatbelt during turbulence? It's such a relief, submitting to the airline's health and safety standards. On this trip, I will submit to the divine air traffic controller in the sky. *Amor fati*: Love your fate.

In Delhi, I passed a few quiet days taking long walks in Lodhi Gardens and around Nizamuddin, filling with anticipation, not quite knowing how to prepare for a pilgrimage to nowhere. "Wet wipes, hand sanitizer, towel, Imodium," my Auntie Neeta Tandon chanted, dropping the items into my duffel. I was staying with her in her flat in Delhi. We are very close but I didn't have the heart to tell her the items would lie forgotten at the bottom of my bag. When Krishna arrived, we split the cost of buying a gold Hyundai, maybe a little flashy for a spiritual expedition, but who says you can't quest in style? Thus began a six-month-long journey of submerging myself into the task of tilling my inner soil, discarding everything I didn't need along the way and yet keeping the conversation going between my mind and my heart by writing in a journal every evening.

I dressed down in Fabindia kurtas and printed baggy pants and cranked my seat back, placing my feet on the dashboard in the car. It took forever to leave heaving, engorged Delhi behind. Outside the city, hot, dry winds swept dust across the road. I loved those rough Indian highways extending across the plains into the mountains. We were eating our way to enlightenment too, stopping at every dhaba that had a fleet of trucks parked outside. Dhabas are usually crudely constructed: a big shell of a building with a wide-open kitchen. A cook in a greasy undershirt will be stirring the dal in his big kadhai. Someone else will be slapping the parathas and rotis, and you can hear the sizzle and taste the heat of the fire. The tables are crowded, eyes tracking the progress of their orders. One of my greatest pleasures is to flop onto a bench in a dhaba and let the experience unfurl. A boy will come up and throw down a couple of glasses of water, which are wedged between some fingers, and whose other fingers are right in the water. With a dirty rag, he'll vigorously wipe down the table, making it even more damp and unpleasant than it was to begin with. I ask what's good, and he will almost always recite: dal, paratha, roti hot off the tava. The boy drops the roti down in front of you on a tin plate, steaming, with a dollop of ghee on top. And you feast like a child. You slurp your tea afterwards and set off after washing your hands and finger-combing your hair at a small sink, completely satiated and ready to hit the road again.

These months, travelling from village to village, plateaus to valleys without plan, maps, or supplies, unspooled like a movie. The flickering, temporary nature of the world had become apparent during my time with the Buddhists, but I was curious—if everything is temporary, then what is real? Does anything last? I needed to hear what others might have to say.

A pattern soon emerged to our days, controlled by a mysterious hand. It was a relief to lay down the mind's habits of planning and be led by hidden currents, the wind in secret sails. We reached the hotel and got the last room. We took the wrong road and ended up in the right place. We left late and arrived on time. It was all very pure, down to the scratchy blankets at night. I saw musical notations in the sky, in the trail of birds impressing themselves in space. I wanted to see how far they could go, stretching beyond the nimbus-covered mountains. This is what it was like to fall in love with the world again. To feel awake. To succumb. To spill your happiness while knowing you exist on a scale larger than this fragile life.

One of my first encounters was with the Seventeenth Karmapa, the head of the Karma Kagyu lineage of Tibetan Buddhism. The Kagyu tradition is more about the experiential practice of meditation, whereas some of the other streams, like the Gelug with its emphasis on logic and debate, are more about the study of scriptures. When I met the Karmapa, he was just a boy, barely in his twenties but magnetic, embodying the energy of a lion. I stood before him, fumbling as I asked: "What is the right practice? What is the right thing for me to do?"

He looked at me and cracked a smile. He leaned in, and via a translator, he said: "Don't worry, your practice is going well, and things are happening as they should. You are finding your way."

He snapped his fingers—a peculiar gesture—and one of the Rinpoche surrounding him removed the white prayer beads form around his neck. He cradled them, mumbled a prayer and then handed them to me.

We all have this impulse within us to think that we are special. Part of the spiritual practice is about loosening the ego's grip on us, but damn, didn't I feel special in that moment! I felt like shouting from the monastery roof: *The Karmapa gave me the white beads!* That's right, World—he gave them to me! I wore them around my neck the entire journey. I was wearing my white mala in Himachal Pradesh when I met the respected Buddhist nun Jetsunma Tenzin Palmo. Born to a fish-monger in East London, she had turned to Buddhism at a young age and for twelve years had meditated alone in a six-foot deep cave in the Himalayas. She was the second woman in Tibetan Buddhism ever to be ordained. This is no small thing; some Tibetans believe that being a woman is punishment, a form of bad karma. Since emerging from her cave in the 1980s, Tenzin Palmo has made it her mission to elevate the status of other Buddhist women. She started a nunnery, reviving an ancient practice for female yogis. She is a hero of mine. Somehow, Krishna and I had ended up at her nunnery, Dongyu Gatsal Ling, which seemed shut for the day. But because I was beginning to pay attention and listen to the world, I felt I was spoken to in a bird that appeared at the right moment, a glance from a woman squatting by the side of the road, a cloud revealing the sun at just the right moment . . . There was nobody in reception, but I saw a gecko flick his tail in my direction and so I followed. We started wandering and opening doors. We walked through the building and up a set of stairs, pushed open a door and there was Tenzin Palmo. She was sitting with a group of nuns, explaining the most compassionate and efficient way of getting rid of Himalayan spiders.

She looked up with the clearest blue eyes, like she was expecting us, and said: "Oh, hello. Would you like to have lunch with us?" So we did. We sat and had lunch with her. She invited me back to her room to have an audience with her. I sat and shared with her my soul's struggle to know itself. She listened carefully and said, "Everything you do has to be aligned with compassion, including your work. Make sure the message you send out is compassion." When I left the nunnery, I walked rapidly to the car, tears tugging at the corners of my eyes, understanding finally the Tibetan idea of transmission: It's not just through words that we learn. It's enough to sit with a presence.

While the rest of the world read the morning headlines and drank their morning tea, Krishna and I drove across Himachal Pradesh to Kulu Manali and then south to Pune. Every morning I rose, prepared to follow whatever path would appear. I found myself scrambling up cliffs in search of hidden shrines and pavilions carved into rock. I heaved myself on to plateaus of solitude in hazy light, coming face-to-face with shaggy haired meditators in one of the many hermitage caves dotting the landscape. "He says, cut the list of your desires," Krishna would translate into my ear. Everywhere I travelled during that time, it seemed, the houses of my horoscope aligned and lingams erupted from the dirt along the side of the road. Krishna and I were welcomed everywhere like old friends; by the monk, the baba, the gardener of an untended estate waving a calloused hand. I took their blessings and touched their feet. Because you never know where the master is hiding. The confusing details of life flattened. Every time I wanted to ask an "important" question or wondered what the clever thing I could say, I told myself to shut up and listen. The lamas I encountered were sweetly dignified and not overly prescriptive. "Live a good life. Look beyond all forms," they said, their faces radiating a luminosity beyond eras. I climbed and climbed to sit on the rocky edge of my vision, in thin air, the sun singeing the skin of my nose. During the day I'd settle my dupatta across my shoulders and just listen, willing the secrets trapped in words to be set free, applying Dettol to my scraped knees at night.

And everywhere I went I wore the white beads that the Karmapa had given me, even when I sat in front of many Hindu shamans. One of them was a female spirit medium who went into a trance. She crouched forward, her long locks hiding her face, and her body started shaking. She had chains in her hands that she started rattling, and she began channelling strange voices, shifting into from female to female before my eyes. Villagers would come with problems, personal, political, spiritual and sit before her as she shape-shifted: "I'm fighting with my neighbour. I think he wants to steal my daughter." And in fiery tongues, she'd give her solution, and a handful of *vibhuti*, the sacred ash. There was no forced sympathy here because it was assumed that your metaphysical wiring was feral and tangled and it was a very normal turn of events to arrive here to set things straight. When it was my turn, she said in perfect English, "Don't listen to others. Only when your life falls apart will you know what you attained." That is some crazy baba medicine, I thought to myself. Afterwards she asked me for rasgullas in Hindi. "Because I told her you are Bengali," whispered Krishna. I gifted her Himachal apples and honey.

I wore the beads as I sat with a white baba, an anti-jadoo baba. I was told I couldn't sit inside the temple because I'm a woman. My brain, of course, said, "This sucks, what's up with that?" But I did sit, in the courtyard, with the damn dupatta over my head, and then left behind my agitation at the injustice. Once my despotic thought storm dialled down, I could sit there for hours and hours. The chants took me into a different chamber of my heart, deep into the spirals of the inner ear and, away from "I'm hot, I'm thirsty, I'm getting bitten by ants, I'm hope there's hot water in the next hotel so I can wash my underwear." At each stop, I was figuring it out, like an athlete who practices again and again.

We kept driving. Sometimes we'd have to deal with a flat tyre by flagging down one of those ornately decorated trucks. *Kya haal hai, paaji?* Voices rang out of the cab of the truck with friendly jibes but when the men hopped down it was with puffed chests and battle-ready vigour. The truck drivers were decorous with me, probably because, when asked, Krishna told them we were on a spiritual mission (bringing to my mind Dan Akroyd's line from the *Blues Brothers*: "We're on a mission from God . . ." But wait, does that make me John Belushi?) We called on them for help on those dusty roads many times.

As the sky darkened, I would start scanning the highway for a hotel to stop for the night. I would check-in to a room with a drain in the middle of the bedroom floor and a stack of fusty towels on the bed and Krishna would disappear into his own. We didn't speak much. Krishna was my jadoo-fixer and trusted guide, but he remained inscrutable to me. Finally, after months, we reached the Osho ashram in Pune, where Krishna had spent so many years. There I traded in my spiritual vagabond look for bewitching, maroon robes. The Osho ashram is the Armani of ashrams in India—very tasteful, done up with elaborate Zen gardens and a serene pond in front of a stunning pyramid-shaped meditation hall with cool marble interiors to hold the silence. Most of the meditations are practiced here. All very high-tech and magical at once, reminding me at times of the lair of a wealthy recluse. Many of the visitors are quite frankly gorgeous, floating around in their robes, like exquisite butterflies. "Zorba the Buddha" was the underlying spirit of the place, a philosophy that combines celebration with meditation, a wholeness of being where nothing is denied, but self-awareness is fundamental. At least that's my understanding of it. Osho famously contradicted himself, as a wry reminder, to remain watchful, even of the teacher. Nadama had made me aware of warring factions within the "Sannyasi" community—a name given to Osho's followers—so I focused on my own inner work and sidestepped the gossip. And there was real work going on; it was humming with an energy unfamiliar to me. The practice there was quite different from the traditional seated *samatha* meditation which I'd been practising, which is the act of observing the breath—rising, falling, rising, falling—to calm the mind. At the Osho ashram, the anchoring practice is dynamic meditation.

"You will clean out the blockages in your body and mind," said Krishna, making it sound as simple as unclogging the plumbing. And in a sense, it was: trauma addressed through embodied practice, the dynamic movement loosening energy blocks and freeing pain trapped at a cellular level. Simple, but not by any means easy. Quite extraordinarily torment-ing at times, in fact.

At the ashram, I learned, there is no conflict between a robust spiritual life and pragmatic, material pursuits as long as every decision and action is taken from a place of mindfulness. And that's the catch. In finding my way, everything becomes permissible in a playground of self-awareness. Everything. As long as you take responsibility for it, which is by far the scariest aspect of it all, and where a lot of people fail. I had not yet learned how to take responsibility for the entire spectrum of my desires. But I was readying myself for it.

At six-thirty in the morning, I joined the line filing into the marble meditation hall for dynamic meditation, a moving meditation of five stages. A sannyasi in a black robe puts on a tape which guides you, step by step. The recipe is something like this: exaggerated breathing, gestalt-like therapy, primal screaming—a mixture of everything, for about an hour. I threw myself into the meditations until my body took over. It's quite powerful to exit the hall early in the morning as the sun comes up, after a deep catharsis, feeling both tranquil and spaced out, a sense of intoxication with existence. I would remember Nadama's words: "It's not your business what is leaving you. It's not your business to try to understand what it is. But don't block the exit. That is your only work." It was another way of telling me to get out of my own way. I do believe a few emotional blockages were cleared.

We continued our trip, the white beads around my neck. But the time in Pune had been intense, and I was getting tired. Many months had passed. One day, I found myself walking barefoot around Tryambakeshwar, an ancient Hindu temple outside Nasik; I was embarking on a Narayan Nagbali pooja. I paused before climbing the stairs to a sacred tank of water to immerse myself and clean past karma.

"Hepatitis . . . cholera . . . oh my god, what about typhoid?"

I saw a reflection of myself as though looking at a photograph: draped in unstitched cloth, wild hair, lips chapped and sunburned. I thought of my father, and my mother back in Canada. I thought of my untended career. I could feel all sorts of internal obstructions that had been transformed: sorrow, guilt, shame, anger—the troubling parts of human life had not disappeared but their strength had dissipated, and they gripped less tightly. The numbness I had carried since the day of the car crash—it had dissolved. Instead, a tender ache spread through the places that had been void of feeling for a long time. I felt I could take in more air. I had been travelling as though my life was on fire, and now it was time to stop. I was replenished. And ready to pursue deeper meaning in everyday life. Which is, as I would later learn, the best way to illuminate all the unnoticed joys about being human.

My spiritual road trip had left me ready to re-engage with my mom and the world. It was time to drive back to Delhi and retire the golden car. It was time to go. I was leaving with a softer spine. I remember looking through my notebook as I sat on the plane to Milan, reading the notes I'd taken throughout. They later formed the backbone of a poem:

The magic lives
outside what is known
in the reclusive bay where fishermen bathe.
This I've always known.

And it's very encouraging
when people don't understand you.
Also,
there are many things not worth knowing.
Like, "Why an 18 per cent surcharge?"
while a tree outside quietly grows.
Talk not to be of inoffensive things,
or the way you hide
behind your crowd-pleasing lives,
or why it is unsafe to travel.
No, I want to hear
the last time your heart was massaged by fingers of delight
or when you found pieces of yourself in broken pottery
or climbed a volcano
and did not tell.
If you change the topic to tell where you get your hair done,
I'll smile.
I may not be strong enough to be despised
but I won't give you the gift
of my wild, unknowing heart.

What! You too? I thought I was the only one—C.S. Lewis

In Milan, I got my hair cut and walked around in a daze, trying to synthesize the clean Western order of this city with the adventures of the past months. It was like leaving a garden bursting with colour for a doctor's waiting room. Within a few days of being accessible, I received an email that my mother had pneumonia. As the doctors had predicted, it would happen more frequently, and each time, it would be more wrenching than the last, and harder for her to recover.

Even though I landed back in Toronto in the middle of a health crisis, I felt very peaceful. Of course, that was my clock, not my mother's. As soon as I saw her, I could tell that something was different: She was much more resigned. When both my dad and I were seated on opposite sides of her hospital bed, she told me to lower the blinds and began asking us to let her go.

"I'm tired of fighting. I need to go now," she said. "I don't want to go through this again." I stared without responding. She had such an incredibly strong will that she had willed herself to hang around for my dad and me thus far. My mother had shaped a kind of life where there was no model, but now, here on this bridge, between life and non-life, she was making the decision to let go. She had managed to befriend an entire network of doctors and nurses at Sunnybrook, from different departments. She wanted us to donate $15,000 to research into lung disease, a charity associated with a doctor she adored. She was, of course, bossy about this, and we assured her, without hesitation, it would happen. She was always organizing up until the last minute. "I want to be cremated. I don't want a big froufrou, jing-bang, bing-bang fuss." She rose from her pillow to make her point. I pulled my chair to her and massaged her arms. For the first time in a long time, I felt like a daughter.

When we met with her doctors, they weren't optimistic about a recovery. She needed constant care and suctioning to remove the phlegm build up. The doctor in Sunnybrook was benignly frosty, a vision of medical well-adjustedness and reason. He recommended a permanent hole in her trachea and a feeding tube. "You want to institutionalize *her? Her?" This woman who left a spark in people that was not there before, even under the sickly godawful lights of your fucking hospital?* I snarled back at him without waiting for a reaction, "Aren't you supposed to *nourish* life . . ." My father dragged me away before I could seize him like a mastiff in a fighting ring. My vision had gone hot and blurry. I needed to be at my mother's side. I walked rapidly back to her room.

It was obvious she had set her intention to go this time. But she needed permission from us. And we would, as a family, decide on *our* terms. My mother was hooked up to machines and clearly in a great deal of pain. We could take her off, and she might recover, but not for long. All it would take is a minute food particle to fall into her trachea and we'd be back. For the next few days I would drive back and forth to the hospital, trying at red lights to make sense of what was happening, stretching my mind across continents, to embody what I had learned in India. At the hospital I tried to bolster my mom with strawberry jello and terrible Buddhist jokes—I hear reincarnation is making a comeback!—and played her favourite Enrique Iglesias songs. I hadn't overcome fears about death and loss, but I was sharpened by silence. I brought her favourite Lily of the Valley scent and tweezers to her bedside, as well as an old ceramic Madonna. I filled in her eyebrows as she directed me through a hand-held mirror. I would finish and observe both our faces through the frame, side by side, documenting our similarities and differences. As I lay beside her in the narrow hospital bed, I felt something other than defeat in her lunar glow. Strength. Conviction. Surrender too, perhaps. I thought deeply of the things I had learned: How love is often mixed up with attachment. It's important to step back and separate the two. The shape of love changes with attachment, distorts in ways we can't always see. But unconditional love asks more of us even as it contains the power to heal. And at the end of it all, is letting go a full stop or a hyphen? We don't actually perish to all that is known, do we? I had been wearing this knowledge lightly, swishing it about my shoulders, but surrendering took a huge leap. My mother's love was unconditional; she had let me go, over and over again. I had to do the same for her. I would sit by her side in a private world of our making, willing her to become better one more time.

"Mama," I'd whisper. "I see you. Close your eyes. What do you see?" I'd ask her.

"I see myself walking into the ocean, and just disappearing."

Her focus was on leaving, and ours was on keeping her. Our grasping was the cause of her suffering. I saw it very clearly. My dad and I had a talk, and I asked, "Can we do it? Do we have whatever it takes to let her go?"

And somehow, with very few words, we agreed that yes, it was up to her, not us. Dying consciously is a very personal moral code.

We stayed by her bedside and my father leaned down and said, "Okay, if you need to go, go, my love. It's okay. You can go."

We both began crying softly, avoiding each other's eyes, my father and I. But I kept trying, after each gulp of air, to stop. One of the Buddhist precepts is that when a soul is passing, it's good to keep the immediate area light and open. Try not to cry, because it's harder for the spirit to leave; sensing sorrow makes the spirit linger. *I am crazed. I know it. How can I endure this loss and have it be a healing?* When I looked at her, another world was in her eyes. "Let's meditate," I suggested, half choking and half laughing because I knew her reaction. "What will meditation do for me?" "Clarity, Mama, peace," I said, seized with desperation. She said, "I don't know exactly what you are thinking, but I know *you*. And you're going to be okay." We are strange and unknowable, suspended by flimsy ideas and mysterious beliefs. I was being sucked into a dark knot in the centre of my being. My mother and I put our hands on each other, and breathed.

We watched her slip away. She closed her eyes and her breathing slowed. We were there in that moment when it simply stopped. Immediately, I felt her spirit leave, her flesh seemed to cave in, taking on a different characteristic. Duller. Flatter. Vacant. The life in her was gone. But unlike her body, she left imperious and unbroken. She left restored. She was free.

15

FUNERAL HOMES, OR parlours or mortuaries, whatever you want to call them, are odd places. Given my penchant for the otherworldly, I had thought I would hit it off with the people who worked in Ward Funeral Home, the place my father and I had chosen for my mother's cremation. But on that red and brown leafed October day, the employees at the funeral home clearly thought that my father and I were absurd. We were still in deep shock but at the same time filled with a strange sense of lightness. I couldn't stop joking around. Looking at the coffins, I said, "Comfy," as I attempted to swing my right leg into one's velvet lush interior. The coffin tilted and creaked a warning. I watched the funeral director's expression curdle in disapproval. Considering the amount of time he spent around cadavers he seemed not to have cultivated a sense of humour about it.

Maybe we had chosen this particular funeral home simply because my father had remembered the sombre-looking brick building in the neighbourhood where we had lived when I was a toddler, before we moved further south in Etobicoke. It was an old-fashioned funeral home, and I can clearly recall the interior; dark and cloaked in thick velvet drapes, like the ones I'd seen in immigrant Italian homes growing up. It wasn't a space of *memento mori* as much as designed to muffle your mind; it reminded me of afternoons in church with my grandma when I had felt suffocated by piety. We needed to find a receptacle for mom's ashes, and none of them were right, all very resplendent, covered in fake silver and gold. We eventually chose a simple dark brown box—my mom would have approved. As we were leaving, the funeral director asked, "We'd like to offer something to your family from ours. Meat or vegetarian?"

And they gave us a frozen lasagne, which made me giggle even harder. Here's what was funny: as the lasagne was discreetly handed over in a plastic bag, I was in the process of arranging a Buddhist *jangwa* ceremony for my mother. Upon special request, monks will perform a purification ritual after someone has died. It was like extending a friendly hand to my mom's spirit in the outer realms (though strictly speaking Buddhists don't believe in the spirit, but a subtle form of consciousness that continues). I had sent a message to a nun I'd met at the Tushita, an American woman who had become a Buddhist nun and a popular teacher. She was also active in a community of end-of-life caregivers grounded in Buddhist ethics. She agreed to arrange the ceremony for me. It would take place simultaneously at monasteries in California and India. So that strange and surreal moment in the dimly lit funeral home, filled with a sense of atonement and frozen food, perfectly underlined for me the difference between Eastern and Western philosophies of dying. While the latter was marked by awkwardness, I took refuge in the former, knowing that far away, complete strangers were praying for my mother's passing in a rich and humane Eastern tradition. Meanwhile, in Toronto, I was being offered lasagne.

I wanted to put our family home up for sale in November and get my father away from the memories it embodied as quickly as possible. In order to do that, I would have to wade through everything stored in the basement, clumsily piled up together like mounds of fallen leaves—the accumulation of a life. There were toys in antique brass-studded trunks that had been brought over from Europe. An old exercise bike. My grandfather's stamp collection carefully preserved between leaves of aged butter paper. Photo albums filled with black and white photos of distant relatives from India staring sternly into the lens. My dad's old stereo, on which I'd spent hours listening to his Beatles records, brought over so carefully from England. But I couldn't find any use for an old hifi in my life and I was momentarily paralysed about what to do.

Next, I unearthed a massive rabbit-fur coat from another trunk. It had belonged to my grandma. It smelled of dead leaves and floral perfume. And Noxzema.

Granny had passed away a week after my mom. She had spent her last few years in Poland in the company of a devoted younger man, and her last few months in the dark, disorienting maze of Alzheimer's. The news came to us one night in the aftermath of my mom's death, through Lech, her companion. He was calling from Warsaw and his voice was cracking as he struggled with his broken English.

"Talk to me in Polish," I said. "I understand."

And he told me.

I clicked into management and efficiency mode. I have a lot of experience packing. We boxed up thirty years of living in that house within a matter of days. We had to be mercenary. We purged quickly, shovelling memorabilia, big and small, into whatever receptacle was available. I was determined that we both clear out the mess. And my father was, remarkably, on board. On one of my trips to the dumpster outside, I walked by the open door of a room, carrying a box, and saw my father sitting and talking into space: "Why would you leave me?" I dipped my head and I let him be. She had been the great love of his life.

It was then that the grief hit me. Really hit me. To say that it was painful, that it was acute, that it tore my heart, would all be understatement. Grief ran through the centre of my chest like a phantom train. One minute I was carrying a box of plastic lampshades, the next I was pedalling through the air, spinning head over heels from the impact. I lowered myself on to a pile of objects, panting like an animal. Remember: *Grief is a practice. That's the riddle of it. Nothing is ever lost.* Even as the pain receded slightly, I knew I would never completely stop mourning for my mother: grief would forever be stitched into the fabric of my life. It would never leave. Nor did I want it to.

But something willed me on through those days of packing. The will to survive, perhaps. Freakish resilience. The idea that reliable salvation lies in doing. I had seen how the contours of my mother's personality could not be crushed. She had been our backbone, even after the crash. She had that improvisational thing going and much later, when I was less girl and more woman, she modelled how the altar I sought was in the core of our being. The knack of befriending squirrels and stray dogs never left her, and even from her wheelchair, she exhorted me to cherish nature and unfettered walks. She had a force in her none of us could contemplate. If that is not a legacy of strength and resilience, I don't know what is.

Everything was either thrown out or donated to Good Will. A truck pulled up to haul things away. I still feel a pang when I think about that house, but I knew we had to leave it all behind if we were going to move ahead. We put the house on the market. It sold within days, and we bought my dad an apartment close to mine in the Beaches.

No matter how loving and close I had gotten to my mother towards the end, I felt a lingering regret. Why didn't I spend more time with her? Why didn't I ask her more questions about her childhood or how she had found the courage to continue? And when I had crawled into bed and wrapped my arms and legs around her, why didn't I remind her that she meant everything to me? Everything. I was for the first time stricken by my choices; bypassing security and accumulation and status in order to express myself as I wished, without traditional boundaries—a migrant by choice. But there had also been a cost—not spending as much time with my mother when she needed me, for instance. Maybe it was time to reassess my ideas about life.

But really, it seems there wasn't a shortcut to the place I find myself in now—accepting the pain. Simply accepting the grief, not trying to rationalize it or push it away. She comes to me often in my dreams. A friend of mine said she'd seen her too. "I saw your mom in front of your old house. Just before she was swallowed up by the earth, she was smiling and she said: Stoicism." I researched the origins of this word, and I don't think she was giving me a stiff-upper-lip directive. In the Hellenic period, Stoics believed that the wise live in harmony with the forces that govern nature and are indifferent to the fluctuations of fortune and pleasure and pain; I like this message better.

After Marco, I had rationed out my energy and time carefully when it came to romantic possibilities. I had been spending so much time in comfortable solitude when I wasn't working, I didn't want to lose myself in another relationship. I'd had enough of an expression of love that screamed, "You are mine." Or the wrestle for dominance that brought out my worst side. I was tired of the hard, ironic edge and of who I became around men. After all, I meditated, I was financially independent, I had frequent-flier cards for every major airline, I didn't even have to solicit a "boss" for time off if I wanted to hike in Patagonia. What did I need a man for? I took my longings by the horns and enveloped myself in aloneness. I was thinking about getting a cat.

I had met Bobcat three years before, on a flight between New York and Toronto, back when the plane was my informal office. (Of course, his name isn't Bobcat, but he was slightly elusive, and I always called him that in my head.) We were seated next to each other. I was wearing a fedora I had picked up in a vintage store in New York and reading a script. He started a conversation with me, and I could tell he was intrigued but a bit restrained. He asked me if I was a writer, and the question pleased me. We had kept in touch for years as friends, but it hadn't become romantic. He was an investment banker and I have always been suspicious of men in suits. I thought we were philosophically at odds. But as we came to know each other, I learned about his youth in the wilds of northern British Colombia—bobcat territory. This explained the whiff of the mountain boy about him, much stronger than the whiff of Bay Street banker. We started to connect from a deeper place.

After I bought my quirky house in the Beaches in November 2007, he'd come over when I was in town and hang out in my kitchen and debate life philosophies affectionately, happy to be together. He would line up all the magnets on my fridge, which seemed a little *American Psycho*. He had been in the military and had a very clean-cut look. I used to tease him about having a double life where he was killing people on the side. Then he'd take off on these wild cycling trips across Europe— daring, independent adventures. Now I was the one who was intrigued.

But then I disappeared for my year of spiritual road tripping. It was only when I returned to Canada that we reconnected. He came over to fix my juicer and I found myself falling for him because, really, small-appliance repair is the route to any woman's heart. One September afternoon in 2008, as I was leaving for the hospital to visit my mom, he appeared unannounced at my door. He insisted on driving me and then politely stood outside my mother's hospital room in the hallway, typing on his BlackBerry. Inside the room, my mother's eyes were closed. She was lying back on the bed, visibly uncomfortable. But then she must have sensed my presence because she opened her eyes suddenly and said, "Oh hello! And who's that out there?" as if she'd been expecting him. I felt that she was acknowledging that he would be a source of comfort to me. My mother had always been extremely intuitive, and I believe she sensed my illness long before I did, and perhaps saw Bobcat as a soft place to fall. Within days of that visit, as if with her approval, we breached our differences, fell into each other, and became romantic partners.

A lot of life is timing, and while we were opposites in many ways—I, the bohemian; he, the businessman—in others, we were similar: both thirsting for pearls of experience. I didn't see any utility to settling down and having children at that time, and we were connected by our mutual disdain for traditional relationships. Ultimately, that's what tore us apart, but what happened between the juicer and our ending was profound. He has said to me, quite poignantly, from the safety of our present friendship, "Perhaps I came into your life to walk with you through that time." After my mother died, I was running on adrenaline, moving my father into his new house, working on projects like one possessed, up all night. I was also thinking about Hemingway, and I became obsessed with Key West. I wanted to go where Hemingway had worked, and I wanted a crazy adventure, which had always been my fallback, and my consolation. I felt I needed to inject a bit of madness into a world that seemed so focused on sombre distractions like the market tanking and year-end financials. The signature of the trip was "no reservations." I just wanted to see where the journey would take us, and Bobcat endeared himself to me by agreeing instantly to these conditions.

We rented a flashy yellow convertible. It was a dreamlike trip. We drove due south along the highway along Key West with the top down. I stood and spread my arms in that classic Bollywood gesture of surrender and rebellion, feeling the wet air on my face. Before the Seven Mile Bridge, we pulled over by the ocean, took off our shoes and walked the salty waves, palming little shells. Key West is a crazy town; it feels like a city of lost souls. We drove by a B-and-B called "The Mermaid

and the Alligator" and threw the convertible into reverse to spontaneously book ourselves into a room. They love their pineapples at the
Mermaid and the Alligator: pineapples were carved into the base of
lamp, wooden pineapples were propped up on consoles and the mantel-
piece. Pineapple watercolours. Pineapple bars of soap. And then, at
breakfast—yes, pineapple.

We had our own little hot tub outside, and stayed for days, drinking
in the kitsch and the heat, remaining entwined in sweaty sheets in a
four-poster bed until past noon. I could totally imagine innumerable
lost bohemian souls gathering in this old, lemony yellow Key West
house. It was a trip of lost souls, but we were celebrating them, not
mourning them, drinking wine, feeling the warm Florida winds. When
I was diagnosed, months later, I used to joke to Bobcat, "Okay, just take
me to Key West. I'm going to live out my days with decadence and
tragedy. No treatment for me! Key West, baby!" It was our favourite
morbid running joke.

Mom had been a firm agnostic, but I thought of my father as a Hindu
agnostic—someone who had been brought up in the improbable, how-
is-this-not-imploding Indian polytheistic milieu could never completely
commit to the non-existence of God. It just depends on which God we
are talking about. His beliefs hinged on evidence. Following my mother's death, my father retreated into himself, trying to bear his pain, and
I wanted to take him somewhere to ease it. We went to a Shambala
retreat centre in Vermont. Shambala Buddhism is an international
community based on the practices and teachings of Chogyam Trungpa,
a radical and colourful teacher of Tibetan Buddhism in the West. His
mission was to offer esoteric Tibetan practices in a secular setting. I was
drawn to his teachings after reading his 2003 book, *Shambala: The
Sacred Path of the Warrior* and it was all I concentrated on as I drove us
through a furious, swirling winter storm to get us to the retreat on time.

It was my father's first direct experience of meditation, but he was
entirely open to it. We were in silence together for several hours a day.
We did walking meditation outdoors in the icy Vermont wind, struck by
dead leaves. I wrote down what someone said to me then: "Sometimes

there are situations in life when words are only smoke on the fires, pointing to something but not capturing it." That was how we were, locked in our sadness and silence, missing her.

That Christmas, the Shambala centre became a wonderful sanctuary from where we could begin a new life without her. A woman called Laura Simms was running our retreat. She was a professional storyteller and humanitarian from New York with an exuberant presence. Laura travelled the world, weaving together oral traditions, and performance art, offering it up as healing and transformation. I'd never met a professional storyteller. But, of course, it's what we each do, every day—we excavate our own lives to create stories: interpreting all kinds of things as signs, or injecting meaning and lessons into the bleakest moments. I thought of Tenzin Palmo, and what she had said to me about bringing compassion into everything you do, and how both these women had broken through their restrictive moulds. On their shoulders, and those of women like them—women who devoted themselves to practices that question, clarify, reveal and transform—I was building a life. My father and I returned to Toronto, quiet and disoriented. My mom's ashes were in their modest box, and it seemed appropriate to take them to India, the country she had loved so much. I had to fly to India for Rado commitments, and before leaving, I spontaneously signed up for a Moksha Yoga teacher-training course to be held at an Ayurvedic resort in south India, deciding I'd do that afterwards. I invited my dad to join me and take in the sights of Kerala while I did my training.

As soon as I arrived in India, my double life was back in full swing. During the publicity tour for Rado I felt a glass wall come up between me and the world. I became a spectator of others around me during assorted shoots and appearances for other products. My view of India upon landing was filtered through stylists and make-up artists, the next generation who spoke confidently about contemporary trends in Indian fashion: "Revivalists are having their day—you must wear a Raw Mango saree to your next event. Did you see Payal Khandwala's show at Lakme Fashion Week? She orchestrates colour and textures so beautifully—layered and minimal. She has such a global aesthetic grounded in Indian textiles. You would rock her look!" These achingly chic girls were schooled in New York, Barcelona and Florence.

I experienced myself being photographed at lavish events with the paparazzi calling for a smile. Here I was, back again in the situation that felt increasingly incidental to my life; the centre of attention. Neither mapped or plotted, I could admit I hated it. But it gave me a unique vantage point to gauge the rapid changes of India. Globalization had brought the collective big dreams and current realities of the world together in one bland formula: the predictable spread of McDonalds and KFC and Starbucks across the landscape. Step out of the airport, anywhere in the world, and you are no longer a stranger. But it was the strangeness of travel that had always been my refuge. And there was no place in the world stranger than India. But I now had to accept: India was changing, striving to construct a new reality, tangible and separate from the past, set apart from the crusted-over buildings and the old bones of tradition.

This contemporary Indian reality was fired by the global mono-culture, by want versus need, but combined with that baffling Indian mixture of conservatism and openness to absorbing new ideas. Materialism and new desires spread through the arteries of India, across sugarcane and mustard fields, through degraded lands and over both Malabar-tiled roofs and urban sprawl, injecting the entire coun-try with a new feeling: Yes. We. Can. This optimism was sublimated by a new tyranny of aspiration to buy new things and craft new identities independent from clans and bloodlines. It was such a seismic change from two decades ago when my middle-class Bengali Brahmin family expressed contempt for people who owned too many clothes and the idea of travelling abroad was neither important nor viable. And yet so much of India had not changed. The same ambitious young women tending me were tentatively bringing patriarchy into discussion. As I got my make-up done, I listened to them talk about how hard it was to break with their conditioning, the old taboos and prejudices. These independent, devastatingly lovely women with "Girl Power" and other slogans on their lips, still grappled with the notion that all their accom-plishments led to one place: marriage and motherhood. And the fetters were not all in society but in their own minds. As they talked, I won-dered how much of these ideas had infiltrated my psyche, because, after all, I too had grown up seeing versions of Indian matrimony both

on screen and in real life, embodied in the elaborate rituals and plat-
ters arranged with betel leaves, vermilion and sweets, the bride with
lowered eyes and tinkling anklets, basking in the triumph of having
achieved her purpose. These conversations helped me see myself in a
new light. In my journal, I wrote: "India is a hallucinogenic trip for
anyone suffering from too much confidence in their own knowledge."
When that part of my life came to a halt, I left for my yoga course at
the southern tip of the subcontinent.

The retreat was run by Ted Grand and Jessica Robertson out of a
resort in Kerala called Isola Di Cocco, the island of coconuts. Kerala
is called the Venice of India, a web of canals with boats of jackwood
and coconut rope punting through the mangroves. Yoga, massage and
Ayurvedic medicine have made for a booming tourist trade, and our
resort had a great swimming pool and treatments that were part
ancient-mystical, part modern-spa. We practiced the Moksha Yoga
sequence of asanas (postures) and had our lectures on anatomy and the
yoga sutras in an elevated thatched hut that overlooked the merge
between the backwaters and the roiling ocean.

Both Ted and Jessica endeared themselves to me with their sincer-
ity and simplicity. Ted in particular made me feel like an old friend.
About a week into the course, his wife, Tara Maclean, arrived with
two angelic blonde girls on her hip. As soon as I saw Tara, I knew we
belonged to each other, like sisters from another lifetime. Tara had
met Ted at the peak of her career as a talented singer and songwriter
in Canada. She soon gave up her touring career to focus on family and
simpler joys, without giving up her artistry. I found in Tara a quality
I had missed after my mother passed: nurturing. Now Tara stepped in
with a tenderness and steadfastness that didn't make sense if you consider we had just met. But I accepted it as one more affirmation that
life is still for me.

Many of the people who came to the retreat were tending to heartbreak, and found comfort in the lush, magical location and atmosphere.
Initially I isolated myself from the group. While I craved aloneness,
part of me was a little sceptical of the community, fancying myself an
outlier. After a few weeks of exhausting public events for my other life,
any social activity in this setting that jostled and forced its way to my

attention caused me consternation. We were practicing two or three intense yoga sessions a day combined with lectures and workshops from morning to night. I was getting very tired. We would end each session with *shavasana*, the corpse pose, lying on the back with the arms and legs lifeless. I'd drift off and when I'd open my eyes, an hour would have gone by. *An hour*. I'd still be there, and everyone would have left. I had come for the same transformation that drew everyone to Kerala, but the irony is that even as I peeled myself weakly off the floor, I didn't figure out what kind of transformation was going on inside my own body during this time.

I did know that something was wrong; my body's messages were breaking through. For instance, I just couldn't keep the sequence of postures in my head. It had been happening on sets too, where I could barely remember my lines and struggled through the day. I would feel sleepy after lunch, the heavy-lidded sleep of a construction worker. So, I had experimented with cutting out carbs, drinking more coffee, waking later, sleeping earlier. I surrendered to Ayurvedic treatments, getting walloped and massaged and locked into a steam box for an alarming length of time. I remember crying out faintly, imagining my bones gelatinized, pouring out like a soup when the sturdy amma returned. Still, nothing seemed to work, so I had ignored it.

But now I could no longer ignore this disturbing failing of my mind. How was I supposed to teach a Moksha Yoga class if I couldn't remember the sequence of postures? Out of desperation I came up with a mnemonic device, matching the English names of the asanas to a nonsensical composition I wrote on the hotel's stationery:

A runner
Chased by a warrior, then two
A running triangle
Point forward, wide legs
The runner toppled my tree
I landed in dancer's pose
I was now the tree
And the tree was a corpse

The wind relieved me
It threaded the needle
Lifted my legs
Into a boat, under a bridge
I saw a cobra, a locust
And a bow on a child

If you fall out of a pose, it's not a big deal, it's yoga! And if I can't remember what pose comes next, it's no big deal, right? It's just yoga!

I was starting to feel drained by all the yoga classes, but I attended the lectures and slowly began to enter the group, like a child creeping out from under a staircase. The training begins and ends with a "sharing circle," which always seemed a little Kumbaya for me. There's a psycho-spiritual crack, and you mine it, sharing what you're feeling, why you're there, what you hope to find. By the end of the sessions, where we'd learned so much about opening the body and the mind, I was finally ready to open myself. I shared what I'd experienced the last few years: the taut feeling clenched in my stomach that never let me rest, the bad love affairs, the attempt on my life, the seeking, the ache for spiritual liberation, and the death of my mother. The effect of starting was mesmeric. I couldn't stop. And when I checked, I wasn't ashamed. I allowed myself to bawl from some part of me I had locked away for years. For the first time, I understood the value of community, something I had shrunk from for many years. Perhaps the sharing circle, corny as it seems, set me down the path of sharing my experiences with the world at large.

My father flew in from Calcutta to join me in Kerala after the course, carrying my mother's ashes in their brown box. One morning we hired a car and driver to take us to Kanyakumari, the southernmost tip of India, a symbolic and sacred place where the Bay of Bengal meets the Indian Ocean and the Arabian Sea. The three bodies of water come crashing on to this strip of windswept coast by a slightly shabby little market town where vendors sell trinkets. On a little island across from the town is a memorial dedicated to the revered spiritual leader Swami Vivekananda, perched on the rock where he is believed to have attained enlightenment, surrounded by noisy tourists and people who come to sit in abiding quietness. It's a fifteen-minute ride in a ferry packed with pilgrims wanting to pay their respects.

My father was carrying my mother's remains in a traditional cloth bag slung over his shoulder. We had been thwarted in our attempt to find a jetty or an appropriate beach from which to scatter the ashes. It was extraordinarily windy that day and I had a strong premonition that my mother's ashes would be carried into the market and end up as an extra coating on some patron's lunch. And while a number of small fishing boats lined the shore, there didn't seem to be any owners to approach with our strange request: "How much to row us into the place where the three oceans meet so I can scatter my mom's remains?" Mind you, in India anything goes, and as a matter of fact, Gandhi's ashes were immersed in the same place. It was a question of how. So, my father and I found ourselves on the ferry to Vivekananda Rock more as a distraction from the mission at hand, than with any real motive.

Once on the island, my father and I sat together in the meditation hall. Outside, the sun was boiling hot, but I was struck by the ingenious, simple solution: paths on the rock were painted white, deflecting the heat and keeping our feet from burning. I remember walking the entire rock on the white path, scanning the horizon, looking for a sign. We finally climbed back on the ferry. As I swayed next to my dad on that creaking old ferry, a warm wind whipped through the boat, laughter and screams from children mixing with the all-pervading sound of the waves. Standing by the railing, elbow-to-elbow with all these strangers, clothing flapping in the wind, my father and I looked at each other and we knew. We had been searching for a formal moment in which to let my mother's ashes fly free, but my mother had always embraced the opposite qualities in life. This was the most perfect moment, in the most appropriate place in the world, to let my mother's ashes mix with the waters. She had loved the chaos and warmth of India, and she had a wicked sense of humour. It was now. My father caught my look. "Now?" It wasn't a question as much as an acknowledgement. "Yes."

I sprang into action. While anything goes in India, I was still conscious that anyone could also object. I felt a sense of urgency; it was a short ride and we were not far from the shore. I pulled the box out from the bag as inconspicuously as possible and stumbled across to the open window. It was a tricky move. Each roll of the vessel was marked by loud cheers and whoops from the passengers. My dad followed cautiously. I elbowed a little room next to the bars that covered the side of the ferry and pretended initially to enjoy the view. I was struck by the setting sun reflecting off the myriad ripples. "Can you see the three colours of the water?" my dad asked.

The ocean was both quiet and joyfully animated. I opened the top of the box, reached in and took a handful of ash. In that moment, I saw my mother's journey collapse in those diamond waves. My father covered my hand with his and we leaned through the bars, letting the ashes scatter through our open fingers. *Fly, Mama, fly.* Flowers were floating on the water—from a devotee on the Rock or perhaps they had travelled down the Ganges, far up north from the delta where the great river mixed with salt water. Who could say? Methodically we continued to dip into the box and hold her ashes to the wind. I saw the ash turn iridescent, like teardrops, like pearls. I left the last handful for my father and we watched as they were massaged into the sea. Such privacy in public is not possible in many parts of the world, but in India, these moments are not just understood but played out again and again. Watching the ash blend into the water sank into a secret place deep within me and filled me with so much lightness I had to laugh out loud from the tickle inside. Nobody batted an eye, of course. At that moment, surrounded by all the chattering people, I felt immense tenderness for that very benevolent, uniquely Indian mixture of the metaphysical and the everyday.

Meanwhile, back in Toronto, Bobcat was growing a little impatient. He thought "no reservations" was cute, but he didn't know my other unspoken life rule: No return date. When he had asked me when I was coming back, I had scoffed. The distance was harder on him than I'd allowed myself to acknowledge. But my priority then was to get my dad to experience the premier bootcamp for spiritual warriors; the ten-day introduction to Tibetan Buddhism course at Tushita, that I'd found so moving the year before. In the burning heat of April, we flew from Kerala to Delhi, and then took a Kingfisher Airline flight to Dharamshala. Kingfisher Airlines was renowned in those days for its nubile air stewardesses dolled up in flashy red uniforms and matching lipstick, as well as its flamboyant owner, liquor baron Vijay Mallya, the self-professed "King of Good Times" who would deliver a personal address onboard in a flat-ironed hairstyle (and who later became so embroiled in financial scandals that he had to flee India). Off we went to our mountain refuge for spiritual learning on an airline named after a beer. Once arrived in the cooler climate of McLeod Ganj, I decided to take whatever course was starting at Tushita, which happed to be "On Death and Dying." A warning shot for my psyche? Spiritual inoculation?

The Buddhist nun who was leading my retreat came from California; she had taken her vows a year before. Her name was Tenzin Chogkyi (real name: Petra McWilliams). She was preternaturally tall with a slight stoop, probably earned during her three years of solitary meditation in a yurt in the Arizona desert. I called her the Cali Surfer Nun, "Surfing the waves of consciousness." We laughed a lot, which makes no sense considering the subject matter. She wrote a brief outline of the course: Death has been seen as a "failure" of medical science and this attitude permeates Western culture. The Buddhist view is it's a natural part of life, not a punishment or failure. In Tibetan culture, we honour the transition, and by contemplating death we can lead more meaningful lives. Death awareness trains you to keep your relationships clean and it's the ultimate dress rehearsal—you're less afraid if you know what to expect!

Buddhists tend to rehearse their deaths, believing that we're constantly being recycled through multiple lives: dying and being reborn. There's never a full stop; we're always in transit, preparing for the next take off. Certain rituals can help prepare us to get rid of the dark mesh of fear of the great transition. Tenzin led us through a visualization of our own deaths. We used our breath to settle our minds, and she said: "You're seated in a doctor's office, and the doctor says: 'You have a very serious disease, and only six months to live.' Let's experience that moment. And what happens afterwards."

Now when I look back at my journals from that course, it stuns me. When Tenzin Chogkyi asked us to write down our motivation and intention for this course, I wrote: "I want to face fear of the unknown, understand Mom's death, and prepare for my own."

On the grounds of the centre is a stupa, a pretty white tea cake of a monument, housing relics from the original Rinpoches—sometimes known as "root teachers"—embedded inside it. All day long, students circumambulate, walking clockwise around the structure. When I had checked in to the Tushita Centre, the young woman at the desk had recognized me from my earlier six-month-long stay. "We're quite full at the moment and we don't often encourage people to stay inside the stupa but would you like to give it a try?" I eagerly consented to sleeping in a windowless room that seemed better suited to a hobbit, beneath the mound-like belly of the stupa. I would slip off my shoes at a small set of hidden steps, open the weathered latch door and crawl into this womblike chamber. It was like entering a chamber of my own heart. I had strong, sometimes disturbing visions while staying there. At night I would feel the room rotating and once, when I woke, I was floating close to the mandala painted on the ceiling, above my body. Other times a myriad of worlds opened behind my eyes, populated by apsaras and demons, terrifying and compassionate. Regardless of whether these experiences happened or not, they felt real to me. But the demons and the angels, in this spirit-ridden crossroads were contained in me. They were projections of my own mind. Once I understood that, I was never afraid. Gradually my nerves loosened and began vibrating to a different rhythm. Later I learned that a teacher who had stayed there had such intense feelings that he fled in the night.

My dad was staying in the regular residences. Because we were all in silence, I'd get little handwritten notes from him: "Do you have any shampoo? I'm almost out." I passed off the goods to him while we walked away from the main buildings and tried not to make eye contact with the monkeys, who were crazed and known to leap on the heads of meditators. There was a lot of activity one night because Lama Zopa, the founder of Tushita, was on the grounds and Richard Gere had come for a visit. He brought with him a white embroidered *khata*, or ceremonial scarf. A burbling crowd of disciples gathered for a glimpse. Richard Gere was an oft-seen presence in the area and a patron. It was even rumoured that he had financed some of the infrastructure in McLeod Ganj.

My father became the honorary mascot of Tushita. He was one of the oldest people to take the ten-day silent retreat, and everyone loved him. I was very proud. Sitting silently for hours and hours at any age is hellish on the back and mind, let alone at seventy-six years old. But I think something was transmitted to him during that experience. I'm convinced, despite his modest, self-deprecating ways, that he success-fully intuited the secret of the universe. As is the case with anyone who has lost their soulmate or life partner, it could have gone either way for him; he might have lost himself too and just shut down, waiting for release. Instead, he came out with a great sense of peace. I wrote down what he said to me: "Papa says that everything changes. You are not who you think you are, and you are responsible for all living beings." I loved that; it was a beautifully distilled conclusion to arrive at after all the pain of the past months.

We returned home in May. At the airport, Bobcat stood back and stared at me. If I look at photos of myself from this time, or even from a year before, when I shot *Cooking with Stella*, I am a zombie. Even with the lighting and make-up, the recent pictures I'd taken for the Rado campaign had captured what was going on. Pasty and sallow, I looked like a dying woman. On the drive home from the airport, Bobcat told me I needed to get tested. I retreated to my constant refrain: "I'm too impa-tient to wait for blood tests and results. I need to keep moving. I can't wait around!"

Bobcat said he would book me an appointment at Medcan, an exec-utive health centre for the Bay Street crowd, a veer into the private system. There, the results would come in the same day, and Medcan would refer me to any specialists back in the public system. As Bobcat presented his case, I caught a glimpse of myself in the side mirror of the car. I was transparent, and I was exhausted. What did they say during the Moksha training again, I thought to myself. Was it: your biography is your biology, or your biology is your biography? I closed my eyes and agreed to the appointment.

16

IT WAS A birdless morning in May in the brick canyons when I zig-zagged my way through the rush hour crowds on the pavement and entered a building off York Street. In the lobby I watched people consent to *not* trample and push each other. Medcan is on the fifteenth floor of one of the lofty buildings off of Bay Street, the financial centre of Canada. I got into the elevator feeling discombobulated; everything was too shiny and much too uniform after India. This part of the city, where people circled profits and losses, had until then existed on the periphery of my consciousness. I was scheduled in for a five-hour long health assessment—the Medcan "speciality"—meant to uncover lurking illness for busy Type-As who expected same-day results. Sounded like me on both accounts. It was to be the first thorough physical I'd had in a decade. Bobcat had, true to his word, made this appointment for me just a few days after I had landed in Toronto.

In the waiting room, which looked like it belonged in a nice hotel, I drank lattes, and snacked on cereal in between getting shuffled from room to room. Blood tests. Ultrasounds. Treadmills. To this very day, my doctor, Dr Susy Lin, feels guilty about making me run to my capacity that day when I was actually on the edge of going into cardiac arrest. But nobody knew that then.

Dizzy after hours of tests, I dressed and went into Dr Lin's office. I sat down in front of her as she flipped through my reports. Then suddenly, as if she had something urgent to do, she got to her feet. Panicked. "How are you even standing?" she said.

"Well, I'm sitting," I tried to joke, but my giggle was nervous.

"A normal red blood cell count is about 120. Acceptable is 90. You're at 30. Before we go any further, get to Emergency. You need a blood transfusion. Then we'll talk."

So the disease of whose insistent presence we were unaware was moving quickly. My plasma cells were growing at such a rapid rate that they had squeezed out the red blood cells. My bone marrow was becoming semi-solid. Red blood cells carry oxygen through the system, and this explained why I'd been having recurring problems with my memory. Finally, an explanation for why, two years ago, I'd really struggled to learn my lines during *Cooking with Stella*. And why, during my recent yoga training, the most basic postures, ones I'd been doing for years, had simply vanished mid-sequence, leaving me standing totally still, unsure of what came next. My red blood cells hadn't been doing the job of bringing oxygen to my brain, and my brain, I now came to understand, had been starving.

"Go to emergency!" ordered Susy Lin. I went immediately to the ER at Toronto General Hospital. After a seven-hour wait, I was given a transfusion. It took two bags to replenish my cells—two pints of blood. A nurse raised her eyebrow. Apparently, this was an alarming amount. The ER doctor went along with my joking around, playing bartender: "Okay, we'll top you up." But he also said he didn't know why this had happened, and that doctors would have to monitor me to see if my red blood cell count dropped again. But once I'd gotten the infusion, I felt terrific. I thought the problem had been solved, and I shrugged off his concern. I emailed Dr Lin with an update:

Hi Doc
This is Lisa Ray—Monday, transfusion girl.

I went to Toronto General and got three units of blood in a transfusion after we spoke! The doctors there did some more investigation—they did a rectal exam (fun!) to see if I was bleeding and more blood work which confirmed all the previous results. The doctors were pretty puzzled about why my haemoglobin was so low, but they recommended doing the transfusion and then following up with a haematologist later. So, they didn't laugh me out of ER at all! I've spoken to Michelle about setting up with the haematologist and now addressing my thyroid. But my cheeks are really red now!

Thanks Doc and let me know if you'd like me to come by again.

Cheers—

Lisa

After two weeks I had my blood checked again and my red cell count had dropped as alarmingly as the stock market months before during the global financial crash. I was given a list of referrals and procedures to rule out internal bleeding as a cause. Both the ER doctors and Susy Lin said the same thing, "Now we wait and watch."

I turned to Bobcat, "Key West it is, baby!"

"Amazing, so happy for us," he answered, poker-faced.

"You are becoming so aah-naal."

"Why can't you just say anal?"

"I don't like the way it sounds."

A fork had appeared along in the road. One was marked Calamity, but I chose the other—Adventure. I was seeing all of this as a new adventure. I swear I even found the colonoscopy interesting.

Thus began months of waiting. It's not like the movies where they take your blood then call you in with the big news. Especially in Canada, where diagnosis is a long, agonizingly slow process, appointment upon appointment, test upon test. In between, I was shooting TV appearances, and agreed to participate in a South Asian Film Festival. All systems go. Everything normal. Meanwhile, my blood had become public property. Because I'd had the infusion at Toronto General, my results were put into the University Hospital Network, where several local hospitals, including Princess Margaret, share information. This is how a haematologist who specialized in multiple myeloma found me, like someone on a dating site stumbling across his perfect match.

Dr Galal had called me as soon as he saw my blood work on the database and left messages. And yet we didn't connect. I've never been good with voice messages. I admit that I saw his name come up on the caller ID a couple of times, and I didn't pick up. I was busy, but I think I also knew why he was calling. Maybe deep down I could feel the urgency waiting for me on the other end of the line. But how fortunate and strange that out in the world was an oncologist—no, a *healer*—trying to find me so desperately, as if he *had* to take care of me. Finally, I listened to his message. Almost breathlessly, he introduced himself as a doctor at Princess Margaret's, a specialist in multiple myeloma, who was concerned about my blood work. Could I call him back, please? It was the first time I had heard the words—Multiple Myeloma. But still I didn't call him back.

Earlier, just a few days before Dr Galal's voicemail, I had gone for a bone marrow biopsy with another doctor at North York General Hospital. The hospital was in the north of Toronto, a little out of my way, but Medcan had found all my tests inconclusive, and had referred me to a specialist to examine my marrow. I took Bobcat, and we agreed that he'd stay with me during the ordeal, which could be gruelling. He had a bit of a swagger because he'd had forty-seven stitches in his own hip; how bad could a biopsy be?

Well, when they took out the giant needle, Bobcat the Military Man passed out. He later climbed up off the floor and staggered into the hall. I didn't see any of it from my position, lying on my stomach on the stretcher. I didn't even know he left the room. Meanwhile, the doctor couldn't get a decent sample, so down he went into my hip with his electric drill over and over, while I sang "Hey Jude" at the top of my lungs. Those high notes really dissipate the pain. I had half the nurses singing along with me. What I didn't know was that the myeloma was so advanced that my bone marrow was no longer soft. It had gone solid; they were trying to pull out steak with a needle.

I never knew that we have sensation inside our bones; they're a part of the body we never touch. During the biopsy, I felt a sense of violation. My body was rising up and closing in on whatever object was forcing its way into my deepest core. You can't freeze bone, but the flesh around the cut was frozen. The shadow in my marrow resisted by going deeper. My bones were not ready for this full disclosure. The more the doctor drilled, the deeper the secret travelled until I thought he would scrape metal, having passed right through me. But after one last tug I felt a release as he removed the sample and stepped aside to let a nurse clean me up. I rested my head on my arms, my breathing jagged, thinking about how to turn this into a funny anecdote later.

I imagine the doctor was wearing a bib, I'd say, *one of those lobster bibs—covered in plastic up to his chin. He appeared a conscientious man, someone who fills out warranty cards for his Harman Karden speakers, which is exactly the sort of person you want mining into the most intimate bits of yourself.*

I think the disease had been progressing in me for about two years. All these medical tests and investigations finally gave me a chance to really tune in to my body. I was short of breath all the time. This had been an issue during yoga practice , which is all about focusing the breath, the delivery system of prana. Yet I had ignored this signal. When I thought I was well, I was always trying to override my weariness. I'd repeat the mantra of the modern world: *I'm stressed. I'm overworked. I've got too much going on.* Discomfort was my normal. As well as feeling uprooted. But if I'd really listened to my body, it wouldn't have allowed me to get out of bed. Maybe I hadn't faced the possibility of serious illness because then I would have to face what was wrong, not just in my body but in my life.

The medical establishment, I'm sure, has a name for it when you are the last patient of the day. Or maybe there's just a look that's exchanged behind reception, as the waiting room empties and they see you, slumping lower in your seat, worn down with the suspense. "There's another one," they think, "about to join the Cancer Club."

I had noticed the sign in the waiting room of North York General Hospital that said "Haematology" but I didn't give it a second thought. I was here to meet Dr S about the results of my bone marrow aspiration, but I didn't think about how I would react to a serious health crisis. Hushed and drowsy by the filtered afternoon light, I just concentrated on waiting. The room was full and bustling while a TV played quietly in one corner. My body ached from sitting. I imagined a guy pitching for the Medical Waiting room contract: "Ready to dress up your hospital's reception area? Our seat upholstery is made of leakproof material, designed to keep patients who pee themselves while waiting for the results of a bone marrow biopsy feeling welcome and comfortable."

There were others like me, stretching and jiggling and tapping in shifty boredom. I smiled at the sad-eyed man opposite me. He looked away. Bobcat was sitting next to me, clicking away on his BlackBerry. He had arrived from "the office" and kept pulling at his tie. I had on a blazer. I almost never wore what I viewed as "corporate" attire, yet here I was, in that hospital waiting room, dressed as if for a job interview, or as a character on one of those television shows I hate about lawyers. I began noticing details in the room, as if stilled and laid on top of each other: a copy of the *Chatelaine* magazine carelessly thrown open to the recipe page (watermelon and feta salad). The haloed head of an old woman's perm. Elongated shadows of patients called into other rooms and nurses passing in the hallway. The room emptying. Peace, and the last patient of the day. Me.

Bobcat was stressed in a way I hadn't seen before. I was annoyed by his anxiety which crawled over my left shoulder in an unmistakable straight line. I needed to intervene before it could enter my mouth and make me spit out the seriousness of this moment. I didn't want to give *this* a name. Not yet. I tried to appear cavalier as the room emptied out, because, after all, who keeps someone waiting this long for good news? Thirty people, then twenty-five. Then twenty. Then it was 2 p.m. Then 4 p.m. I poked Bobcat through his suit and scrunched up my face to get a distracted smile. Around 5 p.m. there was just us. And then the nurse called my name.

The nurse escorted us both into what appeared to be a supply closet. Long, narrow and cluttered, the windowless room had a built-in ply-wood desk that ran its entire length and some very thick, precariously stacked books on shelves at shoulder height. Something like a mop was leaning in the darkest corner. The doctor and Bobcat were seated on a couple of little round rolling stools. I was wedged into an outsized steel-framed chair, too wide to place at any angle except the one where I was, knee to knee with the doctor. Bobcat, gave up on his seat and leant against the desk, staring resolutely at his BlackBerry. The haematologist was jittery. His bleached eyebrows and peaked face under fluorescent tube lights took on the qualities of an albino rabbit. My own grip on reality was in a slow cinematic dissolve. I was waiting for the rabbit doctor to start blurting, "Oh dear! Oh dear! I shall be too late!" before kicking me down the rabbit hole. Instead, he adjusted his glasses and swept his watery blue eyes over me. Hands folded primly in his lap, he began, "We received the results of the bone marrow aspiration." Pause. Count to five. Bobcat's eyes flickered towards me. Oh, am I supposed to say something? Out loud? I smiled. I beamed. Encouragingly, I thought. The doctor recoiled slightly. Aha. Less circus clown smile. Focus. The doctor's mouth was moving.

"You. Have. Multiple. Myeloma." He blinked after each syllable. "Multiple. My-eh-low-maa."

Silence.

"It's a rare blood disease."

He never said "cancer," but I knew, in my marrow, that this was a moment of juncture, one of those unbidden points where the old life meets the new, just as I knew what it meant to be called in as the last patient of the day. The doctor continued doling out the bad news, pausing sympathetically after each instalment of facts so we'd have a moment to digest. Or cry. There were a lot of details. "Serious situation," he said, ". . . not curable . . . fatal." It was like someone shooting you over and over again, word by word. Boom. Boom. He looked at me closely, searching for a reaction. "It's a lot to take in. I know. You will have to pace yourself. Treating this disease is like running a marathon." Bobcat was a blob behind him. I was fixated by the doctor's pale freckled skin, a pulse dancing in his right temple, sweat dampening his collar. Silence. He told me he was going to put me on medications and there would be serious side effects. I just smiled: "Don't worry about it. Those side effects won't happen to me." The doctor was unnerved. I could tell. "Are you sure you want me to go on? It's a lot of information. We don't have to go through everything today."

I smiled. "No, no. Please go ahead. Do you want some water, doc?"

He seemed confused. Did he hear right?

"Would you like some water, doc?" I reached out and patted his hand. "You look thirsty."

So it was that I smiled and nodded as the doctor droned on, giving me information packages, like a high school guidance counsellor giving a teenager pamphlets on the pill. Of course, I didn't hear a thing. I had stopped listening after the last syllable of "Myeloma." Why? Because it simply didn't occur to me that I would not get better.

I didn't need all that information. Statistics. Percentages. Protocol. Bleak arithmetic. I didn't want a statement of the odds. All that data reassures some. Not me. Information, I have learned, is a heavy back-pack. I was defecting to curiosity as a pure, stainless state from which to handle this disease. I didn't want to think, "I know nothing," and panic. I *wanted* to know nothing and begin my MM membership oper-ating from a place of trust.

And that's when I blanked out. I dropped into absolute silence, watching the doctor's jaw moving, the papers in his hand. Bobcat, ready to research, was taking notes. I watched the two men as if they were in a show. I was rocking slightly, bumping knees with the doctor. Up until that moment I had cast myself as the tragicomic heroine of my own life. "Well," I thought, "I'm finally in a situation worthy of that cast-ing." But, it still didn't occur to me that I could die. I will, of course, one day. But not now. And not from this blood cancer called "multiple myeloma." But I could not explain why.

If the doctor had asked, I would have said, we all face different kinds of adversity, doc, but hey, in the words of Mr Charlie Chaplin, nothing is permanent, including your sorrows. But he didn't ask and I couldn't wait to leave. It was only once the doctor finished, and I had walked past the empty reception desk, through the double doors of the hospital to the car, that I could lay my head against the dashboard and exhale. I felt relief. Yes . . . I wanted to lay down my head and bawl with *relief*. Because I had known something was wrong. For a long time I had known it in my blood and bones. And in my life. I had been in per-petual motion for so long. Living in a state of high alert mania, cortisol flooding my brain and body had become my normal. I had been run-ning since sixteen. Too long. And I knew; nothing less than a diagnosis of terminal cancer would give me permission to stop.

On the drive home from the hospital the late-afternoon June sun is all amber heat; I'm grateful for its burn. The light's angle changes as we change our direction while navigating the road. It is now hitting my right cheek, now my forehead. I lower the sun visor and close my eyes.

Bobcat has turned on the radio. Local news, traffic updates and the latest sports round-up create the illusion of a normal ride home. Around us, strapped into BMWs and Toyotas, I catch glimpses of men and women with faraway looks in their eyes, letting their faces go slack on their rush hour commute. When I catch a side glance of Bobcat, his face is stone, like one of those Easter Island statues. Nothing has really sunk in. I think: Well this might be inconvenient, like having mono or strep throat, but in six weeks or so down the line, it'll be over. But as we approach my home in the Beaches, I feel the beginning of anxiety, like tiny wings fluttering against my skin. What do I tell my father?

Bobcat parked the car, leaving me alone to enter my apartment and face my father with the news. My dad stands as I climb the stairs, his features combining in a question. I look at his face and suddenly it's as if the earth has dropped out from under my feet. I put my medical reports on the table and gather myself for a moment. "Well, it looks like I have this thing called 'multiple myeloma.' It's a rare blood cancer." It comes out too fast, like a gulp of air before jumping from a plane. He nods. Something passes between us. A memory of my mother in his eyes. A remembered prayer. A fissure in time. We are both locating ourselves in this moment. Without any words, my father reaches out and holds me, very tight. The mystery in my blood has been solved. The plasma cells in my bone marrow have been rampaging, multiplying, squeezing out the red blood cells. I now understand I've been running on low—oxygen and red blood cells and energy—for far too long. I can finally admit I'm weary and don't know what to do next. I'm yearning for a strong hand. But I haven't asked for help in a long time; I've forgotten how. "It's okay Lisa Rani. We will get through this." My father's green-grey eyes are very present behind his glasses. "Now that we know what's wrong, we can fix it." He envelops me in another hug. Something very strong and bright is restored inside me. I relax in his arms. Now that I know—we know—what's wrong, *we* can do something about it.

Maybe irrational optimism is my legacy. Along with the cancer, it too has infected my marrow. Whether my father is fearful inside but projecting strength, or completely at peace is not my business. I've had enough experiences to be able to distil one truth: Life is unpredictable, so why should we react in predictable ways? Once Bobcat joins us, I settle into the sofa, while he and my father turn their attention to being resourceful.

After I tell my father, the atmosphere in my loft shifts. For the next few hours, it becomes a centre of efficiency. My dad's face is aglow with the light from the computer screen. He is researching multiple myeloma, scribbling on a writing pad while Bobcat has removed his jacket and tie to sit at the dining table, back to Dad, hunched over his "crackberry." Whether he's looking up the prognosis for my rare blood disease or the latest news on the market isn't clear. What is clear is we each have retreated into familiar rituals. Dad is focused on grasping the complexities of this disease. Bobcat, I suspect, is doing predictive modelling and risk analysis. His slavish regard for data is his fatal flaw, in my opinion. But I am not a statistic. I am not a dot on a graph.

"Whatever you do, don't Google it," was the doctor's parting line. I was surprised by this suggestion. It's like telling a surfer not to think of the sea, so, after a quick online search, I hide my phone under a pile of magazines. Myeloma is incurable. It's a relatively rare cancer of the bone marrow (159,985 cases were diagnosed globally in 2018, less than 1 per cent of all cancers[1]). I'm a junior member of the Multiple Myeloma Club in many ways, having been diagnosed at the age of thirty-seven; the average age of diagnosis is sixty-five. Makes the disease not quite as "sexy" as other cancers but we can change that. Apparently, the life expectancy for multiple myeloma patients has increased in the last few years due to new drugs like Velcade and Revlimid and other promising new treatments in the pipeline. That's the good news. The not so good news is it's still considered fatal. There's also a lot of outdated, contradictory information online. I guess that explains the doctor's advice. He thinks if I read "average survival rate one to two years" my skull will spontaneously combust, releasing unpleasant thoughts into the air. But instead of feeling smothered by fear, I'm opening like a sunroof at noon. Sometimes a punch to the stomach shocks you into seeing clearly. I still believe in multiple chances and second lives.

The morning after the diagnosis, the shock starts to wear off slowly. Yesterday is a dream; something that cannot be fully grasped. In the

---

1   https://www.wcrf.org/dietandcancer/cancer-trends/worldwide-cancer-data

living room I spy the multiple myeloma information package, spread out like an unfinished game of Solitaire on my coffee table. The pamphlets are printed with images of old people, bathed in a luminous light and smiling knowingly. They don't seem distressed at all. Maybe they've already passed over, and now they are sending back useful information for cancer interns like myself.

I set water to boil in the kitchen for tea then lower myself slowly on to a chair because, well, I'm weak. Yes, finally I can admit I've been running on fumes for many months. I run my fingers through my bushy hair. It's too much effort to brush this morning. Maybe losing my hair will not be such a bad thing? At least I'll save a ton on shampoo. My mind travels back to the unanswered phone message, and the name that had flashed on my phone so many times before. I spin my phone on the table top, waiting until it stops, then I pick it up and call Dr Galal, "There's something I'd like to discuss with you." Now it was my turn to search for him.

The next day, I'm seated in yet another waiting room, this time on the eighth floor of Princess Margaret Hospital. There is a different quality to this place, I felt it as soon as I entered. "Believe It: We will Conquer Cancer in Our Lifetime" say the banners. I do believe it. This hospital makes me want to skip. I know my reaction to the prognosis of this disease is atypical. Perhaps a tad delusional. Especially when you find out you have what is defined, in one of the MM patient handbooks, as a "catastrophic illness": "A severe illness requiring prolonged hospitalization or recovery. Examples include coma, leukaemia, heart attack or stroke. These illnesses usually involve high costs for hospitals, doctors and medicines and may incapacitate the person from working, creating a financial hardship." And that's the good news, right? After all, what's a bit of financial hardship when you're flirting with death? That's what I'm thinking when the doctor's door opens, and I'm ushered inside.

"I am Dr Ahmed Galal." He stands up from behind his desk and grasps my hand. Dr Galal has thick, solid wrists. He's built like a wrestler. Distinctive dark eyebrows rest above studious spectacles. His thick lips seem to hover somewhere between a cautious half smile and a wide grin. I'm trying to place his ethnicity as I sit, as he's obviously not

Indian but exudes the warmth of the East. I look for clues on his desk. "I am originally from Cairo, Egypt," he volunteers in a light accent, before I can ask. An affability fills the office, but behind it I can sense the divided consciousness of the immigrant. This man understands paradox. He understands inconsistencies and things that don't always line up. He will understand me. He's a hybrid of multiple countries, like me. An accomplice.

He begins to talk to me in a general way, saying he'd seen the results of my blood test. I cut him off, blurting, "Do you want to talk to me about multiple myeloma? Because I was just diagnosed." I smile, earnest and helpful as the volunteers dispensing juice boxes in the lobby. He pauses; he hadn't known that I knew. I'm seeing myself through his eyes. Pale, haggard. "I see," he says, "that's what I suspected." Dr Galal then asks if I would consider being his patient. He has just come to Toronto from Montreal, and he has a bit of Montreal attitude, a touch of swagger. "We are the best myeloma clinic in the country." He watches my reaction and goes on to tell me that together—"If you will excuse my forwardness"—we will kick this disease's ass. Normally, this sort of line puts me off, and the whole war imagery around cancer makes me wary, (no one enlists in this war, and if you die, is it your fault for not fighting hard enough?) but I find myself liking his unorthodox attitude. It's refreshing. I can't deny there's an operation that must be mounted and there's only room for one chain of command. I now feel, deep in my bones, that Dr Galal is my warrior, my commander. I want to submit to this. "Tell me more, doc." Dr Galal tells me he wants to put me on an aggressive, first-line treatment. He has a gleam in his eye. His hands flutter and I notice how gracefully he moves within his brawny frame.

I can't help but keep thinking, as I did when he first left that message on my phone: How fortunate and strange it is that out there in the world an oncologist has tried to find me so desperately, as if he, and only he, can take care of me. Does intuition guide us to mysteries we couldn't get to in a more straightforward way? I'm not sure. But while Bobcat and my dad can continue researching, I now know what I need to know, and I know that I will turn over my care to this man and Princess Margaret Hospital. I made the decision to surrender in an instant. "Yes," I said, as if to a marriage proposal, "I would very much like to be your patient." I watch his fingers flex and rearrange themselves. His desk is piled high with manila folders and papers. "Okay," his voice lowers and takes on a conspiratorial tone. "We're going to hit this thing. I'll give it all I've got. I promise you."

"Look, doc, I trust you. I know I'm going to beat this thing. But do me a favour."

His eyebrows shoot higher and he adjusts his shoulders slightly forward. I clear my throat lightly and lean in to tell him with a stoic face: "I don't want *any* bad news from you." Silence. Slowly a smile cracks across my face. Dr Galal gets it. He chuckles. I laugh. We're both laughing—life-saving laughter—before I get serious again. I take in all the surfaces of his face, like I'm buying an expensive sculpture. "And please, doc, just give me the basics, don't throw statistics and data and depressing stuff like that at me. Knowledge is a heavy backpack. The more you know, the less you understand, right?"

I suddenly realize I'm sharing my esoteric Buddhist philosophy with a medical specialist. He should be giving me an eye-roll. But he's not. We surround ourselves with optimism. And grit.

"Full remission?"

It's the first time I've heard this, and it becomes an invocation.

"Full remission."

We shake hands without moving. At the door, he gives a serious look. "You will have to learn how to be a patient. That's all I ask." I leave his office with a prescription and pieces of paper outlining a protocol for the next few months. My first visit is downstairs to register as a patient of the hospital. "I'm sorry I can't take you there . . . you have to go there yourself," and it seems he is saying something other than what he's saying.

One of the first people I told was Deepa. We may not speak for months at a time, but we have a very strong bond and on some level she's a bit of a mother figure. I trust her intuitive reactions and am inspired by her subversive nature. I felt she would understand. She's weathered so many crises with such panache and style. "It was just wild," is one of her characteristic responses to life's tragi-comedic moments, her dark eyes widening dramatically. I called and almost nonchalantly mentioned that I'd been diagnosed with cancer. I didn't even specify what type, because, *isn't it wild?* The silence on the other end stretched. Then Deepa, in her deep, distinctive voice, said, "NO!" I could feel her shaking her head on the other side of the line. "Oh no, Lisa. NO."

My heart skidding, I rushed to minimize the impact. I babbled about how it wasn't a big deal, how I was going through only a five-minute dose of chemo. I did my best to give the impression of soldiering on with humour and resolve. Deepa took another breath. She told me about weathering chemo with a friend, sitting with her in the day care as she got weaker, her hair falling out in clumps. Her anguish was palpable. "Yes, yes, but this is a radical new treatment. It's just five minutes a dose!" I said. "I won't even lose my hair . . . yet."

"Lisa Rani," said Deepa, "promise me you will call me if you need anything. ANYTHING." But almost before she could finish, I signed off. Her reaction made the cancer real in a way that hearing the diagnosis had not, and I wasn't ready for that reality. I quickly concluded that telling people was disastrous. I withdrew and decided not to broach the subject with anyone else for a while.

Before the treatments could begin, I had to get my teeth in order. Apparently dental health is very important for members of the Myeloma Club. I was told by Nurse Pauline in preparation for treatment that I would have to get my teeth checked and begin to floss. That's because there's risk of osteonecrosis or abnormal death of the jaw bone. "I'm not sure what that means," I said to Bobcat, "but fortunately I'm not married to the idea of talking my whole life. I think I'd rather let my jawbone die a natural death than go to the dentist. Ha. Ha, ha?" I joked. He smiled but then his face became like hardened honey. And then I just knew. He's a big fan of dental hygiene and flossing, but it was more than that. It was even more than the fact that I had avoided any kind of an examination—dental, mental or otherwise—for more than ten years, which I regarded as my crusty badge of honour.

No. It was more than all of that.

Looking at his face, I knew life was going to change. I had just been diagnosed with MM, but I could not start treatment without some gesture, some ritual to acknowledge this passage. In India you break a coconut to symbolize a new threshold. Me, I learned how to floss. I began my cancer journey with a little bit of string.

I was diagnosed with multiple myeloma on Tuesday, 23 June 2009, and started my first cycle of treatment on Thursday, 2 July, that same year. Dr Galal gave me the protocol for oral chemo and steroids, printed out on a piece of paper: Dexamethasone, Cyclophosphamide, Zometa and Velcade. It was like a call sheet for a science fiction movie where the characters were space aliens. "Stay away from the sweets," he said with a twinkle in his eye. He listed some of the side effects, but I had no idea how dramatically the steroids would change my personality or what they'd do to my sweet tooth. All that came later.

The Velcade—a revolutionary new chemotherapy would be one dose a week for four cycles. Because myeloma is considered incurable, there's first-line and second-line treatment—initial treatment and treatment after the inevitable relapse. In Canada, to get some drugs, like Velcade, you have to be second-line, or relapsed. The cost: over $10,000 USD a month, which would fortunately be covered by my Ontario Health Plan, while the Trillium Ontario drug plan would help cover some of the spillover. Dr Galal lobbied the drug company on compassionate grounds, and got me the Velcade even though it was my first treatment. The innate challenge with orphan cancers like myeloma is the cost of the drugs. Everything is deemed "experimental" even if it's the only thing that will save a life. I'm sure I got a discount because I was only thirty-seven years old, which is extremely young to be diagnosed. Mine was an intriguing case, one for the textbooks.

My first journey to chemo day care is a lot like the first day of high school. I wind my way down the fifth-floor corridors of Princess Margaret, peering at signs until I find my way to a new section of the hospital, landing at the check-in counter, in a hallway. "Well, hello there, welcome to chemo day care," I'm mumbling to myself and already looking a bit crazy.

The hallway ends abruptly in a crowded waiting room. There's barely anywhere to sit and the air is stale from many anxious lungs. The diversity on display, however, is impressive—every ethnicity and age group represented. A Korean minister surrounded by his Christian ministry. An older Italian couple holding hands. A shiny-eyed teenager in hijab. Mothers. Executives. Grandfathers. In LA, this sort of room would represent an audition for Central Casting. But here in Toronto, in the celebrated centre of multiculturalism, it just goes to illustrate that this disease doesn't seem to play favourites. *Disease and disaster: the great equalizers.* I introduce myself at reception and immediately joke about getting a Cancer Card. What's the use of being part of this club if there aren't benefits? Do I get frequent-flier points? Can I jump the line if I become a platinum member? The woman checking me in at the computer drops her chin and fixes me with a look over her glasses. Dark eyebrows knit together over her frames. Soon I'll realize this is where social niceties are dropped in favour of frank exchanges. A place of social liposuction. Let's just cut out the fat and get on with it.

"Troublemaker?"

Wow. I decide to banter back, hoping not to show myself to be too rattled.

"Yup. It's the reason I was put here. To stir things up."

She puts her hand on her hip. Sucks her teeth.

"Um-hmm."

And then her expression changes. Softens.

"Well I see you're a new . . ."

"Member?"

"Yes, member. So, here's what you get. You get warm blankets. You get a comfy chair. You even get juice and crackers. You see David with the martini cart over there?" A thin older man, wearing a volunteer's t-shirt is pushing a rattling trolley through the waiting room. He stops to hand over juice boxes to outstretched hands.

"It's always Happy Hour here," she says.

"My cart rumbles on," he sighs. He picks up a crossword puzzle from a Tupperware container and hands it to a man in a tracksuit. What she hasn't alluded to, the woman behind the counter, is the main reason I'm here. The most exclusive privilege of membership. A transfusion of hope. A liquid flush in my veins. Open the gate, I'm chemo blitzkrieging my way to full remission.

I'd been warned about the impossible wait times. A chemo day care hospital tag is dangling around my wrist: Ray, LISA patient 5376. Here I am, branded and part of a group. I have been waiting to be called in for my chemo infusion for a long time, just like everyone else, but I'm still not ready to identify with them. I'm still watching from the sidelines. Dad and I share the same hunting magazine, *Ontario Out of Doors* circa 2006. Dad has driven me and is now waiting with me, having seamlessly stepped into the role of caretaker. Now, well into our second hour of waiting, diversions are thin on the ground. Martini cart David has distributed all the reading material to other patients. Never mind. I've learned a lot about crossbows.

When I look around, I notice some people who refuse to make eye contact. A woman is dabbing at her eyes. One man has been sitting in the corner alone, surrounded by an invisible circle of defiance. In another corner, a large group of East Coasters are playing cards. They are hooting and appear as relaxed as a night out at the pub. I can't even tell which of them is the patient. I see people with nothing more to lose, and everything to lose.

I know suddenly what really binds us together is our otherness. In this room, as in our bodies, the rest of the world is excluded from our battles. In all the faces around me, I see the desire for things just out of reach. Recovery. Comfort. Safety. Empathy. Control. Normalcy. Escape. Luck.

There are so many ways of coping with cancer. There's no smouldering trail of embers that point to a supernatural cause or reason we've been put here together. I also know we are more than just mysterious containers for genes, hormones and electromagnetic pulses. It is our stories, our trusting hearts buried behind fear, that colour and run our lives.

17

I LOOKED UP with a start when my name was finally called, I had settled into a kind of trance. I had started to feel we were inmates, myself and my fellow patients, thighs touching, cuffed to each other in the waiting room. Dad had gone downstairs for a soup and sandwich at the Druxy's in the lobby. There had been a pianist in the atrium when we arrived hours ago. I hoped he was still there and that my dad was enjoying some Mozart with his chicken guacamole sandwich. I entered the day care unit alone. This was as I'd secretly hoped. I needed my first chemo infusion to be without him, because sometimes when my dad was around, I found myself worrying more about him than myself.

Once inside, I try to keep up with the nurse briskly leading me across day care, through a forest of IV poles. I'm aware of other patients as I pass. Some are wrapped in blankets, some gaze up from open books. All of them are connected to a drip through a tube in their outstretched arms. There is a subdued purity of purpose. The nurse guides me to a large beige chair next to the Triage station. She has kept her eyes on my paperwork throughout. As she sits, she asks my name, date of birth and confirms I will be receiving my first Velcade (also known as Bortezomib) infusion, a specialized targeted chemotherapy approved for the treatment of cancer of the plasma cells aka multiple myeloma. When she looks up, she sees I'm seated awkwardly on the edge of the throne, like a new royal reluctant to accept my responsibilities. "Ah—is this your first time?" she asks. "Don't worry. It's just a five-, ten-minute dose, if that. And while you will want to take it easy, you won't feel the same side effects of a lot of other forms of chemo."

Great. I give a weak smile. Then promptly break out into a cold sweat. I feel cold. No, I feel hot. No, it's just a cold sweat.

She's pulling on plastic gloves and fiddling with tubes and labels.

A word about my veins. My veins are terrible; hard to find, painful to penetrate. My veins collapse. They hide. Especially when I'm cold.

And it's cold in here. I suddenly notice how very cold it is. It's summer outside, but in here, the cold has made a home under my skin.

"I have bad veins," I say, sheepishly.

The nurse stops what she's doing, gets up and leaves. I'm a bit startled but she returns with a hot flannel blanket, which she drapes over my chest and shoulders gently. Something about this gesture touches me deeply. She silently hands me a paper cup of water. I anoint her ninja of my veins.

"All set. Now take a look at this. Is this information right?"

She shows me the label on a clear liquid vial: Velcade borttezomib. I see liquid life. The entire scope of faith is a vial.

"Yes," I say.

Now for the needle.

I'm bracing myself. She ties a tourniquet above my elbow, extends my right arm and runs her fingers over my skin, probing for a vein in the soft exposed forearm and crook. No joy. Narrows her eyes, releases the elastic with a snap and picks up the left. I'm making a fist and pumping it helpfully, humming nervously.

"You weren't kidding," she says, tapping my left arm.

"Yah, I know. It's never a little prick for me." I'm playing for laughs and being completely truthful.

"You know, most times I get poked, I normally sing 'Hey Jude'—it's that whole times of trouble line that helps calm me down. Instead of saying ouch I go "Naaa. . . naaaa . . . naaaa . . . na . . . naananaNAAAAH." It helps. A lot. You can sing along too," I add helpfully.

She looks at me, silently. And then, a switch goes on.

"All right, then."

She has to stick me three times. Three rounds of "Hey Jude." It stings but I sing it out, just as I did during the bone marrow aspiration. I'm singing it to my bones. Other patients swivel curiously towards me. They are amused. One exasperated glance. My nurse hums along with the last round.

"Okay. Ready for the Velcade."

I haven't noticed the last successful plunge into my arm, focused as I was on singing. She screws on a vial to the tube dangling at my wrist.

"Okay, let me know how you feel."

I braced myself for a new sensation. She pressed the plunger and that was it—vial number one done and I hadn't felt anything. She removed it and attached another. Repeat, plunger in. One more vial and it's over. "That's it?" I ask, glancing around the room. Almost everyone else was hooked to their IV with a look of resignation and a book or DVD player on their laps. Someone appeared to be giggling with a companion, but everyone else seemed to have checked in for a long stay in the day care.

"That's it."

But, of course, that wasn't it. Within a week or so, I start struggling with chemo brain. One side effect was becoming very vague and fuzzy, forgetful. Up until then, I'd actually continued teaching yoga, though I found the heat in the studio hard to bear and it was difficult trying to keep the postures straight, remembering what came after what. Along with this marked decline in concentration, I began experiencing an intense buzzing through my whole body, like a surge of electricity starting, then suddenly stopping, then abruptly starting again. There was a radioactive dance party under my skin. And then, bam, it would end, and I'd be back to (my new) normal. I started getting worried about driving. When I asked one of the residents at the hospital, he said, "You're just a little wired."

It turned out that my body was starting to have strange secondary reactions. I would take my steroids, four days on, four days off, then oral chemo. The combination caused peripheral neuropathy, a tingling sensation vibrating from the inside all over my body but more acutely in my feet and hands. It felt like wearing vibrating mitts. Or woollen socks full of fleas. Take the scratchiest fabric you've ever worn and multiply that by a thousand. Then put it under your skin. It was, again, one of those things no one really tells you. Bobcat called it "Gently Carbonating" and I started thinking of it as a sign that the medicine was working; the abnormal plasma cells in my bone marrow were bubbling and liquefying. This was early August 2009, and I was still treating the disease like pneumonia: something I'd have, then not have any more. I continued life at my full throttle pace as per usual. I took meetings, signed contracts, read scripts, bought furniture, moved bookcases. Overtaxing my system is my default setting. My drama school training and ability to manufacture an alternate reality also came in handy. But when I lay in bed at night I knew: I'm in denial. I'm treating cancer like it's an inconvenience, managing the stage like a tyrannical Bollywood choreographer. Worst of all, I wasn't looking it in the eye. I was letting the situation tyrannize my heart. I really needed to name it, recognize it and then deal with it head on.

But I wasn't acknowledging it. Not yet. I went to shoot a public service announcement for Plan Canada. Every day the medication was causing more puffiness, more spread, more bloat. I was starting to feel self-conscious, but I still wasn't telling anyone. Under the best of circumstances, sitting in the make-up chair under the bright lights is difficult; an unavoidable confrontation with The Face. All my life I'd believed that my face was too chubby, and now, weeks into chemo, it really was chubby. Craig Goodwell, who was directing the video, came by to see me. I was tempted to offer an excuse for my appearance, but before I could say anything, he noticed the hospital tag around my wrist. Very gently, he took me to the side and said, "Shall we get rid of this?" Of course, those things don't come off easily and we stood there awkwardly while he pulled at the band interminably. I was mortified. He made a joke about the CNE (Canadian National Exhibition, a summer ritual for Torontonians) starting early this year, as if I'd bought a wristband to ride the rollercoaster at the fair. It was his way of giving me permission to talk about what was really going on. I didn't say anything, but it was one of many small moments provoking me towards making a decision to "come out."

Doctors allude to what steroids will do but they don't necessarily spell it out. No one ever really says: 1. YOU WILL TURN INTO A RAGING MANIAC. I read about a husband who said of his Dexed-up wife: "I knew she didn't like the tree in the yard, but I didn't expect her to chop it down." You have superhuman energy. No one says: 2. YOU ARE GOING TO BLOAT. Not in any way that you understood bloating before. Your very frame is going to become distorted and totally different from what it was. I would feel my skin stretch and expand in ways I'd never experienced, bloating up to three times my normal size. It was like putting on a wetsuit. Except it was permanent. Until you stop taking the steroids: then you deflate until the next dose. You may develop the classic "cushingoid" moon face and if you are really lucky, this fascinating fat redistribution may even give you a buffalo hunchback. And there's no way around it. I called it the "Dex effect." On Dex days, I would type out a warning text and send it to Dad, Bobcat and friends in the immediate vicinity: "It's steroid day. Forgive me, I know not what I do."

I would pop those ten small oval pills and immediately, I'd be wound up and ready to go. I craved food that I don't normally crave. That's another side effect: 3. YOU ARE HUNGRY ALL THE TIME. For instance, I'm not really big on red meat and sausages, but there's a place called Meat on the Beach near my apartment where they sell these strange, enticing little food items called pepperettes, mini sausages. I required these spicy fellows. Not craved—*required*. I had a breakdown at the counter the one time they were sold out. I was totally fixated, making the long trek, walking for blocks and blocks like a pilgrim to get my pepperettes. Then on the way back, I'd stop in and sample something at Licks, then the Korean restaurant, then the cheese at the Eastern European deli. There's no better place to have food cravings than multicultural Toronto.

Needless to say, this was strange after years of battling an eating disorder. But I didn't feel like I was getting either my comeuppance or my punishment for all that self-abuse. I might have been flying on amped up optimism, but I was also obeying a call that was much bigger than me. In order to heal, I needed to accept what my body was telling me. I had started moving in that direction from the moment of my diagnosis. Not listening to my body had proved disastrous, and now, if my body was telling me to walk as far as it took to get the damn pepperettes, I would do it. I was in a zone of giving myself permission to eat what I wanted, guilt-free, without judgement.

Meanwhile, after my steroid-sponsored energy had kicked in, I became obsessed with the walls in my home. I looked at the walls, mused on them, and then I marched to the paint store down the street and bought paint. Let me remind you that in Bombay, I had never done anything for myself. Forget DIY wall painting—I had never even made tea.

One night on Dex—because that is side effect number 4: YOU GET NO SLEEP ON STEROIDS—I decided that my bedroom wall needed to be a deep red. I dragged my bed to the centre of the room, taped up the door frame and painted. And painted. I painted about four coats, and I enjoyed it. Then the adrenalized effect of the drugs pulled me down into collapse and I fell asleep, tell-tale cadmium red splotches on the bed sheets. I woke up the next afternoon. Ben Harper was still playing. I looked at the red wall and thought: "Who the hell did that?" Time to repaint. White. All white.

When you become ill, your life is suddenly about administration. Insurance papers. Medical expenses. Dealing with the actor's union about benefits. My father moved into my guest bedroom and helped with the paperwork when I was too tired to do it myself. Of course, I was aware that I might not be able to work. And if I was losing my sole source of income and no longer able to do the one thing I was trained to do in the world, then what? What would I do? I'd always been very cavalier about money and saving, because I'd always somehow magically had enough. I hadn't allowed myself to see my work as a business because I'd been so immersed in the romantic, creative aspect of performing. When one of my more pragmatic friends would cajole me to get my affairs in order, I'd say: "I've gotten this far without ever making a spreadsheet!" But there's nothing like cancer to force a reality check: Acting is business, and my business needed tending.

Slowly, I began to educate myself about saving and planning; found it oddly creative. I got in touch with my inner accountant. If I was going to invest, I wanted to care about it, so of course, I thought of real estate. I've always loved interiors and homes, decorating a new space (secretly, I think this is why I move so much). Buying a house as an investment property and renting it out seemed like the most accessible thing for me to do. I was getting in touch with my inner accountant.

I had identified a particular house that I wanted to buy on a street called Hiawatha. (Great growth potential! Schools! Still reasonably priced!—I was getting good at this stuff). But I lost the house in a bidding war. The day it happened, I was devastated. It seemed hugely symbolic: my life was spiralling out of control, and here was another thing I couldn't control. My angst was way out of proportion to the event.

My real estate agent of Punjabi origin, Noni Fenby, had become a close friend—a sister in the ways we choose our family—on my return to Toronto and she knew I had cancer. She told me that she had seen me managing so well and carrying on so efficiently that she had assumed it wasn't serious. It wasn't until she saw my overreaction to the loss of the house that the scope of the disease became clear to her. My desperation had to do with a simple fact: I didn't know where I'd be physically in a few months. I was facing down a volatile future. I might not have the energy to buy and fix up a house. I needed to do it *now*, while I still could. But my mode of operation had always been about independence and managing. I would never ask for support or help, yet I expected those around me to understand what I needed, intuitively. This, by the way, doesn't work. It was a lonely, and exhausting, way to live. I needed to be able to ask for it and wake up from this trance of denial.

Literally a week later, through pure serendipity, another house came up for sale on the same street. This being Toronto 2009, there was a bidding war. I told Noni, "I have to get this house." And because I asked, she went in like a warrior. We outbid everyone and got the house. It was a trigger for me. I invited a few close friends to dinner at the Beacher Café across the street from my apartment. I took a breath and with the sounds of sizzling meat in the background, I made an announcement: Here's what I'm going through, and I need you to know.

They didn't break. They didn't cry. But they radiated support. I felt transported, magically lifted out of my invented self. In that healing circle in the middle of a busy restaurant each one of them gave me an interesting perspective. My dear friend, Tara, who I had met on the yoga retreat in Kerala, said, "Life gives you these opportunities to take pain and transform it through art, whether it's writing or expressing yourself in some way." Ted Grand, the Moksha Yoga guru said, "You have the power of community to draw from." Ted had introduced me to the concept of *Sangha* or a community with a common vision or purpose. And that our stories can come together like a salve when enough voices participate.

While my personal life was beginning to get real, professionally, I was still undercover, and intensely busy. I'd be doing double duty at the Toronto International Film Festival this year. The film I shot in Delhi with Dilip Mehta, *Cooking with Stella*, was getting a gala presentation at TIFF, and *Defendor*, a Woody Harrelson film in which I'd had a cameo, was also debuting. Then I was supposed to fly west to shoot a film called *Ecstasy*, something I'd committed to before the diagnosis. I had a plan: If I was to be on location on the West Coast, I could come back, do my chemo and then fly back the next day. Easy! Except all of it would require lying. I would have to come up with excuses for my looks, my moods, my absences. I would have to continue the gruelling work of fraudulence.

In my freshly painted white bedroom, I began meditating on my chakras. Believe in them or not, chakras pop up in many ancient Hindu texts. Basically, they're the "force centres" or vortices of energy at different points on the physical body, dotting along the spinal column from the base up to the head. Major energy channels pass through the chakras, which glow with different colours. Yellow is the third chakra, the solar plexus and seat of the will. When I meditated, I would always try to fill my body with yellow, channelling my will, for health, for goodness, for a mindful life. The Sanskrit name for the yellow chakra is *manipura*—the key to personal power and self-esteem. Yellow represented that confidence to me.

Some afternoons, after treatment, when I had stilled my body at last, I would lie on my back, visualizing the yellow entering my body in liquid form. A trickle, then a wave. I would almost start hyperventilating, my breathing would become very laboured, and the pit of my stomach would drop out.

This is why I named the blog I began on 6 September 2009 "The Yellow Diaries." I had never thought of sharing my writing online, I had no experience with blogs, but I started writing about my cancer during a fit of steroid-induced mania in the middle of the night. Those drugs could take me from extreme optimism to picking a fight with whoever was within hearing distance. But I think the steroids also fortified me; they let me be fearless about speaking out. They helped me find my yellow.

And if I was going to be writing, I had to be honest—with the public, and with myself. My moods and my body had changed, and now the rest of my life had to change, too. So many circumstances were colliding in my life, I needed to be able to process it all and writing had always been a covert form of therapy for me. I had a collection of notebooks I had filled as testimony. There was no way around it—it was becoming increasingly clear that as I stumbled deeper and deeper into myself, I had to be open and public about what was happening.

Playing dual roles—patient and actress—was no longer feasible for me. I had kept the diagnosis a secret this long partly because my talent agents had advised me to, partly because I was in shock and mostly because I hadn't understood how much my life would change. Now, well into my second month of treatment, I was worn down with the efforts of my double life. I was also tired from the treatment. Chemo is cumulative; the toxicity accumulates in your system, making you limp. But living on this broken edge was life—my life and the will to keep going. What I was going through was normal. What is abnormal is an unrealistic and painful belief system that, somehow, we are entitled to get through life without suffering.

I was preparing to make my cancer citizenship public in early September. I had told my agent and my publicist that if I was going to walk the red carpet forty pounds heavier than normal, I needed to be open about it. It was time to dismantle this scaffolding of silence and shame. What had I done wrong? Was it my fault a typhoon was gathering in my bones? Should I be punished for being diagnosed with a serious cancer? I was now face-to-face with the impossible standards of celebrity culture, something I'd been wrestling with for years. The physical changes in me would also change people's perceptions of me. A morphing woman's body is public property. (Good thing *you* don't have a face expressing the syndrome resembling hyperactive adrenal cortex with an increase in adiposity, otherwise known as "moonface.") And cancer is becoming a rite of passage, something more and more people are experiencing. It's a crisis that most of us will have to pass through in our lives, personally or from the sidelines as we watch it do its work on someone we love. I didn't want to be an accessory to the taboo any more. I didn't want to pretend that it's possible to achieve perfection at all points along one's path through life.

On 7 September 2009 I uploaded my first entry "From the Marrow" for the Yellow Diaries:

A few months ago my bone marrow started sending me messages . . . It's true the deepest crises are moments of great opportunity. An event that shocks you into seeing with heart. A place
from which to combine survival and celebration. I'm not sure
why [I'm writing this blog] and that's probably the best beginning. Maybe I'm just finally listening to my marrow.

It was out there and out of my hands anyway. Someone in India
chanced upon the blog, and within twenty-four hours my cancer became
national news. Thousands of comments. Overflowing kindness and support. A balm. An unfraying. In India prayers were spoken for me. I had
been chasing love like trying to bottle the wind, thrown off balance or
being swept off my feet, when it was always there, vast and accessible as
the ocean, overlooked in countless small gestures and the spark in the
centre of every heart. My own heart undressed. I sat cross-legged on my
bed, reading messages, shaking my head at the strangeness of it. An
interesting bookend to the way my career had started in India so many
years ago—overnight impact to overnight impact.

I did two interviews in Canada, one for the *Globe and Mail*, and one
for Entertainment Tonight Canada. Both journalists came to my house.
(A sidebar: one of the fun things about cancer is that people will meet
you pretty much anywhere you ask them to. Work that cancer!) My publicist Suzanne Cheriton had briefed Gayle MacDonald from the *Globe
and Mail*, and as we sat out on the deck of my apartment, everyone was
very wired and walking on eggshells, which is a common effect that we
of the sick world can have. I was the only one who wasn't anticipating
anything negative. At this point, talking about it was a compulsion,
because the more I talked about it, the more real it became. And I needed
it to be real, not just something stuffed away in the dark corners of my
life. Finally, I was able to say: "Yes I have cancer." I had never really
connected with the word entirely—it's used surprisingly sparingly in
the medical world—and with its utterance came a deep sense of relief.
We talked about other exceptionally ordinary things too—books, the
apartment—and Gayle was lovely, very gracious. But I could tell she was
scared. "Everything's going to be fine," she said. "Everything's going to
be fine." People say that a lot.

"Yes," I agreed. "Of course, it will."

I was ready to live in the present tense.

One afternoon in early September I was chopping fruit in my kitchen. According to my call sheet of treatments hanging by a magnet on my fridge, I had chemo that afternoon. Before that, I had to attend a launch party for *Cooking with Stella*. I looked down at my bloated hands and saw my fingers were like small sausages. I could hear muffled cries of children and street noises through my small kitchen window. I'd bought a papaya—an extravagance in Canada in the fall. I was stripping the skin, trying to remember how my cook in India did it, turning the fruit, the skin falling off in one long, unbroken peel. I cut through the flesh of the papaya, exposing two symmetrical halves. There is something about this action that is hypnotic, or maybe it's just the things you notice when you slow down. I watched my hands gripping the handle, the tip of the blade slicing cleanly through flesh. I looked at the salmon-coloured centre of the fruit, sweet and yielding, speckled with black seeds. This stillness, this attention I found myself bringing to the most mundane gestures; there's no shortcut to that place. The place I now found myself in.

I knew there was something that must be preserved about my cancer experience. Nurse Pauline had told me my body would shrink once I got off steroids. My hair would fall out and grow back again. All the pain and struggle would fade. So, what would there be to remind me of this time? Because not everything should go back to as it was before. No matter where life takes me, I vowed to remember, I am better for this experience, for having listened to the language of my marrow and letting myself break open. I looked down at the seams in the fruit which I had just cut. It must've been my imagination, but they were decorated with veins of gold.

After attending the *Cooking with Stella* cocktail party launch at the Royal York Hotel, I took a taxi to a few blocks north to Princess Margaret for my chemo appointment. The two worlds can blend: it's okay to cross over from ballroom to chemo day care. But there was one difference: people at the press conference were way more stressed. Come on guys, it's not life and death, is it? And there were no juice boxes in the ballroom. I was really thirsty.

On the day of the premiere, Don McKellar, the talented Canadian actor and film-maker who plays my husband in the movie, and I were invited to open the Toronto Stock Exchange (TSX). I woke to discover that I couldn't fit into the outfit I'd picked the night before. You think of the body as solid but on steroids I seemed to be made of some other kind of material. Sometimes within a few hours, I'd bloat a couple of inches and then subside. The Amazing Elastic Girl. I ended up wearing a simple black sweater while ringing the bell at the TSX. My eyes were also suffering—another side effect. My vision would suddenly become blurry, so I had been goaded into wearing black-rimmed glasses. I barely recognized myself in a reflection on the way into the building.

The cat was well and truly out of the bag. Everywhere I went, I was met with great affection, and some awkwardness. Don McKellar was warm and sweet; in the next year, he would suddenly and tragically lose his partner, the great actress Tracy Wright, to cancer. People I'd never met who were reading the Yellow Diaries came up to me at the TSX, squeezed my elbow or gave me a hug. I ran into Piers Handling, the director of TIFF. I've always thought he has a sensitive face and when he embraced me without words, I melted. The top of my head barely reached his shoulder.

After the morning event, I was dropped back at the Beaches. "I'll be back in a few hours," the driver called to me as he pulled away. I spent the rest of the day wrangling my TIFF outfit and my shoes and my nerves. Suzanne, my publicist, and Jennifer, my agent, were bolstering me, trying to be very upbeat. My stylist Rashmi Varma had put together an outfit with lovely stretch fabric and folds, inspired by the sari. Finally, around three in the afternoon, I left alone for Roy Thomson Hall. Tucked into the curve of the leather seat, I closed my eyes, thinking about the upcoming reveal in front of people and photographers in my purple outfit and lumpy body and why it meant so much. Which way would I be facing? Inwards or outwards? Consumed with my own thoughts or watchful and present? My car dropped me a few streets over from Roy Thomson Hall, where Don and I boarded a cycle rickshaw. I think I let out a whoop on the short ride over and waved to my co-stars Seema and Shriya, who were in another bedazzled rickshaw. We moved slowly, but I heard the wind and I conjured an image in step with my feelings: We were galloping to a place where two worlds meet, where the full bowl of the sky meets the artifice of the red carpet. Then the ride finished abruptly, and I was summarily deposited in the red carpet crush. I remember Don helping me out, escorting me to the centre of the carpet. I was wearing two burgundy wristbands, the colour of Multiple Myeloma Awareness, one dangling from each hand. The mood was buoyant. Photographers clicked and then Don moved so they could take my solo pictures. I smiled like I meant it. Because I did. I was grateful and happy, and I wanted to show it. I had never been this unselfconscious before at a public event, never revealed anything deeper than the colour of my clutch.

I look back at those photographs now and see that I really was very bloated and yet I felt wonderful. Beautiful. I had been surrounded by all these subversive artists for so long, and here was my subversive act: A woman who knew her worth was not conditional on the shape of her body, her style, her racial identity, gender or face. I was swollen and relaxed and living with a serious cancer. I was also standing up for something that was meaningful to me personally: hijacking the spotlight to bring awareness to multiple myeloma. If life is a continuous provocation to go beyond who we think we are, this was one of my greatest moments.

Later in the theatre, I kicked off those ugly chunky shoes and ate a lot of popcorn and M&Ms, as the Dex commanded. I fell asleep for a while on someone's shoulder but came to in time to make it to the after party. Many people didn't know how to interact with me, getting tied up in knots, which is a trademark of serious disease: nobody knows what to say. They're looking for cues. Every time someone asks me a question—How are you?—I want to answer with a haiku:

Barn burn down
Now I see the moon

But that would be a bit too weird, I know. So, if you're wondering what to say to somebody who is ill, here's my answer: I don't know. I was open; I wanted to talk about it. Not everyone does. I do know that it's not the only thing I wanted to talk about. You don't always have to only talk about how I'm feeling. I want to know that life is continuing around me. How are *you* doing? Remember that, even in the face of your own fear. And sometimes it's just presence that we crave. Sometimes words just don't do it, and what we need is to be around people who support us. Sometimes that's enough. You are enough. The essence of being a warrior is this—the refusal to give up on anything or anyone.

Finally, after struggling all this time with my veins, I took the advice of the head nurse of the haematology department, who'd initially suggested I might want to get something called a port or porta-cath. This port is a vascular device that is actually embedded in the chest so the medicine can go straight into the bloodstream, avoiding all that poking around in search of a vein and off-key singing each time I had chemo. I was not excited about this. A foreign object implanted in my body? It seemed like defeat somehow and slightly sinister, like they were fitting a tracking chip, or a portal into my soul. I had resisted it up until now. But when I was getting some blood tests and it took ninety minutes for the nurse to get a vein, and each pinch and dab and poke was making me rise up from my chair, I knew it was time to say: No more.

By mid-September, after my red carpet reveal, I was begging for the port. I called Nurse Pauline and she told me they could expedite the procedure. At Toronto General I joined a long line, as if we are all waiting for our driver's licenses. I lay down in the operating theatre on a table shaped like a cross, with my arms pinned down on either side. I joked with the surgeon, whose face I could not see behind his mask, though he seemed young and cool and relaxed. Clearly this was a matter of routine for him. He silenced me with a look and set about implanting a little bulbous object in my body while I shivered in my skimpy gown. The port is like a cup connected to a catheter, and the needle snaps into it. The nurse patted my bare leg as a medical intern stuck me with needles to numb the area. When the surgeon began slicing into my skin, the nurse held my hand and I turned my head to stare at a blank wall. A quick sharp pain, some dabbing and it was over. I drove home feeling humiliated for reasons I couldn't pinpoint. I reached the Beaches to find a phone message instructing me to return to the hospital immediately— they had put the port in the wrong side. That didn't inspire a lot of confidence. I returned to the hospital, bypassing the line, and the same surgeon took a look from across the operating theatre: "No, it's all good. It's in the right place!" and turned away. I felt relieved, but annoyed. I walked back to the patient's change room, slippers slapping against the floor, trying to breathe through it. My hospital gown was a disciple's robe. Such small dehumanizing moments are part of the patient's life. It was my responsibility to transform them, to find the humour and meaning in them. To survive.

I drove to Tara's home afterwards, to sit on her kitchen floor and blubber. I held her daughter Flora and didn't say a word. Contact with that small, vital body was everything I needed. The porta-cath did end up revolutionizing my experience, diminishing my pain significantly. I still have it in my chest, above my right breast, a hard lump of steel like a small raised tattoo. I call it my "port o potty" and kind of enjoy flashing people with it. It made me feel bionic and ready for reinvention. I'd gotten my cancer stripes.

18

MY FATHER WAS fresh wind during this time. He would drive me to and from chemo, helped prepare meals—especially on my Dex days when food was the centre of my universe—and noted all my appointments and medicine dosages down in a wall calendar with pictures of Canadian synchronized swimmers and field hockey stars. He wordlessly handed me a bowl of pomegranate seeds every evening because he had read they are high in antioxidants. Every time he said, "Lisa Rani" with a fond smile, it no longer mattered if I was five, fifteen or thirty-seven. It was not just my middle name, but a word with such deep connotations in India that it always sounded like an inheritance of courage.

Bobcat was very preoccupied with work post the financial crisis but came when he could. I woke one morning with a very bad reaction to the drugs and a fever of one hundred and four. Even though I was burning up, I saw my father panicking through my delirium, so I reached for the phone, and called Bobcat, faintly, in a voice wet with heat. Bobcat left work immediately and arrived fast, carried me to a tub of cold water, lowered me in, and stayed at my side until the fever subsided. And when it finally did, I started giggling. Then I was shaking with laughter because that's what you do when you come to your senses and find yourself immersed in bathwater up to your neck, fully clothed down to your socks. These kinds of incidents were becoming so frequent, I thought about setting up a camera to make a video of the ways my body was expressing its distress. It was no longer a matter of *will* I have a reaction but *when*. But I wasn't distressed. I let my body take the lead. My body was becoming self-directed, raising its voice, commanding attention. Some days I watched, fascinated, as it dressed itself, pulled on leopard-printed socks, picked up car keys. All done without the cooperation of my brain. The body knew where it needed to go, and I was experimenting with getting out of the way.

My life was upside down in other ways too. Falling sick isn't cheap, not even in Canada, and I had extensive drug bills. My ACTRA insurance covered 75 per cent of my expenses but I still racked up expenses in thousands and thousands of dollars. And these drugs were not negotiable; they are life-saving drugs. Even with critical life insurance, often I had to pay upfront and then it could take a month before I received the actual payment from the insurance company. The amount of paperwork that ensues when you are sick is another thing no one warns you about. But once again my father shouldered that responsibility and patiently filled form after form in his neat handwriting. Still, I was deeply grateful to the universal healthcare system in Canada, along with my Actors' Union's coverage. It's not perfect but I was relatively financially comfortable. I did wonder about Canada's working poor, pulling off minimum wage jobs with no benefits. It made me think about where social compassion starts and stops. I began looking at the men and women brushing by me in the hospital, in and out of chemo day care with awakened empathy.

And then I wondered about the impact of this illness on patients in India. It overwhelmed me just thinking about the challenges they would have to confront every single day. Cancer is a complex group of diseases, each with its own unique prognosis and treatment. For much of India, the word cancer connotes death. It is one of the most feared and misunderstood diseases, even by specialists trained in neutrality. Patients are often judged and isolated. What sort of support is there for the most vulnerable? How do you decide whether to feed your family or pay for chemo? Maybe speaking about what I was going through, bringing it into public discourse in India, would help in some small way. No other Indian celebrity had spoken openly about cancer before, and I just hoped that now, in an age of social media, more influential figures would take the step to share their private challenges. Paying it forward for me at that moment simply took the form of writing and sharing my experience, as frankly and as transparently as possible.

Now I had a "pre-existing condition" that was going to dog me for the rest of my days. When I applied for the mortgage for my investment property, there was an option for critical illness life insurance: if you die, the insurer pays off the mortgage. I ticked the box and the bank called me. After two questions, I was denied insurance.

One of the reasons my team of talent managers and agents didn't want me to go public about my condition is that in Canada, an actor who is employed to be part of a film has to have a health exam, then the production applies for insurance for the main players and actors. Big blockbusters can afford the insurance, but an indie film wouldn't be willing or able to pay that extra premium to hire me. Another strike. Yes, it's the way of the world. But I felt that kind of impotent rage that so many sick people have felt. It really hits you that you're defined by these labels, that institutions marginalize you for a detour that your body has taken for the moment, instead of grasping the magnitude we all carry within. All these statistics, and society's compulsion to place you in a particular box, especially during one of the most vulnerable times of your life, speak to the ways our values, and society itself, are deeply flawed.

Dr Galal always had the vision of a stem cell transplant, but my eligibility was conditional: he needed to see how I reacted to the first few rounds of treatment. I had to be in remission first. Still, I flipped through the booklets: How to Prepare for Your Stem Cell Transplant. The first thing I saw was about sucking on ice chips to prevent the inevitable and painful sores in your mouth. I put the books aside. I kept going to day care, bringing my Scrabble board into the chemo club house. I even looked forward to it, the pastel walls, the warm blankets, the camaraderie. We are such adaptable buggers. The other patients were no longer "grey-faced old man" or "elegant-looking woman in denial," but variously textured. And the more I paid attention, the more empathy arose as I watched how they arranged themselves in surprising new ways. One woman took to brushing her hair, another man planned on building a boat from a kit when he was done. I filled out their back stories in my mind. "This is Shelly. She likes multi-syllabic words, has been compiling the laws of love for the past decade and is pathologically curious about the monarchy. Oh, and she was diagnosed with a parotid gland tumour." My results were optimistic; my blood cells were improving. I wasn't concentrating too much on the numbers. Data was not just sterile and dull but could be brutal too. How can numbers capture the very human ache I felt when my dad wordlessly handed over my medication every morning? I didn't want my mood influenced by charts and numbers. I knew, after all, that I would be fine. It never occurred to me that I could die when I was diagnosed, and I refused to entertain the possibility even now. I needed to humanize the experience as much as possible; numbers wouldn't help.

At the end of four months, I finished my chemotherapy infusions. My final infusion was on Diwali, the festival of light, when oil lamps across India are lit to signify the victory of good over evil within an individual. And then you gamble. Faith mixed with chance. On my last day at chemo day care, I rang a brass bell by the door, which all patients ring once you've completed your cycles of chemo. For me it signalled a chance for renewal in the form of a stem cell transplant. I was told I was probably a good candidate for an autologous stem cell transplant—which is the preferred first-line therapy for younger multiple myeloma patients. That was the good news. The bad news was that because I would be administered such a high dose of a drug called Melphalan I would be pushed into premature menopause. The prospect of banking my eggs had been touched on lightly in the beginning, but now it was suddenly urgent. I had never been inclined towards having kids, but I didn't like the option being taken away from me either. At the same time, given how rapidly things were changing and shifting, I wondered if I was clinging to an old belief system. Wasn't some part of this cancer experience about clearing away old ideas which had taken root in my bones? A nurse spoke to me very bluntly, "If you want to have kids, you need to think about banking your eggs—now." Wow. The future was hurtling towards me quicker than I thought, and it was baby-shaped.

Bobcat and I had been seeing each other for eight months, and surely, they were the most dramatic eight months any relationship could sustain. When you come together in crisis, you don't really know how you'll do outside of it. The "baby daddy" question was far from clear-cut. Between my cancer treatment and the banking crisis, Bobcat was a stress knob, and I was as concerned about him as he was about me. Bobcat had gifted me a BlackBerry, and after overcoming my tech-no-scepticism, we typed each other daily updates, hiding our anxieties behind banter.

> B: Glad u use berry, like chat. I'm completely unfiltered on chat. Bobcat blackberry tip of the day! U only get one per day! Use the button on the left side to change your profile from quiet to nor-mal to vibrate. Good for movies and dangerous situations
> SL: Sure. I'm a bit discombobulated this morning. Nadama taught me when one is confused and in the haze of ego grasping
> B: Tell me
> SL: Go wash your underwear. Brings you in the moment.
> B: Good tip. Adjust volume right key, change profile left key

When all this was over, would he be walking with me still? Or was this a relationship with a minutely timed expiry? How could I possibly know either way?

For a long time, fertility was not my business. I was suspicious of the social pressure around reproduction; it seemed like a way to control women's bodies and sexuality. But once I was pushed into chemo-induced menopause and rendered infertile, I wondered if I would grieve deeply for the greatest gift I had never used. So there was a stopwatch ticking: I had to make the decision about banking my eggs before bank-ing my stem cells, because that extra dose of chemo would be toxic to my fertility. Plus, there was always a line-up for egg harvesting, so if I didn't want to do it right away, the wait could be three months. But I didn't have three months.

Still uncertain, but hearing that ticking, I sat down with one of the gynaecologists at Mt Sinai. They did an ultrasound and explained that I needed to self-inject for a number of weeks, stimulating the eggs. Then I'd return and they'd be harvested. "We hope for a good crop," said the doctor. The language made it sound so simple, like plucking watermelons from a patch. Still, I went in for my second egg harvesting session. I learned how to self-inject and was handed a bunch of requisitions for blood work. I looked at the forms—oh, all these forms—and felt immediately exhausted. In the past few months, there had been too many choices, too many decisions about my body and my future. I just wanted to be cosy and slovenly at home, to scrunch deeper into my blanket and dream. Sometimes in dreams my mother would come to me, sometimes I'd be in an ER bed in a bright pink saree, the nurses discussing contestants on *So You Think You Can Dance*. I was tired of injections, of being poked and prodded. But just when I didn't think I could face one more needle, I listened. And then I made my decision.

It felt essential to do something, to not just be a patient. And luckily, I met many people during that time who had turned their private experience of illness into public good. David Bloom, brash and bold, helped establish the first research chair for myeloma in Canada. He's an ex-CEO of Shopper's Drug Mart and he nudged me into philanthropy by teasingly reawakening my competitive side. Fortunately, I ended up raising $25,000 CAD for him by leading a team walk for multiple myeloma awareness and finding a cure. (Multiple Myeloma M-Moving Together Toward the Cure walk to establish the Molly and David Bloom Chair in Multiple Myeloma Research at PMH.) David gave me stem cell advice: "Kid, they'll tell you to be a two-bag banker, but I'm telling you: bank three bags!"

"Really?"

"Oh yeah! You tell them! Three bags!"

Through David I met Cindy Leder. I had never met a more lovingly committed crusader. Cindy not only joined forces with another MM patient to establish the MM5K Walk in Toronto, but through the organization she advocated for two cutting-edge cancer treatments—Velcade and Revlimid—to be approved and paid for by the Ontario Government which elicited a domino effect across Canada. All accomplished while her husband lived precariously with the more invasive effects of the disease. Cindy's dreams are what kept me alive. Cindy for me, was a true rainmaker, mingling hope with every pragmatic step.

Then there was Sindi Hawkins, an ex-health minister for British Columbia who had been diagnosed with a very virulent form of leukaemia. She had retired from political life and dedicated herself to raising millions of dollars for cancer. She got in touch with me a few days after my blog went public, giving me a call out of the blue. I picked up my cell and stopped in the middle of the pavement, listening to this woman, knocked over by her energy, all hope and optimism. I sat on the kerb and we talked for an hour and a half. She was prepping for her own bone marrow transplant and must have been quite ill, but her life force came barrelling at me through the phone. I felt very relieved: here was someone who had walked down that path and was now taking me by the hand. Sindi is of Indian origin, too, and we talked about raising awareness for stem cell donors in the Indian community. Very few members of ethnic groups donate bone marrow and stem cells. It's a serious problem, leaving so many kids and people vulnerable and in crisis.

She gave me health tips. For her, immunity was a huge issue, and she advised me about the kind of duck-billed painters' mask that's ideal to wear on a flight. She told me that as soon as I got on a plane, I should ask for the pilot's lunch. "Tell them who you are, what you're dealing with, and you'll get the better food!" She was right. "Give me your best food and seat and parking spot cause I'm immuno-suppressed" is a helpful tool no doubt. We laughed and laughed. Even though she was across the country in Kelowna, and I was in Toronto, we spoke every week. She was another who did not clutch tightly to a story of suffering. I'm no expert, but this was how we effectively and humorously managed the storm in our body—observing the fear and wonderment, but not getting carried away.

And then there was Kathy Giusti, diagnosed at thirty-seven. She wanted her eighteen-month-old daughter to remember her, and she and her twin sister started the Multiple Myeloma Research Foundation. She's raised over $165 million USD for this orphan cancer. More importantly, her interest is about comforting and treating the patient, not merely funnelling all the money into a lab. I had heard of Kathy but had never met her, though I'd been given her number. In the middle of a vulnerable moment during chemo, I called. As the liquid burned through my veins my mind was filled with dark thoughts. Then Kathy came on the line. She somehow placed her hand on my brow, from a distance. Calm. Comforting, and with an eye to the future, to a cure. She was given three years to live, and sixteen years on, she's still here.

And yet, despite the sudden emergence of all these people around the world offering themselves in kindness, cancer was a very singular, very individual, very lonely journey. My father and Bobcat were there, as well as Noni. But it was a lot to bear. In a way, I hadn't been back in Toronto that long, and I was still something of a stranger in the city I'd left behind. I don't regret the choices that I'd made before, but I began to understand that I had to make different ones going forward.

All these thoughts were playing in my mind. Preparing for the stem cell transplant, I was finally slowing down. No more yoga. No house renovations. My energy was compromised, and the steroids were making me cuckoo. I couldn't hide from it any more so I might as well let it teach me.

By November, I plunged right into preparing for the stem cell transplant. Say "stem cell" to the average person and an image of a railing George Bush comes to mind. But that controversy involves embryonic stem cells, which make certain people nervous. That's too bad because stem cells are incredible beasts; they are cells produced in our own bodies with the potential to develop into many different kinds of cells—a natural repair system. When injected into the body, they can self-renew and treat all kinds of diseases. Recent research suggests that inhibiting the proliferation of cancer stem cells might actually be the key to a cure for cancer. I support stem cell research in all forms, but the type I needed was, and still is, far from the political frenzy; my stem cell donor would be me. Healthy blood-producing stem cells would be taken from my bone marrow and frozen. Then I'd receive hardcore chemo to kill both white and red blood cells, essentially cleaning out my marrow. Those thawed out stem cells would be reintroduced, and hopefully find their way back to my bone marrow where they would re-engraft and make healthy new blood cells. I gave them a colour, yellow of course, the shade of optimism and the third chakra.

Sounds simple, except that there was a waiting list of at least two or three months for stem cell transplants at Princess Margaret Hospital. If I had to wait that long, then I needed to go back on chemo. That felt unbearable somehow; my life would remain in limbo. I couldn't do a lot or move forward and make changes in my life until after the transplant. My spiritual practice had guided me to accept change and live in my present. But I didn't think Buddhism demanded that I lie down and wait either. I knew something could be done—but what?

I put in a special request. I spoke to the doctors and facilitators, saying, "Look, I don't want you to bump anyone off the list, but is there another solution?" Finally, I was told it might be possible to receive treatment in Hamilton or London, or any smaller town that wasn't strained to over-capacity. I would be farmed out. Outsourced. After a few weeks of plunging headfirst into participating in the Multiple Myeloma M-Moving for the Cure walk, raising awareness through interviews and chronicling my experiences on the blog, ("Pace yourself," Kathy told me wisely when I had to abort a trip to Multiple Myeloma Research Foundation fundraiser because of fever, "you need to concentrate on getting well—then you can give back more effectively.") I woke to a message that I would have my transplant in Hamilton, at Henderson Hospital, late December 2009. The news was a blessing. Many people in the myeloma community and the world fear the words stem cell transplant. I wasn't afraid of the idea at all. I began charting Operation Reboot in my mind, plotting an accelerated overthrow of the marrow status quo.

Preparations for the transplant began immediately. I had a battery of tests on my heart and lungs to make sure my body could survive the operation. Not everyone proves eligible after testing. I tried not to think about the possibility of being turned away. During my electrocardiogram, the technician—a chatty young woman from Newfoundland—and I critiqued the Christmas songs blaring from the radio. I chose "Happy Christmas, War is Over" as my favourite while lying on my back, wires dangling from my chest. "By the way," I quizzed her, "what do you think of murals on the ceiling? I mean I seem to spend all my time on my back staring up."

Another day I had a pulmonary function test at Toronto General with a dourer technician. The device is called a spirometer and the idea is to take a few normal breaths before forcefully blowing out all the air in the lungs into a mouthpiece attached to a machine with a lot of dials. I'd had this test before and always failed miserably. I don't know why, but I can't seem to exhale all the air in my lungs—my body wants to hang on to the last breath. I chalk it up to excellent survival instincts. Very grumpily, the technician kept asking whether I understood the instructions. I repeated the process a few times until I felt light and airy, like a ping-pong ball. I bounced out of there.

For two weeks, I received Neupogen or G-CSF injections from a homecare nurse that stimulated stem cell production. G-CSF stands for granulocyte-colony stimulating factor hormone and "I'm ready for my master's degree." The Neupogen stimulates the bone marrow and increases the number of circulating stem cells. Chemo kills, Neupogen grows. Once the stem cells were released into the blood stream—called peripheral stem cell harvesting—I would go in for the collection in a special "suite" at the hospital. This seemed like as good a time as any to get bald.

I hadn't lost a lot of hair until that point, but before that first dose of mega chemo, I decided that I was going to shave my head as a pre-emptive strike. It was slowly happening anyway. Every morning I woke to a tickle on my pillow from disengaged follicles. The little piles made me think of seaweed tangles washed up on a beach; a reverse sowing was taking place on my head. Sindi had told me how truly traumatic it was when she lost her hair. She also had long, thick Indian hair, and—like me—somehow thought that made her exempt from losing it. But one day in the shower it started coming out in hunks in her hand. She was devastated. "Think about shaving it," she advised, and I listened. It was another adventure, and it's not as if I hadn't done it before. I called Bobcat, former army man, and he brought over his military clippers. We made a little ritual out of it: Bobcat took photographs, leaving wispy Hasidic strands on both sides. Laughter burbled out of me. It was delusional to be this happy about losing my hair, but I was entitled to this happiness. I ran my hands over the spread of my bare scalp, feeling new sensations at the top of my head, a light, tickly breeze. And I remembered that Hindus believe life is *leela*—a play. Be playful and play your role. You will be called to play many roles and your job is to take them on with conviction and commitment. In the Yellow Diaries, I wrote:

An extreme Rapunzel moment.

You know Bobcat, every cancer rookie believes they are different. The Cyclophosphamide or Melphalan is not gonna make ME pukey or constipated or infertile. . ..

I'm special.

Well as it turns out, the Great Cancer archipelago is populated only by special people.

Who are there by special invitation.

Most of my words were drowned out by Bobcat's buzzer. Even in my own head.

That's why I'm happy I'm losing my hair. It's a trap, but I'm entitled to this happiness. This increment of everything. So, I enjoy the increasing spread across my head. There is a lot to be said for the impact of a shiny scalp. And never again will it be so acceptable for someone to find your hair in their food.

By the time we got to the stem cell transplant, I was bald and cold, wearing a little toque all the time with "Tibet" written across the top. I had one session of old-fashioned chemo; no cutting-edge Velcade at this stage of the game. I was given a hit of Benadryl off the top to manage the side effects. Turns out chemo makes me really sick, and though I'd been in treatment for months, I hadn't experienced traditional chemo side effects before. This chemo was different: three to four hours lying on a bed, feeling the rush of coldness as the chemicals hit my bloodstream. The headache was bludgeoning. I couldn't play Scrabble with Noni who sat with me. I couldn't keep up my banter with the nurses. Noni stroked my arm. I couldn't move and lay there on scratchy sheets like a sandbag. The nurse came around with a popsicle and I couldn't even hold it up.

For the harvesting, I was to be hooked up to a dialysis machine so I had to get another catheter put in, this time to connect to a big honking Hickman line. I went to Toronto General to get it, waited in queue and announced, "You know guys, last time you made me come back so make sure you get it right this time! And hop to it—I have a lunch appointment!" In bossing my way through the tension, I was channelling my mother, I think. This time they put this catheter below the collarbone, just above my left breast.

The stem cell harvesting is done in the "Apheresis/Stem Cell Unit" in Princess Margaret Hospital. It's just an ordinary room with about five or six comfortable, beige, wide-bodied chairs with some wicked-looking machines standing sentry behind them. I was in the harvesting suite for two days, with the stem cells slowly dripping out of me via the Hickman line. The entire floor is dedicated to stem cell and bone marrow transplants because of immunity issues. We all stretched peacefully in our beds and chairs, reading books and watching movies and chatting sometimes to find another direction for our attention. I leaned back and watched as the blood was pulled from my body. I watched dials turn steadily on the impressive looking COBE Spectra cell separator machine I was hooked up to. I looked upon it as metallic transcendence. Something close to sacred was taking place as my blood travelled out of my body, spun with a force strong enough to separate the stem cells, and then flowed back into me. When Noni came to sit with me, she asked, "What does all of this mean? Explain this to me." I pointed to a carefully typed, laminated sign on the wall that a patient had left behind. Under a painting of a green, waving lawn was a parable called *Ellen's Lawn: An Analogy for an Autologous Stem Cell Transplant*. It began with the doctor telling this mystery patient: "You are a lawn."

I took over the explanation. "Imagine, Noni, that you are a lawn and the lawn is infested with weeds. Not bright dandelions but the weeds that give no joy. The weeds are growing so fast they are taking over the entire lawn. The weeds are cancer cells. So, we apply pesticide, which is chemo, to kill off the weeds but when we do that, a lot of the grass dies as well. Chemo isn't targeted medicine, it's a bit crude actually so the good cells in our body and our immune system also take a hit. That's also why you lose your hair during strong chemo. Then we prepare the earth for replanting—that's me, don't I look like an earth goddess?—and we replant the grass. The stem cells they are collecting from me are the seeds, and when I go into the hospital, they will clean out my garden completely, so there're no weeds."

"And that's basically a stem cell transplant." I squeezed Noni's hand. "I'm preparing myself for the big reseeding."

I got another spin on my upcoming "ctrl-apple-reset" from my friend Shuvo, a paediatrician based in Montreal. His messages to me during that time blended with the science in a way that gave me solace. Ahead of the transplant countdown he emailed: We recycle every single molecule in our bodies on average every seven years, you are just doing an assisted clean-up of your immune system a little ahead of schedule!

It was getting cold in Toronto. In the days before the transplant, I remember running into friends in the cold weather and saying, almost excitedly: "No Christmas shopping this year—I'm about to get my stem cell transplant! That's more than enough of a gift. Wish me luck! It's a major reboot!" String lights were twinkling, and wreaths were being hung on the doors of houses. I would be getting my transplant on 25 December, Christmas Day, 2009. The thought of it filled me with a warm glow even though I would literally be nuked on that day. To prepare, I was meditating on stem cells and marrow. Filling my body with yellow light. Thinking about protein on the surface of white blood cells. I travelled to Hamilton, about ninety minutes outside of Toronto, to the Juravinski Cancer Centre to meet my new medical team. I saw the suite where I would live for a month after the reinfusion of my preserved stem cells. Families of patients can stay in an off-site hotel attached to the hospital. It was becoming very real. My haematologist laid it all out. First day: mega dose of chemo, strong enough to kill me, essentially.

"We take you to the brink, and on the second day, we bring you back."

"The brink of what?

"Death."

"Oh."

The stem cells would arrive in dry ice, with steam and smoke—very Vegas. There's a preservative used to freeze the cells that can cause a strange taste when it hits your blood—a taste like creamed corn. Oddly, the only thing to counter it is Taveners lemon candy. "We'll have a couple of those," said the haematologist. And ice, too, to suck on to prevent sores on the inside of the mouth. This was all relayed to me in light, drifting conversation. I was ready to get it done. Immediately. "Let's do this. Time for a reboot: Lisa 2.0, newer, wiser, healthier and depending on the kindness of this monstrous operation." My dad ended up moving into my room and sleeping on a cot.

On Christmas eve, I had the dose of chemo. It was considered "the" treatment for multiple myeloma and it was as gruelling as I'd expected. Then, on Christmas Day, they reinfused me, which was the actual "transplant" portion. Despite the dry ice disco look of the event, the beginning of my metamorphosis was pretty simple, taking only about ten minutes for one bag of stem cells to re-enter my body through the catheter. It was the resurrection which would be tough. I lay in my bed, and as soon as the haematologist hit the plunger, the taste of creamed corn welled up in the back of my throat and flooded my mouth. I could smell it too, so vividly that I looked around the room to see if anyone else had registered it.

It took ten to fifteen days for the stem cells to re-engraft. It put me in a very strange, dreamlike state. There was a whiteboard in my room and a black felt-tip pen and the nurses wrote my numbers there after each blood test. I watched the white blood cell count dropping each day until it arrived at zero. Zero. I had absolutely no white cells, which meant no immunity, which meant I felt terrible. The risk of infection isn't just from the outside, but also from within. The natural bacteria in your system notice that there are no white cells around to keep them in check and it's party time for them. I developed horrible agonizing sores through my entire gastrointestinal tract, basically from mouth to ass (or "gum to bum," as the experts put it so demurely). Down below, the diarrhoea was agonizing, while up top, I couldn't swallow. Doctors encouraged me to walk around the hall, dragging my IV, which I named Melvin, because he was my most constant companion. But even that little circuit was unbelievably difficult. My body had shut down. I did not want to walk. I did not want to be awake. All I wanted to do was sleep.

Before, I'd had ideas that I would film my transplant time, or write about it. But it's not possible to do anything at all. Bobcat had gifted me the entire season of the HBO comedy series, *Curb Your Enthusiasm*, but I could hardly focus on Larry David. Bobcat made the two-hour drive to visit at the beginning and I smiled at him weakly from my bed, unable to do anything else. Noni drove up, as well as my oldest friend Tina and her brother Peter, but I hardly remember that time. The only thing I recall is a Buddhist nurse whose name I couldn't remember in my morphine haze. All I knew was that she was originally from Vietnam. We talked, and she loaned me her iPod so I could listen to recordings of an American Buddhist named Jack Kornfield. His talks on dharma and Buddhism are filled with humour and humble insight. One night she came to draw blood from the port in my chest, and I asked her to sing with me, my usual way of comforting myself during the prodding. "You're a Buddhist?" I croaked through cracked lips.

"I'm a follower of anything that gives peace," she said. So, we chanted *"Om mani padme hum"* and another Buddhist chant I was unfamiliar with but repeated after her with growing elation and volume.

"There's no such thing as a 'small change,'" she said, checking my vitals, pausing to dampen my lips with a cotton swab. My father was watching from his cot in the corner. He joined in as we start to make up "blessings."

"May your thoughts escape you and your feelings catch you when you don't expect it."

"May you give birth to the gods and goddess inside you."

"May your inner dialogue reflect the fire of your soul."

"May I you see the other in yourself, and yourself in others."

"May your lottery ticket possess the winning number," I couldn't resist adding, looking up at the nurse's eyes. I meant it.

One night, around four in the morning, in the dark hospital room full of the smell of past struggles, we started chanting. This time felt different, as if I was making my presence known. I visualized yellow releasing into the air around us. It wasn't a religious or even a spiritual exercise. I was chanting out of sheer joy at being able to make these sounds. I grew louder and louder, more and more emphatic as the chant became a battle cry—but a battle waged without anger. Because who was I warring with? Not my body, which had betrayed me as a last resort. The sacred syllables were shaking loose all the forgotten things fed into my bones long ago: memories of the car crash, of slights and suppressed loneliness and childhood terrors, the pain of hungering for connection and always feeling oppressed when it came. At the root of it lived this mutation: "You are not lovable, try harder. You're not enough, and you never will be."

Here, now, in this hospital suite, chemo was purging molecules of
self-hatred and pain along with cancer cells, leaving me emotionally
free. The sounds attracted a crowd of night nurses. They watched in
the darkness as we chanted. What happens in our body derives from the
soul. Whatever emotional sickness of the soul I had been carrying
was also dissipating along with my white blood cells, clearing space.
"Everything can be made spiritual with attention," the nurse told me.
Or maybe she didn't. But I remember those words clearly.

I got colitis, a bad infection in the lining of the colon, so I was sent
to a lab for X-rays. It was a chance to get out of the room at least, that
long, slow walk to the elevator and down to the lab. On other days, while
waiting for my stem cells to begin multiplying and populating my marrow with fresh cells, I forced myself to take Melvin to the sunroom. In
this calm, glassed-in space, I met the others. Belinda was a veteran. It
was her third time there and she had brought her own pink terry cotton
robe. Instant connections were formed, like visitors in a new country
who recognize one another. No one worried about what to say, or how to
be with a sick person. "I really want a shower," I said one day, "when I
have energy, in about a week." We started calling it the spa, a place to
gossip and laugh together, but a sanctuary, I was reminded, that we
would all be leaving soon, in one way or the other. It's weird how time
changes when you are being probed and wiped and drugged. When
you're in the middle of it, you're not sure that you can see the way out,
but it comes. On 11 January 2010, during a short burst of energy I
updated the Yellow Diaries:

Stem Cell Transplant:
It was an odyssey. A trip to the core. The marrow had its way.
Now I'm full of cheerful stem cells, like fields of sunflowers I
travel inside and watch them turn their small, yellow faces
towards me. They giggle and beam.
Go forth and multiply.

I was in there for just under a month, and ready to get out by the end
of January 2010. The new year had started outside my memory and

experience. My father took my bag, and we got into his car. I gulped fresh air for the first time in weeks. "Let's go to Swiss Chalet," I told him. I hadn't had any normal food for weeks—eating was exhausting and painful—so off we went. Under the fast food lights, I relished every bite of this first real meal to celebrate my rebirth. As soon as I got home, I fell into bed. It can take up to a year to recover your energy from a stem cell transplant. My Buddhist nurse had told me, "You're going to discover a new definition of fatigue." A patient told me that she would remove a fork from her dishwasher and then go lie down.

Sindi sent me encouraging little snippets, reminding me that the more joy you find, the better crop of cells you grow. But staying positive doesn't mean you have to be happy all the time. By February, Toronto's grim and grey forecast was beginning to seep into my mind. This is the crucial period that people don't understand: getting out of the hospital doesn't mean it's over; it's when the real healing starts. But everyone around is already spent and drained just from your having been in the hospital. It was the time I most needed support, but I think people assumed that since I was out of crisis, I was okay.

And then something strange happened: I started feeling good. Dramatically different, in fact. I was not dead. I could move and breathe and stay awake for longer intervals. I was even starting to deflate now that I had been weaned off the personality-altering steroids. "Morning Lisa 2.0, you magnificent creature, you," I whispered to a hopeful tune in my head. I wrote in my blog:

This is from a Jorge Louis Borges poem which my friend Sol sent:

"I'll try to make more mistakes—I won't try to be so perfect."

Probably won't find that in the Seven Habits of Highly Effective People. Somewhere, somehow the pursuit of perfection has lodged itself in my very marrow. From making lists to vaulting over myself to achieve, these manifestations of a lack have seeped into the deepest, most secret part of myself.

A lack.

If I don't try to be perfect, it will mean that I am.

All I'm trying to say is that I do not want the cancer to come back.

Therefore, something must change from before.

At home I had surrounded myself with titles like *Practical Yoga Philosophy*, *The Essence of the Bhagavad Gita*, *A History of Food in India* and poetry collections by Indian poets Tishani Doshi and Jeet Thayil. Healing was my priority, but India was also on my mind.

And something else. I could not consent to go back to my old ways. Cancer had thrown me through a window into the central courtyard of crisis and because of that impact, new windows had opened. It wasn't long before an old feeling sprang up: ripples of restlessness. "Not here, not here, elsewhere,"—was that a line from a poem or had I made that up? In my elsewhere, I wore flamboyant colours like rani pink, lime green and marigold and beaten gold on my wrists. I was always in the company of friends you would tell lies for. And everywhere I was show-ered by red dust and tree jasmine, sweat running in maps across my back. To those who understand India, its siren call is beyond dispute. But even they would consider visiting there just a few weeks after a stem cell transplant as a particular sort of lunacy. But for Lisa 2.0, all signs said that it was time to go.

19

MY BODY HAD told me, you're not at the end of the road, journey on. And so in February 2010, three weeks after a stem cell transplant, I found myself on a plane to India. This time, rather than out and out escapism or vagabonding, I was questing to bring the two sides of myself into harmony. In India, I knew my accent and gestures would change, I would slip into my Bombay self, but when I spoke to my Canadian agent on the phone I would go back to being Lisa from Etobicoke. Changing the cadence of my speech to fit the place was a way of life. But now, this no longer felt like fragmenting; it was starting to feel seamless, as if I wasn't denying either side of myself.

Besides, in late January 2010, Aarti Sethi Khanna, the PR manager from Rado's India office had sent me an email. Aarti and I had bonded years ago, when I first signed with Rado, over our taste for the bizarre. Ever since, she had kept sending me photos of weird slogans painted on the rear of vehicles she had spotted around Delhi with "I know you like signs from the universe" in the subject line. Over time we had developed a warm friendship. So, when she asked if I felt up to appearing at store openings in Bangalore and Chennai, the timing seemed perfect. I sourced some wigs in Toronto before leaving, so the bald head wouldn't be the only story at the Rado events. It also occurred to me that my scalp might be shiny. Didn't want to blind the photographers at my first public outing in India after my cancer diagnosis. But I didn't love the heavy, long mane, or the short, coiffed bowl of champagne blush. In the end,

I chose a wig that was less Nancy Reagan and more Michelle Obama—flat and shoulder length. I landed in India, on 15 February, a little drained. I was mindful of my special cargo: fresh stem cells. My "yellow babies" were crying out for a nap. The immigration officer looked at me, then down at my passport and said: "What happened to your hair?"

"I have cancer," I shot back.

"Ah," he said, "medical tourist."

A new category in India: Westerners paying money for surgeries and surrogates and dental work on the cheap. It must be common if an immigration officer was making these assumptions.

As soon as I set foot in Bombay, I felt relief. What I had been yearning for and missing in the Canadian winter was the warmth of solace. That affectionate quality of prodding and advising and caring that hovered in India amongst friends. It was two in the morning when I landed and outside the airport the humidity was an embrace. *Welcome back, why so long? Ah yes, you had cancer. I prayed for you. My family, we went to temple to pray for your health. When will we see you on the big screen?* Every gesture, every emotion would now be amplified, turning my heart into a sponge.

Since leaving the hospital in late January, I had been shedding my steroid induced wetsuit—I had "the shrinks"—and my immunity was steadily improving. I'd even shrugged off my huge moonface like a heavy winter coat. But my body would never be model sleek and thin again. It didn't matter of course and now that I was healing, I was ready to focus on other things. And as I discovered, the terrain had changed not only within me, but outside as well. Contemporary India was embracing everything from luxury brands to fashion blogs to radiance-boosting face masks and matte palettes with a manic fervour. Indian women were buying shades of "because you are worth it" and comparing peep-toe heels, just like women all over the world. And just like elsewhere, marketing had gone rogue. The newest crop of female Bollywood stars presented blank, flawless versions of themselves on the cover of magazines, all the personality airbrushed out of the frame. But they were beautifully styled, and the clothes looked great. It revealed a strenuous effort to manipulate reality, to make women buy things and aspire to an impossible beauty standard. Without championing a notion of authentic beauty in India, we were all complicit. "I will not beat my flesh back into size zero submission. It had to be enough just to radiate health—which in my case is as hard won and precarious as any Bollywood starlet's career," I wrote in my blog.

Over the last decade I had engaged in an uneasy ritual with the Indian entertainment media among whom it had become a sort of sport to get embarrassing or compromising photos of female celebrities. And so, during press conferences or appearances, I would sit with my knees pressed firmly together, hands in my lap with a tense, tight smile. I saw photos of myself with my mouth frozen in a strange grimace or, worse, shot from an angle that almost revealed the colour of my underwear, narrowly avoiding a "wardrobe malfunction." It was humiliating. And the questions shouted by male journalists took on a combative tone: Why are you not married? Why don't we see you on the silver screen? Don't you want to be a mother? What's your fitness routine? What do you think of (insert male Bollywood actor)? It was a public bloodletting that stripped me of any quality of character I might possess and that interfered with the headline they had already composed. I was certainly, in their eyes, a unique failure of womanhood. Any of my answers or accomplishments that didn't fit into their agenda were dismissed. All these years later and my 1990s magazine images were still superimposed on my flesh. All they saw was a *Gladrags* cover with "Voyeuristic peaks at the sexiest women around" next to my cleavage. At least that's what it felt like. I told myself to remain sedate and unruffled, but I would get worn down by the incessant goading until I was bristling with nervous energy, ready to lunge and fight. That is when I felt the room light up. I was snared and finally I had complied with the rules of engagement.

But this time would be different.

I would be different.

I was now a champion of near death.

I would not pull rank. I would not pull back.

I would only ever, now, be me.

The Rado events were exactly as I needed them to be—equal parts uplifting and fun. At the opening of the Bangalore store, I was interviewed by Barkha Dutt, the Christiane Amanpour of Indian television journalism. I was tugging a little self-consciously at my First Lady hair, but it went fine. She didn't make me cry, though I'd heard that was her MO. After the interview I tossed the wig. It was an illusory fix. I was more eye-catching then, without hair, than ever before. Besides, my exposed scalp was an important statement in India, to prove that hair loss during treatment was nothing to be ashamed of. Cancer was neither a death sentence, nor did it ennoble me. It was an experience I had to walk through. Instead of "Cancer Warrior" or "Cancer Fighter" and all the other labels thrown at me in India, I arrived on "Cancer Graduate" after my interview with Barkha, to describe the complex collection of experiences I had lived through. And was still living with and learning from.

Afterwards, Aarti, handed me an issue of *India Today* with my photo on the cover. This was a surprise. They had lifted the picture from my blog. On the cover, I was bald, wearing a white sweater, staring earnestly at the lens in one of the shots Bobcat had taken while he was shaving my head. "Lisa Ray actor, 37, has BONE MARROW CANCER and is undergoing one of the cutting-edge treatments that spell NEW HOPE FOR CANCER PATIENTS." It's cool to be on the cover of *India Today* but I'd always thought they might ask me first. It was a little as if there was a birthday party in my honour going on in the neighbour's house next door, but no one had invited me. I looked at that un-airbrushed cover image for a long time and then wrote on my blog:

This is an image that doesn't manipulate. At least I hope not.
Thank you India Today for urging people to see and feel.
Illness is alchemy.

While in India, I reacquainted myself with old friends, circling back to earlier times but without the Marlboros and youthful posturing and studied nonchalance. I had returned a grown woman. After my Rado events, I met up with my old friend Farrokh Chothia, a confidante since since I was seventeen. And even though I like to call him a grumpy old *bawa* and he is good at playing the reticent artist, he has the softest heart, and immediately took to caring for me.

First, he escorted me to Jaslok Hospital on Peddar Road, for an operation to excise a crop of cysts on my eyelids that had sprung up in the last few weeks. They were known as chalazion, and they were a fallout from

my final blast of chemo and my compromised immune system. The fairly
minor operation to remove them would have taken months to schedule in
Canada since it was elective, so I decided to have it done in India. The cysts
were not serious but ugly. They were the last symbol of illness, bending
my lids and distorting my sight, and they had to go. Farrokh escorted me
back from the hospital, bandaged like a one-eyed buccaneer, and smiling.
A few days later, the bandage was removed, I was restored to sight and he
recorded the moment with his camera. Those portraits he took of me,
were both deeply compassionate and empowering.

At the same time, Farrokh saw the media creating this strange new
brand of celebrity—I had just shot for the cover of *People* magazine
India as a "celebrity patient"—and he said, "Lisa—enough. You have
to get well. You're not going to work. You're not going to run around.
We'll stop now." He had just photographed me for the Indian edition of
Elle magazine, but he understood that my story was more than a passing
headline and he also knew how the hive of opinions in India could
morph into something more biting and unpleasant. And we did stop. I
stayed in Farrokh's flat in Bandra, off Carter Road, hugging the seaside,
recently revamped with a promenade. Farrokh lives according to his
own inner logic: he's a guy with a passion for aviation who doesn't like
to leave the ground. His projects and interests were full of out-sized
ideas that could only happen in India.

His Bandra flat was done up very much in Farrokh's signature SoBo
(South Bombay) understated style: neutral colours, clean lines, concrete
floors. I loved it in this bachelor pad, surrounded by Farrokh's memorabilia: vintage camera lenses, a signed copy of John Irving's *A Son of the
Circus* on top of old copies of the *Onion*, a carefully curated exhibit of our
young lives. I rested and he brought cheese and wine and we ate it sprawled
idly on his floor, listening to his formidable collection of jazz and classical
music or trying to remember the lyrics to the "Lumberjack Song."

In March, we took a road trip to Farrokh's ancestral home in Bulsar
(now called Valsad) outside Bombay. It was an old estate, built somewhere around 1919, the sagging tiled structures competing with the
overgrown garden for my affection. One afternoon, Farrokh pulled out
some ancient LPs that had been sitting in boxes for years: German pop
and Italian arias. "Play at 33 1/3 Revolutions per minute" said the cover.

We sang along to German Schlagers and Chansons de Paris in that sprawling old house with boxed-up memories for days. When I think of my healing, I think of this time, when the house in the mango orchard was filled with silent applause.

My thirty-eighth birthday felt like a rebirth. I had never celebrated my birthday before—they struck me as both juvenile and a relentless promotion of self, year after year. But that year, I didn't hesitate to celebrate my life. I called myself Lisa Rebooted. It was also Easter, which seemed like another symbolic grab from the Christian calendar.

I had a family in my circle of friends in India who I had known in my early life, even though I was a different person then. They threw me a party in Goa. Wendell Rodricks, a writer and pioneer of minimalist resort wear in India who passed tragically in early 2020, was the unofficial ambassador of all things Goan. He lives in a beautiful old house in a village in north Goa, with his French husband Jerome and a collection of pets. Over the years, he had styled me, nurtured me, hosted my parents at his home, and when his father was in the Tata Memorial Hospital for cancer treatment, we had gone together, an unspoken invitation between old friends. Denzil Sequiera, another close friend, photographer and proprietor of Elsewhere, a laid-back eco-beach resort, came with his son, Marc. They arrived at Farrokh's house set at the top of a hillside in Goa we called Breathless, after the view and the climb. Divya Thakur and Anaita Adajania, my girlfriends of the last two decades, flew in from Bombay. Reminiscing was not cool, in our everyday efforts to remain relevant, but that afternoon the conversation flowed, and we laughed over old stories of unfortunate shoot experiences, tumbles out of trees on location and that time we had to reshoot an entire campaign because the *pallu* of the saree was not showing.

"These models are so long now, yaar. Laxmi is like a carrot."

"I've always been a bonsai model."

"Your jeep is open . . . he said. He meant zip."

"The full moon is in Taurus."

"Do you know Hanover Wadia?"

"No, I know Amarcord Singh."

"What do you call an Indian philanthropist? Tax evader."

"I heard Hang over Wadia."

"Did I mention moon's in Taurus?"

"Are you feeling a bit barkish at the moon, FC?"

"He should be Hangover Wadia."

"I did some howling, but the police came and told me to stop."

"Lisa, can you be a part-time lover?" was a throwaway question I took to heart. I closed my eyes, feeling the sun on my skin.

"Until we *adore* ourselves—I mean like head over heels in love with ourselves—we just can't love others. You just can't. But loving part-time is like saying I'm a part-time human. So, I'm a full-time lover. Of everything. EVERTHING. Including suffering. Don't waste your suffering—I read that once. Know it, love it and it won't diminish you."

We threw back our heads, tasting the aroma of the ocean on the wind. The wine and levity quenched us. We drank and ate Kerala pepper prawns and homemade Thai curry cooked in cast iron pots as the sun dipped, bathing us in wistful light.

½ kg fresh prawns—freshwater
2 small onions, thinly sliced
4–5 pods of garlic, chopped
1 fistful black pepper, roughly ground
Handful kari patta
Salt/sugar to taste
Butter

Heat oil and butter in wok—bung in onions till transparent and fragrant. Throw in garlic, stir until fragrant. Add prawns and black pepper. Stir for a couple of seconds till prawns are coated and opaque. Add salt, sugar, and throw in kari patta. Do not overcook prawns! Turn off heat and eat immediately with fragrant mushroom and lime leaf rice—which you should have made by now.

There was a feeling that the world belonged to us, only us, and it was keeping things for only us to see and enjoy. We all ended up jumping into the pool, the girls getting up on the guys' shoulders. Someone piped up: "Let's have a race!"

"Let's play Gladiator!"

Soon the swimsuits came off.

We were recapturing the spirit of youth and hopefulness, but with all the collective experience that we contained. We had been through a lot, and we were wounded, triumphant and accomplished. One of us had seen the love of his life go off and marry someone else. Another had lost their father to cancer. Someone had suffered a marital split, and someone else was yet to find love. We were all citizens of a shared mindscape, spilling warm breath on each other's skin. It was a good reminder for me: I'm not the only one who has known pain. We are all carrying it, some more quietly than others.

That night, under the sway of alcohol and an ample sky, we threw all of it into the pool that Farrokh had constructed. He was always grumbling about this pool with its broken filter that required someone from Bombay to fix it—even that vanished. There was no room for the petty complaints of our daily lives. For one night, we tossed it all away. It was pure joy, Bacchanalian, the kind of fun that is increasingly rare as we grow older. Naked in the water, we glanced around the pool to see who hadn't joined in. There was Jerome, Wendell's partner, this magnificent, massive French man, the picture of gravitas. He was sitting on the pool steps smoking a cigar, half submerged in the water. We all began shouting and pointing at him, the one hold-out: "Come on! Get in Jerome. Stop adulting!"

He put his cigar in his mouth, and very slowly, rose up out of the water, rivulets of pool water covering his huge body, arms extended and yes—he had indeed joined the game already. He was naked. Then he sunk back down in the water, all the while smoking oh-so casually. It was one of those evenings that expands and takes on a shape in my memory that is not proportionate to anything else. Someone set my birthday cake afloat in the pool on an inflatable mattress, and I still carry it around with me, this picture of my first birthday celebration, the candles aflame, faces half-lit, love and deliverance seeping through the shadows. My heart struggled to hold it all. "What if our bodies were transparent?" I thought. "And we could see all our fully experienced heartaches and joys and sadness in shades of glowing, pool water-coloured light?"

The very next day, Farrokh shot me for Indian *Vogue* in his home.

Years before, while promoting *Water* in New York, I had been taken around by an American publicist to the offices of American *Vogue*. It was very *Devil Wears Prada*: I had been paraded around in front of a group of sceptical women in sky-high heels with their thin eyebrows raised. After the meet-and-greet, I was told I had passed the invisible test, and that they'd love to feature me. But the pictures never ran, and later I found out why: They'd rejected the photos because I'd been deemed chubby. And this was when I was rail thin. So, it was vindicating, to be shot by Indian *Vogue*, even bloated on steroids and more or less bald. Anaita had lobbied for the shoot. I'd known Anaita since she was starting out, like me, and now she had moved up the fashion ranks to become creative fashion director at *Vogue* and one of India's most influential stylists. I remember watching her dancing with enviable abandon at parties when I would press myself against a wall. Anaita is warm and unfailingly upbeat, terminally delightful, blending a quirky sense of humour with deadpan endearments: "Daaarling" and "Babes."

Before the shoot was to begin, I sat in hair and make-up, trying to sort through my thoughts about my first big post-cancer modelling shoot. I checked inside myself for the old projections of alienation and unworthiness. The room was clean. The make-up artist's task of fixing individual lashes on to my lids took on a meditative rhythm. Apply glue, blow, apply to my eye. It grew spacious and quiet in my head. The work of our lives is not covering ourselves with achievements but uncovering what lies inside. I understood how ironic an insight it was to have in a make-up chair, but why should there be any division between the worlds I inhabit? It's what caused me to struggle all my life. My yardstick of success had become very clear: to be nothing but myself by uniting *all* my separate selves. This was the only way going forward. And it would begin with this shoot. Anaita came in and gave me a small box. Inside was a silver chain with one small angel wing on it. She had taped a piece of paper to the box: "One cannot consent to creep when you are meant to fly."

It was breezy and late in the morning by the time FC began taking my photographs. Anaita and her team stood outside his sightline. I put my bare legs on the sofa, feeling wild and raw and incarnated. The reflectors flared silver off my skull. It was exhilarating to bare my skin, show off my bones, let my tummy hang out, to revel in the reshaping of my existence after the fall. Farrokh shot me in chiffon, jewels and a draped, full skirted tulle. The caption they chose read: "You can get away with this kind of frock when you don't have any hair. Princess with an edge."

I was surprised when my old friend Sanjay Narang suddenly reached out during my recovery tour of India. He was now recognised as a successful and prominent hotelier and businessman who, along with his sister, Rachna, introduced India to high-end fast food like croissants and delicatessens in the 1990s, Sanjay, Rachna and I had been close friends during our turbulent twenties, particularly after they had been ejected from their massive Pali Hill bungalow after a family feud. Sanjay, always an extremely driven workaholic, had gone on to establish a hospitality empire independent of his family and was one of those forces nudging India into the global future. Sometime in 2007, he sold one of his food catering businesses for millions. He had always been kind, protective and indulgent with friends he considered family, and I had prized our closeness, but over the past decade we had fallen out of touch.

Now, news of my cancer had revived our old friendship. It turned out we were on a similar path. After making his fortune, Sanjay had decided he'd had enough with the entropic spectacle of Bombay and had retreated to the beautiful hill station of Landour. He invited me to visit, claiming there was no better place to rest. I was fascinated by his decision to live with less and closer to simple joys, and immediately took him up on the offer.

My dad was in Calcutta, visiting family at the same time, so I booked him a ticket to Dehradun, the closest airport. Together we climbed into Sanjay's four-wheel drive for the climb up the mountain, catching fleeting looks at snow-capped peaks between hairpin turns, the driver navigating at full tilt as though we were capable of flight. I'm used to the driving in India, but this was harrowing. When you arrive, there's nothing in Landour besides a small bazaar called Char Dukan and a *chakkar* (path) that circles the village. It was perfect. It had been an army cantonment during the Raj, where British military staff suffering from tropical ailments were sent to recover. Even now, the air is crisp and smells of raw piney woods. There's very little development, just a few gabled colonial bungalows, and an old, overgrown British cemetery where many of the officers who never recovered were laid to rest. I was enchanted. Sanjay has purchased two bungalows and developed an old English manor into a small hotel. Landour had always been a quiet creative hub, home to writers, like Ruskin Bond and Steven Alter and alumni from nearby Woodstock International School, many descended from American missionaries with identities even more confusing than mine.

My father and I stayed in a little all-wood chalet guest house off Sanjay's main house. Inside, it was as if Gstaad had been transplanted to this tiny Himalayan hamlet, blonde wood on wood decor, the stone floor layered with rugs and a soaring fireplace. Sanjay was there to greet us the next morning, standing in front of his residence, Bothwell Bank, in his all-American outfit of polo shirt and khaki pants (he had gone to Cornell and must have mainlined the Ivy). But what surprised me about my friend was his new focus: he had become a donor at Woodstock International School, refurbishing buildings at his own expense, giving students from around the world a rock-climbing wall and a squash court. He had the same drive, the same vision, but he had refocused it, and was giving back. I loved that he had installed garbage cans in the town, and renovated an old church. Evenings were passed visiting with friends. A group of us often dropped by Oakville, Steve Alter's bungalow, seemingly unannounced since there was limited cell phone reception on the mountain. But this was the *pahari* (mountain) lifestyle and Steve was always unsurprised and gracious at our determined interruption of his day, ushering us through the grand entry hall while the help laid out tea. He had a gentle but knowing manner and a sly wit, in the way of great observers. I enjoyed listening to him talk about Landour's literary history, about people we knew and local politics and gossip. Steve's lilt lay somewhere between Massachusetts and Mussoorie. I noticed the way he pronounced "Garhwal" like a local and recognized myself in those woven realities.

In Landour, I watched my father come into his own. Each morning he flung a shawl around his shoulders and walked into the mist-filled thin air, emerging hours later with new intelligence. "Did you know Happy Valley, the first Tibetan settlement in India is just beyond the polo ground? The Dalai Lama and his followers walked fifteen days to reach Mussoorie. I tried to get into the Observation Tower, but this is India and of course it was locked. The best view of the peaks is at Lal Tibba. You can see Nanda Devi clear as day. Did you know Landour is named after Llanddowror, a tiny Welsh village? I passed Victor Banerjee's cottage. What a talent! Never got his due. See how they wasted the talents of such a fine actor?"

My father no longer seemed as haunted by my mother's death. He's always had a Zen master-like attitude towards life, but I think he had internalized some of my mom's anxiety over the years. Now he was letting that go. I remember how comfortable he seemed wherever we went. Travelling in India will test anyone's patience, but he never worried about plans falling through. When we were leaving Landour for Delhi, we almost missed our flight. Our driver was driving like a maniac over dusty roads, scattering people and leaning into the car horn and I looked over at my dad, waiting for a freak-out about the plane that was sure to leave us behind. He was absolutely serene. "If we miss the flight, we miss the flight," he said. That serenity was a safe harbour for me during my illness. I was striving every day to absorb it too.

The final stop on my recovery tour was Rishikesh. I've always been attracted to places where mountain meets river, the loftiness dissolving into water. Rishikesh is just such a place and a holy city to boot; a praise song to the miracle and the mess of it all, its moorings deeper—far deeper—than anything on offer in the modern world, where pilgrims gather from all over India to take a dip in the Ganges. Fortunately, when my dad and I drove down from Landour the annual international yoga festival had wrapped. There was a strong scent of crushed petals everywhere.

My dad and I walked away from the noisy, clanging centre of the city to the isolation of the open space by the river. We watched a group of villagers going through private rituals and lowering themselves into the river. The women had removed their cholis and they were standing in the current, wrapped only in their sarees, unselfconscious about their exposed skin. They prayed, pressing joined hands to their foreheads, emptying their souls into the water. According to Hindus, the world begins and ends. And the journey is long. We have to drown through many births before we find our way to the water's edge. I felt the sounds of the river in me, running in my blood. And I began laughing because there it was, finally. That feeling. I was at home in the world . . . with the world. With all its failings and touching faith that there is some meaning to being human.

My dad and I sat on the bank of the Ganges and dipped our fingers in the sacred river. He placed his hand on the crown of my head, leaving droplets in my pilgrim fuzz. We were surrounded by the faithful immersing themselves. Flashes of flesh, fabric flung away, a human ache meets the waters. The waters cleanse it all away, it is said.

Later, in the Yellow Diaries, I wrote:

I'm back from Rishikesh. The holy city of Hindus. Located in the foothills of the majestic Himalayas.

Ganga darshan. A glimpse beyond the bag of bones. Spiritual theatre.

Passed many shaven pilgrims. I have a new vision of myself now. In this city of mystics, mendicants and seekers, my tonsured head blends in.

All through my recovery tour of India, I felt: These also are my people. I mean all of humankind. Perhaps we lack a shared vocabulary, but we share soul-containers for the lingering echo of collapsing stars and shoreless prayers. I've had such a peripatetic existence, always wondering: Where is my place? Who are my people? Maybe that's a sensation many mixed-race kids feel—we're the "third culture" kids, growing up in a world different from that of our parents. Polish, Indian, Canadian—I'd never owned any of those labels. This idea of belonging to a single place was an elusive idea. But with an unnerving taste of mortality behind me, there I was, thirty-eight years old, finally feeling like I belonged. To myself. And just like that, the voices went quiet and I was lifted into my own homemade peace. This is another side effect of cancer: it forces you to appreciate what you have, to live in that elusive present I'd been seeking so long. It bestows the gift of gratitude.

———

After Rishikesh, I understood the word *purna*, a Sanskrit term for fulfilment. I felt that. Healed. And that meant I was well enough to return to Toronto in early June 2010. Of course, a few weeks after my return to my Beaches apartment, my mind started ticker taping: Now what? The great question mark. I wanted to continue the work of reshaping myself from the inside out. I had picked up books on healing and Ayurveda in India, and they lay all over in precarious piles like an errant, long-haired rock stacker had wandered into my apartment. The one I reached for the most in that time was *Anticancer: A New Way of Life* by Dr David Servan-Schreiber. Dr D was a neuroscientist, physician and professor of clinical psychiatry—your garden variety overachiever—who confronted his own diagnosis of brain cancer by radically challenging the medical establishment's established views. When Dr D wrote about the effects of trauma and unhealed wounds on restoring health, my body tingled in recognition but when he went on to propose that cancer cells lie dormant in all of us, all the time, it shook me. "What are the odds," I thought, "that those overachieving cells yearning for immortality will not find hospitable terrain in my body again?"

I busied myself with juicing and researched how food and nutrition could boost my healing. Integrative medicine and inflammation rolled off my tongue, and "Did you know Hippocrates said, 'Let food be thy medicine' while doctors who take the Hippocratic oath dismiss the vital role nutrition plays in our health?" I was preachy enough to merit my own pulpit. My agent called with invitations to give talks to organizations about multiple myeloma and my story. My instinct told me to accept. I felt myself on the brink of becoming a responsible commentator of the cancer experience. I didn't look ill any more, so I knew there was a possibility of returning to acting work. But I didn't feel prepared enough to jump into it full-time and wrangle with competing demands. There were inquiries but I wasn't ready. I was, in fact, feeling cranky and oppressed after returning from India. I spent one afternoon clearing out my medicine cabinet, trying not to linger on the labels. There were so many bottles of pills, with names from a different dimension like apo-metronidazole, apo-granisetron, ran-pantoprazole: "Take 1 tablet 1 hour prior to chemotherapy."

In the Yellow Diaries I wrote:

I have to remember . . . it's not over yet. Because autumn frost
follows the abundance of summer. Because the Jacaranda flowers
unblossom and carpet the ground before I can commit them to
memory.

Because everything changes. From worse to better. Better to . . .
Relapse?

That's when it became clear. I was suffering from battle fatigue. I
had all the symptoms and I was surrounded by the debris of my former
life. Of course, it would take time to recognize myself again. That's
what happens when you return from the frontline. My spirit was tired.
And I knew, if this is how I'm feeling, Bobcat must be battle-scarred too.

After a national media tour for a patient organisation called
Myeloma Canada, I returned to Toronto in the early summer, to find
Bobcat extremely withdrawn. He would disappear for days on end,
and I had no clue where he was. I think that in my head, the trip to
India had been a way to attempt to salvage the relationship: I had
projected this idea that if I left, and got my emotional fill from other
people, that it would take the pressure off him. My take was: I'm not
getting what I need from the relationship. And his was: At every pivotal moment, she leaves. And we were both right.

Finally, I pinned down Bobcat at the end of June and got him to sit
across from me. He wanted to meet at a restaurant, in a public place.
Was he worried I would climb on a table and make a scene? I sat
calmly opposite him in a booth. He kept running his fingers across his
lips when he spoke. It's strange, the things we notice at the end. He
confessed that he was going through a difficult time at work, and that
walking with me through my illness had taken a toll. "Why didn't you
just come out and say something!" I thought, but I was relieved to be
told. The giving from both sides had been large and uncalculated but
I could see he had choked off the airway between us, pulled the plug,
switched off. He kept his eyes on my face as we talked, but it was like
he was looking at a distant landmark. I had already become something remote for him. When we had first met, I was a dramatically

different person. Of course, I had changed; how could I not have changed? And he had changed too, simply by bearing witness. But I knew I couldn't take him in the direction I was headed. Our story had to end and, in fact, when we parted ways, we smiled with kindness. Still, it stung.

Shortly after my return to Toronto, a very old friend of mine I hadn't seen in years, phoned and told me about a small artsy town she had moved to in British Columbia, called Nelson. I first knew Rose when I was a teenager on the club scene in Toronto. After more than twenty years, she had tracked me down upon reading about my cancer coming-out in a Canadian paper. Over the years, Rose had transitioned from a fashionista towards more earthy preoccupations and footprints. She sounded as vibrant as before on the phone, but I couldn't in my head reconcile the two versions, having only a memory of her statuesque fig-ure stalking down Yonge Street in Toronto in thigh-high boots with a matching handbag, all icy-blonde European elegance. "Rose," I paused on the phone, "are you wearing Birkenstocks?" "No," said Rose mildly, "but we do live in a nunnery."

I had never heard of Nelson, couldn't even locate it on a map. There were no direct flights to this former mining town in the middle of the Kootenay mountain range, so of course I was intrigued. I was still recov-ering from the shipwreck of my Bobcat love story, but I was free and in search of restoration. I booked my ticket.

Flying into Nelson meant changing into a propeller aircraft in Vancouver and then landing with a prayer between mountaintops in Castlegar. Rose was waiting at the tiny airport. My mouth hung open at the sheer mass of forest, the endless spread of green on the forty-five-minute drive to Nelson, all untouched by development. I caught a glimpse of the town, nestled against a finger of Kootenay Lake, while turning along a cliff. Even at the first sighting people, something moved inside me. Nelson is a small city of ten thousand people, with restored heritage buildings and even more impressive natural surroundings. It's a place you could say has "character" though that doesn't tell the whole story. It is believed to have been built on a native Indian healing ground so it's one of those places like Sedona, in Arizona, where there's a high vibration. Even if you think everything I just wrote is completely woo-woo, Nelson certainly attracts people who believe that it's a place of higher consciousness, and that's infectious. The town is filled with healers and shamans, draft dodgers from the Vietnam war, urban IT professionals and marijuana growers; people escaping contrived urban lifestyles for a chance at something simple but mythic: a life of small pleasures. Dogs were banned from the sidewalks, and shoes were optional.

When I was in India, I had weathered a lot of healing advice from both friends and strangers. At times, my decision to flaunt my baldness turned me, in others' eyes, into an unnerving vision of mortality, and other times into a symbol of hope and recovery. I was directed to Ayurvedic doctors, pandits who whispered sacred syllables into your ears, and given the number of a homeopathic doctor who had cured thousands of "the cancer." But behind the best intentions, I sensed fear—I had become a target for people's deepest anxieties and hopes about cancer and illness. And when fear meets hope, seeming opposites pushed together, the instinct to seize the narrative takes the lead.

"You're a fighter. You beat it."

"No." I would answer patiently. "I'm not cured. I am living with a cancer that is not technically curable. But that's okay. Nothing is under our control, is it? One day we will all die. We just don't know when."

"You are cured. I read you fought it and now you are cured. See you are okay, god bless you to stand here. Please give me some treatment suggestions, my brother is also fighting."

Sometimes, I learned, it's more important to choose kindness, rather than get locked into our own perception of what is truthful or right.

It had been an overwhelming year. And I was really hoping people would run out of things to say. I needed to retreat into my own inner silence and Nelson seemed the perfect place. Rose and her husband Michael had bought an old convent with original wood-framed doors and windows and converted it into a B&B called "Simply Be and B." Rose, tore down the altar and put her bed there. She and I would cook together, cutting broccoli into spears, chopping and folding garlic into sauce while pasta was boiling on the cooker. We drove a half hour to Ainsworth to soak in the natural hot springs together. We ran errands and draped ourselves on the sofa where the nuns used to congregate for dinner, catching up and reworking our life visions. The one-year anniversary of my diagnosis was coming up on 23 June 2010. Rose decided to take the celebration into her own hands. She had been watching and listening to my stories, noting the gradation in me, the tilt towards trusting my inner compass. "Now that you love yourself, you can love someone else. You're ready. Let's make a list. Time to find your Raja." I had never felt as certain about what I wanted in a companion before. But the idea of asking for what you want was novel. And a bit unromantic. That night on the sofa, Rose plunked down paper and pen and bulldozed me into making a list of qualities in my ideal partner, and I did. "My Dream Lover" (unimaginative title, but a bold step to state my desire so baldly):

— communicates openly and freely with me
— has passion for learning and growth
— is compassionate, he gives back
— helps me see the world in new ways without imposing his vision on me
— is attractive (dark hair, Roman coin profile, just the right amount of chest hair)
— likes spice
— is successful, confident but not arrogant
— accepts my weaknesses, in fact, he doesn't want to change a thing about me
— drops me off at the airport (gate) and picks me up (from the arrival gate)

It went on and on, fifty-two points, getting increasingly specific. Rose looked at the list, and up at me, "Are you sure you didn't forget anything?"

"Oh yes, he fills in those immigration landing forms on the plane for both of us. I hate those and I can never remember my passport number and I have to pull it out of the overhead, and something falls out on someone. But he fills it out without pulling out receipts for all the things we've bought abroad. He's willing to lie a bit, just a teensy bit to the government, and adding things up, you know, rounding up. . .Oh yes, and that's another point, he doesn't round up or down to the last dime.

And he doesn't say things like, "Really, I thought you would have learned to pack better after all these years of travelling," and oh yes, this is important, he carries a notepad on planes that he whips out for me when inspiration hits . . ."

"Now you are pushing it."

"No, no, no wait. It's my list, right? He takes the leg and always leaves me the breast. I hate dark meat, I can't bear it you know and gristle, ugh. He has verve and yet he's very masculine."

"You are asking for the impossible, woman. And that's number fifty-two."

But I was just building to a crescendo.

"He sees me. He really sees me. He recognizes me. Sees me like a novelist sees their characters . . . like, like . . . like Tom Wolfe, you know, someone who will really see me, all of me, even the profane bits, like an X-ray into my soul. My own Tom Wolfe."

"Tom Wolfe? Oh . . . that guy who juggles at the market on Sundays and can read your aura?"

During the day, I would visit Michael Smith, a healer of First Nations descent. He's a bit of a local legend: a former businessman who left a corporate job to start a Chinese school of medicine. I immediately tuned in to his ideas about how the "right relationship" should drive all of our decisions. This means cultivating the right relationship to food, the environment—and each other. I relished the notion of inter-connectedness. In response to everyone's question whether I was "cured," Michael told me: "Healing begins when you realize there's no cure. The disease tells you something is wrong; now you have to fix what's wrong."

He spoke to me about many things I'd heard before. What to eat. What to avoid. How to shift my nervous system out of the stress response and into relaxation. He talked to me about "Larry the Lizard," his name for the amygdala's fight or flight response, programmed into the most primitive part of our brain. In fact, he called his brand of medicine "And medicine" because of all the approaches he threw in. "And" I understood. Everything he spoke to me about. Maybe because I had discovered I had more room inside.

All of this flooded over me in Nelson. I rose for coffee in the early morning, then went down to the lake, kicked off my shoes, feeling small stones beneath my feet and waded into the water. I was thriving by living closer to nature, finding vibrancy in this tiny community and the small, warm greetings that make a life. I found a place that supported a more mindful lifestyle—all the things I had, naturally, scorned when I was younger—meditation, yoga, organic farmers' markets and parties tumbling with children and potluck dishes.

"What's Peru like?" I asked one of the long-time residents of Nelson. Mick Collier had left his home in the north of England in the late 1960s to follow his guru here. The guru left, Mick stayed. He was one of the rotating cast who came to tea at Rose and Michael's. And I quite adored him.

"You know—travelling there just tenderized my heart. *Que linda la vida.* Maybe when I do the Camino this summer, my heart will finally break open," he paused, adjusted his stance and hitched one bare foot up against his inner thigh in a spontaneous tree pose in the middle of Baker Street. "Seems my blood is so sweet some little hitchhikers climbed onboard in Peru to avoid Canadian customs and now we have to bring in the pharma heavies to oust them . . . I have to go to the clinic now. Want to come?"

I knew that I needed to stay. At the start of my second week, I decided I would move there.

As much as spontaneous decisions are part of my make-up, I'm not the first person to up and move to Nelson. I met several people who had shipped all their belongings there within a few days and never left. Others, apparently, had violent reactions to the place and escaped immediately, never to return. One morning over breakfast, I turned to Rose and said, "I need to find a house."

The next day, we went driving by a sweet little cottage diagonally opposite Rose's place. She stuck her head out the window and called to the woman in her yard: "Do you know anyone who wants to sell?"

"I do!" answered the woman. This was too much good karma; I was ecstatic. We negotiated, and even drew up papers, but in the end, the woman was a flaky artist (I've known a few; I may even be one myself!), and she backed out. I was heartbroken, moping around the convent. Rose said to me, "How are you going to find your house if you don't name it? Name it and then you'll know what it is, and you'll find it."

"Oh. Like a mission statement, Rose?"

"Yes, like a mission statement," she said, "but you've been hanging out with too many corporate people lately."

True. On both counts. If you don't know what you're looking for, there's a chance you'll miss it. Earlier that year, 2010, my friend Tishani Doshi had published a book called *The Pleasure Seekers*. She told me that while writing it, she'd spent some time in writers' colonies in upstate New York and Italy. Writers would be taken care of during their stay, dining together at night. I found this idea intoxicating. I wanted to create an artist's retreat, where creative people could sit and nurture their practices. The name of my future house occurred to me as a group of us were hiking next morning up the face of Pulpit Rock, the slumbering elephant shaped mountain on the opposite side of the lake. There, in the summer sun, on the churned soil of the mountain, it suddenly occurred to me that what I was looking for was "The Teahouse"—a place to remind me of my "Alice in Wonderland" journeys, and a gathering place for mad hatters. I could imagine the qualities of the home I wanted to create, and I even visualized myself in it.

Now that I had named it, I had to put the idea into action finally, and get a damn real estate agent. The very first house that agent took me to, I thought, "This is it. This is my house." Tall windows, vintage fixtures, a porch, crown moulding, a big old banister and an unimpeded view of the lake and the mountain. It reminded me of the cosier cottages in Landour. It was what I call "soulful architecture," a house you leave to future generations. Not that kids appeared to be on the cards for me, but it was a nice thought, this heritage home I could leave to my cat. It was also close to the centre of town, within walking distance of Baker Street and Oso Negro, the local coffee shop. The location made it a good investment, satisfying my pragmatic, left-brain side. Mostly, it felt like mine. The best part was the attic: pull a little hatch and the stairs fall down from the ceiling. The tree top room was unfinished and perfect, exactly the studio where I'd want to cloister myself and write. In case I developed survivalist tendencies, I could sit up there and write until the end of the world, which was coincidentally the name of a beachside cafe in Goa that had captured my imagination: Hey, let's walk to the End of the World where we will toast our life-altering defeats and failures. I also had this vision that this house would be a place for my father though I'd never discussed it with him. I put in an offer, but then I was scheduled to leave. I had a trip to New York planned, but as I walked through Nelson, staring at my maybe house from the outside, I thought: No. No leaving. I cancelled the trip and stayed longer in Nelson, which proved lucky, because I got the house.

When I finally returned to Toronto, I called my father. He was actually vagabonding by himself, cheerfully road tripping through Quebec, because he is now the kind of person who does whatever he likes.

I got him on the phone. "Can you come back a couple of days early? I need you to co-sign some mortgage papers." My dad was quiet on the phone, but he did make a U-turn and drive back from the Gaspe peninsula. I sensed he needed a change in environment. I described Nelson to him, and without even seeing it, he signed for the house with me. This could only mean one thing: Road trip! For all my wandering, I'd never really seen the breadth of Canada from the ground, and so we decided to pile our belongings into an old van and make our way 5000 kilometres across the country. I started packing.

The drive was filled with long, comfortable silences. We slept in old motels in small towns like Wawa, on the edge of the Canadian Shield, picking burrs from our sleeves after a hike into the forest for a pee by the side of the highway. Driving across our home province of Ontario itself was interminable. Understanding the vastness of Canada from a map is one thing but experiencing it, something entirely different. Everyone had said, "Oh the prairies will kill you. So boring!" But in fact, the prairies were a great relief. Everything opened up. The skies were endless and alive. We stopped the car and stood by the side of the road, staring up, stars bursting like blossoms above our heads, the expanse of sky watery and dark, all anticipating. It was such a special experience to be on the road together, daughter and father, with our secret language. So much of my father has seeped into the way I see the world, we could talk over our truck-stop diner dinner of steak and fries about what we observed on the road that day and it was like we had the same pair of eyes.

"Did I ever tell you about my grandmother?"

"No, Papa."

"You know rebellion runs in our blood. And I told you Boroma, my great-grandmother, was widowed at young age, and fought the prevailing ideas of how widows should behave. I never told you her daughter also became a young widow but chose to leave Boroma's home with a friend of her husband's who played the violin on All India Radio. This was an incredibly courageous—what do you say, ballsy?—act in 1930s Calcutta. She just followed her heart. Of course she was wiped from family history. But I now think of her often, when I look at you, Lisa Rani."

It's folly to think you can leave behind hurt and grief when you travel, and that was not our intention. But there is nothing like travel to turn over the mind's terrain and make space for fresh encouragement, at least in the case of born nomads, like my father and me.

20

TOWARDS THE END of the long drive across Canada and after crossing the relentless flat of the prairies, my father and I entered British Colombia in early spring of 2010. It was just a few months after my stem cell rebirth. It felt like crossing a threshold that mirrored the steeper parts of the mind. The landscape rose before our eyes: endless mountain ranges covered with thick forest, and the highway snaking through it. I had to pay close attention to the road. The radio turned to static, so I turned it off and cracked open the window. On either side of the car, the forest behaved as if it knew us, beckoning us and drawing closer, firs and giant conifers swaying heavily, whispering like the ocean. It was dangerously hypnotic. A person could forget themselves in this landscape; forget even that most humans lived as though they didn't belong to the natural world. This part of the drive through the interior of BC was exactly like climbing a mountain: the lunacy and attraction of finding a place to rest in a wild landscape being the main force pulling us forward.

When we finally drove into Nelson on a soft spring evening and pulled to a stop at the kerb, the windows and door of the Teahouse were open and Rose and Michael were on the porch, waving at us in a joyous blur. It was the most inviting house in the world. I watched my seventy-six-year-old father shrug off his travel fatigue as he stepped out of the car. He stood on the side of the street, observing the spread of the land, the mountains appearing like resting creatures. The house was set on a steep incline which provided an uninterrupted view of Kootenay Lake, streaked at that hour with the setting light. I watched him taking it all in, his eyes glowing.

Because it was all so right, I had an impulse to do something symbolic, like stab a flag or a trident into the ground in the front yard. When everyone went inside, I stood beneath a lilac tree that arced across the pathway leading to the front door. It was heavy with clusters of lilacs, bowing towards me like curious children. I listened to voices floating from the homes around us. I wanted this home to be a shrine to all of my knocked-together cultures; to Shiva and Jesus and Buddha and Kali, the great god of medical science and chance and the bizarre traditions they could father and mother together. I slipped out of my shoes and went inside.

I think that on a subconscious level I probably bought the Teahouse for my father. He admitted recently that he'd always had a desire to spend the last part of his life in the mountains, something I'd never known about him, but perhaps intuited. According to Vedic Hinduism there are four stages of life: the student, the householder, the retiree and the renunciant, an individual who gives up material pursuits to concentrate on moksha and a simple spiritual life. In Dad's mind, moving to the mountains in western Canada was a form of the last stage, of taking *sanyas*, of living in praise of slowness and observing the sights and sensations of the world churning beyond your window, without getting attached. I love to think of him there, living out his vision for himself in Nelson, where sometimes a poet or a neighbour drops by for conversation and tea, inspired by my father's steadfast spirit.

During our first few weeks in the Teahouse I hung photographs and moved my Ganesha from mantel to mantel. Neighbours from both sides of the street knocked on the door while we repainted the walls, bringing us vegan stews and gifts of fresh-cut flowers. There was even a Nelson "Welcome Wagon" Committee, who left a small houseplant and gift certificates for a free oil change in a straw basket outside our door. I felt like a pioneer in the times when people set themselves to clearing land. Work would pause when people stopped by and we would chat over bread and steaming tea in chipped enamel cups. Much to my delight, Nelson turned out to be a magnet for storytellers, and it seemed everyone had a story to share. Many Nelsonites had had successful careers in different cities before consciously taking a step back from of the pressure cooker lifestyle and the frantic demands of mainstream life. Here in Nelson, it was the constant things in an impermanent existence that brought the deepest joy. "Ah, before I forget, you're going to want to bear-proof your garbage as well," said Deirdre from next door, who worked for a global non-profit of change makers.

Time in in Nelson passed effortlessly that summer after my treatment and recovery. The reclusiveness was good for me. I was serenaded each evening by a deeply refreshing boredom. There were long, solitary drives on mountain roads towards glaciers and rail trails and places where salmon came to spawn, swims far out into the lake and summer festivals to attend, like the Shambala Music Festival and the renowned Garlic Festival in New Denver. Once I slipped into pyjamas, memories would come rushing at me in the dense silence; memories of childhood adventures with my mom. The mustard-coloured bucket she used for catfish on fishing trips. Harvesting honey. Crawling through the forest on our knees to pick mushrooms. The earthy flavour of borscht. I missed her. When Dad and I prepared food together, we served a tableful of guests on my mother's plates. When friends dropped by, we sat together over her recipes. She was everywhere. All those years of trying to know what is beyond the edge of my world had brought me to this place, where I melted and joined with my mother. It had brought me home.

There was another benefit to being tucked away in this remote part of Canada. I was safe from positivity missionaries and all the well-meaning people drawn by the morbid and mystical possibilities of my disease. Living with multiple myeloma made me notice what I thought of as a "tyranny of cheerfulness"—when people don't deal well with the heavier moments of life. But in Nelson I wasn't receiving unsolicited miracle cures, like premixed alkaline baking soda treatment (dodgy looking white powder) or medical cannabis (proven effective). I didn't want to think about my disease just then. I just wanted to be left alone for some time. I immersed myself in the Kootenay lifestyle, slouching around in hemp pants, peasant tops and moccasins. "You look like a Punjabi drug peddler," Bombay friends told me over FaceTime, spinning the hippie-dippy-granola trope on its head. They were kidding of course. But they also didn't get it.

And I enjoyed my singledom. I was single and celibate. I had a brief affair with a charismatic man with a huge personality who lured me out of Nelson by sending chartered planes into the Kootenays. We ended as friends. No more drama!

I was living a largely clean, remission lifestyle; organic fruit, fresh almond milk, wheatgrass, unrefined oils and grains bought at the local farmers' market and weekly Cottonwood Falls fair when residents from smaller surrounding towns, like Winlaw in the Slocan Valley, would venture to the "big city" to sell handmade soaps and dreamcatchers. I even went for the occasional tequila shot at a brand new Mexican taqueria that had opened on Baker Street. It was all about balance.

But by late fall, there was a pull towards a more adrenalized life. Perhaps this high-low formula could work now that I had a place to retreat in the world. The idea of infusing my work with purpose and more substantive intentions had taken hold. My hair was growing back in a halo of tight curls and when I was asked to host a travel series on jewellery traditions in India for television it felt like an opportunity for a strong statement: Here I am, alive and better than before, rocking my chemo cut; cancer hasn't stopped me. My dad stayed in BC, becoming something of a beloved figure: Nelson's unofficial mayor.

Nelson was naturally better at wellness and spiritual pursuits than film and television, so life fell into a rhythm. After I returned from India in January 2011, every two weeks I flew away. I had kept my apartment in Toronto, and it became my basecamp for engaging with the world. When I was in Toronto, I made sure to get my blood work done at Princess Margaret Hospital. I had taken on the responsibility of monitoring my M Protein level seriously, and I had become an expert in reading my blood reports. Once a month I would enter the Ambulance Waiting Area behind the elevators, scribble my name on the sign-in sheet and nod at the others waiting to have blood collected from their ports or PICC lines (peripherally inserted central catheter) or from tubes exiting from their chest. I joined this small club on the couch, feeling the joints in my spine stiffening slightly. It was a natural reaction to living without knowing exactly what was coming next.

Close to the one-year anniversary of my Cancer Coming Out in September of 2010, I wrote one of my last entries in the Yellow Diaries. In it I reflected on the fact that Dr Galal—my guardian angel—had left Princess Margaret Hospital for Saskatoon. While it was too self-centred to believe he was placed by the universe in Princess Margaret just for me, he had been there for a critical period of my treatment, and his departure made me reflect. Nadama and Krishna had also disappeared from my life, quietly. Just "slipped out" as Krishna would say. They had never been big on technology. Nadama never used computers. Krishna had a simple flip phone. When their line was disconnected, I had no way to find them. And it was okay. I remember when I was addicted to travelling the world and looking outside myself for the next spiritual high. Nadama brought me back to the core of all spiritual teachings: Everything you need is inside you. A great teacher shows you the way to self-reliance. They are like a bridge back to your own consciousness. Through this lens, I don't see the parting as sad, but as the natural way of things.

This was the right time to close the Yellow Diaries and lay it to rest. And even though I wasn't in Nelson at the time, what happened next is due in part to Nelson—and Milan and Bombay and LA. In fact, everything that had come before prepared me for the moment when I would meet the person who checked every box on "the list." The cancer, Dharamshala, going West, the men I'd loved and parted from—all of those moments conspired to bring me to a place where I was ready for my husband. I like to say I manifested him. He says, jokingly, that I picked him up online. There was no shortcut to our coming together, but, yes, technology had a role to play.

In early 2011, a good friend, Seamus O'Regan, the former host of the breakfast television news show *Canada AM* (and now a minister in the Canadian government), who I'd gotten to know since my return to Canada, called me. He wanted to tell me that he had just come back from Africa, where he'd been working with a program called Artbound, building the first all-girls high school in the Maasai Mara region of Kenya. Then, in April, when I was called in to be interviewed on Seamus's morning show for a special on stem cell research, he brought it up again, suggesting on air that I get involved, because in 2013 the group would build a school in India. Later, I googled Artbound, and it sounded fantastic: a volunteer organization of artists and arts supporters working with Free the Children—now known as WE Charity—to raise funds to bring arts and education to kids in developing countries. In Kenya, the group had built a pavilion for singing, painting, dance and theatre, attached to a school for girls. I loved the idea of the arts as a tool for breaking the poverty cycle. I found the Facebook address of Artbound's founder, a Bay Street, Harvard-educated, Beirut-born, Toronto resident named Jason Dehni. The fact he had an MBA from Harvard was a strike against him in my eyes, but I decided to put aside my bias for a great cause. I sent him a note on Facebook ending with the line: "I'd love to know more . . ." I'm an ellipsis-abuser. I end many of my emails with that punctuation. But Jason read something into that first interaction; he saw a prescient gesture. He now jokes to people that he opened his email that day and there was a "friend" request from Lisa Ray. "Clearly, she was trying to pick me up," he now says. We met on a Sunday afternoon for brunch at the Four Seasons on Avenue Road. I saw him first: he was wearing a turquoise shirt, sitting with his laptop open.

I sat down, and we stared at each other for a moment before speaking. He was so hauntingly familiar and yet utterly new. "Where the hell have you been?" I wanted to say, but instead, he snapped his laptop shut and we spun off into discussing Artbound, our life experiences, and how not to negotiate your dreams. His eyes settled on me without distraction. I felt like I was lifted from my seat while he was studying me from different angles. He barely broke eye contact. I felt sweaty, pleasantly uncomfortable, aware of a quickening in my blood. He spoke passionately about philanthropy. The recent trip to Africa had been profound, he told me. He hadn't anticipated the emotional effect of actually being in Africa. He kept referring to it as an exchange—he wasn't just ennobled by giving; he had actually gained so much from being around the girls. "I thought we were going there to help them, but they opened up entirely new doors within me," he said. I nodded while thinking: Oh shit! He's the list. What was meant to be an hour-long meeting turned into five hours, to the point where the staff had to escort us out of the restaurant because they had a private evening event waiting to start. I don't remember what all I said in those first five hours of meeting

Jason, but later he told me: "I felt like you were speaking a different language, I couldn't understand some of the things you were saying about manifestation, but you know . . . I wanted to understand."

A lot of life is timing. As much as we try to regulate our lives, it's the moments that knock the breath out of us that we live for. The attraction to Jason was so palpable. We both saw right away that not only did we exert that terrifying power of attraction over each other, but we sensed we could be compassionate towards each other as well. Life had spooked us, tossed us around, bent us over its knee. We could be real partners. We met for the second time three days later and attended an Alicia Keys charity concert. Two weeks later, I moved in.

Jason and I have dramatically different life stories, but the parallels are clear: We're both children of immigrants searching for something other than the obvious. Jason grew up in a suburb of Beirut, in a prosperous Christian Lebanese family. "Ethnically, we are Phoenicians, not Arabs," he clarified. I can understand how important it is to be precise about heritage when you are from a complex land. His father was in real estate development and the family was quite well off, but three years after he was born, war broke out. His childhood was spent in a war-torn country, and mayhem was his normal; weddings and birthdays occurred amidst a rain of bombs. He's shared memories of the dining table shaking between bites. But when the Christian militia came calling for his older brothers, the family took a long vacation to Boston. In the summer of 1983, Jason, his parents and his three brothers went to Boston on a tourist visa and landed as refugees. They left everything behind—all their property, the pretty china and cars. Their bank accounts were seized by the Lebanese government, so the family of six had just $30,000 USD to their name. Jason was eleven years old and spoke only French and Arabic. The only English word he knew was "sneaker." With the economy in tatters, even if they returned, the family fortune had become nearly worthless. This wealthy established family moved near the inner city projects of South Boston, using the only money they had left to buy a corner store where Jason's parents worked sixteen hours a day.

Even now, I can see that young boy, holding his mother's hand as they walk through Boston airport. His green eyes are staring while inside he's already damming a steady stream of memories; the flavour of sumac, broad faces and hands, and warm winds. But I wonder if in the night his heart would shudder with old sounds, of bricks falling and an older generation lamenting.

In 1989, when Jason's two older brothers were at Harvard University, the American government sent a letter that essentially read: "The war in Lebanon is over—it's time for you to go back." The family didn't have green cards to stay in the US, but they couldn't go back to Lebanon either. So, they applied to come to Canada, and were accepted. The Dehnis packed up and drove to Toronto to start over yet again. Jason was seventeen and spent the next two years taking part-time courses at York University and helping his parents get a catering business up and running. Within those first hours of our meeting, he had told me how grateful he is to Canada for what it gave him: student loans so he could get his education; healthcare to help his parents through tougher times. "Canada took me in," he says. And though he eventually went to Harvard for his MBA, he always knew he'd return to Toronto.

At Harvard, Jason experienced a bout of mild depression. His questions of himself were the same ones I've struggled with for years: *I've achieved everything I've worked for my whole life, so why isn't it as fabulous as it's supposed to be?* Although our journeys have been similar, there are differences too: his goal was to achieve acceptance, while mine was to rebel against convention. Like so many offspring of immigrants, he strived to achieve respectability in society. But maybe respectability wasn't enough. He began to imagine Artbound and other philanthropic endeavours that would satisfy his soul even as he worked in the corporate sector as a successful wealth manager for a major bank. And that's when our stories came together.

Those first days of getting to know him were magic in the way of new love but with a twist; I really wanted to show him my scars. All of them. I wanted to bypass the sugary, heady romantic bit and ground our relationship in crucial knowledge of our flaws—the burning of the toast, morning breath, forgetting to pay bills, the sounds that come out of the shower and the bedroom when you think no one's listening. Previous heartaches had given me a wariness, not of love but about time. Cancer does that too, it brings time into focus. After wrestling through morning moods and routines, and sorting through your differences, you land on the deal breakers: What kind of life do you want? What is your version of a life well-spent? I had to find out, and soon, if were we meant to be.

At the time, I was in rehearsals for a theatre piece called *TAJ* that was having a brief run as part of the prestigious Luminato Arts Festival in Toronto in the summer of 2011. It was to be my first stage experience in many years, and I was nervous. I was to play the enigmatic Jahanara, the daughter of the Mughal emperor Shah Jahan, who had built the Taj Mahal as a tomb for his beloved wife Mumtaz Mahal. The director, Tom Diamond, came from a background directing opera and during lengthy rehearsals of dance and music, I could feel myself unfolding as an artist. "What we're doing is C-R-E-O-L-I-Z-A-T-I-O-N," enthused Tom one morning. I thrilled at the sound of the word, even more than a passing compliment during rehearsal. Creolization, a process of evolution and cultural change that has meant different things at different times.

The beautiful little theatre where the play would be mounted was at Queen's Quay on Lake Ontario. Jason lived a hop and a skip away in a loft in an iconic building conversion called Tip Top Building, an old factory, close to the water. Because rehearsals went so late, and I was sleeping over anyway, I asked him if it would be possible to crash for a few weeks—temporarily, I added. Without hesitating, he said: "Of course." I moved in with one suitcase, and I never moved out.

Of course, Jason was "the list," but he was also so much more. There was that ineffable quality in his core that made me think of a line from Rilke: "deep with the winds of homecoming." Really, in the end, it was not about "the list" but the mysterious algorithm of love.

In June 2011, the International Indian Film Academy Awards (IIFA) came to Toronto. Everything in India is amplified, so of course the country has dozens of different film awards, but IIFA is different. It's an extravaganza riding on jet streams, essentially building a bridge between Indian popular culture and the world. Indian celebrities who are jaded by the awards system and the daily tabloid feeding frenzy look forward to IIFA as it pops up in a different location every year. Take the amped-up circus out of India and it suddenly looks different—more charmingly manic, less cut-throat. Of course, part of me recoiled from the gaudiness of the spectacle. But I had softened too; I decided to take it at face value, not judging but just participating, seeing how it went.

I was invited to host a part of the show so during the rehearsal I moved through the warren of tents backstage at Ricoh Stadium, trying to figure out where to go. I kept running into old friends. Supermodel Noyonika Chatterjee, shaking her great mane, was rehearsing. We'd known each other on the Bombay circuit back in the 1990s, and we embraced. Then I ran into Mickey Contractor. "What are you doing here?" he cried. "I live here . . . sometimes, no most of the time, right now!" I laughed.

We sat and joked, and it felt like we were back in Bombay twenty years ago.

Anil Kapoor appeared, and he was as warm and gracious as an old friend. "We are so glad to see you here, and in such good health." Great, happy chaos surrounded the event as Indian actors and actresses rehearsed their dance numbers and models were zipped into their gowns.

The next day was the Awards and people started gathering outside Rogers Centre in the early morning. Teenage girls and grown men and women lined the "green carpet," many dressed as if they were stars themselves, in elaborate sarees and gowns, at the ready to spot anyone famous in the midst. I arrived at the event in an electric pink flowing gown—dramatic (another nod to India) but still simple (J. Mendel again). I didn't feel self-conscious at all as I got out of the limousine, but I reeled at the sheer size of the crowd—at least twenty to thirty people thick on either side of the barriers. As soon as I stepped outside, there was a pause, the "Who is it?" moment where fans try to identify the celebrity. The pause became a whisper, then a ripple of noise that started and gathered into a roar, and then the chanting began: "Lisa! Lisa!" It was powerful, and to my surprise, I got teary. "Lisa! Lisa!" My first name, so familiar, and chanted with genuine warmth. I could feel the pride: *She's one of us.* And I felt like one of them.

But of all the carpets I've walked, this time was different: I wasn't walking the carpet alone or with a co-star; Jason was by my side. He had his hand protectively on my back as we moved through the flashing lights and would gracefully step aside when I had to pose for the paparazzi. He was smiling and content to watch, but not in the manner of an outsider. He was right with me in the experience.

I then did something that I've rarely done, being the introvert that I am: I went up to the people along the barriers. I began holding hands with people, talking and signing autographs. As an intimidating, razor-backed mountain range mellows and transforms the closer you get, the crowd too no longer seemed nameless and thrusting and vaguely menacing as I approached. The hushed chatter, the shrieks and even a quiet exhale of breath, I heard every sound individually, every puff and shuffle, and watched each face separate like a sunflower from the throng. I felt an incredible amount of respect for each of them, and gratitude. I zigzagged down the green carpet to get to people who were calling to me from farther away, bubbly sounds that gathered and rose in a unity of enthusiasm. I'd always found those carpet moments purely performance; a role I'd play because it was required. And I had never got too close before, finding the affection too aggressive when it was direct. But that night, I loved it. Fear was no longer shaping me. I wasn't working my image; I was truly grateful. And full of toothy, genuine joy.

Of course, the show started an hour and a half late, but somehow, IIFA pulled it off. I was in a green room because I was doing the camera links for the TV audience, so I watched most of the actual evening on a screen. But then, I finally went out on stage to present an award. "Hello, Toronto!" I said, and screams swelled up from the audience. I could feel how we all contained the same duality; we were all at home in two cities across the globe from one another. I expect I was under the sway of more maudlin emotions than normal, but I swear I felt a kind of electrically bound awareness in the vast stadium; we were all celebrating together in our adopted country. It was a fever of shared experience.

I'd been told that the makers of the Canadian version of the reality show *Top Chef* had thought of me as a possible host from the beginning of the first season, but I'd been too sick for them to pursue. By the summer of 2011, a producer approached me to come in and talk. Of course, my Canadian agent raised her eyebrows: *Why would an actress do a reality TV show?* But I thought: Why not? I felt healthy in my body. *Top Chef* was an opportunity to take control: food was no longer a trigger for me, and I resolved to use the show to tell this story. I could show people what it's like to be a woman who is content with her body and, at the same time, eat some damn good food. Enough of studied cautious tastefulness, let's take a leap into the spicy reality television bubble!

When I went in for the meeting, Leslie Merklinger, a producer from the Food Network, asked: "What are you going to bring to the show that's different?"

"I'm going to bring my curiosity," I said. "But I am not going to set myself up as a food expert. I'm a food lover but you need someone to ask the stupid questions and you need someone to be able to translate the show to the audience members who aren't the hardcore foodies."

I got the job as host, and almost immediately went underground for a month, shooting every day in September, sometimes for fourteen hours a day. I loved the world of volatile chefs and gastronomy and yes, all that food (when people ask me what it was like, I always say: "Tough work. A lot of chewing. A lot of candour with your mouth full.") On *Top Chef*, I learned that I didn't have to deny myself, a revelation I'd been working towards for years. It is possible to be passionate but not obsessed—healthy eating means neither pushing food away nor overindulging. And of course, my mother's hand was there in all I tasted. My first culinary guru, planting in me all the fresh, redolent, piquant tastes as well as her faith in the power of shared meals to heal and restore, though it had taken a long, long time for my appreciation to take root.

The entire filming was top secret. I had to sign non-disclosure agreements and couldn't tell people what I was doing for many months. I also had to give myself a crash course in culinary terms. "Ambiguity is the salt of life and informs the best, most closely held recipes," I wrote in my dressing room on a break. I came across this quote in the course of researching the master sauces. And what exactly is "umami" again?

I finally surfaced from the *Top Chef* secrecy submarine, ready for a planned getaway with Jason. He had made the bookings, taken time off work, and had meticulously planned the week-long vacation. But right after the show wrapped, I had to break the bad news: I was needed for an appearance in India. Mine is a job without weekends or holidays, and this was hard for Jason to grasp. I was so used to being called away at the last moment, I simply couldn't understand his point of view.

"Stop being such an enthu-cutlet about these things. Chill. Go with the flow," I tried to disarm him.

"I have no idea what an enthu-cutlet is," he replied stiffly. It didn't work.

So, we had a blowout, and I got on a plane.

I landed in Bombay in October 2011 and everywhere in India people were muttering darkly about a growing streak of fundamentalism and bigotry. But a lot of people I met in Bombay and Delhi were talking about women's rights, revivalist movements and social justice in a way I'd never heard before. It was a notable contrast to the clamouring "#stylearmy" and gilded world of celebrity that swelled to larger proportions on every visit. But I felt like a bandit. I wanted to complete my work and run. Normally I would be stockpiling my impressions, but on this trip, even in the buzzing vibe of India I couldn't stop thinking about Jason. I was so unsettled thinking about the friction between us. I remember catching a glimpse of myself in a marvellous mirrored bathroom in the Taj Hotel. I had just finished drying my hands when I looked up into all the different versions of myself reflected in that marbled backdrop. I ran my hands through my curls. What was it about relationships that splintered me, brought out the spectre of a ruthless and righteous side that I barely recognized? *Stop. Sabotaging. Yourself. You need to stop now.* All the Lisas were talking as one.

For one entire week in India I thought about what I might be sacrificing by flying away on that eleventh-hour invitation. I tried to imagine the situation from Jason's point of view and saw how it seemed like I cared more about my work or satisfying my own whims than respecting him. I was being very all or nothing, and all or nothing is the opposite of balance.

I realized: I've got to stop doing this.

Jason was not a sideshow. This was my life. I cut the trip short and came back to Toronto. Jason picked me up at the airport in a bathrobe and boots, looking like a Lebanese Hugh Hefner. He was so unreservedly himself. I loved this man. He could stir a riot inside me even though our messages had been terse while I was gone. In the car, with the evening traffic flowing around us I told him about the panic I had felt when we fought, how I felt like I was drowning in all the unlovely bits of myself that were triggered by the relationship, and how I recognized myself needling him continuously, against my will. And the big question: How to keep the "us" afloat? I heard myself make a vow; "I won't do it anymore. I'm not going to jump on a plane without notice. We're in this together now." In a way, saying it out loud was like a commitment to myself. This was the first relationship where I didn't feel I had to rage against the conventional life, where I didn't have to see making plans as some kind of bourgeois flaw.

And Jason bent, too; he was coming to understand that my life wasn't nine-to-five, and that any defensiveness about my erratic schedule was probably because I felt judged and misunderstood. Back at his loft with its hideous aluminium bar, his face was still impassive. Lips tight, whole expression solid. I stroked his cheek. Fire and water met. We folded into each other, pressed our bodies close, warm breath in our ears. Wrapped around each other in gentle surrender. I was not splitting him, he was not splitting me. For the first time I was with someone whom I wasn't looking to to complete me. I didn't need his skin to shield me. It was an almost preposterous idea: if we are each responsible for our own happiness, only then can we come together in love.

But this business of working on yourself, of opening yourself up to personal self-development and spiritual work is HARD, and it never seems to end. Nadama had explained this to me years ago: the old notion of peeling the onion. Every time you strip a layer of yourself there's another waiting just beneath. The time had come to jet spray as many layers as possible away. I just hoped I wouldn't be swept away as well. As I felt things solidify with Jason after I returned from India, I observed all my mental gymnastics come out to play. And I was done with it. They had to be addressed head-on and pulled out by the roots, these negative, self-sabotaging patterns. So just after Christmas, in early 2012, I booked myself on a flight to Napa, California. I had heard about an eight-day personal growth retreat which would help prepare me for the upcoming depths of my relationship. While I could gauge in myself when stormy thoughts were about to approach, I was still helpless to escape the perimeters of tyranny over my actions—and overreactions. For no reason I would argue with Jason or get triggered by his kindness. "How was your day?" "What do you want to do this weekend?" led to a torrent of eye rolling responses from me. "Stop being so banal, next you'll be saying, TGIF!" "Really, you think I look like a doubles tennis partner?" "How suburban," "I'm feeling suffocated," was a constant refrain. I really wasn't feeling that though. The best I could do when I felt myself get irrational was issue a warning to Jason: "Big fucking thought-storm coming this way."

"Baby. I have to do this. I need to go," is what I said.

The little clapboard farmhouse where the retreat took place had been a spa, tucked away in a subdued forest near some natural sulphur springs (kind of smelly but you get used to it). Those warm, egg-scented pools were said to have healing powers. The program was called the Hoffman Process, a form of group therapy, built on figuring out "negative love" patterns that are heaped on us and embedded from childhood. There were two rules: no physical activity, and don't tell anyone what you do for a living. I loved this idea: I wouldn't be what I did, but who I was—and am.

The eight days proved to be a kind of boot camp for the soul— visualization, talk therapy, written exercises, pounding pillows and shouting it out, all working towards integrating the different sides of one's self. As the days progressed inhibitions fell away, along with family recipes of closely guarded secrets. We all retreat behind walls; it's just a lot of work to remove them. I'm not sure it would have been as effective if I hadn't been doing all the work of self-investigation for so many years already. At one point we were sitting around the room, a knocked together mixture of thirty people, each admitting to a statement of shame. It was a simple act. It was the most devastating moment of the week. When it came to my turn, I could barely speak, but somehow I said: "I'm not worthy." Until that moment I hadn't realized that idea was alive in me, but shame is like that: it lodges itself in you, and you can cover it, and adopt behaviours that lead away from it, but you are never completely free until you acknowledge it. *I'm not worthy.* I heard it uttered again and again in my mind until I saw myself a blur, reconstituting into a figure of a bone-crushing goddess, eyes jewelled with knowing. "*No one can judge my worth because I contain everything. Everything is in me.*" The chant stopped abruptly and I returned to the room. It was a surreal moment. I searched myself, reaching deep for an explanation for this vision. But there was none in me. I looked around to see if anyone had noticed but everyone else appeared rooted concentrating on the testimonial going around the room and learning that everyone felt some variation of the core message: I'm not worthy. One by one, people confessed: "I'm defective." "I'm invisible." "I'm nothing."

"Shit, it's the same shitty, pushy elf inside us all," one of the men said. "I'm done with him."

Now we had to work to see who we really were, and to let go of that statement.

One lamplit evening, surrounded by people who had learned to really listen, I gathered myself in my own arms and heard the urgent longings. In shaking loose from my bones old concepts of who I should be and what life should look like, I uncovered the discrepancy of desire between what the mind thinks it wants and what alchemy happens in the heart when you arrive where you didn't think you want to be to find it's another sort of home.

And that, I realized, was Jason.

On the last day we found out what the rest of the residents did for a living. Without exception everybody in that room would be considered very accomplished and successful. But inside, we all felt fraudulent. That insight—and many more—helped myself set me free from my emotional freight. "And we did it without Xanax, tranquilizers or happy pills. It's a fucking miracle!" trilled one of the women with a crooked smile. We made a vow to stay in touch, knowing it would not happen. I came out of the program realizing: *Now I'm ready. I'm ready to get on with the rest of my life.*

Before leaving, I wrote in the margins of my Hoffman workbook:

Lisa 2.0 Choices

I choose not to observe my wounds and cracks with any sort of regret, but instead decorate them with gold.

I will damn well ask for support when I need it.

I choose not to negotiate my dreams.

Less distractions, more living.

I choose skintight confidence regardless of my weight and the shape of my body.

I will safeguard the port above my right breast and wear it proudly like an honorable pin.

I will not hold myself back to fit in and I commit to supporting anyone else doing the same.

I choose to live as a goddess incarnate, soft and dangerous, striking at darkness, moving with compassion.

I will offer the medicine of my attention when you need it. I will always offer support when you ask.

I choose to love my flaws.

I choose love.

What do you care about?

What matters?

Pursue that

Forget the rest.

I now felt fully prepared to enter into a togetherness with Jason. I had questioned the inherited assumptions about marriage my entire life. I had set up my life so neither family nor wedding would be the natural outcome. When these things had come close, I'd pushed them away. But now, joining my life with Jason's felt as natural as walking in sunlight. I was done with the poorly lit places. When Jason surprised me right after the retreat with a proposal in Napa, my right eye was oozing pus from a bad case of pink-eye and my legs were unwaxed. I collapsed with untold relief at this end to my incessant wandering. Everything comes together in a moment like that. You see complete contentment and it all makes sense. There is a glimpse of what has led to this place, and of travelling down a road with someone you love without fear and then with a gentle ripple, it's covered up again.

We chose Napa Valley for our wedding. We'd both travelled the world but neither of us had been to Napa until we went together. It was a place of mutual discovery and the site of new strides and fresh eyes. Jason had called my dad in India weeks before he proposed. My dad loved Jason immediately and he in turn has basically been adopted by Jason's family. Jason's father had passed away, and he and his three brothers welcomed my father immediately. Our little family is jagged, and extending, with nieces and nephews who fill our weekends with noise and chaos.

When Jason called him to ask for permission to marry his daughter, my dad was on one of his frequent trips home to Calcutta, walking next to the Hooghly, a river that he described to Jason as "mystical." When Jason told me this story of my father giving his consent and blessing, I was surprised by how moved I was, and the yearning that had been lurking inside my bones. Jason cracked me open. That he asked my father for my hand in marriage was a meaningful gesture, magical even. A month later, back in Canada, my father inspected the inscription "*I will love you forever*" etched in Bengali on the wedding ring with a magnifying glass to make sure it was correct. The love story between my parents is still the greatest love story I've witnessed, so I asked him to share his wisdom before Jason and I headed into the great unknown of a life together. And my father's advice was so simple and perfect. "Hold on to each other. And just love. Take care of each other."

Of course, for us, that was, and remains, a loaded statement. My health is something we both grapple with. I'm starting to really listen to a message from myself to myself, which I keep hearing. It's a single word: resilience. And resilience can mean knowing when to push and when not to push; when to let go. Learning those limits is the great reward, and the way forward. One of my cancer buddies, Warner Neumann, had died recently. We had been through our stem cell transplants at the same time, and this shook me deeply. After the engagement, Jason and I sat down together with my haematologist and she was blunt, "The median life expectancy is ten years. Some more, some less." What do you do with this information? You hold hands, and walk out of the office, and cry a little. And then—if you're me—you scoff at the talk of medians and data. "That's not my story," I told Jason. "In my mind, we are living and travelling together, having kids, dogs, buying paintings, our flesh growing saggy and loose. I'm sorry, I don't believe what the doctors say. None of it. My heart tells me I am going to be around a very long time. And my beliefs are fucking magnetic."

I stood before the man I love in the late afternoon of 20 October 2012 in a vineyard in Napa. I wore a dress by Wendell Rodricks, simple and elegant with a hint of India in the folds. After years of red carpets, I was done with aisles. Instead we stood in the centre of a semi-circle, surrounded by people we loved. The days before were lit with pleasure, weaving in Lebanese flair with a big Indian *sangeet*, filled with music and dance. The chef spiced up the food and friends brought poems and songs. It was a weekend to savour. To lose ourselves in tenderness and affection. To stir hope in the cracks of our lives. We welcomed the spirits of our pasts, Jason's father and my mother, by placing a rose each on an empty chair. The symbolism was clear: this is where I'm coming from, but this is where I am now.

What do you care about most?

What matters?

Pursue that.

Forget the rest.

Before the vows, with a harvest moon making a ghostly appearance, I looked out and saw strength, renewal and perennial heartbreak reflected back at me. It was a life I'd created, piece by piece, choice by choice. I felt neither lacking nor complete when I thought about all the places I had touched; the loving joys and hurt and catastrophic sadness, the privilege of having lived at the edge of my capabilities and will. All of my experiences had brought me here. Later, in the moonlit whirl of celebration, I found myself thinking about the importance of storytelling, about the stories that become anchors of faith, that support us and carry us both when we are lost and when we have found meaning. What do we do in the face of life's biggest upheavals and triumphs but make up stories? It's the way of our nature and it's the way of metamorphosis. Spinning gold out of the dark.

The sister of my heart, Tara Maclean, wrote a song she performed for my wedding about love and pain, joy and daring, about how the ways we break and come together may not set you on the path you planned, but on one chosen for you. And, I believe, this idea of a miracle showing up for each of us is a story worth telling, sharing and believing in:

I was lost
But now am found
Here in your arms
On solid ground
I thought that I was destined
To walk the earth alone
Holding on to nothing
Like water over stone

But now we are inseparable
Not even death can break us apart
Now we are two rivers running toward
The same sacred heart

I was blind
But now I see
Your love is grace
And it's washing over me
You know that I'm a gypsy
Always moving right ahead
Now I lay me down beside you
Upon our river bed

And now we are inseparable
Not even death can break us apart
Now we are two rivers running toward
The same sacred heart

No more empty words
This promise is for keeps

And I will follow you
If you flow through me

And now we are inseparable
Not even death can break us apart
Now we are two rivers running toward
The same sacred heart

Afterword

IT SEEMS FITTING that I first sat down to write this on 1 May 2018—the anniversary of having met Lisa in Toronto seven years ago. I say this because Lisa resides firmly in a place of manifesting what she envisions. Just like how we met on that day. "I manifested you," she would later say to me, as my alpha ego nervously chuckled.

Married for five-and-a-half of the seven years, we cannot imagine our life any other way. When we do, we would simply design a new one or a variation of it, and then manifest it together. That's been the hallmark of our love and commitment to each other.

But that wasn't always the case, at least not in our first year of marriage.

Within a week of returning from our honeymoon, we abandoned the two-bedroom trendy loft I had been living in for five years and moved into a "grown-up" four-floor house that we had purchased in a posh neighbourhood. Two days later I started a new job at a new company as head of strategy for one of the largest insurance companies in the world that was struggling to come out of the financial crisis, working for a volatile CEO who had graciously waited two hours after I landed on the first day of work to fire (or force into retirement) my direct boss. I don't think I had figured out where the washroom was yet. And on that very same day Lisa had to travel to India for a seven-week gig leaving me with the responsibilities of running our grown-up house and our crazy Persian cat who randomly took creative liberties in order to show me her displeasure at Lisa's absence and my lack of attention.

And while this drizzle had put a slight damper on the post-wedding euphoria, I was still paddling forward, with Christmas holidays in sight. I managed not to burn the house down, got a good handle on my new job and eventually sequestered the little fluffy devil in a corner of the house where she could do little damage. I had this.

I just didn't see the tsunami wave that was about to hit.

Back in Toronto and shortly after New Year's, Lisa went in for a routine blood test. She had missed the last few tests as life got increasingly busy. And on a bone-chilling day in January 2013, I found myself in a tiny sterile room in Princess Margaret Hospital, sitting between Lisa and her oncologist, staring in at Lisa's blood report. Her markers were off the charts. Lisa's incurable fatal cancer was back. I thought I had this.

Happy 2013.

Looking back on that year, it's hard to explain the roller coaster of emotions that ensued. I tried to set aside my own anxieties and give Lisa the support she needed. I monitored her blood markers closely. I built an Excel spreadsheet with trend lines going back three years of blood test results—with graphs, correlations and sensitivity analysis. We set up a juicing station in our basement and for an early birthday present, I sent her on a two-week course to one of the best nutritional healing retreats in the world. Anything to make me feel useful or in control. But in reality, I was neither. I was just masking my own fears.

Lisa's fierce determination, however, to take charge of her own health through holistic healing and beat back multiple myeloma was nothing short of remarkable. "You need to be the CEO of your own health," she would say at speaking events. "You need to pick up and complete the circle at the point where Western medicine stops." Her second stem cell transplant scheduled for April was cancelled as the cancer quickly retreated, and till this day there's been no sign of it. I continue to be inspired by Lisa's courage and ability to manifest her deeply held beliefs. While I stayed up late at night reading and worrying about the statistics of the disease, Lisa never once allowed herself to entertain such foolishness. She only focused on the inevitable manifestation.

And as the months went by, and the waters calmed, the differences in personality that we had found endearing in each other at the beginning of our relationship turned threatening to me and suffocating to

Lisa. An undercurrent of resentment and anger that had built up on both sides began to surface. And on the very day of our first wedding anniversary, we broke up. I took off my wedding ring and that was that. I started mentally plotting my retreat back into the life I had before.

But as usual, Lisa managed to alter my course once again.

Unbeknownst to us at the time, we were both consumed in our own feelings of love, of what each felt about the other. And in so doing we were unconsciously testing the other against the image and feelings we had of them, wondering whether they could ever be the person we wished them to be. We were each paddling in separate directions, trying to create a love we each desired in the other for ourselves.

Egos aside and with open hearts, we realized that we still wanted to be with each other for reasons that were far more meaningful and real than those that pushed us apart. What we needed was simply to modify what has become the narrative thread of our relationship.

And so, we did, and the course of our life followed.

We decided to make up our own rules and unapologetically design the life we wanted to live, shedding all imposed expectations and norms. We started loving each other in a way that the other needed to be loved. We set out to create a safe space for the other to be who they are, as they wish to be, with no judgement. The modification turned into a complete rewrite of our story, and for the past four years we've travelled long distances, supporting and propping each other up along each ocean crossed, no matter how choppy the waters. We designed a life that seems unimaginable to us from our first year of marriage. The love we have for each other continues to grow deeply, while the feeling of being loved by the other deepens even more. And by the time this book is published, we will have welcomed two beautiful souls into our life, a creation of the pure magical powers of our co-manifestation.

With gratitude
Jason Dehni
May 2018

"The privilege of a lifetime is *being* who you are."
Joseph Campbell

Acknowledgements

THIS BOOK IS an offering. My way, hopefully executed with a modicum of humility, to end this practice of running our lives in the shadows. It's not easy to write about defying majority opinion or challenging the rules without support from other seekers, learners and defiantly fearless souls.

I am indebted to the team at HarperCollins India, my editors Shreya Punj and Diya Kar who gave this book a home and just "got it." My lit agent Jaya Vasudevan who is my tireless compatriot and who "gets me." Preeta Sukhantakar, who connected me with Jaya and who is a woman who inspires me—and challenges me—daily as any true friendship must. Siddharth Shanghvi who has been seminal in not only guiding this book to fruition but in nurturing this incredibly terrifying and at times thankless task of serving language with integrity. Sid also connected me with Bron Sibree, an incredibly compassionate and skilled editor, who helped me shepherd the story to its final version. Rohit Chawla, who accommodated this wandering spirit in Goa when I reached out, without introduction or preamble, and asked him to shoot the cover of the book. Thank you, Bonita Vaz-Shimray, for going along with this scheme.

Thank you to Amy Black, Emma Ingram, Sharon Gill, Danielle LeSage, Ashley Dunn and Abdi Omer, for believing in this travelogue of the soul to travel across the world, back to an audience at home. And very special thanks to Bhavna Chauhan, for rallying so sensitively and resolutely around these words. I'm filled with gratitude.

To my closest friends, family and supporters, I love you. Intensely. I won't name you all for reasons of privacy and to preserve something sacred in a world where secrecy and intimacy have become luxuries, but thank you for summoning up your support and vulnerability when I needed it. Thank you for resisting the voices telling you how to live your lives. Thank you for helping me confront my doubts and fears, for all the conversations and love.

There is no story without my father and mother. My strongest models of unflinching and quiet heroism. The most gracious faces of resistance. I'm forever indebted.

Thank you, Boroma, for living with incurable passion and passing on the fire in your veins. All the women of your lineage—including my daughters—are richer for it.

To India, my most enduring lover and source of inspiration. To life itself. For all the teachings. I want to honour all the teachers of my life, especially the ones who reacted from essential ignorance of reality or unresolved pain: thank you for your powerful teachings.

My husband. I'm finally at a loss for words. I bow in silence to your spirit. My babies: Sufi and Soleil. You are my teachers and the source of non-stop love and delight. To be pulled in the direction of the search of the soul has brought me to this place where I find myself as your mother. I'm so excited to watch you play your parts in this leela, to guide you to witness the action but not identify with it. You are free. And these words have been written for you.